Issues in Philosophy

Related title from Palgrave Macmillan

Julian Baggini, *Philosophy: Key Texts*

Julian Baggini, *Philosophy: Key Themes*

Anthony Harrison-Barbet, *Mastering Philosophy*

Jenny Teichman and Graham White (eds), *An Introduction to Modern European Philosophy, 2nd edition*

Issues in Philosophy

An Introduction

Second Edition

Calvin Pinchin

First edition 1990

Second edition published 2005 by
PALGRAVE MACMILLAN
Houndmills, Basingstoke, Hampshire RG21 6XS and
175 Fifth Avenue, New York, N.Y. 10010
Companies and representatives throughout the world

PALGRAVE MACMILLAN is the global academic imprint of the Palgrave
Macmillan division of St. Martin's Press, LLC and of Palgrave Macmillan Ltd.
Macmillan is a registered trademark in the United States, United Kingdom
and other countries. Palgrave is a registered trademark in the European
Union and other countries.

ISBN 1–4039–3394–4 hardback
ISBN 1–4039–3395–2 paperback

This book is printed on paper suitable for recycling and
made from fully managed and sustained forest sources.

A catalogue record for this book is available from the British Library.

Library of Congress Cataloging-in-Publication Data
Pinchin, Calvin.
   Issues in philosophy : an introduction / Calvin Pinchin.—2nd ed.
      p. cm.
   Includes bibliographical references (p.) and indexes.
   ISBN 1–4039–3394–4 (cloth)—ISBN 1–4039–3395–2 (paper)
   1. Philosophy—Introductions. I. Title.
BD21.P485 2005
100—dc22   2004057786

10   9   8   7   6   5   4   3   2   1
14 13 12 11 10 09 08 07 06 05

Printed in China

Contents

Introduction

This book is intended as an introduction to philosophy for students of philosophy at secondary and degree level and by those taking accessory courses in certain areas of philosophy. The book also serves as a useful introduction for the general reader into a number of traditional branches of the subject.

My approach has been to connect up a number of problem areas in philosophy with relevant texts. The aim of this approach is to create an integrated course which should help students to understand why the writings of the great philosophers of the past have relevance to modern philosophical problems. *Issues in Philosophy* has been substantially revised and expanded for this edition. Changes include a new chapter on the Philosophy of Science, a new section on Personal Identity and Biological Naturalism. The text has been updated throughout to reflect recent developments in research and teaching.

As each of the chapters contains its own introduction, I am not going to provide further introductory comments here. I shall, however, make some introductory remarks about philosophy in general. The importance of philosophical problems can hardly be doubted. The briefest perusal of the kinds of questions to which philosophers have addressed themselves will reveal that this is the case.

Philosophers have concerned themselves with questions relating to:

(i)   Our knowledge of the world and what justifications our claims to knowledge have.

(ii) The relation between mind and body, together with the teasing out of the implications that the different available theses have.

(iii) The existence of God and the problems which face the religious believer.

(iv) What we mean when we say that a particular course of action is 'right', or a particular state of affairs is 'good'. Philosophers have concerned themselves with the rationality or otherwise of our moral judgements. Some have sought to lay down criteria for testing moral judgements or maxims.

(v)   The issue of political obligation and the justification of power together with related questions concerning the relationship between the individual's freedom and the state's authority.

The author believes that the importance of these questions is self-evident and that many of them will inevitably touch our lives in one way or another. To think seriously and rationally about such issues is the best definition of philosophy that the author can give. It is hoped that the definition will contain its own impetus for study. To someone with no interest in the aforementioned questions, the author has nothing to say. To the reader who has either felt the weight of such questions, or can see how that weight could be felt, the author sincerely hopes that something of use will be found in these pages.

The philosophical approach adopted here is predominantly that of linguistic or conceptual analysis. The author believes that most philosophical problems are concerned with meaning and the implications of what we say. In the field of ethics, philosophy has at least a vital clarificatory role to play. Whether it has a role to play in the deliverance of moral judgements is an issue which the reader is invited to consider for himself.

The author wishes to express his gratitude to the following philosophers for their stimulating conversation and more than useful suggestions: Mr Maurice Charlesworth, Mr Richard Beardsmore, Mr John Daniel, and Ms Eluned Price – especially for her lengthy philosophical correspondence.

A special debt is owed to the person who fired my interest in the subject and kept it fuelled, Professor C. W. K. Mundle.

Deganwy, N. Wales   CALVIN PINCHIN

1 Perception and Knowledge

▶ Epistemological theories

An epistemological theory is a theory of knowledge. Such theories are concerned with the questions of how we know what we know and with how we distinguish knowledge from belief, opinion or faith. What we mean by 'knowing' involves an analysis of the meaning of our statements. There are two opposed epistemological theories. They are the theories of Rationalism and Empiricism. In considering the two areas on which they disagree, the reader will become acquainted with important philosophical terminology.

Rationalism and Empiricism: an introduction

The two central areas of disagreement concern (a) the source of our ideas, and (b) how we know necessary truths. We shall discuss in some detail the epistemological theories of some important philosophers (Sections II to ?). Let us first of all clarify the nature of the disagreements and equip ourselves with the technical terminology.

We shall begin with the issue of the source of our ideas. Empiricists claim that all our ideas are derived from experience. By 'experience' they mean sense-experience plus introspection. Empiricists do not claim that a person can only form ideas of things he himself has experienced. They draw a distinction between, (i) ideas given in experience, and (ii) constructed ideas such as mermaids and atoms. According to empiricism, all of our ideas must either be of things or properties presented to us in our own experience, or they must be derived from, and analysable into, ideas of the former kind. This thesis involves the conception of the mind as a 'blank sheet' which receives impressions from the external world via the sense organs.

All Rationalists agree that many of our ideas are derived in this way. They do not, however, agree that this account of our ideas is an exhaustive one. The father of modern philosophy, Descartes, was a Rationalist but he

1

conceded that many of our ideas are derived from sense-experience. Descartes describes such ideas as obscure and confused, and not important in gaining knowledge and understanding of the world. The important ideas for Descartes are what he refers to as 'clear and distinct ideas'. By this he means abstract ideas, such as cause and effect, substance and attribute, and especially the ideas of mathematics. Examples of these would be equality, number and straightness. He held that such ideas are innate. They are implanted by God, not derived from sense-experience. When humans reach thinking age, they are able to relate in terms of cause and effect and so on. A modern Rationalist may support this thesis by appealing to recent psychological experiments which indicate that the ability to perceive depth is innate in humans. He is, however, unlikely to follow Descartes in the claim that God implants such ideas or dispositions.

The Rationalist thesis was not invented by Descartes. Many early Christians held such a thesis. In the pre-Christian era Plato adopted a Rationalist theory of knowledge in which 'knowledge' could only be applied to the Ideal Forms rather than to the world of sense-experience.[1]

The second issue about which Rationalists and Empiricists disagree concerns how we know necessary truths. This issue is nowadays expressed in technical language by asking: 'Are there any synthetic *a priori* propositions?'. Let us now examine the meaning and importance of this question.

An '*a priori* proposition or statement' may be defined as a statement which can be recognised as necessarily true simply by considering its meaning and without needing to appeal to the evidence of sense-experience. The proposition '$2 + 2 = 4$' is a necessary truth. We do not need to verify its truth by repeatedly counting things, adding two pairs of oranges, two pairs of matches and so on, to make sure that the sum is always four. Its truth is independent of experience. Compare this with a generalisation which is believed to be true but is not a necessary truth, for example, 'All metals expand when heated'. This does need to be verified by the evidence of experience. We have to make observations, heat metals of different kinds and measure them before and after heating. In advance of such experiments we could not know whether heating a metal would cause expansion, contraction or have no effect on its size. Moreover, however much experimental evidence we have accumulated, all of it supporting the generalisation, this will not make the generalisation a necessary truth. It will always remain possible that some special circumstance will be found in which some, or all, metals do not expand when heated. Propositions which are to be verified by experience are called 'empirical' or 'contingent' propositions. The term 'contingent' means that their truth is not necessary. (They are also called *a posteriori*.)

Rationalists and Empiricists agree that some of the propositions which we know are necessary truths and that a great deal of the propositions which we know or believe to be true are contingent. The issue about which they disagree concerns the nature of necessary truths or *a priori* propositions. Empiricists hold that all necessary truths are analytic; Rationalists hold that some necessary truths are synthetic ('synthetic' meaning 'not analytic'). What is meant by 'analytic' in this context?

An 'analytic' proposition or statement may be defined as a statement whose truth follows necessarily from the meanings of the words in which it is expressed. An analytic statement simply unfolds or makes explicit all or part of the meaning which we have given to some word or expression. Examples of analytic statements are 'bachelors are unmarried' or 'a triangle has three sides'. Those are necessary truths as 'bachelor' *means* 'unmarried man', and 'triangle' is *defined* as 'a three-sided figure'. In the case of any analytic statement there is no difficulty in understanding why its truth is necessary, for its truth is determined by the meanings we have given to the words in which it is expressed. A person only has to understand it to see that it is *self-evident*.

We can now recast the technical question, 'Are there any synthetic *a priori* propositions?', as 'Are there any necessary truths which do not derive their necessity solely from the meanings of the words in which they are expressed?'. Empiricists answer this question in the negative, Rationalists in the affirmative. Examples of propositions which Rationalists have held to be synthetic and *a priori* include some moral judgements, for example, it is wrong to break a promise, the principle that every event has a cause, and the axioms and theorems of mathematics. Let us briefly consider the latter, since Descartes considered that mathematics provides the model of clear and certain knowledge.

Arithmetical equations like '2 + 2 = 4' or '5 + 7 = 12' are necessary truths, but are they synthetic propositions? A Rationalist may support the claim that they are with two arguments:

(1) '4' does not *mean* '2 + 2', nor does '12' *mean* '5 + 7';
(2) such equations do not merely unfold the meanings of the symbols used, they also provide information about the world as $2 + 2 = 4$ applies to everything in the world that can be counted.

An Empiricist may challenge these arguments. Regarding (1), it is plausible to say that '4' does not *mean* '2 + 2' (rather than '3 + 1'). But what does '4' mean? Surely it means '1 + 1 + 1 + 1', and '2' means '1 + 1'. And so, by substitution, we get: $'2 + 2 = 4' \equiv '(1 + 1) + (1 + 1) = 1 + 1 + 1 + 1'$. This latter equation is explicitly analytic.

Regarding (2), does '2 + 2 = 4' report a necessary truth about everything in the world that can be counted? In that case '2 + 2 = 4' would be a brief way of saying that if 2 things of a certain kind are added to 2 other things of that kind, then there will be 4 things of that kind. But on this interpretation,

$2 + 2 = 4$ is sometimes false. We get less than 4 pints of liquid by adding 2 pints of one liquid (if it is alcohol) to 2 pints of another (if it is water). As a theorem in pure arithmetic, '$2 + 2 = 4$' is necessarily true. It does not, however, tell us how *all* physical things interact with each other.

The Rationalists seem to have a stronger case when they claim that the theorems of geometry are synthetic *a priori* propositions. It is a necessary truth that a cube must have 12 edges. This can be recognised simply by considering the structure of a cube. But the property of having 12 edges is not part of the definition of 'cube', and many people use the term 'cube' correctly without knowing that cubes have 12 edges. So the statement that a cube has 12 edges is not analytic. The same is true of Euclidean geometry. It is not part of the meaning of 'triangle' that a triangle has the property proved by the first theorem, namely, that the sum of its angles is 180°. So this theorem is not analytic, yet it seems to be a necessary truth. We prove it once and for all by deducing it from Euclid's axioms; and these, in turn, seem to be synthetic *a priori* propositions. That a straight line is the shortest distance between two points seems to be a necessary truth, but seems not to be analytic, for surely straightness is one property and being the shortest distance between two points is quite a different property.

In view of such considerations, it is natural that many Rationalist philosophers should have held that geometry provides clear examples of synthetic *a priori* propositions, or of 'innate knowledge', to use Descartes' language. (It was not until the eighteenth century that the terminology of 'synthetic *a priori* propositions' was introduced by Kant.) Until the nineteenth century it was taken for granted that Euclidean geometry applies to and accurately describes the structure of physical space and all objects which exist in physical space. So long as it was believed that Euclidean geometry comprises necessary truths to which everything in the physical world must conform, explaining the origin of such knowledge posed a major problem for empiricist epistemology.

However, it can no longer be taken for granted that Euclid's axioms are necessary truths to which everything must conform because other systems of geometry, which are internally consistent, have been developed. They start from axioms different from those of Euclid, and, according to physicists, a non-Euclidean system fits the facts better when one is dealing with inter-stellar distances.

Some modern philosophers have claimed that some of the propositions which we know *a posteriori*, that is, through sense-experience, are necessary truths. This claim is made on the basis that there are some propositions which are known *a posteriori* which could not be other than they are. Their truth is therefore held to be necessary rather than contingent. This doctrine has particular application in the case of identity statements, and this is discussed in Chapter 2.

▶ Descartes' Rationalism

Today the disciplines of science and philosophy are distinct. Very few philosophers make scientific discoveries and very few scientists make important contributions to philosophy, though their findings may give rise to philosophical problems. This was not the case in Descartes' time.

In the seventeenth century physics was known as natural philosophy. Descartes uses the word 'philosophy' to include science. He said that the roots of the tree of knowledge were metaphysics, the trunk was physics and the branches were the other sciences. He used the term 'metaphysics' in a way that differs from modern usage. His use of the term includes what we now call epistemology together with the meaning it was given by subsequent philosophers. Metaphysical questions are concerned with ultimate reality. Thus a typical example of a metaphysical question would be: 'What are the fundamental constituents of the universe?'. Those who answer such a question in terms of physical particles of some kind are known as Materialists or Physicalists, those who answer in terms of minds or spirits are known as Idealists. Descartes held that both mind and matter were real and that position is known as Dualism. Metaphysical questions then are concerned with the nature of reality. Epistemological questions are concerned with how we know.

Descartes had an ambitious idea of the philosopher's task. He thought that all laws of nature could be discovered by *a priori* reasoning. It would be a matter of drawing out the implications of premises which were necessary truths.

Descartes' famous method, known as Cartesian doubt, was initially designed for making scientific discoveries and later used for dealing with philosophical problems. In the *Discourse On Method* we are presented with the following rules which are held to constitute a method for obtaining knowledge of the world:

(1) We should not accept as true any proposition which it is possible to doubt. The feature of a proposition which makes it impossible to doubt is that it is 'clearly and distinctly' shown to the mind. He adopted the principle that any proposition clearly and distinctly 'perceived' is true. Later he made the same claim for 'conceived'. This is Descartes' way of saying that the proposition is *a priori*. In the *Regulae* he says that there are two mental operations by which we can claim certain knowledge. They are intuition and deduction. Intuition is a faculty of reasoning independent of the senses and the imagination. Deduction is the process whereby propositions are logically derived from other propositions. If deduction is to succeed, then the initial propositions must be obtained by intuition. An

intuitive proposition is known *a priori*. It is presented clearly and distinctly to the mind.

(2) Divide the problem into as many parts as needed (analysis).

(3) Start from the simple and work to the complex (synthesis). Thus, if we have a complex proposition, the first stage is to analyse it into simpler ones until we reach propositions that are so clear and simple that they can be known by intuition. We then start with the simple and self-evident and construct a deductive argument whereby we can prove the initial complex proposition. There is a parallel here with Euclid's thought with which Descartes was much impressed. Euclid had begun with the simplest propositions about space. Descartes was, however, taking much for granted in thinking that such rules had universal application.

(4) Check one's argument.

In conjunction with these rules, the success of geometry[2] had led Descartes to believe that all things of which man can have knowledge are capable of being discovered by deductive inference starting from *a priori* propositions. This is an example of Rationalism in its most extreme form. He is claiming that all human knowledge is deducible from *a priori* propositions whose truth is independent of sense-experience. All knowledge about the world can be arrived at by a process of deduction starting from our simple, intuitively certain ideas. Given that Descartes held such ideas to be innate, it follows that he was claiming that all we can know can be discovered by working out the logical implications of these innate ideas. This is plausible in regard to mathematics. The problem is that Descartes thought it applicable to all the sciences. His error was the subordinate role which he assigned to sense-experience or to empiricism in general. Knowledge concerning how the physical world works is not to be obtained by deductive inference from *a priori* propositions. It is observation and experiment, that is, sense-experience, that is all important in obtaining such knowledge. Even though Descartes did much experimental work in anatomy and optics, he underplayed the importance of sense-experience in the quest for knowledge. We shall see further evidence of this in the following section.

The quest for knowledge in the *Meditations*

In the *Meditations* Descartes is seeking the indubitable starting point for knowledge. He wanted to start with the existence of something that was logically certain, that is, something that could not be doubted. He decided that in order to discover the correct starting point, he would systematically doubt all his previous beliefs until he arrived at something that could not be doubted. The conclusion of this procedure was that the existence of a thinking self is what cannot be doubted. This conclusion and what it implies are discussed at the start of the following chapter. For our present purposes we are concerned with how the method of doubt was applied to the existence of the external world.

The first point to clarify is what Descartes meant by 'doubt'. He should be understood as meaning the suspension of judgement. In applying the method of doubt, it would, he says, be an endless task to consider each of his beliefs individually. He therefore does it in classes. He lumps together beliefs of the same sort and applies the method to very general classes of beliefs. Thus if certain members of a class of beliefs have been shown to be false, then this will serve to cast doubt on the entire class.

Descartes selects a very extensive class of beliefs, namely, all the beliefs that he has acquired through his senses. (An Empiricist would claim that these are all the beliefs he could have, except those involving introspection.) He is doubting the independent existence of material things. He thinks that these beliefs can be doubted on the grounds that they have sometimes been mistaken. The form of the argument is: My senses have sometimes deceived me, therefore, they may always deceive me. He admits that it seems paradoxical to say that his senses might always deceive him but decides that he can claim this without being classed insane. We are then presented with a second argument.

He has often dreamt that he is sitting by the fire and such dreams have deceived him, so how does he know that he is not dreaming now? He concludes that there are no certain marks to distinguish waking from sleeping. Let us now examine these arguments.

Starting from the premises, (1) My senses sometimes deceive me, Descartes goes on to assert (2) I will consider myself without hands, eyes and so on. I do not or may not have any senses. Clearly, if (2) is meant to establish that he has no senses, then (1), the premiss which supports it, would have been demolished. We should understand the term 'senses' as having two meanings. In (2) he is referring to his sense-organs, whereas in (1) he should be understood as meaning his sense-experience or sense-data, that is, the experiences he has via his senses. Descartes is casting doubt on the existence of physical things, including his body, and not on his having of sense-experiences. We might, for example, doubt that there is water on the road ahead of us on a sunny day, but not that we are having the sense-experience of seeming to see water.

In the case of dreaming, Descartes seemed to think that being deceived by one's dream is the same as being deceived by one's senses. Again, 'senses' should be interpreted as meaning sense-experience and not sense-organs. Descartes uses confusing terminology to refer to sense-experiences. He refers to them as 'ideas'. If, for example, you are looking at an apple, then in Descartes' terminology, you have an idea of an apple. The term 'idea' is used by Descartes to refer to sense-experiences, objects of thought, and imagination.

There are problems concerning the coherence of the doubt that Descartes is proposing. The obvious problem with the case of arguing that sometimes my senses have deceived me, therefore, they may always do, is to say how one knows that one's senses have sometimes deceived one. In order to recognise a deceptive case, I must know of a veridical one. If I do know of a veridical case, then the claim that my senses may always deceive me must be false. Austin in *Sense and Sensibilia* has remarked that talk about deception only makes sense against a general background of non-deception. A similar problem arises with the example of dreaming. To say that I know I have been deceived *by my* dreams on some occasions presupposes that I have the distinction between dreaming and waking. The deception cannot therefore be used to obliterate the distinction. The distinction is a prerequisite for recognising the deception.

A further argument to show the unreliability of the senses is offered in *Meditation* VI. There is a tower seen in the distance and from a distance Descartes' sense-experience led him to believe that it was round. On closer inspection it turned out to be square. A critic of Descartes can ask how he knew it to be square and thus be able to judge his first belief false. The evidence for saying that the first belief was false is the evidence of the senses. Descartes would therefore be assuming that the evidence of his senses was not deceptive on that occasion in order to show that the first case was deceptive.

Readers coming to philosophy for the first time might well feel puzzled at the ease with which Descartes persuaded himself of the viability of doubting the existence of physical things. This can best be explained through a consideration of the theory of perception he held.

Descartes held a Representative theory of perception as opposed to a Realist theory. We can elucidate the difference between these theories by considering an example. Suppose that you are looking at and touching a round, green apple. You think that what you see and feel is part of the apple's surface. The surface is round, smooth and green. The Realist theory endorses this view. Realism holds that the immediate objects of vision and touch are the surfaces of physical objects. Realism, in what is known as its 'naivest' form, asserts that physical objects possess the kinds of properties which we perceive them to have. The Representative theory rejects this and holds that the roundness, greenness and smoothness which you experience are private objects which exist in you. They are transitory objects which last only as long as they are experienced. They are caused by the apple and in some way represent the apple. What is important for our present purpose is the notion of a 'private object'. According to the Representative theory, a person's sense-experience acquaints him with his own sense-data, or 'ideas', to use Descartes' terminology. These sense-data or ideas are private objects so a person cannot observe a physical object directly and compare it with the sense-data. All he can do is compare different sense-data. This has been a highly influential notion in philosophy, that is, that in perception the perceiver is aware of his own ideas (Descartes and Locke), or his own ideas of sense (Berkeley), or his own sense impressions (Hume), or his own sense-data (Russell), or his own sense-contents (Ayer). We are going to discuss this fully when we come to Russell. Suffice it to say here that if you accept that what you are directly aware of in perception are your own sense-data or ideas, then you have a wedge driven between what you are aware of and the external world. You are never *directly* aware of such a world. It is because Descartes accepted this thesis that doubt concerning the existence of the external world was easily generated. Once you have accepted such a thesis, the problem is to say how you know that there is an external world given that you are not directly aware of it.

Descartes' answers to this are unsatisfactory. In attempting to demonstrate the existence of material things (*Meditation* VI) he tells us that his faculty of imagination persuades him of their existence. He distinguishes imagination from his essential nature, namely intellection. Intellection is the grasping of conceptual content or meaning. We can grasp the concept of a triangle, chiligon or myriogon without forming any mental pictures. Indeed, we cannot imagine complex figures in terms of forming mental images, but this does not detract from our ability to grasp their conceptual content. He claims that as the imagination is not part of his essential nature it must therefore depend on something other than mind. He postulates body as a possible answer to the question of what it is dependent on. Thus imagination is regarded as a faculty of knowing whose application is to body. He does not regard this as a proof of the existence of material things, though he thinks it renders the existence of body probable.

He has another reason for believing in the existence of material things. He describes the faculty of perception as passive and asserts that his ideas of sensible things (sense-data) must be produced by an active power which must belong to some substance other than himself as a thinking being. The main reason for this conclusion is that ideas of material things appear independently of, and contrary to, his will. He then asks what kind of a substance it is and considers three possibilities: (a) body, (b) God and (c) some other creature superior to body. He dismisses (b) and (c) on the ground that God is no deceiver. God has endowed him with a strong natural inclination to believe in the existence of material things. There are problems with this.

First, some of our natural inclinations lead us astray. He cites the example of a man suffering from dropsy who craves drink which in turn worsens his condition. Descartes struggles with this problem but with little success. He attempts a physiological solution but fails to acknowledge that God could have made creatures in such a way that their natural inclinations did not harm them.

The second problem can be brought out by considering further Descartes' views on perception. In philosophy there is a traditional distinction between the primary and secondary qualities of a physical object. The primary qualities include such qualities as an object's shape or size or its property of being extended in space. The secondary qualities are an object's colour, taste, texture, smell and felt temperature. Descartes was a subscriber to what is known as the Secondary Qualities Thesis. This asserts that it is only the primary qualities of objects that are objectively real. The secondary qualities are effects *in us* which are somehow caused by the object. They are subjective. The physical object itself does not possess the secondary qualities, although it does possess properties which make us experience them. Descartes was endorsing a thesis of Galileo's that the primary qualities are objective and the secondary ones subjective. Descartes introduces his thesis of the essential nature of physical objects at the end of *Meditation* II. He invites us to consider a piece of wax before melting and lists its sense-given qualities. When the wax is melted, we say that the resultant liquid is the same stuff as the solid wax even though all its sense-given qualities have changed. Its smell, colour, solidity have all changed so what is it that remains the same in spite of changes in the sense-given qualities? His answer is that nothing remains the same except the properties of extension (that is, being extended in three-dimensional space), flexibility and movability. It is these properties which are held to constitute the essential nature of matter. The secondary qualities do not. They exist only in the observer and if there were no observers, then there would be no colours, sounds and so on. The problem this creates for Descartes is that we have a strong natural inclination to believe, for example, that physical objects are coloured. We are disposed to believe that the apple we are eating is firm and green. If it turns out that objects are not really coloured, then it could be said that God, in giving us the inclination to believe they are, is deceiving us. Descartes does seem to realise that his argument for the existence of material things is not that strong. He talks of giving the ground from which matter can be inferred and ends by saying that his aim was to show the existence of the self and God to be the most certain.

I shall conclude our discussion of this aspect of Descartes' philosophy by providing the reader with further evidence of the subordinate role which Descartes assigned to sense-perception in the acquisition of knowledge. At the end of *Meditation* II, Descartes was not just introducing his thesis of the essential nature of physical objects, he was also attempting to defend his Rationalist theory of knowledge. He claims that the essential nature of the wax is grasped in an abstract way by the intellect. It was this which led him to conclude in the final paragraph that bodies themselves are not properly perceived by the senses or the imagination, but by the intellect alone. We can grant to Descartes that in judging the melted liquid to be the same as the wax, there is more involved than just sense-experience. The identity judgement requires some interpretation of the sense-experience. We cannot, however, accept the implication that the senses play no part in perceiving the wax.

Consider the second example he gives concerning the city street. We look down from a high building and see hats and coats below. From the sense-experience we 'judge' that there are people under the hats. The use of the word 'judge' implies that we consciously distinguish between sense-data and the objects to which we attribute the sense-data. These so-called 'judgements', however, are unconscious, spontaneous and involuntary. In discussing this example Descartes draws an extreme conclusion, namely, that what is seen with his eyes is judged only by his mind. This claim is highly eccentric. Suppose I look down on a city street and see the top of a hat and I infer that there is a person under it, then, according to Descartes, my mind makes a judgement. What he neglects to mention is that the evidence for such a 'judgement' is that of my past *sense-experience*. We might well ask Descartes how we could discover wax, fires, hats and people without sense-experience.

Having discussed an extreme form of Rationalism and Descartes' method in the quest for knowledge, we now turn to a very different kind of philosophy. The philosophy of David Hume may be described as radical empiricism.

▶ Hume's theory of knowledge

In his *Treatise of Human Nature* and *Enquiry Concerning Human Understanding* Hume's avowed purpose is to provide an account of human knowledge and how we acquire such knowledge. He is going to inquire seriously into the nature of human understanding and such an inquiry will reveal the limitations of that understanding. Hume's project is going to be based on the experimental method. He tells us in *Enquiry I* that the project will not involve any metaphysical speculation. Metaphysics is not to be regarded as a genuine science. Hume is telling us that his project will not be concerned with questions about ultimate natures or realities. This is a point which we need to get clear.

Hume's method

As an Empiricist Hume holds that all sciences must be based on observation and experiment. Knowledge about the world can only be obtained in this way. The science of human nature will be no different from other sciences in this respect.[3] In order to understand what Hume thinks such a science of human understanding can achieve we need to consider a passage from the introduction to the *Treatise*. He tells us:

> that the essence of mind being equally unknown to us as that of external bodies, it must be equally impossible to form any notion of its powers and qualities otherwise from careful and exact experiments, and the observation of those particular effects, which result from its different circumstances and situations. And though we must endeavour to render all our principles as universal as possible, by tracing up our experiments to the utmost, and explaining all effects from the simplest and fewest causes, 'tis certain that we cannot go beyond experience, and any hypothesis that pretends to discover the ultimate original qualities of human nature, ought immediately to be rejected as presumptuous and chimerical.

This impossibility of explaining essential natures or ultimate principles is not regarded as a defect which is peculiar to human science. Hume holds it to be a common feature of all science. Let us now try to get clear just what Hume means by this kind of impossibility.

Hume is writing with the natural science of his time firmly in mind. In particular he is writing with Newton's *Principia Mathematica* in mind. It is not so much the picture of the world presented by Newton's physics which interested him, but rather Newton's views on scientific method. Newton believed that experiment and not what he called 'hypothesis' (what we might call 'speculation') is the basis of science.[4] Newton believed that mathematics was just a mechanical tool useful to scientists in their attempt to describe relationships between natural phenomena. It does not describe the structure of the world. Hume is not particularly impressed with mathematics. He regarded geometry as a fairly imprecise and uncertain discipline. His general view of mathematics was that it was a corpus of *a priori* propositions which had no direct descriptive relation to the world. A proposition like '2 + 2 = 4' does not describe the world in the way that 'heat iron and it will expand' does. It is important to realise that Newton distinguishes between discovering the laws according to which physical things behave, such laws being expressible in the form of mathematical equations, and the discovery of the real physical causes of such phenomena as the laws of gravity and motion. To provide laws in mathematical terms is one thing, to seek their causes is another. Newton held that no one can ever discover such real causes. The most that can be achieved is the discovery of laws or principles by which things behave. It is this methodological ideal which Hume proclaims himself to be following. Such a method would have the twin advantages of providing us with the most secure knowledge of human nature that we can have and also showing us the limits to which we can go in our understanding of human nature. In the same way that Newton dismissed the possibility of attaining a knowledge of the real causes of natural phenomena, Hume was equally insistent that his philosophy would show how we could never hope to attain knowledge of the essential nature of human beings. We can only discover the laws according to which they behave and think.

Metaphysics, the science which claims to deal with ultimate realities, is not regarded by Hume as a possibility. He believed that the only way to deal metaphysics a fatal blow is to 'inquire into the nature of human understanding and show from an exact analysis of its powers and capacity, that it is by no means fitted to deal with remote and abstruse subjects' (*Enquiry I*). In the *Enquiry* Hume wants to delineate the various areas of the mind, as he says, to sketch out a geography of the mind. Such a science as that would be possible as there are obvious distinctions to be made between the various mental faculties, for example, the will, the imagination and so on. Having delineated the various aspects of the mind, it will then be possible to find out how they work. We can go as far as finding analogous laws to those to which we referred earlier concerning Newton. We discover the laws by which the different mental faculties work.

There are inconsistencies in Hume which should be noted here. We have so far been discussing his enthusiasm for the experimental method. Book I of the *Treatise* and *Enquiry I* are not, however, founded on the experimental method. They are founded on what Hume refers to derogatively as 'abstract philosophical principles'. Although Hume was impressed by Newtonian method, he was also impressed by the *content* of Newtonian science. He was impressed with the corpuscular theory of the natural world, that is, that the real nature of material things is to be constituted by corpuscles, or, in modern terms, atoms. This was a theory concerning the ultimate nature of the world and, on his own principles, Hume had no right to be impressed with it. There is also an inconsistency in the fact that although Hume did not accept the corpuscular theory (he did not subscribe to the thesis that secondary qualities are subjective, holding that the arguments which supported such a thesis could be adapted and applied to show the same of the primary qualities) he was also so impressed by the corpuscular theory that he thought he could treat the human mind on the same model. That is to say, he thought he could regard the mind as being composed of corpuscles of thought and that he could discover the laws which governed those 'atoms' of thought. There is nothing in Hume to suggest that the corpuscular model was being treated as a convenient fiction. He took himself to be describing the *actual* contents of the mind.

The contents of the mind

It was from John Locke that Hume inherited the 'atoms' of his theory of human nature. Locke thought of the human mind as comprising discrete simple ideas of sensation or reflection which could be combined to form complex ideas. Thus, for example, the idea of gold would be a complex idea formed out of the simple ideas of yellowness, hardness and so on. These ideas were regarded as sorts of images. This is Hume's point of departure.

Hume set out to describe exactly the totality of the contents of the mind and how they come together in order to give rise to human knowledge. Like Locke, he regarded these contents as being various ideas and impressions. Unlike Locke, he regarded these ideas as exhausting the contents of the mind. There was nothing else over and above them, whereas Locke had believed that in addition to the contents of ideas and impressions there was also a mind which made judgements about them. In Locke you have the notion of substance in which the various sense-given qualities inhere together with the self which makes judgements about the ideas. In Berkeley's system God plays a vital role guaranteeing the objective reality of the ideas. In Hume there is no recourse to substance, self or God. There are just the ideas and impressions.

Hume's classification of the contents of the mind is as follows:

Hume tells us that if we look into our own minds, we find that all the contents resolve themselves into two distinct kinds. The most important distinction is the one which he takes to be fundamental in *Enquiry II* between impressions and ideas. The difference between them is held to be essentially one of force or liveliness. He says that everyone will readily perceive the difference between feeling and thinking. The distinction he is getting at here is that between actually seeing, for example, a tree, and merely thinking about one, or between actually being in love and just thinking about it. The impressions are what impress themselves upon us and they are more lively and vivid than when we just think, imagine or conceive such things. He tells us that we will all readily perceive the difference between an impression we feel when an object is present and the idea we have of that object when it is remembered or thought of in anticipation. This difference in force is used to explain the difference between impressions and ideas. Hume admits that this vividness or liveliness can be approached in fever and dreams. This problem does not bother him. He says that this notwithstanding, they are generally different and even when our impressions are weak and feeble, no one will quibble about the distinction.

In Hume's classification there is a departure from Locke's use of 'idea' (and from Descartes' use of 'idea'). Hume uses the term 'perception' instead. This is done to avoid any misleading connotations with the term 'idea'. Hume is going to restrict the term 'idea' to its proper sense.

Hume's classification is meant to be – indeed it has to be – an exhaustive one. The impression/idea dichotomy must describe and explain all there is to describe and explain concerning the workings of the human mind. There must be no residue.

In all else except force and vivacity, impressions and ideas are alike. Every idea seems in fact to be a copy or reflection of some impression. Hume tells us that all perceptions of the mind are double, and appear both as impressions and ideas. What Hume is getting at here is the relation of memory or imagination to original perception. He regards all of these as awareness of the same mental images differing only in their force or vivacity. His challenge to anyone who doubts that simple ideas and impressions always and necessarily correspond is to ask them to look into their own minds and see if they can find a simple impression that has no corresponding idea or a simple idea that has no corresponding impression.

There is, however, some uncertainty on this question of correspondence when complex ideas and impressions are concerned. We can, for example, have complex ideas, like the idea of a Brave New World, to which there is no corresponding impression. Similarly, we can have complex impressions, like London, the details of which cannot be reproduced in memory or imagination. This problem is not too damaging for Hume whose point is essentially concerned with simple perceptions.

This constant conjunction of impressions and ideas does not, according to Hume, occur by chance. If we apply the methodology of Newtonian science to it, it becomes clear that one is dependent on the other. The ideas are dependent on the impressions. According to Newtonian method, 'being dependent on' is defined in terms of 'constant conjunction'. If we note the order of appearance of ideas and impressions, we find that the impressions always precede their corresponding ideas so we must say that impressions are the causes[5] of ideas, and not vice versa. Hume thinks that this is confirmed by the fact that where, owing to deficiencies in our perceptual organs or in the absence of them, there are no ideas because there are no impressions for them to correspond to. If there are no eyes, then there will be no remembered or imagined sights. There is one exception to this which Hume notes: if all the different shades of a colour except one be placed before a man who has sight, he will be conscious of the blank and be able by his imagination to supply the deficiency even though he has never had a corresponding impression of that shade. Strangely, this potentially dama- ging counter-example does not bother him. He skates around it by saying that it is so particular and single (which is exactly what a good counter-example to a generalisation should be!) that ''tis scarce worth observing, and does not merit that for it alone, we should alter our general maxim.' He thus takes himself to have proved the general proposition, 'that all our simple ideas in their first appearance are derived from simple impressions, which are correspondent to them, and which they exactly represent'.

This then is Hume's account of the contents of the human mind. There are serious difficulties with it especially in respect of the supposed criterion of demarcation, force and liveliness. If that is the sole criterion, then it is difficult to see how vivid perceptions associated with hallucinations and so on, are to be excluded from the realm of impressions and how feeble and weak perceptions are to be included in that realm.

Hume on mental operations

Hume's account of mental operations is covered under the general term 'thinking'. Ideas and impressions are the basic building blocks of thought. Hume approaches this matter by making a distinction between (a) ideas of imagination, and (b) ideas of memory.

An impression which has been present in the mind may reappear in one of two ways, in memory or imagination, and these are distinguished in two ways. The first distinction is the already familiar one of force or liveliness. The second difference is that ideas of imagination are not tied down to the order and form of their preceding impressions. Ideas of memory are so tied in relation to order and form. On Hume's account, we cannot properly be said to 'remember' an event other than the way it occurred. We can remember an event out of order with other events, but in respect of any particular event, our idea has to be of a certain order for it to count as a memory. Hume would say that an idea was not a memory if its order were different from the original impression. He wants a considerable degree of correspondence in order. This does not apply to the imagination where we can put ideas together without such correspondence. Hume takes this to be shown by fables of winged horses, dragons and so on. The impressions have never occurred in that order. We have had impressions of wings and of horses but not of winged horses. The imagination puts the separate ideas together into a form which has no corresponding impression. Even though the imagination has the greater freedom, it is not completely free. It is guided by a universal principle, namely, that it is uniform with itself in all times and places. This means that we imagine in much the same way as we see things. Even in the case of *rara avis*, there are marked similarities with actual creatures. This circumstance is held by Hume to be due to some bond or union, some associative quality by which one idea naturally introduces another. Ideas tend to go together in certain ways. A particular shape tends to be associated with other qualities. We get complex ideas of imagination which are like complex impressions. For Hume, this is not an inseparable relation, but should be regarded as a gentle force which prevails and forms a constraint on the imagination. Hume believes this association of ideas to be based on certain qualities in the actual ideas that are associated. He does not regard association as arising out of some element in the mind making the associations. As there is no corresponding impression of such an element, it follows from Hume's thesis that we could not have an idea of it. To postulate such an element or disposition would be to indulge in metaphysical speculation. Hume is accepting the association of ideas as an observed fact and asking what are the laws which govern it. We cannot say what lies behind association. Thus his interest is in a question like, 'According to what law should a particular tune in my mind be associated with a particular person, place or event?', Hume is interested in the laws that govern such associations, not in their secret causes.

His answer to the question of what governs association is that wherever there is association there will always be found, as an observable matter of fact, certain relationships between the ideas themselves. The relationships are:

(1) Resemblance. By this he means that our imagination runs easily from one idea to another which resembles it.
(2) Contiguity in time or place. Here he means that in the same way that the senses in changing their objects (that is, by moving from one object to another) take them as they lie contiguous to one another, so must the imagination, by long custom, do the same.
(3) Cause and effect. This presents a serious problem.

It is in the principle of association that Hume thought that he had found the equivalent in human science of the principle of universal gravitation in physics and astronomy. It was Hume's belief that the three principles of association underlie *all* thinking. They underlie all connections in the mind. This was Hume's belief when he wrote the *Treatise*. By the time he came to write the *Enquiry* dissatisfaction with association was apparent. In later editions of the *Enquiry* the section on association was cut to three paragraphs.

We have seen Hume's general theory of what goes on in the mind. Let us now move on to a critical discussion. There is an obvious problem in his distinction between memory and imagination. Given that he requires such a high degree of ordered correspondence in memory, it is unclear what account he could give of the undoubted fact that we can remember in a muddled and confused way.

Secondly, there are a number of difficulties concerned with the principles of association. Resemblance will not do the work Hume requires. Without a human mind *as agent* to note the resemblances, there is simply no way in which the resemblance of two ideas can be regarded as responsible for their association. It is not even clear what 'resemblance' means here. Hume tacitly acknowledges this problem in the *Treatise* when he suggests that such ideas would be found to be associated with closely connected cells in the brain and this would be the real cause of their association. He is here in danger of contravening his own precept about not making speculations and searching for secret causes. Consider his second principle of association, contiguity in time or place. Ideas, considered as mental images, can be related in time but how can they be related in space? What Hume has done here is to switch from talking about ideas as mental items to talking of them as objective realities. We can have an idea of a book on a table, but this is not a case of our *idea* of the book being *on* our *idea* of the table. This confusion becomes clearer to us when we consider the third principle, cause and effect. There can be no doubt that when, for example, our thought of a gun calls up the thought of a dead man, there is some principle of association involved and one in which a grasp of causal relationships plays a part. The causal relationship, however, is not a natural relationship between ideas considered as mental images. It is not that our *mental image* of a gun is causally related to our *mental image* of a dead man. It is not even clear that mental images can enter into causal relations with each other. It seems, therefore, that of Hume's three principles, only half of the second one (contiguity in time) is even a possibility.

Thirdly, there is a major problem with the philosophically speculative basis of Hume's science of human nature. This is his acceptance of the truth of Locke's claim that all we are directly aware of in perception are our own ideas. This claim is not argued for by Hume, but it is clear that it is not a proposition to be arrived at by any observation or experiment which are the procedures Hume is supposed to be following. Such a claim is totally at odds with what we take ourselves to be aware of in perception and yet it is a cornerstone of Hume's position.

Knowledge and belief

Strictly speaking Hume limits the term 'knowledge' to relations between ideas. These relations are logically certain and cannot be denied without contradiction. They follow as a matter of logic from the content of the ideas as in mathematics. Such ideas do not, however, tell us anything about the world. It would be possible in principle to sit in a room and work out the truths of mathematics through a consideration of the meaning of the ideas. We could not, however, work out truths about how things in the world behave just by sitting down and thinking about it. Relations of ideas are purely *a priori* and do not carry a descriptive load relating to the world.

The sphere of belief is not as objectively certain as a true relation between ideas. Belief is concerned with matters of fact or real existence and the contradiction of a matter of fact is conceivable by the mind. If you said that silver did not expand when heated, you would have said something empirically false but not self-contradictory. If you said that a square had five sides, then you would be saying something self-contradictory. Although belief does not share the logical certainty of relations between ideas, Hume regards it as far more important. It is more important precisely because it is concerned with matters of fact. It is belief which more deeply concerns man as a moral being. A moral being has to act, and action requires belief. We are also forced by the necessities of life to pass judgements on matters of fact. If the mind is not to be limited to contemplating the ideas of sense as they occur, it must be by processes other than strict knowing that it escapes from such a limitation. If mind is to transcend its immediate ideas and impressions, then it must do so by belief. There is no other way. The most important relation in the acquisition of beliefs about the world is that of cause and effect.

Belief and fiction

In part two of *Enquiry V* Hume discusses the nature of belief. He contrasts belief with imagination and tells us that the imagination is free to form all manner of fictions. We can, in imagination, join the head of a man to the body of a horse. (These remarks are similar to our earlier ones concerning memory and imagination.)

The question Hume is interested in is how we distinguish such fictions from beliefs. What constitutes a belief as opposed to an imagined fiction that we cannot believe? He dismisses the idea that the difference consists of some idea attached to one and not the other. If that were the case, then there would be nothing to stop us attaching such an idea to a fiction and the road would then be open for believing anything. Hume holds that the difference lies in some sentiment or feeling which is attached to the belief and which is absent from the fiction. This feeling is not subject to the will in the way that the attaching of an idea would be. It is purely natural. We *feel* differently about one than the other and this feeling will have come about through custom. Belief is the name of this feeling. It is described as a more vivid, lively, forcible, firm, steady conception of an object than we get with imagination. The way this more vivid conception of belief arises is through the constant conjunctions through custom of an object present to the memory or the senses.

We have now reached the end of this aspect of Hume's philosophy, namely, his attempt at explaining what the contents of the mind are and how they interact according to empirical laws. The distinction between ideas considered as logical entities and ideas considered as real items of the world (real existents) ought to have led Hume to question the project of attempting to explain all thought in terms of empirical laws. The truths of logic (relations between ideas) are not ascertained by observation of the way we think. They are not empirical laws, they are the laws we *must* obey if we are to think at all.

We have not been able to have detailed discussions of Locke, Berkeley and Kant due to space limitations. Hopefully, this defect can to some extent be remedied in our discussion of Russell's *The Problems of Philosophy*. This will also provide us with the opportunity of broadening our discussion of issues in this area of philosophy though the reader should realise that it is very much an introductory work and by no means represents Russell's most technically refined position.

▶ Russell's *Problems of Philosophy*

Knowledge of the external world

Russell begins by asking whether there is any certain knowledge. He considers the case for saying that our immediate sense-experience provides us with such knowledge and invites us to reflect upon that experience. The reader should now be aware that this is the starting point for all empiricist epistemologies.

In considering his present sense-experience, he tells us that he 'seems' to be sitting in his chair, at a table. He looks out of the window and sees the sun. He has various beliefs about it and so on. Russell holds that all of this can reasonably be doubted. His grounds for this doubt are expressed in what is known as the argument from phenomenal variability. The argument is meant to establish that in perception we are not directly aware of physical objects.

Let us take Russell's argument concerning the table. In looking at a table we find that there are a number of perceptual variations or differences. To different observers, or to the same observer from different points of view, and under different lighting conditions, the table will appear to be of different colours. There is no *one* colour which can be regarded as *the* colour. To say that there was would be unjustified favouritism. The shape of the table is equally problematic. Again, there is much perceptual variation, depending on the observer's viewpoint. Thus the variability of our perceptions of the table applies to both its primary and secondary qualities. These different experiences we have from different viewpoints (for example, dark brown, light brown, shiny and so on) are what Russell calls 'appearances' of the table. What we call the real table is inferred from these appearances. There is a distinction drawn between what we directly perceive and what we infer, or between appearance and reality. We take it that there is a real table underlying the various appearances, but what we are immediately aware of are the various appearances and not the table *itself*. Russell concludes that the real table, assuming that there is one behind the appearances, is not the same as what we immediately experience via the senses. The real table is not directly knowable to us.

He then introduces a distinction between what he calls 'sense-data' and physical objects. What he means by 'sense-data' are the colours, shapes, smells, textures, sounds and so on, which we experience. The sense-data are the immediate objects of our experience. They are what we directly perceive and what we are immediately aware of. The awareness itself is called a sensation. It is from our experience of sense-data that we *infer* the existence of physical objects. 'Sense-data' correspond exactly with Hume's impressions of sense.

If what we are immediately aware of are sense-data, then the question arises as to the relation of these sense-data to physical objects (assuming that there are such things). Obviously, given the way in which Russell is using the key terms, the relation cannot be one of identity. We cannot talk about sense-data in the same way as we talk about physical objects without producing nonsense. He gives examples of this, you can buy and sell a table considered as a physical object but you cannot buy and sell your sense-data. Your sense-data of the table last only as long as they are experienced, whereas the table is more or less permanent. The important point to grasp here is that sense-data are essentially private objects, whereas physical things, like tables and chairs, are public objects. They are taken to be permanent and observable by different people. Sense-data, on the other hand, are private to each individual and they are transient. Sense-data exist only as long as the individual is perceiving them. To put it in technical terms, the essence of sense-data is to be perceived; they cannot exist unperceived. This is known as the *esse est percipi* principle.

Physical objects are held to be inferences from sense-data and, inasmuch as they are inferred rather than directly perceived, their existence is problematic. The existence of sense-data is not. You could doubt the existence of the table, perhaps it is a dream table, but you could not doubt the existence of your sense-data. There are two questions for Russell to answer:

(1) If what we directly perceive are sense-data, then what reason do we have for thinking that they are caused by physical objects or that there are physical objects underlying the sense-data?
(2) Is it true that what we are directly aware of are sense-data?

If the answer to (2) is no, then (1) becomes pointless. As Russell answers yes to (2), we need to discuss both.

Russell's answer to (1) is that the external world, that is, the world consisting of publicly observable physical objects which are permanent and exist independently of our perceiving them, should be seen as a postulate or hypothesis. This hypothesis would constitute the simplest explanation of the occurrence of the sense-data. Such a postulate would be consistent with the sense-data. What this means is that, for example, the many different sense-data I have when looking at a table and touching a table are most economically and systematically explained by the postulation of a physical object which causes the sensations of being aware of brownness, hardness in me. Thus, on Russell's account, the external world never has the status of anything more than a hypothesis.

Problems with Russell's solution

If all we are aware of are sense-data, then we can never *know* that there are physical objects which underlie them. This is an important point as it is a major difficulty with any representative theory of perception. If all we are aware of in perception are sense-data, then how can we know that they represent physical objects? How can we know anything of their external causes?

There is a further problem which arises from the previous one. Not only do we not know what they represent, neither can we know that they are representations. To see why this is a problem, consider the various ways we use a term like 'representation'. We might, for example, say that a picture represents a building, but note that it is only because we have knowledge of the building independently of the picture that we can legitimately describe the picture as a 'representation'. The problem is that any theory of perception which restricts what we know to sense-data or representations rules out what corresponds to independent knowledge in the case of the picture. We could not *describe* something as a picture if all we were aware of were pictures.

Another difficulty concerns Russell's initial claim that he 'seems' to be sitting in his chair and so on. Now when we use the word 'seems' we are normally making a guarded claim. We are allowing for the possibility that what we say could be wrong. Thus, for example, we might say that this ring seems to be made of gold, where the use of 'seems' allows for the possibility that it is made of some other metal. The point here is that there are always procedures which we can adopt to see whether what seems to be the case is the case or not. It is the possibility of adopting such procedures which gives a sense to 'seems'. The problem with Russell's use of 'seems' is that there are no procedures for finding out whether what seems to be the case is the case. No matter how closely we scrutinise or how hard we concentrate or who else we ask, there remains an element of doubt. He is quite prepared to use an expression like 'what seems to be the case' without saying what its counterpart, 'what is known to be the case' means. He could therefore be accused of using the term 'seems' in a philosophically objectionable way.[6]

Russell might claim that his use of 'seems' was legitimate on the grounds that what he says seems to be the case could reasonably be doubted. But how reasonable is this doubt? There are innumerable ways of checking what we would ordinarily call the reality of the situation. For Russell, however, even after all these ways have been exhausted there remains the possibility of doubt. It seems that all we can understand by 'doubt' here is that it is *logically* possible to suppose all these things to be false. That is to say, we do not involve ourselves in a formal contradiction by supposing them to be false. This does not, however, mean that the doubt is reasonable. There are many things that are logically possible and yet it would be quite unreasonable to believe in their actual possibility. It is logically possible for Snowdon to turn into a lump of cheese, but it is not reasonable to suppose that it might.

The argument from illusion

We now turn to the second question, namely, whether it is true to say that what we perceive are sense-data and not physical objects.

As we have seen, Russell's version of the argument from illusion concerns the variability of our perceptions. It is usual for sense-data theorists to add the notion of qualitative similarity to that of perceptual variation. What this means is that the observer looking at Russell's table from different viewpoints would not only experience slightly different colours and shapes, but also that the colours and shapes would change gradually rather than abruptly. Successive colours become darker and so on. There is no intrinsic difference in any of the perceived qualities. We can make the point of this addition clear by considering a summarised form of Ayer's argument from illusion.[7] The argument is based on the case of the stick which appears bent when half-immersed in water. The reader will note that, unlike the Cartesian arguments, no claim to *know* which appearance is veridical is made.

(1) The stick cannot be both straight and crooked and cannot be supposed to change its state back and forth depending on whether it is partly immersed in water.
(2) Therefore one of its appearances is delusive.
(3) But even in the case of the delusive appearance we are still seeing something with that character, which it is convenient to call a sense-datum.

(4) But there is no intrinsic difference in kind between the perceptions we call 'delusive' and those which we call 'veridical'. Nor is it possible to draw a line distinguishing veridical from delusive perception; the two shade indistinguishably into one another.

(5) Therefore, if delusive perceptions are perceptions of sense-data, so must veridical ones be likewise. What we directly and really perceive must always be sense-data and not material things.

(6) Therefore we cannot be sure that material things exist.

The point concerning qualitative similarity appears in (4) above. Ayer has identified a common core of the various arguments from illusion. 'This argument', writes Ayer '... as it is ordinarily stated, is based on the fact that material things may present different appearances to different observers, or to the same observer in different conditions, and that the character of these appearances is to some extent causally determined by the state of the conditions and the observer... The familiar cases of mirror images, and double vision, and complete hallucinations, such as the mirage, provide further examples' (*Ibid.*, p. 3).

There is another argument which can be used to show that in perception we are not aware of the external world and its existence is thus dubious. This argument may be described as the scientific argument and it comes in two forms:

(a) *The causal argument.* If perception involves a causal chain of events, all we can be aware of in it is the final event in this chain. How then can we be sure that there is a physical world at the beginning of the chain?

(b) *The argument from physics.* If the physical world reveals itself to the physicist as being quite unlike what we perceive, then what we perceive cannot be any part of the physical world. Therefore, we cannot be sure that there is such a world.

Let us now consider whether these arguments are valid. We shall begin with Russell's argument concerning the variability of perceptions.

The problem with Russell's argument is that it simply does not establish that what we are aware of in perception are sense-data rather than physical objects. We *expect* the table to look different under different conditions and we can explain why this is so. The facts that the way we see things varies according to variations in perceptual conditions and that we can predict the patterns of variation are exactly what we should expect. The fact that things behave in accordance with our expectations affords no ground for saying that they do not have the qualities we perceive or that what we perceive are not physical objects. Consider the following quotation from Thomas Reid:

Let us suppose for a moment that it is the real table we see. Must not this real table seem to diminish as we remove further from it? It is demonstrable that it must. How then can this apparent diminution be an argument that it is not a real table? When that which must happen to the real table, as we remove further from it, does actually happen to the table we see, it is absurd to conclude from this, that it is not the real table we see.[8]

There is another important objection against the argument from illusion. We can bring this out by considering Ayer's bent stick argument. (The objection applies equally to arguments appealing to double vision, hallucinations and so on) The objection is that the arguments commit the fallacy of the reification of appearances. What this means is that such arguments as Ayer's bent stick argument assume that there really is *something* which is bent and which is really seen. In the case of hallucinations it is assumed that there is a *thing* which we see and mistake it for a physical object. It is these assumptions that can be questioned. Step (3) in Ayer's argument can be rejected by saying that when we see a straight stick looking bent in the water, we are not seeing a bent *something* called a sense-datum. It is simply a straight stick which appears bent. In the case of hallucinations, there is no *thing* which is seen.

The scientific argument, in both its forms, also fails. The arguments are self-contradictory. In order to show that we have no direct awareness of the physical world and therefore cannot be certain of its existence, it is first of all assumed that there is such a world. Instead of supporting scepticism about the existence of the physical world, they exclude it. Consider Russell's argument in Chapter 3 of *The Problems of Philosophy*. The argument is that as it takes the sun's light about eight minutes to reach us, what we are seeing now is the sun of eight minutes ago. If the physical sun had ceased to exist within the last eight minutes that would make no difference to the sense-datum we call 'seeing the sun'. Arguments such as these require factual statements about physical things to serve as premises, and yet their conclusions, if true, would show that we could never know that there were physical things as all we have are sense-data. We might also note Ayer's comment, namely, why should the time interval make a difference? Is it any more paradoxical to say that our eyes see into the past than it is to say that we do not see physical objects?[9] We can conclude that Russell has not shown that what we are directly aware of in perception are sense-data.

The secondary qualities thesis

Although the scientific argument fails to establish grounds for doubt concerning the existence of the external world, it can be used to try and show that the secondary qualities are not part of the external world. This move is made by combining the causal argument with the argument from physics. The latter argument tells us that the secondary qualities are not possessed by physical objects as they are revealed to us by physicists. The former argument tells us that they are contributed by us. Russell argues like this. The physicist's account of the physical world includes wave-motions, light waves and so on. These are not the sorts of thing that could, for example, be coloured. They interact with optic nerves and cause us to have the experience of colour. Colour might well *represent* some property of an object, but the object is not *really* coloured.

This thesis seems quite non-controversial for certain of the secondary qualities. Indeed, it might be regarded as the common-sense view for smells, tastes and sounds. We might not, for example, think that the smell and taste of bacon and eggs belong to the objects themselves in the way their shape or size do. The problematic case concerns the senses of sight and touch – colour and texture. In these cases common sense sides with Realism. As we remarked in our discussion of Descartes, we regard the apple we are eating as really being solid and green. A proponent of the secondary qualities thesis will claim that scientific arguments can and do upset our common-sense beliefs. The history of science has many examples of this. The reader might, however, feel some reservations concerning his apple. If he is told that the apple he is about to eat is 'really' colourless and consists mainly of wave motion so that it cannot be described as solid, then he might feel that something has gone wrong. Perhaps what is wrong is the notion that the physicist tells us what the world is 'really' like.

Let us consider the property of solidity which we attribute to chairs, tables and so on. On a physicist's account of such objects they are wave motion, mainly empty space. This is the basis for saying that they are not 'really' solid or firm. When we use the term 'solid', however, we mean that the objects we are talking about are able to support us or books or whatever. We distinguish solid things which can support from non-solids, like quicksand, which cannot support. This notion of an ability to support is a criterion for ascribing solidity to objects. Clearly, when a scientist describes these very objects as non-solid, he is not saying that they will not support things. He feels no qualms about sitting in his chair. It seems, therefore, that what he, or the philosopher influenced by physics, is recommending is a change in our criterion of solidity. Thus when a scientist describes physical objects as non-solid he means that electrons can pass through them. This need not be incompatible with our use of 'solid'. We use the term 'solid' to distinguish what will support from what will not, what is firm from what is not, what is hard from what is not and so on. If that usage constitutes its meaning, then its meaning is left untouched by the physicist projecting electrons through solid objects. Furthermore, if we revised our concept of solidity so that anything which can have electrons pass through it is to be called 'non-solid', then we are going to have to say that just about everything is non-solid. The problem then would be to give a meaning to 'solid', and if we could not do this, then how could 'non-solid' have a meaning?[10] It is very difficult to operate a solid/non-solid distinction in a world consisting of wave motions.

Berkeley's Idealism

In Chapter 4 Russell discusses the philosophical doctrine of Idealism. This is the thesis that what is known to exist must in some sense be mental. As we shall see later, this is not to be taken as a denial of the reality of physical objects and this is why it was a misunderstanding on the part of Dr Johnson to think that he could refute Berkeley by kicking a stone.

Berkeley is best understood as the successor to Locke. According to Locke, a certain number of our simple ideas go together to form a complex idea. Let us take an example to clarify this. Consider the idea, or sense-datum, of the sun which we have when we look upwards. The idea of the sun is, for Locke, the aggregate of a number of simple ideas such as bright, roundish, hot and so on. The idea we have of any material object is held to be a collection of these simple ideas. (Locke, of course, holds that what we are aware of in perception are our own ideas.) Words like 'sun' or 'horse' represent complex ideas – they are composed of simpler ideas. Locke sees a problem here, namely, we cannot imagine how these simple ideas going constantly together could subsist by themselves. Because of this we assume a substratum in which they inhere. This substratum binds or holds together the different qualities. Thus, in the case of an apple, the ideas (qualities or attributes) of greenness, firmness, sweetness and so on, are held together by something called substance. A physical object is substance plus attributes. The problem for Locke is that we are unable to say what this substance is. The nature of the material substance is, for Locke, unknowable, secret and abstract.

Berkeley's Idealism contains an assault on Locke's theory of material substance. He is denying the existence of Locke's matter and claiming that common sense is left undisturbed by such a denial. He points out that on Locke's theory of language words stand for ideas but as there is no idea corresponding to material substance the term must be meaningless. He also argues that Locke's theory of matter contravenes the empiricist standpoint that all ideas come from experience. Matter is something distinct from ideas, yet all we are said to be aware of are ideas. Thus on Berkeley's denial of Locke's matter no actual object of experience is lost. He claims that the road to scepticism about the existence of the external world will be closed as on his scheme there will be no problem of connecting ideas to things we know not what. On Berkeley's scheme all there will be are the ideas. Material objects are collections of ideas (sense-data) and their being is to be perceived (*esse est percipi*). For Berkeley, the immediate objects of sense are the sensible qualities and nothing other than them. To say that their essence is to be perceived means that they cease to be anything if they are not perceived. Berkeley's use of 'perceiving' includes sensing, imagining, conceiving. He holds that true knowledge is acquaintance with our ideas of perception.

It would be a gross misunderstanding of Berkeley to think that his *esse est percipi* principle committed him to saying that objects spring in and out of existence depending on whether they are being perceived or not. The clearing up of this misunderstanding is a good antidote to those who think that philosophers spend time wondering whether the objects they are looking at cease to exist when they are not being looked at. As Russell remarks, it would be difficult to understand how an unperceived cat gained an appetite during a period of non-existence! (The body of the cat being a collection of ideas.) Berkeley, however, does hold ideas to be mind-dependent (remember that 'ideas' for Berkeley includes what is appre-hended through the senses). Now we cannot just call up ideas of sense and make them vanish at will. Berkeley realises the inadequacy of saying that their existence is dependent on, and guaranteed by, individual human minds. They do persist when we are not aware of them. The *esse est percipi* principle carries an implication of mind-dependency, but not necessarily that of human minds. The mind upon which they are dependent is that of God. Such a mind is infinite and eternal.

Russell wants to attack the notion of mind-dependency. He points out an equivocation in Berkeley's use of 'idea'. In its proper usage it is quite permissible to talk of ideas being in the mind, but in Berkeley's usage there is a danger of regarding the material object itself as being in the mind. Russell holds that Berkeley was correct in saying that the sense-data (ideas) which we are immediately aware of in perception are dependent on there being a perceiver. The point he wants to attack is that whatever can be known must be in some mind or in some sense mental. Russell is not calling into question the thesis that ought to be questioned, namely, the thesis held in common by Locke, Berkeley and Hume that what we are directly aware of are our own ideas. Indeed, Russell endorses this when he says that what we are directly aware of are our own sense-data. Where he differs from Berkeley is over the nature of the sense-data or ideas which Berkeley holds to be mental.

Knowledge by acquaintance and knowledge by description

Following his brief dismissal of Berkeley, Russell moves to a discussion of whether any other reasons can be adduced in support of an Idealist position. It is here that we are introduced to Russell's famous epistemological distinction between knowledge by acquaintance and knowledge by description.

The distinction is introduced through a disapprovingly quoted saying: 'We cannot know that anything exists which we do not know.' Russell wants to reject this as he wants to say that matter is something we do not know (directly) and yet we can know that there is such a thing as matter. So how is such knowledge possible? The first distinction which Russell introduces is that between knowledge of truths and knowledge of things. He wants to distinguish two senses of the word 'know' and claim that the saying referred to is seen to be false when this distinction is made apparent. The two senses of 'know' are:

(1) The sense in which knowledge is opposed to error. This is the sense in which what we know is *true*. Truth is predicated of propositions and it is in propositions that judgements, beliefs or convictions are expressed. When we know these to be true, then we know that something is the case. This is *knowledge of truths*.

(2) The second sense of 'know' is that in which we know *things* rather than truths. It is this knowledge of things which Russell here refers to as knowledge by acquaintance. This is the way in which we would know sense-data. We are acquainted with them. As we shall see, we are also said to know things by description. We shall come to that shortly.

If we now rephrase the saying, 'We cannot know that anything exists which we do not know.', in the light of the above distinction between knowledge of truths and knowledge by acquaintance we get, 'We can never truly judge that something with which we are not acquainted exists.' Russell then claims that such a proposition is false as there are things with which we are not acquainted and yet we can and do truly judge them to exist. He cites the Emperor of China as an example to support this (there was such a person at that time). He can truly judge such a person to exist even though he is not acquainted with him. There is, however, a problem here.

The example he uses is itself problematic. It looks as if it is very plausible as long as we regard our non-acquaintance with the Emperor as just being a *factual* matter. If the example is taken in this way, then the analogy with the existence of matter is destroyed. In the case of judging matter to exist, we are dealing with something with which it is *in principle* impossible to be acquainted given Russell's claim that what we are directly acquainted with in perception are sense-data. This is the status of Locke's matter; it is essentially unknowable. In citing the Emperor example, Russell has switched to our ordinary way of talking in which we say that we are acquainted with physical things. On his own premises he has no right to do this. In the case of acquaintance with the Emperor the most that Russell can say is that we are acquainted with certain sense-data from which we *infer* the existence of the Emperor. We cannot be acquainted with the Emperor himself any more than we can be acquainted with the physical object itself. In order to be consistent, the initial saying should be recast as: 'We can never truly judge that something with which we *cannot* be acquainted exists.' Now this might well be false but the problem for Russell is to say how we could ever *know* it was false. The problem, of course, arises from the claim that what we are acquainted with in perception are sense-data and not physical objects.

Russell holds that it is possible to have knowledge of things with which we are not acquainted. This kind of knowledge is referred to as knowledge by description. Strictly speaking, our knowledge of the Emperor of China should have been referred to as knowledge by description rather than by acquaintance. All our knowledge of physical objects is by description. Russell's table, for example, would be known via the description, 'the physical object which causes such and such sense-data'. Knowledge by description will ultimately rest on knowledge by acquaintance. In the case of the table, our knowledge by description will rest on our sense-data with which we are acquainted. In order to have knowledge of the table, we need to know truths which connect it with things with which we have acquaintance (sense-data). As Russell remarks, we are going to have to know the truths of the form: such and such sense-data are caused by a physical object. The difficulty though is how we can ever know truths like these when all we are aware of are sense-data. We can never pass beyond the world of sense-data and see whether they are caused by physical objects. The contention that they are so caused remains a hypothesis, and a hypothesis is distinguishable from a truth.

In addition to sense-data Russell also held that there were other objects of acquaintance. We are said to be acquainted with our own mental states and states of awareness, with a self denoted by 'I', as distinct from the mental states themselves, though Russell was to change his mind about the self later. At the time of writing *The Problems of Philosophy* Russell thought that the pronoun 'I' had to refer to something. He later came to think that the self could be analysed in terms of its experiences.

Russell held that we were also acquainted with universals. By these he means abstract and general concepts like whiteness or squareness. These are eternal, whereas particular things exist only for a certain time.

The theory of descriptions

Russell is concerned with the nature of our knowledge concerning objects in cases where we know that there is an object corresponding to a description but we are not acquainted with such an object. He wants to elucidate the nature of this knowledge.

The kind of description with which we are concerned is a *definite description*. This is a singular expression of the form 'the so and so'. Examples of such definite descriptions would be 'the last King of England', 'the man in the iron mask', 'the first Roman Emperor' and so on. When we know that there is an object corresponding to a definite description, we know that there is one and only one (*the* so and so) object which has a particular property.

Russell has a distinction between genuine or logically proper names, and the ordinary proper names of grammar. A genuine proper name can only be used in conjunction with some object of direct acquaintance. Russell's favourite candidates for such names were the pronouns 'this' and 'that' used to denote some immediate datum of sense. At the time of writing *The Problems of Philosophy* he thought that we were acquainted with a self, thus when a person uses his own name he would be referring to an object of direct acquaintance. This is the only occasion in which an ordinary proper name can function as a genuine proper name. The crucial point about the use of genuine proper names is that they secure uniqueness of reference. They pick out and identify an object of direct acquaintance. Ordinary proper names do not do this. They are disguised descriptions. This means that whenever we use an ordinary proper name the thought we wish to convey in the proposition in which it occurs can be expressed, without changing the meaning, by replacing the name with some definite description. Thus, to use Russell's example, the ordinary proper name 'Bismark' can be replaced by the description 'the first German chancellor'. Russell held what is known as a denotation theory of meaning. For a genuine name to have meaning there must be some object which it denotes; its meaning is the object it denotes. Now all manner of ordinary names, like 'Zeus', and what might appear to be complex names, like 'the present King of France', can occur in meaningful propositions. It would seem that, in order for them to do this, they must have a meaning. If they were genuine names, then they would have to denote objects in order to acquire this meaning. This would mean admitting a great many strange entities into the world. Russell's theory of definite descriptions is intended to remove this difficulty by showing that such names and expressions do not function as genuine names. They are disguised descriptions. Genuine proper names cannot be used in conjunction with existence and non-existence. Given that 'this' used as a genuine name refers to some object of direct acquaintance, a sense-datum, then once we had named such an object 'this' there would be no point in going on to say 'this exists'. Once we have got the object, we know it exists. If we said that it did, all we would produce is a tautology. If we denied that it existed, we would say something self-contradictory. Ordinary proper names can be used in conjunction with existence and non-existence and, for Russell, this shows that they cannot be genuine names. He tells us that: 'Whenever the grammatical subject of a proposition can be supposed not to exist without rendering the proposition meaningless, it is plain that the grammatical subject is not a proper name, i.e., not a name directly representing some object'.[11] It would be analysed away according to the theory of descriptions which replace the ordinary name. Thus in denying the existence of Moses we would be saying: 'There is no object X such that X was called Moses and X received the ten commandments'. This avoids the problem of admitting Moses as a kind of object.

I have given this brief outline of the theory so the reader will understand why the notion of a definite description plays such an important part in Russell's epistemology. We can now turn to the nature of knowledge by description. Let us take Russell's example of 'Bismark'. The first point to note is that the use of that name by its bearer in making a judgement about himself would be a case of knowledge by acquaintance. He is acquainted with a self which the name denotes.

However, if someone other than Bismark used the ordinary proper name 'Bismark', he would not be securing that uniqueness of reference which Bismark himself would secure. The other person would not be using 'Bismark' to refer to something with which he was directly acquainted. What he is acquainted with are, at best, certain sense-data which he infers to be representations of Bismark's body. Bismark is known to him by the description 'the entity which causes such and such sense-data'. What is important here is that the description contains a reference to particulars, that is, sense-data, with which the person is acquainted. This is what is meant by saying that knowledge by description rests ultimately on knowledge by acquaintance. If knowledge by description is to give us knowledge about the world, then the description must always make a reference to some particular with which we are acquainted. If no reference is made to a particular, then we do not have any knowledge of the world. In such a case our knowledge would be confined to what was *logically* deducible from the description. This is the point of Russell's example of the description, 'the most long lived of men'. Such a description makes no reference to particulars but consists entirely of universals. It is because it does this that our path to real knowledge is barred. All we would know from such a description is that he lived longer than any other man or whatever else could be *logically* deduced from the description. We do not know any *facts* about him.

Suppose we ask how it is possible for us to have knowledge of something with which we are not acquainted, for example, Julius Caesar. Russell's answer is that the ordinary name is replaced by a description such as 'the man who crossed the Rubicon' and this contains a reference to a particular 'Rubicon', and we are acquainted with this either via the sense-data experienced from standing by the river or obtained from looking at maps and so on.

The importance of knowledge by description is that it enables us to transcend the limits of our immediate and private experience. It enables us to have knowledge of things which we have never experienced. We will never be acquainted with Bismark or Caesar, but we can have knowledge of them through description. Such descriptions will ultimately rest on things with which we are acquainted though these things will not be the objects themselves.

There are problems with the thesis. The problems centre mainly on the idea of knowledge by acquaintance and Russell's theory of names. We cannot pursue technical criticisms here but we can note a point made by Ayer.[12] Russell assumes that all descriptions are ultimately linked to objects of acquaintance, mainly one's own sense-data (and universals). The problem is that sense-data are private to each individual. If that is so, then how can we be said to be referring to the *same* particulars? Is it not necessary to do this in order to communicate about, and agree on, our descriptions?

Russell on *a priori* knowledge

Russell agrees with the Rationalists that we do have knowledge which is independent of experience. As the reader will know from the introduction to this chapter, such knowledge is referred to as *a priori* knowledge. Russell gives examples of *a priori* knowledge: (1) principles of logic, (2) some ethical judgements, and (3) the truths of mathematics.

Russell refers to the elementary principles of logic as 'the laws of thought'. We need to realise that this should not be understood in a psychological sense, but in a logical one. What distinguishes a logical law from a psychological one is its necessity. To put it another way, a logical law, such as the law of non-contradiction, *could not* have been different, whereas a psychological law, such as a law of association, could have been different.

The problem of *a priori* knowledge is that it appears to legislate for experience and yet is known independently of experience. Russell tells us that although such knowledge is independent of experience, it is nevertheless caused and elicited by experience. This is not an important enough point to embarrass the Rationalist. It is still the case that logical principles are known *a priori*. Even if we say that all propositions which we know are experiental in the sense that we require particular experiences to know them, we are still going to have to make a distinction between those which need to be confirmed by the way things are in the world and those which do not. The problem is not going to be solved by this kind of move. In Chapter 8 Russell moves on to a discussion of how *a priori* knowledge is possible.

Kant had argued that we have *a priori* knowledge which is not purely analytic. Kant claimed that *a priori* knowledge provides us with knowledge of how things in the world must behave. It does not just unfold the meaning of the subject-term as analytic propositions do. According to Kant, there can be propositions which are synthetic (telling us something about the world) and *a priori* (known independently of experience). The problem is to say how it is that we can have knowledge of things we have not experienced or how we can anticipate how they will behave. As Russell says, Kant's answer to this is difficult and technical. We can, however, give an outline of it.

Kant holds that in every experience there are two elements. One is due to the object and the other is due to ourselves (our nature). What are due to the objects are those qualities given in sense-experience, what Russell refers to as sense-data. On the other hand, the categories of space, time and causality are supplied by us. They are forms imposed by the mind. It is necessary for the mind to do this in order for us to have experiences. Unless an object had those forms imposed on it, it could never be an object of experience for us. These are the forms to which all our experience must conform. The same would apply to bug-eyed Martians. Although they might see things differently in some respects, they would still see objects as spatial and so on. These forms are necessary conditions for the having of ordered experiences.

The objects which we experience are referred to by Kant as 'phenomena'. We who have these experiences are also part of the phenomenal world. The self of experience is called the phenomenal self. Physical objects themselves, without the forms of space, time and causality imposed upon them, can never be known by us. In order for anything to be known to us it must have those forms imposed on it. The thing-in-itself – what Kant refers to as 'noumena' – remains unknowable. All objects of study for any science are phenomenal objects, that is, objects located in space-time and subject to the law of causality. The reader may wonder why Kant thought that there were noumena behind the phenomena instead of being content with just the phenomena studied by the sciences. Briefly, the main reason for this was that Kant, as we have seen, held that whatever appears to us appears conditioned by our senses and understanding. They are not, however, the products of our senses or understanding. We do not choose what we see – if we look around, it is not a matter of choice that we see tables, chairs and so on. Whatever it is that causes us to see tables is something we cannot know as all we are aware of are the tables, which are conditioned by us.

Any phenomenon is bound to have those characteristics supplied by us. This is central to Kant's account of *a priori* knowledge. It is to those characteristics supplied by us that *a priori* knowledge is applicable. That is why *a priori* knowledge is true of all actual and possible experience. Without the imposition of the necessary forms of experience (space, time, causality and number) there simply would not be any experiences. Kant held that *a priori* knowledge was of those forms and that explains how it is also synthetic. It lays down the forms to which experience must conform.

Russell is critical of this solution. We noted earlier that the hallmark of logical laws was absolute necessity. Russell does not think that this necessity is adequately explained by saying that it is contributed by us or is somehow a part of our nature. There is no hard and fast distinction in Kant between what we could broadly describe as psychological laws on the one hand and logical ones on the other. This distinction was made apparent in the writings of Russell and Frege.[13] This dismissal of Kant is too simplistic but further inquiry is beyond the scope of our present purpose.

The necessity of *a priori* knowledge cannot be accounted for by saying that it is applicable to physical things or to our thought processes. These are both covered by empirical laws and such laws do not carry the necessity of logical laws. We can express this by saying that there are possible worlds in which our empirical laws do not hold but there are no possible worlds where the laws of logic do not hold. Russell tells us that *a priori* knowledge is concerned with entities which do not, properly speaking, exist in the mental or the physical world. The entities to which it applies are universals.

Universals

In Chapter 9 Russell inquires into what kind of being universals can be said to have. The problem, like many philosophical problems, goes back to Plato. Russell follows in Plato's footsteps for a fair way on this issue. What are universals? He takes Plato's classic case of asking what is justice. We start to answer by considering a number of particular just acts and seeing what they have in common. The idea is that there is a common feature which is shared by all just acts and nothing else. This will be the essence of justice or the universal 'justice'. All just acts must participate in this essence (or Form) in order to be called just. Now this principle does not only apply to moral or aesthetic terms, but also to terms such as whiteness, squareness, triangularity. It applies to any general term. What Russell refers to as universals and Plato refers to as Forms are the same. They are not objects of sense-experience. Thus, for example, particular white things are objects of sense-experience but whiteness itself is not. It was through a consideration of the eternal, immutable, indestructible, non-spatial Forms that Plato believed that the world of sense-experience was only a pale reflection of the world of the Forms which exists outside experience.

A universal will be anything that can be shared by particulars but is not itself a particular. Particulars constitute the world of sense-experience, universals populate a quite different realm. Russell tells us that when we examine language we find, in the main, that proper names refer to particulars, whereas other nouns, adjectives, prepositions and verbs stand for universals. No sentence can be constructed that does not contain at least one universal. It follows that all truths will involve universals and all knowledge of truths will involve an acquaintance with them.

There are universals which express properties and substantives (denoted by adjectives and nouns) and those which express relations (denoted by verbs and prepositions). Russell argues that those which express relations are fundamental. His reason for saying this is as follows. In order to avoid admitting the reality of universals, traditional empiricists had claimed that we form an abstract idea of whiteness, for example, from particular sense impressions of white things. Russell points out a difficulty with this. Suppose we ask the question, 'How do we know that some particular thing is white?'. The traditional empiricist reply would be that we know by comparing the thing before us with some particular patch of white and if it resembles it sufficiently, then we would know it was white. Thus what would be crucial would be the resemblance it bore to the selected sample of whiteness. But, Russell argues, all this achieves is the admission of another type of universal, namely, the *relation* of resemblance. This relation would be between a great deal of things as there are a great many white things. The problem cannot be avoided by saying that the resemblance in question need only be supposed to hold between the problem case and the chosen sample and some other sort of resemblance holds between other white things. If you said this, then you would have to say that the various resemblances resembled each other, and again, you have to admit the relation of resemblance as a universal. You would have to say that the various resemblances resembled each other in order to account for why we use the same word to describe all the pairs in question. Russell takes this to show that universals expressing relations have to be admitted.

Taking himself to have established that there must be universals, the next question concerns the status of their being. Russell wants to reject the notion that universals are mental. He has two arguments against the mentalist thesis (or conceptualism as it is sometimes called).

(1) A true proposition containing a relational universal (for example, north of) is true independently of whether we think that it is true. If there is nothing mental in the complex fact signified by the proposition, 'Edinburgh is to the north of London', then there cannot be anything mental in any of its constituents. One of its constituents is the relational universal 'north of'.

(2) If universals were mental, then this would rob them of their universality. Our ideas, considered as mental contents, can differ and so can one person's at different times. Russell takes universals to be possible objects of thought but not to be thoughts themselves.

Universals are said to belong to a world which can be apprehended by thought, but this is not a world created by, or dependent on, thought. He concludes by saying that he will reserve the term 'existing' for those things that are in time. Thus the world of particular things can be said to exist. Universals, being non-temporal, cannot be said to exist. Nevertheless, they have being and Russell refers to this being as 'subsisting'. He describes the world of universals as unchanging, rigid and exact. It is the world studied by the mathematician, logician and metaphysician. It is contrasted with the world of sense-experience which is full of imprecision, it is changing and transient. He regards both those worlds as real and he holds it to be a matter of temperament as to which one we choose to study.

We can now see how Russell intends to solve the problem of *a priori* knowledge. The possibility of such knowledge is going to be explained in terms of his theory of universals. The solution is expressed by saying that all *a priori* knowledge deals exclusively with the relations of universals. You will remember that the problem of *a priori* knowledge was that it seemed to legislate for experience independently of experience. It appeared to tell us the way things must behave in experience and yet it was not derived from experience. Russell's answer to this is that if you take the classic example of *a priori* knowledge, mathematical or logical propositions, like $2 + 2 = 4$, then you see that the proposition asserts a relation between the universal '2' and the universal '4'. This is concerned exclusively with relations between universals (concepts) and makes no reference to particulars (sensible existents). No *a priori* proposition asserts or implies anything about the *existence* of actual *particular* things. Propositions asserting existence can only be known to be true through experience, they are never known *a priori*. Nowadays, this would be expressed by saying that no existential proposition is logically necessary.

This connects up with Russell's conception of philosophy. In the final chapter he tells us that we can never answer questions concerning what there is in the universe through *a priori* reasoning. This is the point of his criticism of Hegel's conception of philosophy. Hegel thought, through what he called the process of synthesis and antithesis of either ideas or things, we could arrive at some fundamental idea, some ultimate reality – the whole. What this means is that if you think of something in abstraction, then necessarily it is incomplete. It has to be linked to something else and that in turn must be linked to another thing and so on. What is important in this linking process is that these things or ideas are not accidentally linked. What something is linked to is contained in its own nature. Thus it is through a consideration of separate things that we discover the links and eventually join everything up in a whole which requires no further linking. It is like doing a kind of logical jig-saw. Each piece contains the possibility of its relations in its own nature and by considering that nature we could tell what is linked with it. A piece of the jig-saw existing on its own would be an abstraction and only a part of the picture of reality. Hegel held that things by their very existence presuppose the existence of other things and that we can discover these presuppositions by *a priori* reasoning. We would therefore discover reality through pure reasoning. It is this that Russell believes philosophy can never achieve. We cannot, through the purely logical procedure of *a priori* reasoning, answer questions concerning what exists or must exist. *A priori* reasoning is concerned solely with the relations between universals and they cannot be said to 'exist', they 'subsist'.

There are problems here, especially in connection with Russell's account of universals. The most I can do here is indicate some lines of thought which the reader might like to pursue. First, there is a difficulty of understanding what is meant by 'subsisting'. Russell tells us that relational universals (for example, 'on', 'in', 'under') do not seem to exist in the full-blooded sense that the things they relate (that is, physical objects) exist. The problem is whether we can think of 'existence' in a strong and a weak sense. It might be claimed that existence is an all or nothing affair.

Second, readers should consult Chapter 4 of this book, dealing with Plato's theory of Forms. Aristotle offered an alternative. Universals are real (that is, they exist) but they are not real or existent as *abstractions*. They exist only as the essences of *actually* existing particular things.

Third, an influential alternative approach has been that of Wittgenstein. He held that things referred to by a common name *need not* have anything in common. Wittgenstein thought that the search for generality was responsible for a number of philosophical confusions. He claimed that it is a mistake to think that we must always find a common essence in order to account for our use of a general word in referring to a number of particulars. Consider his classic example of the general word 'game'. There is no feature common to all games and yet we use the term 'game' to refer to them. There is no common feature to cricket, skipping and ring-a-ring-a-roses. Instead, we find that there is a complex network of similarities and relationships all intertwined with each other. Some similarities are more marked than others:

> What ties the ship to the wharf is a rope, and the rope consists of fibres, but it does not get its strength from any fibre which runs through it from one end to the other, but from the fact that there is a vast number of fibres overlapping.[14]

We now move to the most influential philosophical movement of the inter-war years, Logical Positivism.

▶ A. J. Ayer's *Language, Truth and Logic*

Ayer holds that the way to solve philosophical disputes is to establish precisely what is the purpose, method, function and scope of a philosophical inquiry. Metaphysics considered as a subject which reveals some transcendent reality beyond the world of sense-experience is regarded as a non-starter.

The method of Ayer's attack on metaphysics is to show that any proposition purporting to describe such a reality is nonsensical or is not significant. This method is intended to be a purely logical mode of criticism and not a psychological one. Ayer is not saying that our minds are incapable of dealing with a transcendent reality, but rather, propositions which purport to describe it are meaningless. Now in order to make judgements like this concerning the nature and scope of meaningful discourse, you need some criterion for distinguishing between what is meaningful and what is meaningless. The criterion in question is the verification principle.

The verification principle

According to this principle of meaning, a sentence is factually significant to any given person, if and only if, he knows how to verify the proposition which it purports to express. He must know what observations would lead him to accept or reject the proposition.

Although Ayer uses the expression 'factually significant', it is clear that with the exception of analytic propositions, factual significance is the only kind of significance that is relevant to a proposition's being meaningful. Thus we can say that any proposition which is not analytic and of which we cannot say what observations would be relevant to its acceptance or rejection is to be regarded as meaningless.

It is not necessary for us to be able to *actually* verify the proposition, but it is necessary for us to know what observations would be relevant to its truth or falsity. This is what Ayer means by a proposition being verifiable in principle though not in practice. As long as it is verifiable in principle then it can be admitted into the realm of meaningful discourse. It might not be practically possible to verify a proposition about a distant galaxy, but it would in principle be possible. Such a proposition would be regarded as meaningful as we could say what observations would be relevant to its truth or falsity. It is just that we cannot make those observations.

In addition to the preceding distinction, there is a further distinction between conclusive and probable, or strong and weak, verification. Verification in a strong sense would mean that it must be possible to conclusively verify a proposition by experience. Ayer rejects this and opts for verification in a weak sense. Verification in a weak sense means that it must be possible for experience to render a proposition probable. The reason Ayer takes this line is that general propositions stating scientific laws could not be regarded as meaningful if the strong sense of verification were adopted. We say that all metals expand when heated but this could not be conclusively verified in experience. We could never examine all the metals that there are as there is an infinite amount of them. Neither could we ever know that all the metals we had examined were all the metals that there are. In spite of this we would not want to say that such general statements were meaningless. Weak verificationism allows them in as meaningful as we can say that they are probably true given that we have found no exceptions. There is a similar problem with statements about the past. They are probable and yet we would not wish to write them off as nonsense. Ayer therefore adopts verification in a weak sense.

Applications of the principle

Armed with this principle of meaning Ayer sets out to show the kinds of things that could be ruled out by it. The claim that the external world is unreal or mere appearance would be an example of a piece of nonsense because there is no observation which is relevant to determining its truth or falsity. The metaphysical dispute concerning whether reality is one substance or many is also ruled out. Again, there is no observation relevant to settling the dispute. The dispute is not a genuine dispute in direct proportion to the lack of relevance of factual evidence. The same applies to the dispute between Realism and Idealism. Talk about God is also regarded as a species of nonsense as are moral judgements.[15]

It is, of course, also the case that such metaphysical pronouncements are not *a priori* propositions. If they were, then they could be admitted as meaningful. Ayer allows empirical and *a priori* propositions into the field of meaningful discourse.

One of the most important ways in which metaphysical beliefs arise is from a failure to understand the structure of language. The linguistic fact that a word can appear as a grammatical subject in a proposition should not be taken to imply that there must be some entity to which it refers. Ayer uses the problem of substance to illustrate this. In our language we cannot give the qualities or attributes of something without mentioning it as a subject term. We say, for example, 'the apple is green', 'the apple is sweet', 'the apple is round'. This is said to lead to the confusion that in addition to the sensible qualities of greenness, sweetness and roundness, there is *something* else to which 'the apple' refers. This leads to Locke's supposition that there must be a substance in addition to the various qualities and in which they inhere. Ayer holds that logical analysis reveals that 'the apple' is nothing more than the sum total of its sensible qualities and the way they are related to themselves rather than to something other than themselves. As we shall see, this is a position close to that of Berkeley.

Philosophy as analysis

Ayer regards the entire function of philosophy as critical and not speculative. It analyses and provides us with a certain kind of definition.

Now when Ayer says that philosophy is an analytic discipline, he does not mean that it sets out to dissect things into parts in the way a chemical analysis does. What he is concerned with is the way in which we talk about things, that is, what it makes sense to say. The propositions of philosophy are of a linguistic character rather than a factual one. Philosophy is said to be concerned with definitions and the formal consequences of those definitions. All philosophical problems are seen to be a demand for definitions. The problem of perception will reduce to 'what is the nature of a physical object?' and this is a demand for definition. If philosophy is a demand for definitions, then how is the task of the philosopher to be distinguished from that of the lexicographer? Ayer's answer to this comes at the start of Chapter 3. He distinguishes explicit definitions from definitions *in use*.

(a) *Explicit definitions.* An explicit definition is simply the replacement of one symbol or symbolic expression with a synonym for it. The condition of synonymity is satisfied where the replacement yields two different sentences which are equivalent, for example, (1) There is a puppy on the mat, (2) There is a young dog on the mat. These are different sentences but they are equivalent. 'Puppy' and 'young dog' are synonymous expressions. Ayer's condition of equivalence is that two sentences, p and q, belonging to the same language, are equivalent if and only if every sentence which is entailed by any group of sentences together with p is entailed by the same group together with q. Each sentence taken in conjunction with a particular group of sentences must have the same entailment properties. This is the kind of definition which is of interest to the lexicographer. What is of interest to the philosopher is the second kind of definition.

(b) *Definitions in use.* To define a symbol *in use* is not to be taken as meaning that it is replaceable with some synonym or other, but rather as meaning that any sentence in which it occurs can be translated into equivalent sentences in which neither it nor any of its synonyms occur. Russell's theory of descriptions is a classic example of this. Any definite descriptive phrase, the so and so, can be eliminated in favour of sentences which make no reference to it or its synonyms. Any expression which is amenable to such an analysis is said to be 'logically eliminable'. If we apply this procedure to language in general, we find that by listing the various types of sentences which are significant, and by showing the relations of equivalence that hold between them, we are thereby revealing the structure of that language. Ayer regards the procedure of giving definitions *in use* as resulting in the display of the logical structure of a given language.

Logical constructions and the problem of perception

We remarked earlier on a similarity between Ayer and Berkeley. Berkeley had claimed that a material object is a collection of ideas. Ayer replaces the word 'idea' with 'sense-content' and claims that Berkeley was right to think that a material thing could be analysed in terms of sense-contents, even though his own analysis was faulty. The thesis that a material thing is definable in terms of actual or possible sense-contents (sense-data) is known as *Phenomenalism*.

In attempting to solve the problem of perception (which Ayer regards as a demand for a definition of a physical object) Ayer wants to say that symbols which represent physical objects can be replaced by symbols which stand for sense-contents. The resultant analysed sentences will be equivalent where 'equivalence' is defined in terms of common entailment connections. It is here that the notion of a logical construction comes in.

To say of something, e, that it is a logical construction out of b, c and d, does not mean that the *object e* is constituted or made up of the parts b, c and d. What it means is that any sentence in which a symbol for e appears can be translated into a set of equivalent sentences which do not contain a symbol for e or any of its synonyms, but do contain the symbols b, c and d.

It is called a logical construction because we are concerned with the translation of *sentences* about one thing into *sentences* about another. It is essentially a linguistic thesis. To say that a physical object is a logical construction out of sense-contents (such as 'brownness', 'hardness') means that the resultant sentences will be equivalent in that they have the same entailment properties. It is important to realise that Ayer is not saying that the symbol 'table' can be explicitly defined, as in dictionary definitions, by merely replacing it with sense-content symbols. If you did that, then you would produce nonsense. The sense-content symbols are not to be regarded as synonyms for 'table'. This thesis is known as Linguistic Phenomenalism.

On Ayer's account then, to say that one is seeing, touching and so on a physical object is the same as saying that one is experiencing certain sense-data. This is a thesis concerning what it means to say that one is perceiving a physical object. One of Ayer's criticisms of Berkeley is that he got the relationship between ideas/sense-data and material things wrong. Material things are not composed of them; they are logical constructions out of them.

There are some questions for Ayer to answer. What relations must hold between our sense-data in order for them to count as elements of the same material thing? How are different sense-data (such as visual and tactual) to be correlated so that they count as belonging to the same material thing? Given that sense-data cannot exist unperceived, what account is to be given of material things existing unperceived? Ayer's answers to these create problems for him.

His answer to the first is that to say of any two of one's sense-data that they belong to the same material thing is to say that they are related by resemblance and continuity. Ayer's answer to the second question is that any two of one's visual and tactual sense-data belong to the same material thing when every element of the visual group which is of minimal visual depth forms part of the same sense-experience as an element of the tactual group which is of minimal tactual depth. This notion of perceptual depth cannot be defined, it can only be pointed to. Minimal depth is that which is nearest to the body of the observer. There is going to be a problem here as Ayer is bringing in a reference to a material thing, that is, the observer's body, in his attempted reduction of material things. He blames this on the poverty of our language. This should put the reader on his guard. If it is held to be a defect of all natural languages, then this might well suggest something wrong with the theory rather than language in general.

His answer to the third question is that to say a material thing exists unperceived is to say that *if* an observer were to stand in such and such a position, *then* certain sense-contents would be experienced. All sentences about unperceived material things can be translated into hypothetical sentences about sense-contents. It is because he holds this that he endorses Mill's notion of a material thing as a 'permanent possibility of sensation'.

Criticisms

There is a problem with the claim that statements about physical things can be translated into statements about sense-contents. No statement about sense-data *logically* entails a statement about the existence of a material thing. It might render it highly probable, but not logically certain. Ayer had recognised this by the time he came to write *The Problem of Knowledge*. It is expressed there (pp. 124–5) by saying that the existence of a physical object is not a sufficient condition for the occurrence of the sense-data. And, conversely, the occurrence of the sense-data is not a sufficient condition for the existence of the physical object. There is no relation of logical deducibility between statements about actual or possible sense-data and statements about physical objects and vice versa. Phenomenalism requires a relationship of deducibility in order to effect a thoroughgoing translation of statements about physical objects into statements about actual or possible sense-data. Ayer is now saying that this relationship cannot be guaranteed.

Second, we are told that if the translation of statements about material things into statements about sense-data is to work, then the resulting sentences cannot contain symbols which refer to material things. If they did, then the sentences would not have been fully analysed. This is where Ayer's notion of perceptual depth causes a problem. We cannot give an account of what perceptual depth is without incorporating a reference to the perceiver's body. The body is, of course, a material object. We cannot use any physical object term to stand for a reference point in picking out and identifying whatever terms are to be analysed. Ayer later realised that it is inadequate to talk of placing a normal observer at a certain vantage point under normal conditions and saying that he would experience such and such sense-data. Tests have to be carried out to determine normality and these could involve a never-ending series of hypotheticals.

Third, we regard physical objects as public, whereas sense-data are private. On a phenomenalist account, to say that two people are looking at the same object reduces to saying that they are experiencing similar sense-data. But how can a phenomenalist explain *how* it is that they are experiencing similar sense-data? He cannot say because they are looking at the same physical object as all he has is an appeal to sense-data.

We shall leave the issue of phenomenalism and end our discussion of Ayer with some general remarks. Ayer sees philosophy as forming a unity with science. It analyses and clarifies concepts used in science. It does not discover facts about the world. Factual discoveries are the domain of the empirical sciences. Philosophy deals with the logical or conceptual aspects of science, whereas science deals with the framing of hypotheses, empirical inquiries and so on. Knowledge of the world can only be obtained through science. For Ayer, all *a priori* knowledge is analytic. Analytic propositions are nothing more than tautologies. The whole of mathematics is tautological in nature. Its validity follows solely from the definitions of the terms it contains.

Much controversy has centred on the verification principle. According to Logical Positivism there are only two kinds of meaningful or significant proposition, namely, the empirically verifiable and the *a priori*. But what about the proposition asserting the verification principle? It does not seem to be either. It is not seen to be correct by observation and neither is it true in virtue of the meaning of its terms. What status can it have?

Another problem that some have found is this. We normally inquire into the meaning of words or sentences. A proposition is what a sentence means rather than something that itself has a meaning. It is propositions, however, which we verify, so how can verifiability be identified with meaning? In the preface to the second edition of *Language, Truth and Logic*,[16] Ayer tells us that it is a statement, rather than a sentence or a proposition, that is verified.

The reader should read the section on Ayer's ethical thesis in Chapter 4 of this volume. He should bear in mind that whereas some form of verificationism is appropriate for factual meaning, we cannot assume that factual meaning is the only meaning that there is.

▶ **The concept of knowledge**

Knowledge and doubt

If we adopt Descartes' approach to philosophy we find that it is only those propositions of which we are logically certain that we can properly be said to know. This would cover those propositions which lie beyond the possibility of theoretical doubt such as the cogito and mathematical truths. We find something similar in Plato. Knowledge can only be of that which is eternal and immutable; it cannot be of that which is subject to change and decay or is in constant flux. Given that the external world known through the senses is in a state of flux, it is going to follow that we cannot have knowledge of it, but only belief or opinion. For Plato, knowledge could only be applied to the world of the forms, a perfect unchanging world beyond the senses. It cannot be applied to the world of appearances (see the simile of the cave in Chapter 4).

On both of these theses our knowledge becomes extremely limited as we cannot properly be said to know any empirical propositions at all. At best we can have belief. Many philosophers would want to reject such an extremely limiting view. They may point out that it is quite at odds with the way we ordinarily use and apply the concept of knowledge. In everyday language we do talk of 'knowing' things about the world as opposed to merely believing things. The knowledge/belief distinction is made *within* the world.

Empiricist philosophers like Russell, have tried to locate knowledge about the world in our immediate sense experiences. They cannot be doubted. Indeed, since the time of Descartes there has been a pre-occupation with the rule of doubt in the search for knowledge. For Russell, once we go on to make inferences from our immediate sense experiences, for example, this is a dog, we open up the possibility of error. Certainty tends to be located in the non-inferential reporting of sense experiences, for example, this black or blackness here. Such reports as these make no presuppositions about what objects there are, they merely record the occurrence of sense-data. No inference as to what such sense-data may represent is made. A major difficulty with this approach is whether non-propositional utterances can be regarded as knowledge at all. The idea behind this approach is the elimination of doubt. To that extent, there is a similarity with Descartes.

There are, however, some points that need to be made in regard to this pre-occupation with doubt. The fact that a proposition is logically contingent, that is, that it *could* have been otherwise, does not imply that it *might be* otherwise. The logical possibility of doubt does not mean that there is anything inherently dubitable about the proposition in question. It simply means that I do not involve myself in a formal contradiction in supposing it to be false. The mere fact that I can imagine it being otherwise is not in itself grounds for supposing it to be otherwise and does not constitute a rational ground for doubt. Doubt requires a context and some possible means of resolving it. This is a problem which a global sceptic must deal with. To see what is at issue here, consider the recent *Matrix* films, and, by extension, Descartes' evil demon.

The *Matrix* hypothesis requires that the experiences in the deception are experientially indistinguishable from those we call 'the real world'. A pint of beer tastes the same in the Matrix. However, we can and do distinguish illusion and reality within the world in which we live, for example, mirages and the like. If a global sceptic claims that we are not entitled to use such distinctions to establish a reality claim on the grounds that these deceptions occur within an even greater deception, a difficulty emerges. Once you allow deceptions within deceptions you open up the possibility of an infinite regress. How can the controllers of the Matrix know that their world is real? Not by appealing to any of their experiences, as they would be the same. Neither can it now be done by distinguishing the perpetrated deception from reality as it has now been allowed for such distinctions within a total deception. The same will also apply to the team of gods who are manipulating them and to the demon who controls the team. Somewhere we have to stop and say *this* is reality in order to generate a deception hypothesis. Once we do this we set out the criteria for the reality judgement, and if we wish to be global sceptics, we must say why those criteria do not hold for our world and our experiences of it. This is the only way that a meaningful hypothesis can be generated. (It was also a stroke of good fortune that words retained their meaning within the Matrix!)

Our ordinary use of the concept of knowledge does not imply the logical impossibility of doubt. What is needed is an enquiry into the nature of acceptable evidence that would be relevant in justifying claims to knowledge. One of the most famous attempts to give an account of knowledge is that of describing it as justified true belief. It is to this that we now turn.

Knowledge and belief

As we said at the end of the last section, one very influential account of knowledge is that of justified true belief. Thus a person, S, is said to know a proposition, P, if and only if P is true. S believes that P is true, and S is justified in believing that P is true. When these conditions are satisfied, S knows that P. There is, however, a famous objection to this thesis and a number of examples appear in the literature to illustrate the problem. I shall now give an account of the problem in its original form and consider some possible replies.

The Gettier Problem

Gettier describes the knowledge as justified true belief thesis in the way we outlined above:

(a) S knows that P IFF: (i) P is true
  (ii) S believes that P
  (iii) S is justified in believing that P
  (IFF = if and only if)

Gettier wants to show that conditions (i), (ii) and (iii) can hold and yet S would not know that P.

He introduces two conditions:

(1) The sense of 'justified' being used here is that of good evidence. He allows for the possibility of S being justified in believing a proposition which is in fact false. If one did not allow for this, then the thesis would become true by definition.
(2) For any proposition P, if S is justified in believing P, and P entails Q, and S deduces Q from P and accepts Q as a result of this deduction, then S is justified in believing Q.

We can now move on to one of Gettier's examples. Suppose Smith and Jones apply for a job. Smith has strong evidence for:

(b) Jones is the appointee and Jones has ten coins in his pocket.

The strong evidence for the appointee belief is that he has been tipped off by a reliable source (the boss). The strong evidence for the number of coins is that Smith has counted them.

Proposition (b) will entail:

(c) The appointee has ten coins in his pocket.

Smith deduces (c) from (b) for which he has strong evidence. Smith is clearly justified in believing (c). But it turns out that Smith gets the job, and also, unknown to Smith, he has ten coins in his pocket. Now (c) is true, though (b), from which it was deduced is false. So:

(i) (c) is true,
(ii) Smith believes that (c) is true
(iii) Smith is justified in believing (c) is true.

Even though these conditions hold, it is clear that Smith does not *know* that (c) is true. What makes (c) true is the number of coins in Smith's pocket of which he is ignorant. He bases his belief in (c) on counting the coins in Jones's pocket, whom he falsely believes to be the man who will get the job. Thus we have a case of justified true belief but not of knowledge.

Responses to the Gettier Problem

An immediate response that needs to be made is that Gettier's 'Jones is the man who will get the job (appointee) and Jones has ten coins in his pocket' is not of the logical form P, but rather P and Q. It is clearly a conjunction of two propositions. So rather than represent this as a case of S believes that P, it should be represented as a case of S believes that P and Q. Gettier's proposition (a) should be amended accordingly. The knowledge as justified true belief thesis in this case should read:

S knows P and Q IFF:

(i)   P is true

(ii) Q is true

(iii) S believes that P

(iv) S believes that Q

(v) S is justified in believing P

(vi) S is justified in believing Q

Had the thesis been presented in this way, it would have been seen that condition (1) was violated. It also seems to be the case that the conjunction is being used in a philosophically objectionable way. It is by using a conjunction that Gettier is able to carry out the deduction referred to in his condition (2). Where P and Q are logically independent propositions, Gettier cannot deduce from either of them individually proposition (c), in which the specific reference to Jones is removed. Its removal is essential to the argument but the entailment which achieves it is dependent on the conjunction.

It may also be argued that Gettier removes the reference to Jones with 'The man who will get the job has ten coins . . .', and this is an ambiguous description. It fails to identify any one individual in the way 'Jones' does. Yet the belief S has depends on the ambiguous description uniquely identifying Jones. He does not believe that the man who will get the job, *whoever he is*, has ten coins in his pocket. Thus, in order to be plausible, an integral component of the belief is omitted. If Gettier had stuck with a uniquely identifying description, proposition (a)'s condition (1) would again have been violated.

Some have complained that Gettier omits any psychological references from the knowledge-is-justified-true-belief thesis; for example, S strongly believes that P, or S feels certain that P, and so on, and then go on to argue that S would not have sufficient evidence to guarantee this degree of conviction. It seems, however, that the example(s) could be simply amended so that S would have the appropriate psychological conviction. This objection makes little philosophical impact but at least it raises the issue of justification.

Justifications seem relative to circumstances and, sometimes, to the state of our knowledge. Attempts to make them watertight have failed. One is reminded here of Plato's ultimate dismissal of knowledge as justified true belief, or, as he called it, knowledge as belief plus true discourse or account. In the *Thaetetus* he discussed the case of Hesiod's wagon. To know it was Hesiod's wagon you were seeing you would need to know not just the axles, wheels and cover, but every component. This would include all the planks and you would have to be able to recognise them in all situations. This is clearly not possible and if this is what is implied by 'justification' or 'true discourse' then we are hardly going to know anything at all. It seems right to say, with Gettier, that it is possible to have good reasons for believing a proposition which is false. Much will now depend on what is meant by 'good reasons'. However, to have a good reason does not imply that one could not have a better reason. The nature of the reason is all important. Up until fairly recently many believed that Richard III suffered from certain physical deformities. History books said so, Shakespeare said so, contemporary paintings depicted him so. This seems to constitute good evidence or a good reason. Spectrographic analysis, however, now shows that the deformities were added to the paintings at a later date. This evidence was not available until recently and thus, what is good evidence can be succeeded by better evidence. Justifications can be subject to shifts and they must always be appealed to in knowledge claims. We must also remember that the presence of a justification does not guarantee knowledge.

Finally, one very common criticism of Gettier is that he omits any reference to knowledge being caused by the appropriate object. Perhaps it would be better expressed by saying that knowledge must be directed at the appropriate object. I prefer this statement as it is not clear that it makes a great deal of sense to talk of knowledge being caused. A similar version of this criticism involves a further consideration of Gettier's condition (2). When Gettier tells us that S deduces Q from P, we should have added that the deduction is made for the right reason. There is some conflation in condition (2) regarding logical relations between propositions and logical relations regarding our attitudes to propositions.

2 Problems in the Philosophy of Mind

The question of the relation between mind and body is one of the most fundamental and intractable problems of philosophy. Solutions have been offered, but, it could be argued, they raise as many difficulties as they have attempted to remove.

Mind and body appear to be two radically different kinds of things and yet they also appear to be intimately connected. What is the nature of this connection? Are there really two things at all? These are two of the questions which we shall discuss in this chapter. We shall find that the kind of solution one settles for here will carry implications for the positions that *can* be held on a number of other major issues in philosophy. It will carry implications for what we can say regarding the possibility of disembodied consciousness, the problem of free will and responsibility, personal identity, our knowledge of the mental states of others and what it is possible for a science of the mind to achieve. The importance of such questions can hardly be doubted. We shall begin with the philosopher who is regarded as the father of modern philosophy, Rene Descartes (1596–1650). The reader is strongly advised to read Descartes' *Meditations* in conjunction with the following.

▶ Cartesian Dualism

Descartes' mind-body theory used to be known as psychophysical dualism. It is now referred to as Cartesian Dualism and was dubbed 'the ghost in the machine' by Ryle. According to Descartes' theory a person's mind is an immaterial substance which is independent of the body. Descartes believed that some states which we normally regard as mental states are dependent on the body. These are exemplified by sense perception, which is dependent on our sense organs, imagining (the ability to form pictures in the mind's eye) is dependent on prior acquaintances with shapes, sizes, colours and so on, which in turn are dependent on our senses. There are other states which Descartes would have regarded as body-dependent such as pain, hunger, thirst and sexual desire. These states which are to some extent body-dependent do not, for Descartes, constitute the essential nature of the mind. Although they are in some sense mental, they are not what is essential to the mental.

On Descartes' theory, the mind, through its independence of the body, is capable of surviving the death of the body. It could continue to exist for an indefinite period after the dissolution of the body unless God chose otherwise. Now whatever is said to survive bodily death cannot be dependent on the body. It follows that those mental states which are designated body-dependent, such as perception, hunger and sexual desire, will play no part in the activity of the mind after the death of the body. It is only the essential nature of the mind that will survive. Descartes holds that this essential nature is intellectualism. We shall now turn to his arguments in the *Meditations* to see what he means by this.

In order to arrive at an indubitable starting point for knowledge, Descartes is supposing to be false all that he had once held as true. It must be realised that Cartesian doubt is *not* sceptical doubt. He is not attempting to doubt all his beliefs in order to show that nothing can be known. He is doubting in order to arrive at something which cannot be doubted. This would then serve as the starting point for knowledge. It would be the only possible starting point.

He doubts all those beliefs which are based on the evidence of his senses. This doubt covers a large general class of beliefs, namely, the existence of material things. He is not doubting that he has various sense experiences or sense-data, but rather that there are material things which cause them. Even if his belief in material things is an erroneous belief, is there not, he asks, some power which puts those thoughts (that is, the various experiences) in his mind? This too can be doubted. His ground for saying this is that it is possible for such thoughts to be self-produced. The question that now arises concerns the nature of this self. He has already supposed that the existence of body, including his own body, can be doubted. He could not, however, persuade himself that he did not exist. We are told: 'I existed without doubt, by the fact that I was persuaded, or indeed by the mere fact that I thought at all.'[1] Given that he cannot doubt the existence of the self, whereas he can doubt the existence of body, he wants to claim that the nature of the self is not materiality. In the above quotation Descartes is using the verb 'to think' in a wide sense which includes doubting, understanding, imagining and perceiving. There is a *prima facie* inconsistency here as he also held that one cannot perceive without a body. He should be understood as claiming that whenever he has a conscious experience, then he exists. Even if he supposes himself to be constantly deceived by a cunning deceiver, he still cannot be deceived about his own existence. As a matter of logic, a deceiver requires *someone* to deceive. Descartes should be regarded as saying that as long as he thinks (in the wide sense) then he is something. He concludes the paragraph by saying that he must, 'take as assured that the proposition I am, I exist, is necessarily true, every time I express it or conceive of it in my mind.'[2] One of the most famous propositions of philosophy, *cogito ergo sum* (I think, therefore, I am) is not presented in the form of premiss-conclusion in the *Meditations*. It is presented in that form in part four of his *Discourse On Method* and it has aroused considerable philosophical controversy. Briefly, some have argued that the inference from *cogito* to *sum* is invalid without the inclusion of a major premiss like 'All things that think exist'. Descartes has been accused of circularity in that the truth of his conclusion is said to be presupposed, rather than proved, by the premiss. I shall not pursue these matters here. Suffice it to say that in *Meditation* II Descartes is presenting the argument as a necessary truth. Whenever he thinks, in the wide sense, he exists, as thinking implies existence. Existence is a logical prerequisite of thinking. This does not mean that everything that exists thinks, but rather, if anything thinks, then it must exist.

Descartes then addresses himself to the question of the nature of this self. He is looking for the essential nature of the self. The self has indubitable existence and the question concerns what can be said to constitute such a nature. As we have seen, the properties of body are regarded as possible objects of doubt. They could not, therefore, constitute what has indubitable existence. The same applies to those attributes which are body-dependent, such as eating or walking. The self cannot be essentially an eating or walking substance. In the case of perceiving we can be deceived, as in dreams, but what we cannot be deceived about is the having of conscious experiences. Even in cases where we are deceived by our senses, we still have certain sense-experiences. Thus, for example, in the case of a mirage although you might be deceived into judging that there is water on the road ahead of you, it is still the case that you have the sense-experience of seeming to see water. The mirage example is a case where it is appropriate to say that one is deceived by one's senses. The case of dreaming is not to be described as a case of being deceived by one's senses. It is permissible, however, to describe it as a deception of sense experience. If, for example, you dream that you are climbing a mountain, then you have certain sense-experiences such as seeming to see colour and so on. Given that the having of these experiences, as opposed to making judgements about them, cannot be doubted, Descartes locates the essential nature of the self in thinking in the wide sense referred to earlier. This is held to be the one attribute which belongs to the self and cannot be separated from it. He tells us: 'I am therefore, precisely speaking, only a thing which thinks'.[3]

We are told that this 'thinking' includes doubting, perceiving, affirming, denying, willing and imagining. Descartes holds that it cannot be doubted that the 'I' is the subject of these attributes. Even in cases where there is error, for example, imagining[4] or perceiving, the capacity for imagining or perceiving does not cease to lie in the self. It is the subject of those various attributes whose existence cannot be doubted. They require a subject as a matter of logic.

In *Meditation* II the nature of the self is a thinking thing. In *Meditation* VI it is a substance whose whole essence lies in thinking. These terms require some clarification. In using the terms 'substance' and 'essence' he is using terms taken from scholastic philosophy. When he describes the mind as a substance, he means that it is a thing dependent on nothing except God. Each mind is a separate substance, whereas there is only one physical substance. Physical objects do not constitute distinct substances. To say that the mind depends on nothing except God for its existence implies that the mind could cease to exist if and only if God chose to destroy it. It would not, on this thesis, cease to exist on the dissolution of the brain as it has no dependence on the brain. We now need to say something concerning the use of the term 'essence' so that we can get a clear understanding of what talk about 'essential natures' means and also what it means to say that the essence of mind lies in thinking.

Descartes uses the term 'essence' in the Aristotelian sense. Objects of the same class possess an identical property which constitutes the essence or essential nature of that class. Thus to take a simple example, it is part of the essential nature of a square that it has four sides. Members of a class may have some properties which are not shared by other members of that class. Thus, for example, some men will have blue eyes and others will not. Aristotle refers to such properties as these as accidental properties. The important point to bear in mind is that a member of a class cannot lose its essential property without ceasing to be a member of that class. It can, however, lose or gain an accidental property and continue its membership of that class. There are some problems here for Descartes.

Given that Descartes is claiming that the essence of mind lies in thinking, or in the having of conscious experiences,[5] it is going to follow that if a mind lost its consciousness, then it would cease to be a mind. It would have lost what was essential to its being a member of the class 'mind'. The problem for Descartes is that as we are all unconscious for some of the time, he is implying that our minds cease to exist from time to time. It would be somewhat implausible to suggest that minds are always conscious. It might be thought that during sleep we are always dreaming and are thus having certain experiences even if we do not remember them. This is not in fact the case. We dream during only some of our sleeping hours. We have several periods of dreaming, but these periods do not occupy the whole of sleeping time. As it is difficult to claim that minds are always conscious, it seems that on Descartes' premises, God must be creating and destroying minds intermittently throughout the night. We can grant to Descartes that whenever he is conscious then something exists, but there is a problem here in the case when he is not conscious.

There would be another problem in claiming to know that his mind had existed indefinitely. The reader should bear in mind that Descartes' *cogito* argument occurs within the context of applying the method of Cartesian doubt to those classes of beliefs which can be supposed false. It seems that, in the name of consistency, he should have applied this method to the supposition that his mind had existed indefinitely. How does he know that his mind is a continuous thing? How does he know that his mind has existed for forty-one years? The evidence for such a claim is that of memory. At the start of *Meditation* II he says, concerning the application of the method of doubt, 'I persuade myself that none of those things ever existed that my *deceptive memory* represents to me' (my italics). In spite of this, he ignores the implications of doubting his memory. One such implication concerns the claim to know that his mind has existed indefinitely, 'Am I not this same being who doubts of almost everything' (*Ibid.*, p. 107). If he had doubted his memory, then he could not claim to know of any past event. If he seriously entertained the hypothesis that he was being deceived by a malignant demon, then how would he know that he had not just been created by such a demon along with a set of memories which give the impression of continuous existence?

It is, however, possible to come to Descartes' assistance here. If he had applied the method of doubt to memory claims, then he would have found that ultimately we are forced to accept some such claim as veridical. The idea that because memory is sometimes unreliable, therefore it could always be, is part of a more general mistake of supposing that because something is sometimes the case, then it might always be the case. There are many examples where this will not work. Consider a case in which one might say that one's memory had let one down. How would one know this? Perhaps by appealing to other memories or to the memories of others. Sooner or later we shall have to rely on a memory claim in order to show that our memory had let us down in a particular case. Similarly, in the case of dreaming and being awake, I can only know that I have been dreaming if I also know of occasions when I am not dreaming. The fact appealed to in *Meditation* I concerning vivid dreams and hallucinations cannot be used to show that such may be our permanent condition. We need to have the dreaming/waking distinction in order to recognise the deceptive case and describe it as deceptive. This is an important point to bear in mind.

In addition to revealing the nature of the self or mind, *Meditation* II is also intended to establish the independence of the mind from the body. This presents serious problems for Descartes. Let us just recap for a moment. We have seen that he dismisses the idea that he is an eating or walking substance on the grounds that such attributes require having a body. Given that he is doubting whether he has a body, it follows that he is rejecting those attributes which are body-dependent as constituting his essential nature. It is important for the reader to remember that this is not sceptical doubt. He is doubting what is *possible* to doubt in order to arrive at what is *impossible* to doubt. As we have remarked, he is not doubting the various sense-experiences, but rather, that they are caused by physical things. We saw that he identified thinking as an attribute of the soul. He claimed that this attribute belonged to him, that it is inseparable from him, and concluded that he is, precisely speaking, a thinking thing. From the premiss that thinking is an attribute, he claims that it is an inseparable one (that is, a necessary one). He then leaps, without explanation, from the inseparability of the attribute of thinking to the conclusion that it is the *only* attribute. His whole nature was said to lie in thinking. We saw that this left him vulnerable to the example of the dreamless sleep.

After concluding that he is only a thinking thing, he goes on to say that he is not the assembly of members of a human body. He takes himself to have demonstrated the mind's independence of the body. This argument, however, involves a fallacy. Consider what he says on p. 106, 'It is most certain, however, that this notion and knowledge of myself, thus precisely taken, do not depend on things the existence of which is not yet known to me'. By the latter phrase he is referring to physical bodies and this includes his own body. If, in the above passage, he had claimed that knowledge of his existence was not *derived* from such things, then it would have been permissible. The problem is that he uses the term *dependent*. His premises are:

(1) I know that I exist as a mind,
(2) I do not yet know that I have a body or that there are any bodies.

What can be inferred legitimately from these premises is that his knowledge of his mind is not derived from knowledge of material bodies. His conclusions, though, were:

(A) My knowledge concerning my mind is not dependent on my having a body. (*Meditation* II)
(B) My mind does not depend upon my body. (*Discourse*)

These conclusions do not follow from the premises. The premises permit a very different thesis from the one Descartes wished to maintain. This is the thesis of physicalism which we shall come to in due course. Things which we know to exist may very well depend on things which we do not yet know exist. Thus, for example, we can know that diseases exist and yet they can be dependent on bacteria which we do not yet know to exist. There is nothing in premises (1) or (2) which excludes the possibility that his being conscious may depend on a state of his brain or, at least, on his having a brain. This is not to say that his conclusion is false, it is to say that such a conclusion is not entailed by his premises.

Consider premiss (2) and conclusion (B). If this argument were valid, then it would be equally valid to claim that he did not yet know that God existed and conclude that his mind was independent of God. This is an argument which Descartes would have found unacceptable. He claims that his mind must have been created by God and, it should be remembered, its being created by God is a necessary prerequisite for describing it as a distinct substance.

On the arguments thus far presented, Descartes is not entitled to argue from *cogito* to the independence of the mind and body. Even if we accept the subtitle of *Meditation* II that the mind is easier to know than the body, it does not follow that the mind is *independent* of the body.

In *Meditation* VI we are offered further arguments to demonstrate the independence of the mind from the body. It is to these that we now turn. The first argument begins with the claim that whatever can be clearly and distinctly conceived can be produced by God exactly as they are so conceived. Descartes moves from this premiss to the claim that it is sufficient for him to conceive clearly and distinctly one thing (mind) without another (body) in order for him to be certain that one is distinct and different from the other. In appealing to God's omnipotence he establishes that God has the power to create anything separately that can be conceived as separate. He concludes the paragraph with the claim that his mind is entirely distinct from his body and may exist without it.

The difficulty with this argument is that from the premiss that God *can* do something all that follows is that He has the power to do it. That is to say, He has the power to create mind and body separately. It does not, however, follow from this that God has exercised that power. Descartes needs that in order to establish that minds and bodies have been so produced. To say that they can be thought of as separate and that God has the power to produce them as separate will not suffice to show that they are actually separate or independent. Descartes needs the *exercise* of that power by God. His concluding sentence (p. 156) that the mind 'may' exist without the body leaves it unclear as to whether he had recognised the difference between the exercise and the possession of a power.

Having emphasised the independence of the mind from the body and stressed their different and distinct natures, Descartes introduces a new way of talking about the mind-body issue (pp. 159–60). In an interesting passage, which is difficult to reconcile with his other writings, he tells us that nature teaches him that he is lodged in his body in a strong sense. The nature of this 'lodging' is not just like that of a pilot in a ship, but of being conjoined or intermingled in an intimate way, 'that I form as it were, a single whole with it'. What he is getting at here can be elucidated by considering what he says about the feeling of pain.

It is because of the close relation between his mind and his body that he *feels* pain rather than merely perceiving a wound. If his mind were just the guide of his body in the sense that a pilot is a guide of a ship, then he would, for example, only perceive a gash in his hand in the way a pilot would perceive a hole in the hull. There is thus a sense in which his mind pervades his body that does not apply to the case of the pilot and the ship. At the end of the paragraph he speaks of a union and a mingling of mind and body. This passage is at odds with a thesis for which Descartes is well known. The thesis in question is that the mind and the body interact at the pineal gland. We are now told that the mind pervades the *whole* body.

The official theory of Descartes is that of two distinct entities, a mind and a body. The appropriate predicates of the former are terms denoting states of consciousness, whereas of the latter they are terms denoting bodily states. On the official theory it would be inappropriate to apply the language of bodily states to a self whose essential nature consists in thinking. By switching to talk of a mind 'lodged' in the body, Descartes was reverting to the usual way of talking about persons. Both mental and bodily states are appropriately attributed to persons in normal discourse. In this passage of *Meditation* VI Descartes is implying that he is a complex mind-body substance. He is talking of his entire self as being composed of a mind and a body. This is a quite different claim from the one that he is purely a thinking thing. To say that the mind is lodged in the body is to talk metaphorically. The mind, lacking spatial properties, cannot be a party to the spatial relation 'in'. To talk in this way does not explain the interaction of mind and body. In spite of what Descartes had said in this passage concerning the union and mingling of mind and body, he went on to emphasise his official position by presenting a second argument for the marked distinction between mind and body (p. 164).

This second argument involves the claim that the mind is indivisible, whereas the body is divisible. He can distinguish parts of his body but not parts of his mind. The reader should note that Descartes does not regard the faculties of the mind as constituting separate parts on the ground that their exercise requires the entire mind as subject. In this passage he is reverting to the official theory. Although mind and body appear to be closely united, if, for example, you lose a limb it will not affect the mind, the mind remains whole and entire throughout such physical changes. Again, we have the conclusion that the mind is entirely different from the body.

The thesis that the mind is indivisible is one which can be questioned. We shall say more of this in our discussion of psychoanalysis. There are also psychological phenomena, such as split personality, which are difficult to explain on the indivisibility thesis. Setting these problems aside for the moment, let us consider whether we can move from the claim that mind and body have such distinct natures to claim that the mind may survive the destruction of the body. Descartes believed that the mind could exist without the body.

Presumably, if the mind is so distinct from the body, then it is not the sort of thing that can be destroyed (unless God chooses to annihilate it). Now it may well be the case that a mind cannot be destroyed in the same way as the body can be, but this does not imply immunity from destruction. It seems quite permissible to say that those who are described as 'human vegetables' have had their minds destroyed. Indeed, this would seem to be the criterion for so describing them.

A modern-day dualist maintaining the independence of the mind from the body would face a number of difficulties which were not apparent in Descartes' time. These difficulties point the way to alternative solutions of the mind-body problem. A modern critic of dualism can appeal to the evidence of neurophysiology to demonstrate the dependence of the mind on the brain. He can, for example, appeal to the effects of brain damage, the effects of the removal of parts of the brain or the effects of electrical stimulation of parts of the brain. By applying electrodes to the occipital lobe of the brain a visual sensation can be made to occur. It would, therefore, seem implausible for a dualist to claim that the ability to have volitions has no connection with the brain. A dualist might, of course, claim that the production of such sensations by electrical stimulation needs to be distinguished from the actual volition to form a particular mental picture. He might, that is, claim that the volition is a mental act, an act of the will, and this is something which is not produced by electrical stimulation. He might also claim that there are some mental activities which could be performed in the absence of a brain. If he were to follow Descartes, then he would hold that thinking (conceiving) was such an activity. This would present him with a serious problem. Certain parts of the brain have been identified as the speech areas. Extreme damage to this area of the brain can result in aphasia, the loss of association between words and their meaning. Given that our ability to think is dependent upon our linguistic capacity, it is going to follow that if this latter capacity is brain-related, then so is the former. It seems that in order to avoid this a dualist will have to claim that our ability to think does not depend on our capacity for using words. There are grave problems with a claim like this. The reader should consider the point that the use of symbols is essential to our ability to refer to absent objects and to our ability to think in an abstract way.

There are other examples which a dualist critic can appeal to. Amnesia can be caused by brain damage. Changes in character can be effected by frontal lobotomy surgery. When confronted with examples such as these a dualist may claim that damage to the brain results only in the loss of the power of expression. He may claim that the brain is an instrument and that damage to it means that it no longer serves its purpose. This view cannot be conclusively refuted but it will imply that we can never know what a brain-damaged person's mind is really like. A further general implication of Cartesian dualism is that no matter how detailed our study and knowledge of the brain might become, it will never provide us with knowledge about the human mind. For, *ex hypothesi*, such knowledge would concern the instrument, and its greater detail would be detail about the instrument and not the mind.

We have noted a number of difficulties facing a dualist. If one holds that mind and body are two distinct entities – immaterial substance and material thing – with different natures, then one is faced with the difficulty of saying how they interact. The central problem of dualism is to specify the nature of this interaction. The problem was well expressed by Hume when he remarked that the union of soul with body is one of the strangest of all nature's principles. How does a spiritual substance acquire such an influence over a material one that the most refined thought is able to actuate the grossest matter?[6]

Indicating difficulties is one thing, finding a plausible alternative is another. We have seen that maintaining the independence of two radically different things is problematic. It is also problematic to specify the nature of their interaction. In attempting to solve, or avoid, these problems some philosophers have advocated the thesis of physicalism.

▶ Physicalism

In addition to avoiding dualist problems some have thought that a physicalist or materialist theory of mind is required in order to have a unified science. According to physicalist theories of mind, the mind is not to be regarded as an immaterial substance. There are no immaterial substances. Physicalist theories hold that a person is a complex physical organism whose states of consciousness and mental abilities either depend on or are identical with processes in the brain. Those who hold that such a thesis is required in order to have a unified scientific picture seek a unity of kind in the entities that there are and in the explanations that will ultimately apply to all phenomena. This involves the claim that all explanations will ultimately reduce to physical ones. It is then held to be far more plausible to claim that brain states, electrical impulses or neuron firings could be expressed in terms of physics and chemistry than it would be to claim that such 'things' as hopes, wishes, after-images and pains could be. This is a strong motive for attempting to identify the mental with the physical. The goal of such an enterprise would be to reduce psychological phenomena to the neurophysiological and that in turn to physics. We shall now consider three versions of physicalism.

The mind–brain identity theory

This thesis, which is also known as central state materialism, asserts that a conscious state simply is a brain process. The first question that arises here concerns what it means to say of two apparently different things – a mental state and a brain state – that they are identical. To say that they are strictly identical implies that any property possessed by the one is possessed by the other. In more formal language, if x and y designate the same object, then whatever is true of x is also true of y and vice versa.

When this relation is applied to the mind–brain identity theory a difficulty arises. Let us take pain as an example of a conscious state to see what the problem is. According to the identity theory my pain is identical to a state of my brain. The reader must realise that the theory does not say that pain is *caused* by a brain state, but rather, that pain is a brain state. The properties which I attribute to my pain such as intensity, stabbing, throbbing and so on, must also be attributable to the brain state as they are held to be identical. It will also follow that any property possessed by the brain state will also be possessed by the pain. Thus, for example, to say that one's neuron motions are swift or amoeboid will entail the proposition that one's pain is swift or amoeboid. Opponents of the identity theory have held that mental events and physical events possess different properties and therefore cannot be identical. Thus, for example, physical events are located in space but mental ones are not, therefore, they cannot be the same.

An opponent of the identity theory can also argue that whereas one experiences a throbbing pain, one does not experience an amoeboid motion of neurons so how can they be the same? He might claim that it is *logically*[7] possible for that motion of neurons to occur without pain being experienced but it is not logically possible for the throbbing pain to occur without it being experienced. Again, he would want to conclude that they could not be the same. Alternatively, an opponent of the identity theory might interpret the theory as a theory concerning what we mean by making identity assertions and then go on to claim that it is ridiculous to say that when I describe my pain as intense, or talk about my mental states in general, what I *mean* is a description of my brain. One can talk about mental experiences without knowing anything about the brain, so how could such talk *mean* something about the brain?

A standard reply to these objections is the claim that the identity theory is not being put forward as a theory of what we *mean* when we talk about mental items, rather, it is a factual or empirical theory concerning what mental items are as a matter of *fact*. This is the approach of J. J. C. Smart.[8] The kind of identity proposed by Smart is contingent or factual identity. Smart offers an example to illustrate what he means by contingent identity.

Consider the case where we say that lightning is identical to an electrical discharge. It is something that is discovered as a matter of fact. To claim a factual identity between what appear to be two different things does not imply that statements about one are translatable into statements about the other as a matter of logic. The linguistic fact that two expressions are not inter-substitutable in all contexts will not in itself show that the two expressions do not have the same reference.

In Smart's hands the identity theory is an empirical theory. Whether or not a mental state is a brain state is a question which is to be settled by empirical methods. Empirical questions are not to be settled by the way we talk. Linguistic usage cannot be used to legislate as to what the facts are.

The upshot of considerations such as these is that when Smart is presented with objections such as neuron motions are elliptical or amoeboid, whereas pains are not, therefore, they cannot be the same; he replies that this begs the question against his theory. If he is right, and this is supposed to be a factual matter, then, as a matter of fact, pain will be elliptical and mental experiences will be in physical space and so on. There are a number of difficulties with this theory.

We can bring out the first difficulty by considering what Smart says about the case of the after-image (pp. 94–5). Smart claims that a person who reports having an after-image is, as a matter of fact, reporting a brain process:

> The man who reports a yellowish-orange after-image does so in effect as follows 'What is going on in me is like what is going on in me when my eyes are open, the lighting is normal etc., and there really is a yellowish-orange patch on the wall.' In this sentence the word 'like' is meant to be used in such a way that something can be like itself: an identical twin is not only like his brother but like himself too.

He goes on to say that for this account to be successful, it is necessary that we should be able to report two processes as like one another without being able to say in what respect they are alike. His reason for saying this is that as we are not acquainted with our brain states, we are not able to say in what respects they are similar. How plausible is this account?

All cases of similarities or resemblances are similarities in a particular respect. If we do not know or cannot say what the respect is, then our similarity judgement is without foundation. The purpose of Smart's remark about a sense of 'like' according to which something can be like itself is to allow for the possibility that what is said to be like what is going on in me and so on, should turn out to be identical with what is going on in me when there is a real colour to be seen. Perhaps this could be contrasted with someone saying, 'The man I saw yesterday was exactly like you' and getting the reply, 'He was me'. The problem here is that the fact that he was me would rule out the claim that he was like me. It is also difficult to see how we could describe two people as being exactly alike without being able to say in what respects they were alike. Likeness or resemblance is a relation and it is unclear how something can be related to itself.

Secondly, Smart seems committed to saying that it is a straightforward factual matter whether, for example, our thought of a white Christmas is two inches to the left of a pain in our foot. This implication arises not through saying that when we think or are in pain something occurs in our brains, but through *identifying* our thought or pain with a brain state. There is a difficulty here with the idea that we could, as a result of an empirical test, say that our thoughts and pains were in space. We can, of course, carry out empirical tests in order to discover the properties of brain states, but the step of identifying the brain state with the mental state does not seem to be a purely empirical one. The reader should note that making the identity involves us in linguistic oddities that are not paralleled by the assertion of identity in Smart's lightning example.

Thirdly, some philosophers[9] would claim that the concept of a contingently true identity statement is a confused concept. If a statement is contingently true, then, according to the empiricist tradition, it is known by *a posteriori* methods. It is also a defining feature of contingently true statements that they need not have been true. This is not to say that they are inherently doubtful, but just that the world might have been different. To say, for example, that it is a contingent truth that I live on a hill simply means that I might have lived somewhere else, but, as it happens, I do not. The truth of the proposition is, of course, determined by *a posteriori* methods. To find out where I live, you look and see. If we apply these remarks to the case of identity statements, then we find one or two problems emerging. The main problem is whether it is ever correct to say that an identity statement is contingently true. We have remarked that a contingent truth might not have been the case. If we now examine an identity statement such as 'Tully is Cicero', we find there is a problem in saying how this *could* have been different. What is a contingent fact is that these two names refer to the individual in question. It is not, however, a contingent fact that that individual was the individual he was. To claim that it was would be to claim that Cicero might not have been Cicero which is senseless. If this is a correct analysis of identity statements, then they are necessarily true and not contingently true. This points the way to the other problem here. According to empiricism all necessary truths are known *a priori*. There are, however, identity statements which are known to be true *a posteriori*. Thus, for example, you might learn the truth of 'Bruce Wayne is Batman' by seeing Mr Wayne in the act of changing his clothes. This is something which you would discover by looking and the identity assertion would certainly be informative. The point that could be made against Smart is this: if mind–brain identities are genuine identity statements, then they are necessarily true and it is completely against the grain of empiricism to say that necessary truths can be decided on by laboratory tests or any other empirical test.

A fourth problem concerns whether the claim that a mental state is a brain state is a genuine identity statement. Let us write out a group of identity statements thus:

(1) The Evening Star is the same . . . . as the Morning Star
(2) The Green Plover is the same . . . . as the Lapwing
(3) Dr Jekyll is the same . . . . as Mr Hyde
(4) Tully is the same . . . . as Cicero
(5) A mental state is the same . . . . as a brain state

In examples (1) to (4) the blank can be filled in with what is known as *a material* concept, such as (1) planet, (2) bird, (3) man and (4) person. Example (5) can only be completed with the addition of a purely *formal* concept, such as thing, event or process. There is simply no third term which designates the background area against which the discussion of the identity of the mental with the physical takes place. The philosophical issue here turns on how significant this linguistic revelation is.

The fifth problem concerns the problem of rationality. This is a serious problem for all physicalist theories of mind. The problem of rationality is a serious one which requires a great deal of care and attention if we are to avoid the grosser errors of modern identity theories. In a recent work[10] Patricia Smith Churchland has suggested that new knowledge about the brain may alter our conception of what it is to be rational. There are many problems with claims like this. We may note the following:

(a) Investigations concerning the workings of the brain must proceed according to rational principles, but how could such investigations show that *those* principles were mistaken? Such a move would cut its own ground from under it.

(b) If we were to change or revise our concept of rationality, then we would be adopting some other standard of rationality. The problem here concerns what we could appeal to in order to justify the change and within what framework such an appeal could be made.

(c) Churchland thinks that we can come to revise concepts and change attitudes in the light of new knowledge. In other words, we can behave rationally by giving reasons for our changes and revisions. These reasons would constitute a justification. She also thinks that thoughts *are* neuron motions, which, presumably, are governed by physical, causal laws. How are these two positions to be reconciled? Her official philosophical position is that the mind and the brain are the same, but, in order to advocate the revision of concepts, she is forced to use the conceptual structure of rationality as distinct from the purely causal framework in which the investigation of the motions of neural impulses takes place. There can be no question of *justifying* neural impulses.

Finally, some identity theorists have thought that their thesis can be strengthened by refusing to admit mental items as kinds of 'things'. The tactic here is to avoid the difficulties of identifying one kind of object (mental) with a different kind (physical). It has been claimed that many terms which might be thought to refer to inner mental states are susceptible to a behaviourist analysis. They do not, that is to say, refer to the occurrences in a private mental world or a Cartesian soul substance, but to publicly observable bodily behaviour or dispositions to behave in a particular way. We shall discuss this later. For our present purposes we need to note that there are some terms which have proved peculiarly resistant to behaviourist analyses. An identity theorist seems stuck with an irreducible core of mental objects which present him with problems when he tries to make the identification with the physical. We need to consider an attempt to deal with this problem.

The attempt I have chosen concerns U. T. Place's treatment of the case of the after-image.[11] This case presents an obvious problem for the identity theorist. If an after-image is a brain state, then how does one explain that whereas the image is not located behind the eyes, the brain is? And how does one explain that whereas the image can vary in colour, the brain remains the same colour?

Place has attempted to solve the problem by saying that it arises out of the commission of the phenomenological fallacy. The fallacy in question involves the reification of the afterimage. Place is claiming that it is a mistake to regard the after-image as a kind of object. It is not, and, according to Place, it is sufficient for a physiologist to give a causal account of how we come to have the experience of, for example, seeing green when nothing is green. A similar argument could be applied to our earlier example of pain. Thus, in attributing properties to my pain, I am not, on this account, listing the qualities of an object in spite of grammatical appearances to the contrary. This version of the theory is also open to objections.

First, if experiencing a pain or an after-image is a neural process, then, in observing the relevant state of a person's brain, we would not *infer* that he was having a particular experience; we would be *seeing* his having of the experience. Consequences such as this will follow if we replace the private object with the public object rather than avoid object-talk altogether. In regard to this point, the reader should consult the following section on the double-aspect theory.

Secondly, there is a problem with Place's causal account. The claim that a neural process *causes* us to have a particular experience needs to be distinguished from the claim that having the experience is a neural process. A cause cannot *be* what it causes.

Thirdly, there is considerable controversy over the alleged success of the exorcism of the mental. Smart, for example, holds that in the case of pains or after-images, we are reporting something in a 'full-blooded' sense of report. Perhaps the reader would like to consider the issue of the banishment of the mental in the light of a modern neurophysiological theory known as tensor network theory. This theory holds that the role of the cerebellum is that of a 'translator'. Thus, for example, the cerebellum translates an intention to move your arm into a set of muscular movements. The question to ask here is what is the nature of this intention that is said to require a translation? It cannot be the bodily behaviour as that is yet to occur, and how can it be a brain state given that such states do not require translations? Brain states simply *cause* other states and movements. A dualist would want to claim that the intention was a mental act or occurrence.

For a discussion of the issues involved in a behaviourist analysis, the reader should consult the section on behaviourism in this text.

The double-aspect theory

This theory asserts that a conscious experience is the subjective or 'inner' aspect of a brain process. The 'outer' aspect is what a physiologist could observe if he were observing the relevant part of a person's brain. The theory holds that having a conscious experience is a brain state and the brain state has two aspects. This is one attempt to avoid the objection we referred to earlier concerning the possibility of *seeing* the having of an experience by another when we observe his brain.[12] On this account what we observe is the 'outer' aspect of his experience and what he experiences is the 'inner' aspect of what we observe. In as much as the theory holds that there is the one state – a brain state – it presupposes the truth of the identity theory.

A recent statement of this theory has been offered by J.-P. Changeux.[13] He assumes the truth of the identity theory, that is, the mind and the brain are said to be the same thing. To talk about the mind and to talk about the brain is, according to Changeux, to talk about two aspects of the same thing. There is the language of introspection in terms of thoughts, intentions and so on, and there is the language of neurophysiology in terms of neuron firings, cell membranes and so on. The two languages are held to refer to the same events.

A major problem for a theory such as this is to specify the relation between the two languages. It is not as if the two languages attempt to describe a referent which can be specified independently of either language. What is described, be it a brain state or a conscious state, is internal to, and a part of, the language of introspection or neurophysiology. To say that there are two 'aspects' of the same 'thing' or 'event' is rather vague.

Changeux believes that positron emission tomography (PET) can be a useful tool in understanding the mind and how it works.[14] A consideration of this claim will point the way to difficulties with the theory. By injecting an isotope into the bloodstream, PET enables the physiologist to detect areas of neural activity by measuring increased blood flow in those areas. The difficulty though lies in understanding how this provides information about the way the mind works. Even on Changeux's own premises it gives information about the outer ones. The question to ask here is this: if there are two aspects of one event and PET provides information about one aspect, then what is the relation between these aspects for it to provide the same information about the other? If the relation is one of identity, then the double-aspect theory collapses into the identity theory and faces the objections referred to earlier.

We may also inquire as to the nature of this information in relation to thoughts, wishes and so on. Consider the thought that Richard III has had an unjustly bad press and consider what it is to formulate such a thought. The problem is to understand how the measurement of blood flow or the scanning of neural activity gives us knowledge about the thought or how it was formulated. The formulation of that thought is based on a consideration of evidence, such as listening to historians and their interpretation of documents. The thought has a *rational* base and our formulation of thoughts follows evidential procedures. The thought has the property of intentionality. This means that it is *about* something or is *directed* at something. PET provides information concerning that which has a physical base and has the property of being in motion. Such motions may well occur when we formulate thoughts, but Changeux does not explain how PET information constitutes information about the thought or *why* it was formulated. It is not very helpful to talk of 'two aspects' as that merely transfers the problem to how information about one aspect is also information about the other.

There is, of course, a clear sense in which thoughts can be said to have an external dimension, namely, when we tell others what they are. The relation, however, between this external dimension and the one alleged by Changeux remains unclear. His conception of the external dimension of a thought concerns the neuron motions which a physiologist could observe.

I shall conclude this part of the discussion by remarking that attempts to reduce the language of introspection to that of neurophysiology face a number of difficulties. Let the reader try to give a neurophysiological translation of a statement such as: 'I am thinking about the synapses of my brain'. It must be remembered that the personal pronouns must also be translated.

The problem of qualia

When philosophers talk about 'qualia' they are talking about the subjective feel of our experiences. There is something that it is like to see red or hear Mozart. It is this qualitative aspect of our experiences that has been regarded by many philosophers as providing a powerful argument against materialism, or at least against certain kinds of materialism. It has been argued that this qualitative aspect of experience is irreducible. It cannot be reduced to brain states or replaced by descriptions of brain states without leaving something out. Thus, the qualia argument is frequently invoked against eliminative materialism, that is, that version of materialism that wishes to eliminate mental states from a complete description of what there is. Proponents of the qualia argument will want to say that any description of what there is given in purely physical terms will be incomplete. It will be incomplete in the sense that it omits the experiential aspects of our mental lives.

Although there has been much interest recently in the qualia argument, the issues it raises are not at all new. Russell writing in *The Problems of Philosophy* (1912) discussed the difficulty of explaining what our experience of light is like to a blind person. We could explain a physicist's concept of light. We could, for example, explain wave motion by appealing to a sea voyage and so on. However, light as we experience it, would remain unknown to the blind person. Russell was making an important distinction between what it is like to experience light and the physical description of light. The latter could be grasped by the blind person, but not the former.

Recent arguments

I now want to describe two influential versions of the qualia argument. Probably the best known is Frank Jackson's 'What Mary didn't know'. Jackson invites us to consider the case of Mary, a scientist with expertise in colour vision. She has, however, spent all her life in a black and white room. She has studied the physics and physiology of colour vision. Let us suppose that Mary knows all there is to know about such matters. She knows the brain processes that occur when looking at contrasting colour patches. Thus, when people report the experience of seeing blue or red, Mary knows the neurophysiological differences. She knows the causal connections between light rays impinging on optic nerves and the succeeding brain states and she has such knowledge right across the spectrum. It looks as if there is nothing left for her to learn. She has a complete physical description. The problem for the materialist who accepts that there is nothing left to learn becomes apparent when Mary steps outside the room for the first time and *experiences* colour for the first time. The materialist will be committed to saying that on seeing a red rose for the first time, Mary does not learn anything new. She cannot learn anything new as she already had a complete physical description. Jackson wants to say that she clearly does learn something new, namely what it feels like to experience redness.

The second argument is similar to Jackson's but appeals to an experience with which we are not familiar and for that reason makes a slightly different impact. This argument is sometimes referred to as 'The Navigating Bird'. Consider the case of a bird that navigates through sensitivity to the pull of the earth's magnetic field. Imagine that a scientist knows every detail regarding the physiology of the bird's brain and of the presence of magnetic fields. He can even plot the flight path of the bird and predict every twist and turn. The entire flight path can be accurately predicted on a computer screen. It looks as though his knowledge is complete and there is nothing left to add. However, it can be argued that something has been left out. No matter how detailed his knowledge is, or can be, he still does not know what it *feels like* to be sensitive to a magnetic pull. This argument supports the claim that there is an irreducible qualitative aspect of experience that detailed physical descriptions fail to capture and, therefore, such descriptions are incomplete.

We must now consider how a materialist may respond to these arguments. I now wish to consider a recent attempt to refute Jackson's argument. At the Richmond Philosophy Conference 2003, David Papineau delivered a paper entitled 'Brains and Feelings' in which he attempted to refute the qualia argument, or at least Jackson's version of it.

Papineau's 'Brains and Feelings'

We have seen that Jackson had argued that the physical description available to Mary in her black and white room was incomplete. Papineau wants to refute the claim that there is some element of colour vision, the experience of what it is like to see, for example, red, that is non-physical.

Papineau invites us to consider this story. Jane has a list of all the children at Bristol Primary School in 1920. This list includes Archie Leach. She then learns something new: she learns that Cary Grant was at Bristol Primary School in 1920. Can we conclude that at least one child from Bristol Primary School in 1920 (Cary Grant) is not on Jane's list? We cannot conclude this as Jane has not learned about a new *child*. Her list includes all the children. What she has acquired is a new *name* for an old child.

Papineau wants to claim that this story is analogous with Jackson's Mary. Mary has not learned about some new element of reality, what it is like to experience red. Her old knowledge included all aspects of reality. Rather, she has acquired a new name a new concept for something she could always talk about in other terms. According to Papineau the physical description concepts only leave out qualia or feelings in the sense that they do not *use* them. They can, however, *refer* to the feelings.

Replies to Papineau

(1) One way of responding is to question the analogy. The best strategy here is to find an uncontroversial analogy with the Leach/Grant case, note what they have in common and then argue that the analogy with Mary breaks down at a crucial point. Consider the case of Ben's film collection. Ben has all the films directed by Sam Peckinpah, including 'Ride the High Country'. He discovers a film for sale, directed by Peckinpah, called 'Guns in the Afternoon'. He then learns that this latter title is simply the British release title of 'Ride the High Country'. Ben learns something new, but not in terms of an extra film, because he already has a complete collection. He learns a new name for *something* he already knew and could describe in other

terms. However, in the cases of Jane and Ben, this 'something' can be unpacked in terms of material concepts, person or film. The Mary case cannot be unpacked in this way. Consider the following:

(a)   In order to know that Leach is Grant, Jane must know that Grant is a person.

(b)   In order to know that 'Ride the High Country' is 'Guns in the Afternoon', Ben must know that 'Guns in the Afternoon' is a film.

(c1) In order to know her experience is a brain process, Mary must know that her experience is a brain process.

(c2) In order to know her experience is a brain process, Mary must know that her brain process is a brain process.

When cashed out in the way above the disanalogy becomes clear; (c1) merely presupposes the very point at issue whereas (c2) is clearly trivial. It is of no use to attempt to use formal concepts like 'thing', 'event', and so on, as that merely confirms the disanalogy. There is no need for such a move in the cases of Jane and Ben.

(2)   An objection closely connected to the above is that the Jane and Ben cases involve a two-term relation of name and object. It could be argued that the Mary example involves a three-term relation: name, object *and* the experiential dimension of what it is like to experience the object. Papineau is assimilating the different cases and, strangely, claims not to be an eliminativist.

(3)   *What* Mary talks about on leaving the black and white room is given in the terms of the description. These features are essential to identifying the experience and for distinguishing it from other experiences. These features are experiential and subjective.

(4)   Papineau describes Mary as acquiring a new *concept*. This does not seem to be the case for Jane and Ben. They merely acquire names. They subsume named objects under pre-existing concepts. When Mary experiences red for the first time we may well wonder what pre-existing concept this is subsumed under. Papineau realises the difficulty here but should have seen that this difficulty puts the alleged analogy under considerable strain.

(5)   The recognition and distinction of phenomena via different sense modalities is not to be explained solely in terms of being able to talk in different ways. The qualitative feel of different modalities enables us to talk differently but this does not imply that there is *just* different talk.

The reader may also consider our other argument regarding the navigating bird and consider how plausible Papineau-type arguments are in countering that. It would seem odd to say that the scientist, with his complete description, already knows what a magnetic pull feels like when this is precisely what he does not know. Another interesting approach is to examine how plausible such arguments are in relation to other sense modalities. Imagine a previously-deaf person hearing Beethoven for the first time. He may have had perfect knowledge of the physics of sound waves but what would his deaf state distinction between music and sound have been like? It is implausible to say that he can now appreciate what he already knows in different terms.

Epiphenomenalism

This version of physicalism asserts that a person's conscious experiences are produced, or caused, by his brain states. The conscious experiences, however, are held to possess different aspects from those possessed by the brain states and therefore cannot be identified with them. On the epiphenomenalist thesis the causal relation is one-way. It is always the brain states, together with the environmental stimuli, which cause the mental state. Mental states do not cause brain states. The relationship between brain and mind is often likened to that between a tree and a shadow of a tree. It is always the tree, in conjunction with environmental conditions, which causes or fully determines the shadow. It is never the other way around. On this thesis mind is a by-product of cerebral processes.

We can get clearer about the differences between epiphenomenalism and dualism by considering a remark of Plato's. He said that the mind can and does control the body by performing a mental act. A bodily desire can be curbed by the mind, and, from this, a dualist will want to say that the mind is independent of the body and can determine it. The issue can be represented schematically. We shall adopt the following symbolic representation: W = act of the will, B = brain state, A = bodily action, S = stimuli, C = consciousness and → represents the causal relation. The dualist holds that:

$$W \rightarrow B \rightarrow A$$

The epiphenomenalist holds that:

$$B_1 \overset{\nearrow W}{\rightarrow} B_2 \rightarrow A.$$

In this case W is an offshoot of B. On this account any C is determined by B and every B is determined by previous Bs plus S via the sense organs. C cannot change, affect or alter B.

According to a dualist, B may be influenced by C plus S plus previous Bs. C may be caused by previous Cs. The full schematic representation is:

(a) *Epiphenomenalist thesis*

(b) *Dualist thesis*

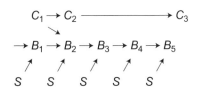

The advantage that the epiphenomenalist seems to have over the dualist is that he can accommodate those neurophysiological facts referred to in our discussion of dualism. They caused the dualist a number of problems. Before we become too enthusiastic though, there are problems with epiphenomenalism which must be mentioned.

In the first place it might be objected against epiphenomenalism that it has not provided an adequate account of what the mind is. What it has done has been to provide the causal antecedents for our mental states. Although this might be of considerable interest if the antecedents were made specific, it does not get to grips with the question of the nature of mind. To give a causal history of some object, event or experience does not tell us what that object, event or experience is. Explaining *what* something is needs to be distinguished from explaining *how* it occurred.

The second problem is that which affects all physicalist theses, namely the problem of rationality. On the epiphenomenalist account all our actions are going to have physical causes. This seems to conflict with the idea that we act as a result of rational considerations. A problem that will crop up here concerns the nature of action. Brain states are physical events and they will cause other physical events such as the muscular movements involved in the performance of actions. The problem is that a human action is not *just* the muscular movements. There is more to understanding human actions than specifying the movements that are involved in those actions. In raising my arm I might be greeting someone, giving a salute, making a signal and so on. The *same* physical movements would be involved and yet we have three *different* actions. How could this be so if the actions were *just* the movements? I now want to say something about the difficulty involved in giving a causal account, in physicalist terms, of what would be described as a rational action. Let us consider an example.

Suppose that I am undecided as to which politician to vote for at an election. As a result of listening to arguments put forward by the parties, I reach a decision and vote accordingly. The decision is a result of reasoned argument. The activity takes place within a rational and social framework which is a necessary condition for identifying and describing the act in the way we do. What account though is to be given of our conscious experiences of listening to and evaluating arguments, and making decisions on that basis? In what sense can these experiences be an accidental by-product of brain processes? In other words, if the causal chain which results in action is to be specified in purely physicalist terms, then what account are we to give of the procedure of evaluation, decision-making and action? Arguments do not appear to be the sorts of things that are easily accommodated within a physical causal chain. The American philosopher Daniel Dennett has attempted to show that arguments can be part of, or have effects on, a physical causal chain. He tells us that:

> Presentations of arguments have all sorts of effects on the causal milieu: they set air waves in motion, cause eardrums to vibrate and have hard to identify, but important, effects deep in the brain of the audience.

Later he says:

> one's perceptual system is designed to be sensitive to the sorts of transmissions of energy that must occur for an argument to be communicated.[15]

There are a number of points to be made about this.

First, one can only say of an utterance that it is an argument when a framework of rationality is presupposed. We can only be said to argue when rational considerations are a possibility. Two dogs do not argue *with* each other; they growl *at* each other. It is not clear that what we mean by 'rational possibilities' can be elucidated in terms of energy transmissions and sophisticated perceptual organs. The perceptive reader will have noted that the term 'sophisticated' cannot be defined in terms of receptivity to rationality without making Dennett's claim circular.

Secondly, there is a difference between being convinced by an argument and being moved by atmospheric perturbations. In the latter case the rationale is omitted thus we have no ground for saying that the subject-matter of our discussion are arguments as distinct from noises. Arguments should be described as persuasive forces, where the possibility of persuasion has its roots in a rational framework, rather than causal forces. In concentrating his attention on the physical processes involved in a spoken argument, Dennett has presented us with the properties of sounds in general. But we cannot get from sounds in general to arguments in particular by just spelling out in greater detail what these physical processes are. (The reader should note that talk about energy transmissions has even less appeal in the case of written arguments.) There is nothing in

Dennett's account to distinguish arguments from any other linguistic activities such as singing, joking, greeting, questioning, and so on. Dennett does not provide physically necessary conditions, let alone sufficient ones, for marking off arguments in particular. We can, of course, give a list of physically necessary conditions for us to partake in linguistic activity. These conditions, however, are not peculiar to arguments. If the reader thinks that they are, then he should try imagining a case in which precisely *those* conditions did not hold. Imagine a tribe that could perform the same as us linguistically with one exception, namely they could not argue. This does not mean that they could not argue well, but rather, they could not argue at all. In what sense could they ask questions, make assertions or hold beliefs? The reader should consider whether this is a *logical* possibility.

Perhaps one of the attractions of an epiphenomenalist thesis is the idea that there is something fundamental about physical explanations. This idea is often expressed by saying that physical explanations have epistemological priority over any other kind of explanation. In the case of the mind-body problem the physical explanation will be that explanation is couched in terms of neurophysiology. The central claim here is that if we had a neurophysiological explanation for some phenomenon of consciousness, then we would not need to bother with any other explanation. The other claim is, of course, that all phenomena of consciousness will ultimately be explicable in neurophysiological terms. To see how such claims might be challenged the reader should consider the following example from Dennett and the reply to it.

Dennett holds that purposive explanations (that is, explanations in terms of the purposes, intentions and so on, of the agent) are undercut by the neurophysiological. He considers the case of a man who cannot or will not say the word 'father'. The pronouncements of the layman and the psychoanalyst would be undercut:

> if a neurosurgeon were to establish that a tiny lesion in the speech centre of the brain caused by an aneurism was causally responsible for the lacuna in the man's verbal repertory – not an entirely implausible discovery in the light of Penfield's remarkable research.[16]

But how plausible is this example and what exactly does it tell us?

The psychoanalytic explanation would run into difficulties if he could use terms for 'father' such as 'dad', 'pa' or 'papa' which are more affectionate, and 'pater' or 'male parent' which are more formal. It is then left wholly mysterious as to why this one word should be problematic. The hostility towards his father appealed to in psychoanalytic explanation, unconscious or not, would seem to be aimed at the *word* 'father'. The psychoanalytic explanation would be rejected, not on the grounds of epistemological poverty, but on the grounds that it simply does not adequately account for the facts.

The next question to ask is whether he could say words which syntactically resemble 'father', such as 'farther'. If he can say this latter word, then the discrepancy in his repertory would not be noticed unless we are supposed to believe that a lesion in the brain can make it impossible for him to combine possessive pronouns with adverbs of distance, that is, 'my farther'. This supposition would confuse a physical law with a rule of language. Given that the differences in pronunciation between 'my farther' and 'my father' are negligible for conversation purposes, it seems that what we are supposed to believe him incapable of is using the word 'father' where 'father' is seen as having a meaning content. It is not just the physical movements involved in pronouncing the word that he is incapable of. The brain lesion is supposed to be causally responsible for the absence of the meaning content embodied by the word 'father'. But if he uses expressions like 'dad', 'pater', 'male parent', and so on, then in what sense does he not have the meaning? The most one can say is that the lesion in the brain is the cause of his inability to master an almost imperceptible nuance of pronunciation. The problem now is to see what is of philosophical importance in Dennett's example. The neurophysiological explanation no longer enters on the scene with epistemological priority stamped upon it. In this example it just so happens that this explanation *fits the facts* better than the layman's or the psychoanalyst's. The reader must realise that this is not the same thing as Dennett envisages with his talk of 'undercutting' and of the other two candidates having the rug pulled from under them. There is nothing of philosophical importance in saying that speech impediments or pronunciation defects are logically appropriate objects of neurophysiological inquiry. What Dennett's example requires is that meaning contents can be logically appropriate objects of neurophysiological inquiry and it is precisely at this point that his example becomes implausible. Perhaps the reader would like to note an actual example[17] of people having difficulty saying the word 'father' even when their father was addressing them. I am referring to the children of Hitler's architect, Albert Speer. In this case 'meaning' is responsible for the absence of the word. It is not plausible to say that (one day) we might undercut their explanation of why they will not use the word.

We have now examined Cartesian dualism and physicalism and we have seen some of the problems associated with them. I now want to draw the reader's attention to a modern alternative.

▶ Persons

We have seen from our discussion of the mind-body problem that the Cartesian dualist takes the idea of a self whose essential nature lies in thinking as being the logically primitive concept. It is upon this foundation that we construct our knowledge. Dualism affords priority to the mental. It is said to *control* bodily action. On a physicalist account the mental is to be explained by either identifying it with the physical or claiming that it is a by-product of physical processes. Physicalists adhere to what is known as the 'bottom up' approach – we start with knowledge of physical processes and it is from that base that we construct our knowledge of human beings and everything else.

Some modern philosophers would want to reject the idea that either a body or a mind was the logically primitive concept. They would want to say that a person is not to be split up into two different things. The concept of a person is itself taken as the logically primitive concept. The concept of a person is not to be further analysed; it is a cornerstone of our conceptual scheme.

In an important work[18] Strawson has endorsed the implications of our everyday talk about persons. He wants to reject Cartesian dualism. In our ordinary discourse we attribute to each other both states of consciousness and bodily states. We saw an equivocation in Descartes regarding this matter. The reader will remember that on his official theory it was inappropriate to attribute bodily states to a purely thinking thing. We were then presented with a switch to the self as a mind-body substance which would accommodate our ordinary ways of talking. Strawson wants to say that our concept of a person is that of a single substance to which both states of consciousness and bodily states are attributable. This is held to be the concept with which we must start. A person is not 'essentially' a thinking thing or a complex amalgam of mind and body. Strawson takes it to be a necessary truth that a person is embodied. We cannot here go into the details of this thesis, but I shall mention one of Strawson's main arguments for accepting his account. Consider the following propositions:

(1) I could not ascribe a state of consciousness, like pain, to myself unless I could ascribe pain to other people. (This does not mean that I could not *feel* pain unless such a condition were satisfied. Strawson is concerned with *ascription* of conscious states.)

(2) I could not ascribe such states of consciousness to others unless I could, at least sometimes, verify the statement.

(3) It is possible to verify this statement only on the evidence of that person's bodily behaviour.

Strawson concludes from this that the meaning of words like 'pain', 'depression' and other terms denoting states of consciousness must involve a reference to characteristic patterns of bodily behaviour which are publicly observable.

What is of great importance here is that Strawson is rejecting an assumption implicit in Descartes, namely, that terms such as 'pain' are simply *names* of states of consciousness. If one were to accept the Cartesian view, then serious epistemological problems would arise. Thus, for example, if each person can only be acquainted with his own states of consciousness, then he will not know what a word like 'depressed' means unless he has been depressed. Problems will arise in making such ascriptions to others, and, ultimately, in making them to oneself. There will be no check that words are being used in the same way if their meaning derives from a private baptism of our own sensations. We shall discuss this in the following section.

On Strawson's account, the way out of these difficulties is to take the 'person' as basic. A person is a single particular of which material object predicates (*M*-predicates) and person predicates (*P*-predicates) can be attributed. A person is to be distinguished from a material object in terms of the attribution of *P*-predicates such as, 'is depressed', 'is indignant', 'collects stamps' and so on. These *P*-predicates could not be ascribed intelligibly to a material object. The ascriptions are based on observations of people's behaviour. This provides the logically adequate criteria for ascribing *P*-predicates.

We cannot pursue a critical discussion of this thesis here, but the reader is invited to consider the following problem. If persons are to be distinguished from material objects in the way Strawson suggests, then will it always be possible to distinguish a person from a sophisticated robot? The problem is that if we ascribe *P*-predicates (which are what distinguish people from material objects) on the basis of behavioural criteria which are logically adequate for the ascription, then what happens in the case of a robot that behaves in ways similar to us? It might, for example, clean houses, go shopping, do sums and a number of other things besides. The lines of thought that the reader might like to follow here are:

(a) whether Strawson's account does justice to the idea of 'inner feelings' themselves as opposed to the observed bodily behaviour through which we ascribe such states; and

(b) whether a group of robots *could* ever be said to constitute a community and, if not, why not?

▶ The problem of other minds

In adopting Descartes' approach to philosophy one never has the same evidence for the existence of other minds as one has for the existence of one's own mind. The reader will remember that the existence of his own mind is the one proposition that Descartes held to be indubitable. He has certain knowledge of his own mind and mental states.

The problem that arises is how can I claim to know, in Descartes' sense of 'know',[19] that others have minds. This problem is generated through the notion that the individual has privileged access to, or direct acquaintance with, his own mental states but not the mental states of others. I am not directly acquainted with your mental states. They are something I infer from your bodily behaviour and it is, in principle, possible for such an inference to be mistaken. There will be no logical impossibility in doubting that others have minds. The sceptic's question is: how do you *know* that others have minds? This is something we would all claim to know, but can we justify our claim to knowledge? Can we dispose of sceptical doubt?

Until about fifty years ago it was thought that any doubt could be dispelled by use of what is known as the argument from analogy. Recently, philosophers have put this argument under considerable pressure and many have rejected it. There are two traditional versions of the argument. One is presented by Russell and the other by J. S. Mill.

Both versions assume that the premiss of the argument involves a causal statement of the form X causes Y. The individual is said to know from his own case that mental states cause bodily states and then he argues by analogy with his own case that the same applies to others. The reader should note that there is a difference between arguing from cause to effect and arguing from effect to cause. When arguing from cause to effect one argues:

X causes Y, X occurred, therefore Y occurred or will occur.

This involves the premiss that Xs are always followed by Ys. When arguing from effect to cause one argues:

X causes Y, Y occurred, therefore X must have occurred. This involves the premiss that Ys are always preceded by Xs.

Let us now turn to Russell's version of the argument. He claims to know from his own case that mental states cause bodily states or actions (bodily states are always preceded by mental ones) so, the argument runs, if I observe a particular bodily state (BS), such as a grimace, in a particular person, then I may infer the mental state (M) of feeling pain in that person. If I observe $BS1$ in P, I can by analogy with my own case, infer $M1$ in P.

Am I, however, entitled to claim that $BS1$ is, in my own case, always preceded by a specific mental state, $M1$? It might be a legitimate claim in cases where the bodily action is, for example, difficult to perform. One could claim that in such cases the bodily states were preceded by volition, intention or deliberation. This does not have to be the case though for all our actions. There is a difference between moving a limb in a dexterity competition and simply scratching your head. In the latter case the bodily action need not be preceded by mental states – you just scratch.

Let us assume that I do know in some cases that my bodily actions are preceded by mental states. The question then becomes whether it is legitimate to infer that other people are like this. We can consider this in the light of an example. Consider the case where I alter my bodily behaviour in order to avoid something. This behaviour is dependent on my having particular visual experiences. When I see another behaving in the same way am I entitled to think that his behaviour is guided by the same experiences? I have sometimes said 'there are nettles' and this has been preceded by a particular visual experience. If I hear another utter this sentence and see that he is looking in the same direction, then can I not conclude that he is having the same visual experience? What makes this kind of example convincing is the information content of the sentences.

The problem with this argument is that the sceptic can claim that it does not *prove* the existence of other minds. His reason for claiming this is that the argument assumes that the other means by his words the same as what I mean when I use these words. If this is so, then the argument assumes what it purports to prove. I shall say more about this later.

I now want to consider Mill's argument. In this argument $S =$ stimulus, $M =$ mental state, $BS =$ bodily state. I know from my own case that:

(1) $S1$ causes $M1$ ($S1$ is always followed by $M1$)
(2) $M1$ causes $BS1$ ($BS1$ is always preceded by $M1$)

If I observe, in connection with a person P, both $S1$ followed by $BS1$, then I may infer $M1$ in P.

The question to ask here is whether every $S1$ is followed by a particular $M1$ in my own case. It is permissible to claim this in cases where the stimuli are, for example, loud noises or flames coming into contact with the body. It is not, however, always true. My eyes could be stimulated by an object in close proximity, but it does not follow that I shall always see it. It is also the case that the repetition of the same stimulus can produce different mental states as in the case of jokes. In the case of reflex actions there are no intermediate mental states. There is just S1 followed by $BS1$.

In spite of these objections common-sense tends to side with Mill. From introspection I know that if my hand touches a hot iron, I experience pain, wince and withdraw my hand to treat it. When I observe others I see that they behave in the same way. Am I not thus entitled to infer that when others are burnt they have the same experiences/sensations as I do? If we consider cases where we observe only $BS1$ or $S1$, then the argument is not decisive. If we have both, then the argument seems to fit well with common-sense. The problem though is that appeals to common-sense do not necessarily solve philosophical problems or silence sceptical critics. As we have seen, there are objections to the common-sense view. In the light of some of these objections the argument from analogy has been amended.

When analogical arguments are used in other contexts we do not always expect there to be causal laws of the kind envisaged by Mill and Russell. Consider the case of a doctor who discovers a particular set of symptoms in a patient and he concludes that the patient *probably* has mumps. The premiss in this case asserts that these symptoms are *usually* associated with mumps, rather than always or invariably associated. (The causal form of the premiss in the original argument involved the use of 'always'.) Thus, some have argued, in the case of other minds all we require are probability arguments. We would then argue analogically with the example of the doctor: $S1$ is *usually* followed by $M1$ in my own case and so on as before. This has been held to avoid the objections which centre on the use of 'always'.

However, many have rejected the amended version, along with the stronger version, on the ground that they both involve the fallacy of generalising from a single case. They are held to assume that all other people are like oneself. There is evidence of considerable differences in mental powers and experiences and this has been regarded as a warning against generalising from a single case. In 1883 Galton reported the extent to which people differed with the mental imagery which accompanied their thinking. He discovered that not all people had visual imagery. Many scientists claimed that mental images were unknown to them, and even some artists who painted from memory made the same claim. Galton regarded them as having a mental deficiency of which they were unaware. Investigations such as this might be held to warn us against assuming that all people are like ourselves. Appeals to investigations such as this will not, however, show that all individuals might be fantastically different. We shall consider this later. For the present the reader should ask what assumptions about others it was necessary for Galton to make in order to begin the investigation. What were the preconditions of conducting such an investigation?

There are differences between the Mill–Russell argument and the analogical case of the doctor. The doctor's diagnosis is not based on the single case, theirs is. It could be said that it is *because* the doctor's diagnosis is not based on a single case that it is permissible to talk of probabilities. A second difference concerns verification. The doctor's conclusion can be verified but when the conclusion is that another is, for example, having the same sensation as I do when I feel pain, then the matter is different. To talk in terms of the other wincing, crying and so on, only prompts the question of how it can be known that the same sensation is being experienced when all there is access to are bodily manifestations. The verification procedures in the two cases are not comparable.

In relation to the question of verification, the verification principle was taken as self-evident by a school of philosophers known as the Logical Positivists. According to A. J. Ayer, the leading British exponent of the doctrine, a statement is meaningless if you cannot say what would verify it. The school adopted a slogan, 'the meaning of proposition is its method of verification'. When Ayer applied this principle to the problem of other minds he adopted a paradoxical conclusion. He argued[20] that if I interpret the statement 'John is in pain' as being about a sensation of which only John can be aware, then the statement must be meaningless for me as I cannot verify it. Quite obviously such a statement is not meaningless and Ayer attempts to avoid saying that it is by adopting a behaviourist account. Thus the statement 'John is in pain' said by Ayer would refer to what Ayer could observe, that is, bodily behaviour such as wincing or crying. What is paradoxical is that as Ayer did not adopt a behaviourist account for first-person reports, words like 'pain', 'depression' and so on are all going to have two meanings depending on whether Ayer is talking about himself or others. When Ayer says 'I have a pain', he is talking about a state of consciousness. When he says 'John has a pain', he is talking about behaviour. Ayer later abandoned this position and reverted to the argument from analogy.

The argument from analogy, even in its strongest form, is an inductive argument. Mill thought that his argument was as strong as any inductive argument could be. One could be satisfied with this argument and say that although our knowledge of other minds is not *logically* certain, this does not mean that we cannot claim to know that others have minds. After all we do not restrict our use of 'to know' to only those propositions of which we are logically certain. We cannot be expected 'to know' that others have minds in Descartes' sense of 'know'. If one accepts this, then the thesis of solipsism remains a logical possibility. It is a logical possibility that there are no mental states other than my own. There are, however, other ways of attacking scepticism.

We have already hinted at one such way in raising the question of the presuppositions of conducting tests such as Galton's. In order to ask questions and evaluate answers so as to draw conclusions from them, it was necessary to assume that others understood the words and that their words have the same meaning as when used by the person conducting the investigation. We are, therefore, assuming the existence of a common language.

It can then be argued that language is necessarily public in nature. It would not be possible to engage in the kind of linguistic activity we do engage in, were it not for the existence of common meanings and the application of rules. If it can be shown that this is a logical precondition for having a language, then it can be argued that the sceptic, in using language, raises and expresses a doubt where the presuppositions of his doing so show such a doubt to be nonsensical. The sceptic, in asking the sceptical question, would be partaking in a *public* activity, namely language. This is the only way in which his scepticism can be expressed. What the sceptic must deny is that language is necessarily public in nature. He must assume the possibility of a private language in which he names his sensations, considered as private objects, by a kind of private, internal baptism. This would then let in the problem of how two people could ever know that they were using words in the same way or having the same experiences. It was this possibility of a private language that was denied by Wittgenstein.[21] The argument is too technical for our purposes but we can note some of its most important features.

First, the activity of naming is one which takes place within a public language. We can, of course, give private names to things, but we can only do this because we already participate in a public language. Naming presupposes a certain amount of stage-setting within a language.[22]

Secondly, there is the problem of how a private language user could be said to be using his words correctly or incorrectly. *Ex hypothesi* there are no public rules against which the usage can be checked. The notion of rules which are private in nature is fraught with difficulty. The only criterion for saying that such a rule was being obeyed or not is whether it *seemed* to the private language user that it was.[23]

Wittgenstein argues that a criterion tells you whether what seems to be so is actually so, therefore, 'seeming' cannot *itself* function as a criterion. Where one cannot speak of a rule being obeyed or disobeyed, one cannot say that there is a rule. If there is no rule, then there is no language either as it is the existence of rules which distinguishes language from sounds. It might be thought that memory could provide a criterion for whether a sign in a private language was being used in the same way and, hence, in a rule-governed way. There are, however, problems with this. There will be no *external* check on the memories of a private language user; all there will be are memories. The deep problem here concerns how the private language user can be said to check the meaning of the sign which he has matched with a particular sensation. If he wants to use that sign to refer to future occurrences of the sensation, then he must know what the sign means. In order to know what it means, he must be able to recall the sensation that goes with it, but in order to recall *that* he must already know what the sign means. The memory of what the sign means would be used as a check on itself and this is why Wittgenstein likened such a procedure to that of a man who bought several copies of the same newspaper in order to assure himself that what it said was true.

If the notion of a private language can be shown to be incoherent, then scepticism in relation to other minds will turn out to be inexpressible. The sceptic must assume that words referring to his mental states acquire their meaning by an act of naming a private object with which he is directly acquainted. The Wittgensteinian attack is an attempt to show that words cannot acquire meaning in this way. As a general point, Wittgenstein held that it is not sufficient to establish a sign as a name in language by making a particular noise when confronted with an object.

Wittgenstein wanted to pinpoint a confusion in the Cartesian idea that one is said to 'know' one's mental states. Wittgenstein and his followers would hold that the argument from analogy merely endorses the confusion by accepting the initial premiss, 'I know from my own case that ...'. The reason why Wittgenstein thought there was a confusion here was that he held it was only possible to talk of knowledge in cases where it was at least possible to talk of doubt. It is not possible to doubt, for example, that one is in pain, thus, the argument runs, it is not possible for us to say such things as 'I know that I am in pain' without filling in a special background in which the expression is given a use. The point is that if doubt is logically excluded, then so is talk about knowledge. Opponents of this view will hold that if doubt is logically excluded, then our knowledge must be all the more certain. We cannot pursue these matters here. The reader might, however, like to ask just what it is that he is supposed to 'know' in the case of his own mental states. If you think that it is an inner 'object' of some kind, then there will be both object and knowledge of the object. This implies that it is not so much pain that is distressing, but rather the knowledge of pain. Readers who think that it is possible to doubt whether one is in pain should consider the following questions:

(1) How is the doubt to be resolved?
(2) What would count as making a mistake?
(3) What difference could it make if one made a mistake?

I shall conclude our discussion by raising a further question mark against the sceptic. Let us assume that the sceptic puts his question in the following way: how do you know that another is having the same experiences as you? It can be argued[24] that the sceptic has failed to give a sense to this question because he has excluded all possible answers from the outset. He would not permit an answer in terms of using the same words and neither would he accept an answer in terms of the same neural processes occurring when, for example, we are in pain. It seems that he will only be satisfied by the *having* of another's experience. The difficulty lies in understanding what this means. If this is a genuine demand, then the sceptic ought to specify what state of affairs could be said to satisfy the demand. It would be unreasonable to smuggle in an unspecifiable standard of knowledge and then complain that the standard, whatever it is, had not been attained.

▶ Behaviourism

There are two versions of behaviourism that need to be distinguished.

Psychological behaviourism

Behaviourism was, and to some extent still is, a highly influential methodological principle of psychological science. Psychologists influenced by J. B. Watson held that it was not necessary to assume, postulate or attribute mental states in order to predict or explain human behaviour. To put it another way, if such states do occur, then they are of no interest to the behaviourist psychologist as he can go about his business of explaining and predicting behaviour without making any appeal to them. For all practical purposes this is tantamount to claiming that such states do not occur.

During the second decade of the twentieth century psychology came to be regarded as the study of behaviour pure and simple. On a strictly behaviourist account the attribution of mental states or an 'inner life' to others will add nothing to explanations of their behaviour. The explanatory model is simply that if the organism is presented with a particular stimulus, then he will make a particular response. The ultimate goal of the enterprise is to be able to predict the response from a given stimulus, or, if you were given the response, to be able to say what stimulus had produced it.

Everything intangible was to be replaced by its most tangible manifestations. Thus, for example, sensation and perception would be replaced by discriminative responses, thinking was regarded in terms of problem-solving performances and talking (very quietly) to oneself, emotion was not to be regarded as an inner feeling but as various bodily movements such as those of glands and muscles. Peirce summed the theory up when he remarked that if we consider what effects, which might conceivably have practical bearings, we conceive the mind to have, then our conception of these effects is the whole of our conception of the mind.

As we shall see, one of the most important explanatory concepts was that of the reflex. This was a term which came to have many varied meanings. The standard criteria for distinguishing the reflex from other kinds of response were that it was involuntary, unlearned, predictable and uniform, and unconscious. The reflex came to be regarded as a kind of behavioural atom out of which all other responses were composed. The use of the concept certainly goes back to Descartes. He had used it in his theory that animals are complex automata whose behaviour is governed by a rigorous cause and effect relationship. Man, thanks to his possession of a soul, was, according to Descartes, free to influence the workings of his nervous system. Man could, if necessary, override reflex action. Behaviourist psychologists did not adopt Cartesian dualism. They took over the concept of a reflex because they thought it would make the behaviour of man amenable to the same kind of cause and effect relationship that Descartes had spoken of in connection with animals. We shall have more to say about the concept of a reflex during our critical discussion.

Logical behaviourism

This is a philosophical thesis concerned with the correct analysis of statements about the mental or 'psychological' statements. The central idea here is that statements which purport or appear to be about the goings on in a private mental world can be analysed or translated into statements about overt bodily, publicly observable behaviour, or dispositions to behave in a particular way. The seminal text advocating this position is Ryle's *The Concept of Mind*. Ryle was mainly concerned with an attack on what he regarded as Descartes' two worlds myth. The two worlds in question are the mental and the physical. He dubbed such a view 'the ghost in the machine'.

We can list some examples of how the translation procedure is supposed to work. To say that John is in pain means that John is behaving in a particular way, such as crying, wincing and so on. To say that John is angry means something like John is going red in the face, waving his arms, shouting and so on. To say that John is experiencing a green after-image would mean that John has a disposition to assert that something is green when in fact it is not. To say that John intends to go to the cinema means that if John is not prevented, then he will go to the cinema. In these examples terms which we might take to refer to mental items or states of consciousness, such as 'pain', 'anger', 'an after-image' and 'intention' can be analysed into descriptions of publicly observable bodily behaviour or dispositions to behave in a certain way. For such an enterprise to be successful, the translation procedure must not involve any loss or change of meaning. If it did, then a critic could complain that the mentalist terms and the behavioural ones were not equivalent in meaning.

The theses of psychological and logical behaviourism are obvious allies and they are, of course, historically related.

Criticisms

(1)   We have already referred to one problem during our discussion of the other minds issue. To say that John was in pain would, on behaviourist principles, mean that John was behaving in a particular way. In the case of first-person locutions, however, we do not mean by 'I am in pain' that I am behaving in a particular way. It looks as if we are going to have different meanings for mentalist terms depending on whether we are talking about ourselves or others.

(2)   Some philosophers have attempted to apply a behaviourist account to one's own mental states, though not very successfully. Ryle argued that if words like 'pain' referred to private feelings, then I could never know that another was in pain[25] as the argument from analogy is too weak, but, Ryle says, there are occasions when we do know, therefore, pain cannot be a private experience. It is a behavioural response. Now whereas this sort of move might work with words like 'vanity', it does not work at all well with words like 'pain'. To say that someone is vain is to say that they have a tendency to show off, and this has to involve some reference to bodily

behaviour. But if all we meant by 'John is in pain' was 'John is disposed to behave in certain ways', then we would have no reason to think that there was anything wrong with pain except that the noises he made were unpleasant *for us*.

(3) If 'pain' simply refers to bodily movements, then how is it that we can and do distinguish pain-killing drugs from paralysing drugs? There are many similar arguments to this one. Consider a strictly behaviourist elucidation of the difference between anger and indignation. The bodily movements constitutive of anger are more pronounced. Indignation thus becomes a kind of muted anger. Given that animals are capable of bodily movements which constitute anger, we could say, by simply diluting these movements, that animals feel indignation.

There are many other problems with a behaviourist account of the emotions. If all we meant by 'sadness' was crying and so on, then how can a behaviourist account for why peeling onions and garlic is not a source of emotional upheaval in our lives? A behaviourist will, of course, say that not all cases of movements in the tear ducts will count as sadness. The problem for him though is to distinguish those cases which are from those which are not *within* the strictures of behaviourism. Perhaps it would be more accurate to say that crying is a *measure* of sadness, that is, it tells us how sad a person is.

(4) There is a criticism concerning pretence behaviour which requires considerable care. The criticism is that if a description of bodily behaviour is synonymous with the ascription of the mental state, then how is it ever possible to distinguish, for example, someone who is really afraid from someone who only pretends to be? Their bodily behaviour could be the same and, on a behaviourist account, there will be nothing else to go on. One way of answering this[26] is an appeal to limitation analysis. The idea here is that there comes a point when it no longer makes sense to say that someone is pretending. The behaviour, that is to say, becomes so pronounced that it simply is not feasible to say that a person is pretending. Thus to be certain that an ascription of, say, 'fear' is appropriate all we need is more behaviour and this will settle any doubt. Although there are cases where this will work, it is not the infallible guide that some have supposed. To see why it is not the reader should consider the following example which I have borrowed from the cinema.

In the film *Angels with Dirty Faces* the central character is a gangster admired by the local slum boys. When he is sentenced to the electric chair the local priest asks him to feign fear at the execution so that the boys will no longer think him a hero and aspire towards his life style. The gangster refuses to do this. When he is taken to the electric chair, however, he screams, pleads for his life and so on. Part of the appeal of the film is that we do not really know whether he had acceded to the priest's request or whether his nerve had finally failed him. He had a close relationship with the boys and was a childhood friend of the priest so he had a motive for complying with the request. On the other hand it was important to him not to be regarded as a coward and we also know that people do break down at the sight of the electric chair. The point about this example is that even if we had had more screaming, shouting and so on, we still would not know whether he was afraid. Limitation analysis has its limitations.

It is, of course, true that pretence behaviour is only possible against a general background where behaviour is connected with the ascription of mental states. This 'connection', however, is hardly sufficient to give the behaviourist what he wants, namely a relation of synonymity between descriptions of bodily behaviour and ascriptions of mental states.

(5) A major problem with behaviourism considered as a scientific theory concerns the idea of the environment consisting of a set of stimuli. The problem is that nothing is seen as meaningful in the environment. Ultimately it will be regarded as a matter in motion which causes us to move in particular ways. These latter movements are held to constitute behaviour or actions. The whole cause and effect process is held to occur automatically and mechanically. Let us consider an example to see what is at issue here.[27]

In Skinner's version of behaviourism, conditioning represents a purely automatic process of learning. But consider the use of the teaching machine in the light of this claim. We find here that what corresponds to the reinforcement (the rewards in conditioning) is the information received by the subject which tells him whether his response (answer) was the correct one or not. The problem is whether this can be regarded as a case of automatic imprinting which just increases the probability of the occurrence of this kind of movement in future situations of a similar kind. There are a couple of points to be noted about this.

First, when we talk about 'similar' situations in the future, then the subject needs to *see them as* similar. In other words, he must be able to pick out the relevant features of similarity in order for him to get down to the business of answering.

Secondly, to regard information as a purely biological reward is a gross distortion. The reader should consider the conceptual framework to which the concept of information belongs. It is related to the activities of questioning and answering which can only have a meaning within a framework of rationality as opposed to that of movements. To exist within a framework of rationality has other important implications. It implies that agents are capable of taking a point of view which they may attempt to justify by appeal to argument. They are capable of holding and altering beliefs in accordance with information received. They can weigh up evidence and see its relevance. In other words, they interpret their environment and are not just the passive recipients of external stimuli which cause their bodies to move. Thus it is not just a case of the automatic imprinting of information; there is also the *rational appraisal* of information. Indeed, the behaviour theorist must assume this in the case of his own activity of theorising. He cannot regard that activity as an automatic series of motions which is initiated and sustained by bare stimuli impinging on his sense organs. On such an account as this the question of rational justification cannot arise. It makes no sense to talk about justifying movements. It is, of course, the hallmark of scientific theories that they can be justified by appealing to rational considerations.

(6)   We have just seen that regarding the environment as a collection of bare stimuli raises difficulties. There are, however, cases where it is feasible to talk in this way. You need not interpret anything in order for your knee to jerk in response to a hammer tap. The difficulties arise when it is claimed that all our responses are to be assimilated to the case of the hammer tap. Many behaviourists would want to avoid making such a claim. In attempting to do this it might be claimed that whereas not all responses are like the case of the hammer, they are, nevertheless, composed of such basic responses.[28] The idea here is that you can somehow break down complex responses into a series of simpler ones, and these simpler ones are of a reflex variety. This was the point of our earlier remark that the reflex came to be regarded as a kind of behavioural atom. There are further problems with this move:

(a)   If there is no rationality in the single reflex (it is just a movement) then it is difficult to see how a collection of the *same* reflexes can produce rationality.

(b)   It might sound reasonable to claim that a response which takes time to make or perform can be broken down into smaller elements. But meaningful responses have got nothing to do with length of time. A response can be immediate, momentary *and* meaningful, as in the case of the wink of an eye.

(c)   Many responses can only occur and can only be described when rule-governed and meaningful criteria are presupposed. Consider the example of Sir Galahad riding past a tower and seeing a white handkerchief being waved. The handkerchief is not just a bare stimulus like a hammer tap or pin prick. Galahad knows what it means and this presupposes a level of interpretation. Furthermore, his response presupposes a form of life in which the concept of chivalry plays a role. This is an activity governed by rules, and the rules and concepts which constitute that form of life must be taken into account and accepted for what they are if we are to describe and specify responses made in that form of life.

(7)   No distinction is drawn between the cause of an emotion and its object. Behaviourist psychologists do not take into account the object-directedness of our emotions, or what Wittgenstein referred to as their

'target'. The difference can be brought out by considering emotions which are projected towards the future, such as dread. As the object does not yet exist, it cannot be regarded as a cause or some environmental stimulus. An effect cannot precede its cause. We cannot pursue this topic here, but interested readers are recommended to consult the works listed in the Notes.[29]

(8)   There is a circularity problem in the behaviourist analysis of mental states. Critics often bring this problem out by considering the cases of belief and desire. Suppose that John believes that we are about to have a storm. If we analyse this in terms of his behaviour, we may appeal to his checking that the doors are closed, that all the windows are closed and so on. The problem is that this presupposes the fact that he does not *want* to get wet. So the analysis of belief in terms of behaviour rests on another mental feature, namely, desire.

(9)   It can also be argued that behaviourism, like epiphenomenalism, denies what we all know to be true. We all know that mental states can cause bodily actions. My desires, affections, feelings, issue in subsequent actions, and it is hard to see how they can be *identified* with the actions or with dispositions to act.

(10)   The notion of a 'disposition' has never been made transparently clear. If we analyse, 'John intends to go to the cinema' in terms of something like, 'John will go to the cinema if he is not prevented', the problem will be what is meant by 'not prevented'. Presumably a terrorist attack on the cinema, falling and breaking his leg, would count as preventions and so might receiving a phone call from a famous model inviting him out for a meal. It would be natural to call this latter option a change of mind but this is not something to which we could refer in the initial analysis. It also seems that a full analysis could involve a never ending list of hypotheticals which are somehow part of the meaning of John's intention.

I shall conclude this discussion of behaviourism by saying that when the stimulus-response model for explaining human behaviour is interpreted in a narrow sense, where we are working at the level of physical movements, then the theory is inadequate. When it is given a wide interpretation, then of course it is true to say that all our actions are responses to stimuli because 'stimuli' has now come to mean 'anything to which we respond'.

When 'behaviour' comes to mean anything we say or do in a social context, the psychological theory becomes trivialised. Even so, it is by no means clear that all mentalist terms can be analysed along the lines suggested by the logical behaviourists.

We have discussed one highly influential psychological theory in relation to the mind-body problem and the nature of human action. We are now going to discuss another. This is a very different theory from that of behaviourism. It is one which has had important effects in many different areas of the intellectual map.

▶ Freud and psychoanalysis

Freud's most important conception is that of an unconscious mind. His conception is said to differ from that of his predecessors in that it was with Freud that it became a scientific concept. The unconscious refers to processes, phenomena and forces that are mental and of which the person is unaware. It should be distinguished from the pre-conscious. If a particular phenomenon is pre-conscious, then the agent can be made aware of it by normal means. If, on the other hand, it is unconscious, then it cannot be brought into consciousness by normal means but through analytical therapy.

Among the most important of the contents of the unconscious is repressed material. Examples of the kinds of things that can be repressed are: impulses, wishes, desires and memories, especially those related to the experiences or fantasies of the child.

Freud regarded the unconscious as a dynamic force. This dynamic nature means that the unconscious is not to be regarded as a mere container of ideas. The source of its dynamism is said to be derived from the energy of the instinctual drives, sexuality and aggression. In order to show the kind of influence that the unconscious can have on normal persons, Freud formulated the theory that such things as slips of the tongue, lapses of memory and other shortcomings in psychological functioning could be traced to material relating to the unconscious. This work of Freud's was called *The Psychopathology of Everyday Life*. It should be noted, however, that much of Freud's data had been drawn from studies of persons suffering from neurotic disorders.

The theory of the unconscious was greeted by some with a sense of discovery. William James wrote:

> In the wonderful explorations by Binet, Janet and Freud of the subliminal consciousness of patients with hysteria, we have revealed to us whole systems of underground life, in the shape of memories of a painful sort which lead a parasitic existence, buried outside the primary fields of consciousness, and making irruptions thereinto with hallucinations, pains, convulsions, paralysis of feeling and motion, and the whole procession of symptoms of hysteric disease of body and mind.[30]

Although James' remarks are concerned with abnormal cases, the theory of the unconscious is intended to apply to normal persons. It is not just abnormal aims and goals, but also normal ones, that are held to be mainly determined by the unconscious. Normality is simply the harmony between unconscious goals and conscious aims.

After 1900 Freud postulated two great drives: (i) Self-Preservation, and (ii) Procreation (the preservation of the species). He gave the name 'libido' or sexual energy to the procreative drive. When Freud first used the word 'sex' in his theoretical writings he intended it to be understood in its everyday sense. During this period, however, important changes in usage occurred. The term came to be applied to any pleasurable sensation relating to the bodily functions. Through the concept of sublimation it was applied to tenderness and friendship. This means that the sexual energy was channelled in directions other than the primary aims of sexuality. Freud came to use the term 'sex' to refer to what we would call desire in general. His reasons for defining the word in this way were:

(1) Sexual relationships are not restricted to persons of the opposite sex.
(2) Sexual intercourse is not necessarily the object of sexual behaviour.
(3) Some actions observable in children resembled actions of adult perverts. (Freud once referred to children as 'polymorphous perverts'.)

Libido is regarded as drive energy whose main components are sexual in this all-embracing sense of the word. In its most basic state libido is regarded as a dispersed distribution of energy throughout the whole body. It becomes focused in the mouth area, at first passively, and then actively and aggressively with what Freud describes colourfully as the 'eruption of teeth in infants'. Libido is thought of as a closed system of energy regulated by the physical law of the conservation of energy. In Freud's theory of wit, laughter is seen as an 'explosion' of energy which was previously employed to repress anti-social tendencies which society is prepared to accept in a disguised form.

After 1920 Freud developed a new conceptual scheme. He claimed that there were two basic instincts: (i) The Life Instinct (Eros), and (ii) The Death Instinct (Thanatos). These concepts are related to what had gone before. The concept of a life instinct includes the earlier concept of libido and partly that of the self-preservative drive. The death instinct represents an innate destructiveness and aggression directed mainly at the self. The death instinct is unconscious. It was at this time that Freud formulated the theory of the tripartite structure of the mind: the ego, the id and the super-ego.

Freud held that the ego, the mainly conscious part of the mind, performs the function of self-preservation. He postulated that the ego utilised a number of defence mechanisms. Amongst the most important are:

(1) Rationalisations. These are reasoned justifications for an act conditioned by an unconscious urge that is seen as repugnant.
(2) Projection. This is the attribution to another of an inner attitude which is felt by the projecting person to be repugnant.
(3) Regression. This represents a retreat to an earlier stage of development in order to avoid coping with mature impulses.

The ego can be said to represent reason and sanity, the id contains the passions (it contains the instinctual drives) and the super-ego is said to discharge the functions of a conscience. It contains the social norms acquired in childhood and its effects are felt in the ego.

The concept of aggression plays a crucial role in Freud's thought. He held that inwardly directed aggression can be combined with sexual energy to take the form of sadism and masochism. Aggression is also held to play a part in supporting the dictates of the super-ego. He thought that war could be understood as a nation's attempt at self-preservation. If it did not direct its energy outwards, then it would destroy itself with internal feuds.

In Freud's *General Introduction to Psychoanalysis* we find another conceptual use for aggression. It plays an important part in his concept of sublimation. As we have seen 'sublimation' refers to the channelling of the sexual and aggressive drives in directions other than the primal aims of sexuality and aggression. The sexual drive is channelled into socially accepted aims which are thought to be higher than the purely sexual aims.

He also postulated a pleasure principle which urges the organism towards drive gratification. It is, however, opposed by the reality principle (that is, considerations of what is permissible or possible). We are here introduced to the important idea of mental equilibrium. Freud tells us in *Beyond the Pleasure Principle*:

> what consciousness yields consists essentially of excitations coming from the external world and of feelings of pleasure and unpleasure which can only arise from within the mental apparatus.

Tension within the mental apparatus can be reduced through dreaming. Freud regarded dreams as the symbolic representation of unconscious desires. The dream represents the unconscious desires as satisfied, and this is how the tension gets reduced and the equilibrium restored. This notion of symbolism had a fairly wide application. It was applied to art and architecture where sexual acts or organs are said to be symbolised. Unconscious symbolisation may involve the representation of words or phrases in a disguised form which have an emotional significance for the person. An example of this is Freud's case of a patient, an Austrian debutante, who was suffering from the physically inexplicable complaint of pains in the right heel. Elucidation of the symptoms revealed its connection to a deep-rooted fear that upon her first appearance in society, she might not find herself on a 'right footing'.[31]

I have given a brief account of some of the key developments and concepts in Freud's thought. Hopefully, the reader will now have sufficient familiarity with the major concepts to enable us to proceed to a critical discussion.

Criticisms

(1)   We saw that Freud has an eccentric usage of the term 'sex'. In ordinary discourse we can and do distinguish sexual desire from other desires, such as friendship. The distinction is important for many purposes, yet such a distinction seems closed to Freud. There is no reason why we *must* interpret the term 'sex' in the way Freud does.[32]

(2)   There are straightforward logical problems in accepting the unconscious as an explanatory concept of normal behaviour. We can see an example of such a problem by considering an instance of neurotic behaviour, such as compulsive hand-washing. We find that in normal cases of hand-washing we wash our hands in order to get them clean. This is the purpose of the act and it points to nothing beyond itself. The important point here is that we can only *recognise* some cases of hand-washing as irrational because we already understand the purpose of normal cases. We do not need to attribute the normal cases to unconscious motives. There would be no point in making such attributions when we already have an understanding which is logically presupposed by the explanation in terms of the unconscious given for the irrational case.

There is a similar point in connection with Freud's concept of a rationalisation. It should be realised that it is only when a person's reasons for acting sound suspicious that we begin to think that we are not getting the real reasons. This suspicion is logically dependent on there being genuine explanations in terms of conscious reasons. I can only know that a person is not divulging real reasons if I also know what it is to divulge real reasons. Some of Freud's key explanatory concepts will thus presuppose, rather than replace, our ordinary understanding.

(3)   Perhaps one of the most famous philosophical objections to psychoanalysis is the problem of falsification. Karl Popper has argued that Freudian theory has not developed in a way that is characteristic of the empirical method. The difficulty with Freud's theory is to specify some set of observations which, if instantiated, would count against the theory. Alternatively, if one rejects a falsificationist theory of scientific method, one could ask just what set of observations *could* validate such a theory. A similar point has been made by Glover:

> It is often said that Freud was ready to alter his formulations when empirical necessity called for a change. But although this was true as regards certain parts of his clinical theory it was not in my opinion true of his fundamental concepts.[33]

The trouble here is that if a theory is compatible with virtually *any* set of observations, then it lacks explanatory power. It will fail to pass Popper's test of scientific credibility. Glover's point is that the real basics of the theory, such as the concept of the unconscious, are going to be made compatible with any observation. If correct, this point would seriously detract from the Freudian claim that the unconscious was an explanatory concept in a scientific sense.

(4) There is a problem concerning the postulation of unobservable entities. Although it is true that a Freudian can appeal to the case of physical science for a precedent, there is still a problem concerning how close the analogy is. In the case of physical science, we can ask the cost of not making such postulations. We can spell out that cost in terms of lack of predictive power or of some level of accuracy that would not otherwise be attainable. The problem with some of Freud's concepts, such as the super-ego, is that their postulation does not seem to make any difference as far as predictive power is concerned. We can and do make perfectly good predictions by regarding the person, together with his conscience, as the agent of moral decision. The cost of not making such postulations as the super-ego is the collapse of an edifice and the removal of a particular way of classifying behaviour, but this does not bring about a corresponding collapse of predictive power.

(5) Some philosophers have thought that the idea of an unconscious mind is a confusion. The difficulty here has centred on the idea of thoughts, desires, wishes, motives and so on, which the person is said to have and yet be unaware of them. It has been said that it is contradictory to claim this as the mind is transparently aware of all its contents. The objection is that terms like 'wish', 'intention', 'desire' or 'motive' designate, or refer to, aspects of normal *conscious* life and this is held to be presupposed by our ordinary linguistic usage of these terms. Thus when we talk of someone's intentions, thoughts or motives, we are talking about what he is aware of and responsible for. This is why they figure in what we mean by a person's character. To refer to these as unconscious, the objection goes, is a contradiction.

MacIntyre[34] considers this claim concerning ordinary linguistic usage and argues that such usage can and does accommodate the use of the term 'unconscious'. He offers examples, such as the use of 'unconscious' to refer to something inanimate or to persons in a trance or coma. He has a second and more important use, namely, 'unconsciously' used in an adverbial sense. That is, we might use it to refer to some action or behaviour performed under certain conditions. The conditions could include 'without conscious intention or effort', 'inadvertently' and so on. In this sense the term 'unconsciously' can perform an excuse function, as in 'I didn't realise that I'd done that'. So to speak of actions performed unconsciously, or to speak of doing something without being aware of its goal or purpose, is permissible in ordinary language. MacIntyre concludes:

> The terms 'wish', 'fear', and so on do not in ordinary usage describe and refer to only private moments of consciousness, to inner mental events, but are in part at

least – and it is an essential part – descriptive of patterns of behaviour which are publicly observable. These patterns may go unrecognised and so be denominated 'unconscious'.

We can accept the point about adverbial or adjectival uses of the concept, but it was the substantive sense or noun usage that was all-important to Freud. He wanted to talk of *the* unconscious and thus regard it as a kind of entity. MacIntyre's appeal to ordinary usage may well show that the various uses of the concept are not to be ruled out *en masse* in an *a priori* manner, but the question of its legitimate use as a substantive is not answered by appeal to adverbial usage. There is the further problem that Freud was using the concept of the unconscious in a technical sense. It is those phenomena which cannot be brought into consciousness by normal means (for example, recollection, pausing to think and so on) that he designated 'unconscious'. MacIntyre's examples of doing something inadvertently or without thinking of its purpose and so on, need to be distinguished from cases in which the purpose can only be brought into consciousness through psychoanalytic techniques. What many philosophers have found *difficult* with the concept of the unconscious can be brought out by considering one of the defence-mechanisms described by Freud. In the case of projection, the projecting person projects an attitude which is *felt* by the projecting person to be repugnant. Is this repugnance held to occur at the conscious or the unconscious level? If it is unconscious, then he seems to be aware of it and not aware of it. He is aware of it in the sense that he does something (projects the attitude) *because* he feels it, and yet if it is unconscious, then he cannot be aware of it and neither can he become aware of it through normal means. It is by no means clear that ordinary language sanctions this kind of talk.

(6)   The issue of substantive usage has given rise to other difficulties. There are times when Freud treats the unconscious as a purely scientific phenomenon (a system of energy) which causes us to behave in particular ways. On this interpretation there is no intentionality in what it does any more than there is intentionality in chemical processes. On the other hand, Freud also talks about the unconscious in intentional terms. It 'wants' to do things, it 'represses unwelcome material', which presupposes that it distinguishes the welcome from the unwelcome. There is a strain in Freud between two kinds of explanation, one in terms of mechanical causes and one in terms of reasons.

We have briefly surveyed two influential psychological theories. They both offer explanatory models of human behaviour and they also make assumptions about mind and body. Behaviourists hold that we can do without the concept of mind and utilise descriptions of bodily behaviour in talk about human actions. Freudians, on the other hand, take a quite different line and uphold the reality of the mental. Both theories take an essentially 'determined' view of human actions. They differ, of course, in their accounts of what it is that determines our actions, but they do not leave room for free will. The free will problem is a major issue in philosophy and no discussion of the problem areas in the philosophy of mind would be adequate without some reference to it.

▶ The problem of free will and determinism

This is a problem which arises through a supposed conflict between scientific and moral thinking. The scientific view is that everything is subject to natural law. The moral view is that people are responsible for many of their actions and it is this responsibility which permits us to talk of praise and blame. Determinism, which has been held by many to be a precondition of scientific thinking, may be defined in the following way. If an event is determined, then that event could not have occurred other than it did unless the event(s) which determined it were also different.

It is this presupposition of determinism which is held to give a sense to our attempts to control, predict and explain situations and events. It is, for example, by applying the laws of motion that we can predict eclipses. This kind of predictive success led to the idea of the universe as a determined and mechanistic system. The idea is amply expressed in the words of Laplace who said that if a superhuman intelligence could know the position, mass and velocity of each particle of matter, he would be able to deduce every event in the history of the world. This way of presenting determinism shows the close link with the notion of prediction. Every event is governed by laws which are such that the occurrence and nature of any event could have been predicted with precision and certainty by one who knew the laws and the relevant facts.

Determinism begins to raise problems if we consider that psychologists and physiologists are constantly adding to our knowledge of human beings. It has been discovered that some types of behaviour which were thought to have been voluntary are now regarded as involuntary. A case in point is shellshock. This was once regarded as cowardice and hence worthy of moral blame. Investigations revealed its real causes and removed it from the area of moral blame. The threat that determinism might pose to our moral thinking is that the more we understand about the causes of human behaviour, then the less sensible or rational it will be to hold people morally responsible for their actions. Determinism, if true, will imply that people could not have acted other than the way they did given the causes that were operating. We are, of course, still far away from formulating laws of human behaviour, though it is believed by many that knowledge of such laws is attainable. The assumption is that there are such laws.

Determinism is a thesis which is nearly always held by those who accept physicalism. It may also be held by a psycho-physical dualist. This seems to have been Freud's view. The reader will realise from our previous discussion that Freud regarded our actions as determined by conscious and unconscious desires. These in turn would be determined by past experience, especially infant-experience.

As we have seen there is an apparent conflict between determinism and an assumption of our moral thinking, namely, responsibility. When we judge a person morally we imply that he could have acted otherwise. It would be pointless to say that he ought to have acted differently if it were causally impossible for him to have done so. To say that a person ought to have acted in a particular way implies that he could have done so. Ought implies can. The problem is that determinism implies that it is never true to say that a person could have acted differently. The action is an inevitable result of the person's character and situation. It would be possible, in principle, to predict the action given sufficient knowledge. Some determinists have suggested that we scrap our moral vocabulary. Punishment would no longer be regarded as something that was deserved. It would become analogous to medical treatment. The notion of moral desserts would lose its application.

Some philosophers have attempted to resolve the conflict between free will and determinism by claiming that the conflict is only apparent and not real. One famous attempt was made by David Hume. In S VIII of the *Enquiry Concerning Human Understanding* Hume offers what is known as a compatibilist account of the free will issue. He aims to show that there is no genuine conflict between the notions of liberty and causal necessity.

Hume starts by remarking that whenever there has been a long controversy with no solution an ambiguity in the terms used by the disputants is indicated. If the terms can be clarified, then it will be seen that there was really nothing to argue about. The whole 'problem of free will' is really a pseudo-problem which would have been solved if the disputants had assigned a precise meaning to their key terms. This is what he sets out to do.

First, Hume wants to get clear about the notion of necessity. We regard the motions of matter as necessarily determined. The idea we have of necessary causation arises purely from the experience of repeated constant conjunctions of objects and the determining of the mind by custom to infer the one from the other. These two circumstances are present in what we call the voluntary acts of men. We all realise this through living or from the briefest survey of history. We all recognise this, and if that is all that is meant by 'necessity', then there is no conflict between necessity and voluntary action. There is the same uniformity in human action as there is in the motions of natural phenomena. He allows for some individual variation within the general uniformity. We must, for example, allow for diversity of character, prejudice and opinions. Such individual variations, however, are found everywhere in nature. When we find some irregularity in human behaviour it is not due to some non-causal principle. It is just that other causes which are not immediately apparent are at work. The connection between all causes and effects is equally necessary. Any seeming uncertainty will be due to the operation of contrary causes. On this account we could explain and predict any irregular conduct if we knew the full facts. This uniformity in human action is the basis of our making inferences about future human actions in the same way as uniformity is the basis of making inferences about natural phenomena. We feel no difference between describing a series of motions cemented together by what is called 'physical necessity' and in the description of a series of human actions. (The reader should refer to Hume's example of the prisoner being led to the scaffold in *Enquiry* VIII.)

Such a doctrine of causal necessity is taken to be so obvious that no one would doubt it. Where then lies the conflict between liberty and necessity? Hume locates the source of the problem as follows. In our experience of natural phenomena what we have are constant conjunctions of objects. The mind is carried by a *customary transition* to infer the existence of one from the other. Although this is all that happens, we also *feel* that there is some kind of necessary connection or compulsion in the phenomena. If we transfer this to the human mind, then we find that we do not *feel* any compulsion or necessity between motive and action. It is because we have no such feeling in the latter case, but do in the former, that we go on to assert that there must be some real difference between the two cases. When we realise that we know nothing of causation beyond constant conjunctions and the subsequent inferences, we see that the two cases are not different at all. There is then nothing left to argue about. Hume is saying that once we get clear as to what causal necessity means, we see that it applies equally to bodies and minds.

Secondly, Hume attempts to clarify the notion of liberty. He makes the very important observation that we do not mean by 'liberty' some sort of randomness or caprice. What we mean is a power of acting or not acting according to the determinations of the will. Hume tells us that what is required of any definition of liberty is that it be consistent with the known facts and logically coherent. To say that something is caused is to say that it is necessary and this is based on the repeated constant conjunctions we experience. Nothing can exist or occur without a cause and thus human actions will be the effects of various causes to which they are necessarily connected. This does not, according to Hume, conflict with our notion of liberty of action. By 'liberty of action' we do not mean chance, and it is chance that would be the logical opposite of this doctrine of necessity. What we mean (that is, what Hume means) by freedom or liberty of action is the absence of constraint. If our actions are not subject to constraint, then we say that they are free. Thus we are offered a compatibilist account asserting no inconsistency between the concepts of liberty and necessity. A human action can be necessary in the sense that it is the inevitable outcome of causes. It can also be free in the sense that it is not subject to constraint.

There are a number of difficulties with Hume's account. Consider the following argument which Hume seems committed to:

(1) All events are caused.
(2) Caused events could not be other than they are (unless different *causes* intervened).
(3) Human actions are events.
(4) Human actions are caused, from (1) and (3).
(5) Human actions could not be other than they are, from (2) and (4).

The reader should consider whether this is compatible with saying that people have free will and are responsible for their actions. It conflicts with the idea that an act is free if the agent could have chosen some other act in the same circumstances. Hume is going to have to say that there must be some difference in the circumstances in order for this to happen. It might be said that a person could have acted differently had his desires been different. The problem though is to say how his desires could have been different as they are determined by equally binding causes. If we say that a free act is one which is determined by the strongest desire of the person, then it will follow that the actions of a maniac are free.

Further difficulties arise through Hume's inadequate account of both necessity and liberty. Repeated constant conjunctions are neither necessary nor sufficient for saying that two objects are causally connected or necessarily determined. Thus they can hardly be appealed to as an adequate account of what we *mean* by 'necessity'. The reader should also note that although Hume claims that the connection between all causes and effects is necessary, he cannot find anything in the cause which necessitates the effect. Consider also the notion of absence of constraint. The problem here is that the absence of *felt* constraint is not a sufficient condition for describing an act as a free act. The fact that the agent *feels* neither pressure nor constraint will not suffice for describing the act as free.[35] If we drop talk about felt constraint and concentrate on just constraint, then we face the difficulty of knowing when constraints we do not feel are operating.

A third problem with Hume's account concerns the running together of human actions and material motions under the single heading of causality or necessity. A critic can argue that human actions can be changed by *rational* rather than *causal* considerations and this distinguishes them from material motions. A criticism such as this involves making a distinction between reasons and causes. Philosophers normally make such a distinction by saying that causal accounts tell you *how* something happened, whereas accounts in terms of reasons tell you *why* an act was performed. The latter type of account is a candidate for a justification of an act, but the former is not.

Finally, in connection with Hume, there remains a problem with moral responsibility. If we could not have acted otherwise given the causal conditions operating, then how can we be praised or blamed? Where, we might ask, do the notions of punishment and reward fit into this? Perhaps we are to regard them as just determinants within a series of constantly conjoined events. Punishment, however, is not just *a causal* factor introduced to prevent or promote certain effects. Any theory of punishment (or reward) must take into account what is deserved. Attempts have been made to show that responsibility is compatible with determinism. Honderich, for example, attempts a reconciliation via an appeal to the legal concept of strict liability. 'That an action of mine was an effect does not entail that I cannot be held responsible.'[36] Such an appeal as this does not advance matters. It is difficult to imagine a legal system that consisted entirely of strict liability, that is, that took no account of intentions, duress, undue influence or provocation. The point is that there has to be some connection between moral responsibility and legal responsibility. In order to *explain* the concept of strict liability, it has to be contrasted with cases where your intentions and so on are taken into account. The fact that you can be *held* responsible does not establish moral responsibility in any important sense of that expression. There is a distinction between being held responsible and being responsible. Consider a fortunately imaginary example of a dictator with unusual views on the nature of autism. A law is passed to the effect that autistic children will be beaten if they do not make progress with their schoolwork. It follows from this law and Honderich's remarks about strict liability that the children can be held responsible for their lack of progress. Their inability is an effect. It certainly does not follow from this that they *are* responsible or that there is a morally relevant sense in which they are. The difference between being responsible and being held responsible is manifest. I shall close this brief discussion with some general remarks for the reader's guidance.

The first point concerns the notion of prediction. We have seen that predictive success in the natural sciences was a cornerstone of the determinist's thesis. It is not, however, obvious that prediction is all-important in discussing free will. Does the fact that you can accurately predict how someone will behave in a particular situation entail that the act was not a free act? Surely not, you can know how a person will act without in any way impugning the freedom of the act. It might, for example, be *morally* impossible for that person to have acted differently. A moral constraint needs to be distinguished from a causal one. Whenever a causal determinist appeals to the notion of prediction, he must state precisely what he means by 'prediction' and on what basis the prediction is to be made. Accurate predictions of human actions can and do take place without undermining the freedom of those actions and without there being 'laws' of human behaviour.

Secondly, it is not clear how supportive of the determinist thesis are the kind of examples we referred to earlier, such as shellshock. The fact that behavioural scientists can identify some aspects of behaviour as not being under the control of the agent, and thus remove them from the sphere of moral judgement, does not show that all aspects of our behaviour could be like this. The reader might like to consider how it would be possible to distinguish shellshock from cowardice if there were no genuine cases of cowardice.

Thirdly, much care is needed with the claim that our actions are determined by *our own* desires. It must be remembered that they are not something external to us. There are cases when we refer to a person as being a 'victim' of his desires, a 'slave' to his passions, 'at the mercy' of desire, but such descriptions cannot be the standard case. A determinist must be able to distinguish such cases from the normal. The libertarian must distinguish his thesis from the claim that free acts are those which occur *in vacuo*. To pursue this topic would require a detailed analysis of the concept of desire. Any reader who wants to take this on might start with a distinction between wishes, desires and cravings. He might also consider the nature of our evidence for the attribution of desires and what it means to say that a person is in control of his desires.

Fourthly, the reader should be wary of any attempt by a libertarian to import ideas from quantum physics into the free will discussion. As Hume pointed out, a free act is not a random act. Even if it were discovered that random, unpredictable events occur within the brain, it is not at all clear how this could contribute to a solution of the question of what is meant by a 'free' act. It should also be realised that in the case of human actions it is precisely those acts which are random, those which bear no relation to what has gone before, that tend to arouse our curiosity in the direction of causal explanation. Free acts are not maverick acts and it is for maverick acts that we seek explanations in terms of causes rather than reasons.

This last point leads us to an influential modern attempt to solve the free will problem and related problems in the philosophy of action. This attempt involves a rigid distinction between reason and cause. It is the concepts of rationality, purpose or goal, rather than the concept of cause, that are to be used in explaining, understanding and predicting human behaviour. On this account human behaviour is not a caused phenomenon at all. The uniformity in human actions that Hume spoke of will not, on this account, be due to the operation of causality, but to shared principles of rationality and purpose. A thesis such as this will carry important implications for the nature of the social sciences and for their appropriate methodology. It will carry practical implications. It is necessary to have a sound philosophical base for practical procedures. We shall conclude this chapter with a discussion of some issues in the philosophy of social science.

► The philosophy of the social sciences

The human sciences aim to understand, explain and predict human behaviour. Given the success of the natural sciences in dealing with natural phenomena it was hoped that the methodology of the natural sciences could be applied to the study of human behaviour and achieve the same kind of success in that field. The prized objectivity of the natural sciences was located in the empirical method of observation and experiment. It is on this basis that we discover the causal laws which govern the behaviour of natural phenomena. The question is whether the same methods will provide us with similar causal laws of human behaviour. There are differing views on the viability of this aspiration and there are differing views on what will count as objective knowledge of human beings and on what can be said to count as a theoretical understanding of human behaviour. Indeed, not all social scientists think that gaining a theoretical understanding is important. Let us examine an example of this.

Consider the following statement of the ideal objective method for psychology provided by B. F. Skinner:

> When we have achieved a practical control over the organism, theories of behaviour lose their point. In representing and managing relevant variables a conceptual model is useless; we come to grips with behaviour itself. When behaviour shows order and consistency, we are much less likely to be concerned with physiological or mentalistic causes. A datum emerges which takes the place of theoretical fantasy.[37]

This is thought to represent science in its most rigorous objectivity and to show how that objectivity is to be incorporated into the human sciences. There are problems with a position like this.

It is obvious that this seeking to control without paying any attention to theoretical understanding flies in the face of what we normally understand by the scientific enterprise or the scientific spirit. Skinner decries the use of conceptual models, but also talks of 'representing and managing relevant variables'. The problem though is that unless we have a conceptual model or *some* theoretical backing, we shall be unable to distinguish the relevant variables from the irrelevant ones. We cannot banish theoretical assumptions in the name of objectivity. To think that in getting rid of theoretical backing one is successfully adopting the methods of natural science reveals a misconception of natural science. It is by theorising and conceptualising that we obtain knowledge. The mere imprinting of data, if they could be called data, would put us in a position where knowledge was unattainable. It is by theorising that observed events take on the status of conveyors of information. We classify things and events according to theoretical assumptions and this is the base from which predictions can be launched. We do not objectify science by demolishing that base. Furthermore, there is no precedent in natural science for such a move.

Explanation in social science

Granted that some theoretical assumptions are necessary, the question concerning the nature of those assumptions, and hence of the appropriate kind of explanation for human actions, remains to be discussed. Such a discussion will bring out the most important differences that are alleged to exist between natural and social science.

We saw during our discussion of behaviourism that some assumptions had to be made concerning the agent interpreting his environment and the meaningful nature of the environment in which human action takes place. This is an obvious assumption to make in the study of social institutions. In the case of the natural sciences we make no such assumptions concerning the subject-matter of physics or chemistry. The major philosophical issue here revolves around the importance of this difference.

Some philosophers would hold that the difference is unimportant. It just means that explanations of human behaviour will be that more complex. The explanations will still be of the same kind as those used in natural science. That is to say, the model of mechanical causality will be the appropriate category of explanation in the human sciences as well as in the natural sciences. There are other philosophers who would want to push this further and claim that the causal laws of the social sciences should not be regarded as a final result of scientific inquiry, but rather as a kind of interim result. The final result would be the 'reduction' of such laws to what are regarded as genuine laws, namely, the laws of physics and chemistry. It is this aspiration which is at the centre of the modern controversy between some neurophysiologists and psychologists. A number of the former hold that psychology is 'reducible' to neurophysiology. This means that when we understand the physical causes and basis of behaviour, then mentalistic concepts and constructs will become obsolete. This is known as favouring the 'bottom-up' approach (starting with the physical and working up to the mental) rather than the 'top-down' approach (starting with the mental and working down to the physiological mechanisms which underlie mental performances). Psychologists often defend their position by claiming that even if physiological explanations are attainable, this does not mean that we can eschew talk about the mental. This claim may very well be correct, but if that much is conceded to the reductionist, then serious questions can be raised against the ontological status of psychology's theoretical constructs. They would, for example, appear to be theoretically eliminable from a complete description of what there is. The fact that we cannot help talking about them will not in itself guarantee them a place in the final ontological roll-call. What needs to be shown is that the conceptual structure in which mentalist, rational and social concepts have their place enables us to say things, make descriptions and specifications, give reasons and so on, and that such activities are not reducible to purely neurophysiological descriptions. It needs to be shown that a purely physicalist description is necessarily incomplete. This is a philosophical issue of great importance. The resolution of this issue involves a detailed analysis of the concepts of action and movement.

In opposition to those schools of thought which hold that mechanical causation, be it mental, physical or in terms of social 'forces' is the appropriate explanatory category, there are those philosophers who claim that causal explanations are appropriate for explaining what *happens* to a person, but inappropriate for explaining what a person *does*. In other words they are opposed to the use of mechanical causation as an explanatory category for dealing with human actions. There is a distinction between actions and happenings. This distinction is not always easy to draw; for example, falling in love shares characteristics common to both. It is something we do and we also say that it is something which happens to us. Borderline cases will not, however, show that there is no distinction. Let us then pass to a discussion of the implications of making such a distinction.

Rule-governed activity

Philosophers who reject mechanical causation in explanations of human actions emphasise the distinction referred to earlier between actions and movements. Actions involve physical movements but are not to be identified with them. It is then argued that the causal model is appropriate for explaining movements but not actions.[38] In explaining human actions we must realise that persons are aware of what they are doing. They act according to rules which they are capable of formulating. Explanations of actions must accept such rules for what they are, rather than attempt to explain them away in terms of something else. The conceptual argument here is that actions, such as getting married or voting, *logically* presuppose a network of rules. They are rule-governed activities. Unless one takes these presuppositions into account, then not only will we fail to explain actions, but also we shall fail to specify or describe them. In other words, we shall be in danger of losing our subject-matter. The use of action-descriptions logically implies a network of rules and rationality. The descriptions we have of the phenomena to be explained are *internal* to, or *generated by*, the various networks of rules. Thus, for example, we could not even describe a behaviour sequence as 'conducting a transaction' unless we presupposed a rule-governed background of economic exchange. The terms we use in the description, 'money', 'deal', 'property' and so on, can only be generated by the system of rules which constitutes the economic framework. An economic transaction is not *just* marks on paper followed by changes in spatial position of the paper. The reader can multiply examples such as this. Soccer is not *just* kicking a piece of plastic or leather around a field and so on. Thus if we ignore the rule-governed nature of these actions and attempt a purely physical description, then we shall fail to describe and explain what we set out to.

Before we proceed to a detailed discussion of the rule-governed model, I want to draw the reader's attention to how fundamental the concept of a rule has been regarded. We are not concerned with rules considered in a petty sense, but rather in the sense that they can be said to be the fabric out of which social existence is constituted. It would thus be an irrelevant counter to say that people break rules every day or act without thinking about rules and so on. The point is that unless we take rules into account, then we shall be unable to describe behaviour as action. Even the social rebel or the recluse derive his status *as* rebel or recluse from a reaction against, or a withdrawal from, certain rule-governed activities. We need the concept of a rule in order to *specify* his mode of being. He requires the concept of a rule in order to effect a 'rebellion against...' or 'a withdrawal from...'. The reader should see from this how deep-rooted a concept this is. Neither the rebel nor the recluse abandons *all* rules; he adopts different ones.[39]

One of the most important arguments for the employment of the rule-governed model is that put forward by Peter Winch.[40] His central claim is that social behaviour is rule-governed behaviour. As we have seen, this means that understanding and explaining human action involves employing the concept of 'rule' rather than that of 'cause'. Winch argues that the identification of the events to be explained is necessarily dependent on understanding the rules which make them count as events of whatever kind they might be. Thus, for example, if you wanted to explain the occurrence of a war, you would have to adopt political and military criteria in order to pick out or identify a particular act as an act of war or as a declaration of war. Political and military systems are constituted by collections of rules. It is only against such a background of rules that a particular event can count as a declaration of war. It is only against such a background that reasons for, and justifications of, actions can be given.

An implication that has been drawn from Winch's thesis is that when we examine social phenomena, then we are bound to employ the criteria which the agents themselves employ. When, for example, we examine politics or religion, then we employ political or religious criteria. This would mark an important difference between social and natural science. By employing the same criteria as the agents who are having their actions explained, we are much more nearly participants in the events than could ever be the case in the natural sciences. This implication is drawn by Alan Ryan[41] and is correct as far as it goes. There is, however, a deeper point to be noted. Winch's argument is not just that we employ the criteria of the activities we examine. He is also saying that in order to examine any activity at all we must participate in language and it is within language that conceptual structures are given. Winch tells us:

> Our idea of what belongs to the realm of reality is given for us in the language that we use. The concepts we have, settle for us the form of the experience we have of the world. (*ISS*, p. 15)

Ryan, on the other hand, claims that social scientists do not have to stop at the level of explanation which the agents themselves give of their actions. They can go on to seek out the 'real' explanation of what the agents are doing or why they are doing it. Ryan holds that conceptual claims are vulnerable to factual proof and disproof, 'new facts may make us change our minds about what it makes sense to say about the facts' (*PSS*, p. 167).

Winch's point, however, is that what counts as a fact will be determined by our conceptual framework. Ryan holds that there is a realm of *facts*, as distinct from *things*, which is independent of any conceptual scheme. The problem with this claim is that these facts can only be known and stated if you already employ *some* conceptual scheme. Thus, whenever you criticise one conceptual scheme (as the social scientist would do in by-passing the agent's own account) then, necessarily you do so from the point of view of another one. What Winch is saying is that there is no *independent* realm of facts or reality to which competing schemes can appeal. Indeed, the whole idea of conceptual schemes competing with each other is problematic as that would imply that they shared some common goal, and that some were better at attaining it than others. But in order for us to say this and judge their relative merits we would have to be able to specify this goal and describe it independently of the conceptual schemes which are attempting to capture it. This, according to Winch, is what we can never do. There is no absolute vantage point from which we can survey different conceptual schemes. This is a major issue in the philosophy of social science and has given rise to much controversy. I shall discuss briefly some of the problems associated with it.

Ryan (*PSS*, pp. 162ff) has pointed out two problems. The first concerns the possibility of criticising conceptual schemes different from one's own. Ryan holds that if you agree with Winch, then this kind of criticism will be extremely problematic. He goes on to say that even if there is no absolute vantage point, it is still the case that we do criticise other conceptual schemes or 'entire ways of life' in the case of some primitive tribes. But this does not really come to terms with the deeper issue here. Winch's thesis is concerned with the *logic* of criticism and not with the *psychology* of it. The issue is whether what is *intended* as criticism *can* be regarded as criticism. The logical point is by far the deeper and more fundamental one. There are two points to note about this matter.

First, in order to criticise a conceptual scheme or form of life different from one's own, it is necessary to understand that scheme or form of life. The fact that you *intend* to criticise is not in itself sufficient to establish your remarks as a criticism. You must understand the alien scheme, compare it with your own, establish a common goal, and then claim that your scheme is better at attaining that goal. We have already seen that there are difficulties with such a procedure; it constitutes the *logical* requirement of criticism.

Second, even if there are difficulties in criticising *entire* forms of life, it does not follow that all criticism is ruled out. It may well be possible to establish strong areas of overlap between conceptual structures. It is also possible to criticise morally without there being absolute values. Winch's claim is that if you do criticise a particular vantage point, then you must do so from another one. The project of criticism does not have to be frustrated by the absence of the absolute.

Ryan's second problem is one we have referred to earlier. It concerns the possibility of the social scientist disbelieving an agent's own account of an action and going on to give the 'real' account. Ryan sees the Winchian thesis of employing the agent's criteria as being a barrier to this possibility. It is going to point the way to a participant understanding and thus reveal an important difference between natural and social science. There are, of course, unproblematic senses in which we can disbelieve someone and go on to reveal the 'real' reasons for his action. This happens in the case of the liar and the deceiver. In such cases the agent is aware of his reasons but tries to disguise them. We call them the 'real' reasons because he is aware of them and because his awareness is part of the project of lying. The cases we are here concerned with are those in which the agent is not aware of the real reasons or causes of his action, but has them revealed by the social scientist.

Ryan offers examples of cases where it would be in order to disbelieve the agent's account and go on to reveal the real one. The examples are the use of psychoanalytic and Marxist explanations to account for the enthusiasm of the working class towards the outbreak of the First World War. The Marxist account of what they were 'really' doing could be stated in terms of their lining the pockets of the arms manufacturers. The joy which they felt could be explained in terms of a holiday mood engendered by a change of routine in their alienated lives.

The Freudian account could be framed in terms of sexual jealousy and rivalry. Thus in going off to war the young men would become more attractive to their potential sexual mates. The older men would have a motive for sending the young off to war, namely, that of getting rid of their sexual rivals.

Ryan holds that the agents could not accept such explanations of their actions, but they could, nevertheless, be legitimate explanations, 'their behaviour could only have taken place as it did, so long as they did not conceptualise their world in this way; and thus we seem a long way from Winch.' It is sufficient for Ryan to establish that such explanations are logically respectable scientific candidates for accounting for the behaviour in question. He does not need to show that they are in fact correct. There are, however, counter-arguments to the claim that such explanations are logically proper and scientifically respectable.

First, Winch's point would be that the agents who are having their behaviour explained must be able to *understand* the explanatory concepts. Ryan seems to be aware of this when he says of innovatory explanations, that in order for them to be understandable, they must be attached to what was understood before. The interesting question here concerns the nature of this attachment. Does it, for example, mean an extension of our *ordinary* concepts? This would have to be distinguished from a scientific neutral account of their actions.

The second problem can be brought out by considering the Marxist claim. When we refer to lining the pockets of the arms manufacturers, we are referring to an *effect* of their actions. The danger lies in confusing an effect of their action with either a description of the action itself or with the cause of the action. Such a confusion would destroy any analogy with explanation in the natural sciences. A cause must precede its effect. Even if it is argued that in celebrating the outbreak of war, the working class was, as a matter of fact, helping the arms trade, it will not follow that the reasons they give for the celebrations are not real or genuine reasons. Criteria have to be laid down for distinguishing real from spurious reasons.

A third difficulty concerns the idea of *explaining* joy at the outbreak of war in terms of a change of routine from their alienated lives. The problem is that a whole manner of different and diverse activities are going to have the same explanation. Thus, for example, so long as there is a level of description at which we can say that the particular group has had a change of routine, then we can account for any and every joy they might feel by appealing to the change of routine. It is not clear that this is a scientifically respectable development.

That there are important differences between natural and social science is brought out by Ryan's own remarks. He says, quite correctly, that both Marxism and psychoanalysis depend on teaching people a new conceptual scheme, 'within which events wear a different significance'. This admission is not as far from Winch as Ryan had earlier supposed his position to be. A defender of Winch can claim that, for example, Freudian concepts have to have *some* significance for the agent and this will distinguish explanations which utilise such concepts from those given in terms of purely mechanical causes. Winch will, of course, also hold that the descriptions of the events which take on a new significance will be *internal* to the various conceptual schemes. It is not the case that we first of all specify and describe events and *later* endow them with significance as we learn different conceptual schemes.

Explaining and explaining away

A charge that has often been levelled against social science theorists, or at least some theorists, is that they tend to confuse explaining some social phenomenon with explaining away the phenomenon. We need to consider an example to see what the issue is here. The example I have chosen is taken from a review by Anthony Storr[42] of a work by J. H. Crook. It is a work of ethology, a subject pioneered by Lorenz and Tinbergen. What is important for our purposes is the nature of the explanation offered for a particular kind of human behaviour. The behaviour in question is altruistic behaviour.

Storr tells us that altruistic behaviour, so difficult to explain in terms of 'the survival of the fittest' model, is now explicable in evolutionary terms. Instead of regarding altruism as a counter-example to the claim that the 'survival of the fittest' is an adequate all-embracing explanatory concept, it has to be accounted for in terms of that principle. In attempting to do this Crook and Storr transform Darwin's blind natural force into a force capable of the most ingenious scheming. Storr writes:

> Reciprocating altruism not only favours survival of a social group, but because it allows for recurrent verbal exchange, leads to the conceptualisation of identity, and to the possibility of empathy.

(The reader will be reminded of an earlier point in which we saw the danger of confusing a *description* of an activity with an *effect* of the activity.)

Let us consider the concepts of 'survival' and 'social group'. If we apply these concepts to the case of Captain Oates walking out into the blizzard in order to save his fellows, we find that there is an unproblematic sense in which they can be used. It is quite correct to describe this act of altruism as ensuring the survival of a social group, namely, his colleagues on the expedition. It is problematic, however, to say that Oates acted in order to ensure the 'survival', in a Darwinian sense, of the society to which he belonged. The talk about reciprocating altruism suggests that one does not act altruistically as a result of the way one sees the interests of others, but rather because of the probability that one's favours will be returned, and that the mutual swapping of favours will tend toward the survival of the social order. Oates' action is a counter-example to the claim about reciprocation. What is important in this example is that the 'real' motive for altruism offered by the ethologist is one which could not be given by the agent. This kind of explanation is known as a 'hidden purpose' or 'functional' explanation. It is an attempt to *explain away* the essentially altruistic features of the act.

We are now in a position to formulate a very important difference in approach between the ethological theorist and the natural scientist. We can contrast our ethological example with a possible case from astronomy in order to bring out the difference. Let us suppose that a group of astronomers construct a model of a planetary system belonging to a distant star, and that the model allows for the possibility of five major planets. Following the improvement of observation techniques, perturbations are noticed in the orbit of the fifth planet. The astronomers begin to question their earlier model. After further improvements in observation techniques a sixth planet is discovered. The astronomers then abandon their earlier model. The point is that they do not attempt to explain away the observation by saying that it is not 'really' a planet, it is something else. This is because there are agreed criteria concerning what is to count as a planet and what is not. There are no agreed criteria for saying that an act is 'really' altruistic within the ethological framework. The astronomers approach their enquiry by saying that if certain observations are made, then there may well be another planet as there is no necessity in our earlier model being correct. The ethologists approach theirs by saying that no matter what we observe, this act cannot be 'really' altruistic as our 'survival of the fittest' model *must* be universally applicable. The trouble here is that if you ask why the model *must* be correct, then you will be told that it is because certain types of action cannot happen; and if you ask why they cannot happen, then you are told that it is because the model must be correct.

The claim that 'real' altruistic acts *cannot* happen should be treated with great caution. What is the force of this 'cannot'? It is not a conceptual truth as we do not contradict ourselves by supposing there to be such acts. But neither is it an empirical truth as we have seen that no matter what is observed, the act cannot be 'really' altruistic. The attempted exorcism of the altruistic nature of actions is not effected by conceptual analysis or empirical discovery. The practice of explaining away is characteristic of a theorist who has a particular conception of human nature and wishes to impose that conception on a mass of data irrespective of how well it fits. The explaining away procedure is the way of dealing with awkward data. This practice needs to be distinguished from that of giving genuine explanations. Our astronomical example typifies the latter kind of explanation. This is not to say, of course, that explaining away is the standard practice of social science, or that it is exclusive to social science, but just that it needs to be identified and exposed wherever it occurs.

There are many other problem areas in the philosophy of social science which we cannot pursue. I can merely indicate, under broad headings, some further lines of thought that the reader should pursue in connection with natural and social science differences.

(a) Independent evidence. Consider the Freudian explanation Ryan offered as an explanation for the joy felt by the working class at the outbreak of the First World War. Ryan told us that in covering themselves in glory, the young men would make more suitable sexual partners. The term 'suitable' needs unpacking. It presupposes value judgements which have already been made. It presupposes conceptions of bravery, masculinity and femininity. These are the bedrock upon which talk about suitability in this context rests. In order for the Freudian explanation to get off the ground, the agents must already have these values. It is not just the fact, if it is a fact, that war-glory makes a man a more suitable partner that explains their behaviour, there must also be a sense in which they *believe* it to be true. If the agents claim not to have such a belief, then it is said that the belief must be unconscious. The problem is that the only 'evidence' for such beliefs is that they are required by this explanation. The question that needs to be asked concerns whether there is any *independent evidence* for the existence of such unconscious beliefs. It might turn out that the theorist requires the unconscious beliefs more than the agents do!

(b) Prediction. There are problems concerning the extent to which social scientists rely on genuine causal laws for making predictions. Popper[43] has argued that the genuine causal laws of the natural sciences are universal in form, that is, they apply in all places at all times. The 'laws'[44] of society, on the other hand, are confined to what takes place on one planet. Popper holds that they should be regarded as general trends rather than laws. Trends can always change. The reader might like to consider whether this has any unacceptable implications for biological science.

A second problem is that in social science the predictions themselves can interfere with what is predicted. Thus the prediction which arises out of a causal story becomes an actual part of the story. An economist who predicts a price increase in a commodity might bring about such an increase through panic buying. The prediction might become a self-fulfilling prophecy. Much depends, of course, on who is making the prediction. Consumers understand what the prediction means, they have certain purposes and act accordingly. This is quite in keeping with the economist's assumption of rational behaviour on the part of the consumer. Assumptions of rationality are not made about the phenomena of the natural sciences. The assumption of rationality carries many important implications concerning the subject-matter of social science.

(c) Scientism. The reader who is acquainted with the social sciences will have noticed the importation of many terms from the natural sciences. We meet with terms such as 'social dynamics', 'social statics', 'sublimation' and so on. The importation of such terms tends to suggest that it is, for example, the business of the sociologist to study the 'physics' of society. As physics is concerned with matter in motion, there is a danger of creating a misleading

impression of the nature of social science. An interesting approach to the problem of scientism is to express the matter in the following way. Either there is enough similarity in the uses of the terms to justify the transference, in which case the similarity can be stated; or there is not, in which case the whole procedure stands in need of a justification. The reader would do well to try this out in practice. Trace a particular expression to its original use in natural science and then test for any conceptual differences in its subsequent uses. This is a fruitful method for discovering whether there are differences between the natural and social sciences.

▶ Artificial intelligence (AI)

A recent development in cognitive psychology which has implications for the philosophy of mind concerns the use of computer models to explain the workings and nature of the mind. The strong version of the thesis claims that computers have mental states. They can, for example, be said to understand, have beliefs or thoughts, and various other cognitive states that are attributable to people. Such a claim is based on the kind of performance which a machine is capable of. The way in which it carries out the performance is held to explain what human minds do when they carry out similar performances and are said to understand things. The central issue is whether what a computer does is a sufficient condition for saying that it understands.

One of the most famous attempts to show that it is not is the one offered by J. R. R. Searle.[45] Searle's claims are that a computer cannot be said to *understand*, and that what it does fails to *explain* human cognitive abilities. Many arguments are presented in support of these claims. The most well known and controversial is Searle's example of the Chinese room.

Searle wants to attack the claim that a computer which has been fed a story and can print out answers to questions about that story, even when the answers are not actually stated in the story, can be said to understand the story. He invites us to consider the case of a person who speaks English, but not Chinese, and who is put into a room into which different sets of symbols can be passed in and out. Searle makes the following suppositions. The non-Chinese speaker in the room is given:

(1) a batch of Chinese symbols;
(2) a second batch of Chinese symbols, together with a set of rules in English for correlating symbols from the second batch with those from the first – the correlation is achieved by matching one set of symbols with another according to their shapes;
(3) a third batch of Chinese symbols with more English instructions in how to correlate members of the third batch with members of the first two batches.

The rules tell the person how to return Chinese symbols of a certain shape in response to the shape of the symbols given in the third batch. Suppose also that the people outside the room call the first batch a 'script', the second a 'story', the third 'questions', the returned symbols 'answers to the questions' and the manipulation rules a 'programme'. The point that Searle wants to make is that no matter how good the manipulation rules are in terms of producing the right 'answer', and no matter how adept at following instructions for matching one Chinese shape with another the man in the room becomes, he will not thereby understand a word of Chinese. So long as all he does is match one symbol with another according to their formal properties, that is, their shape, then he will not understand what the symbols mean. Even if the answers given are always correct and even indistinguishable from answers that would be given by a native Chinese speaker, he still cannot be said to understand. The case is held to be manifestly different from the case in which the whole procedure is carried out in English. In this latter case, the man, who is an English speaker, would know what the questions *meant* and what the story was *about*. He would have semantics as well as a syntax. In the Chinese case, all he has is a syntax. That is to say, he just has a set of syntactical rules for manipulating undefined symbols according to their shapes. Although the correct answers are forthcoming in both the English and Chinese case, it is only in the former case that we can talk about understanding.

Searle wants to conclude that, given that a computer manipulates uninterpreted symbols according to their formal properties, this cannot be a sufficient condition for understanding as the man in the Chinese room can do all of this and yet not understand a word of Chinese. This is held to dispose of the AI claim that machines can literally be said to understand.

In regard to the claim that the model of instantiating a programme is an explanation of how the mind works, Searle argues that no reason has been given for supposing that when a person understands English, or anything else, what he is doing is implementing or instantiating a programme. A 'programme' is, of course, defined as the manipulation of uninterpreted symbols according to their formal features.

There is a further general problem with AI in stating the criteria for saying that a programme is being instantiated. If the criteria are stated too widely, then the thesis becomes trivial. Thus, for example, if it is sufficient to say that a programme is being instantiated when there is some level of description at which we can say that a given system has input, processing of input, and output, then a great number of systems can be said to instantiate programmes. Given that AI holds that it is the instantiating of a programme that constitutes the essence of the mental, then all sorts of things turn out to have minds. Fridges, stereos and kettles, for example, will turn out to have minds. Alternatively, if we restrict the criteria for saying that a programme is being instantiated to the manipulation of symbols according to their formal features, then we find that we do not have a sufficient condition for understanding or a satisfactory explanatory model for our cognitive abilities.

Searle's attack on AI involves the strategy of examining what computers do and then claiming that people can do the same things without understanding anything. An alternative strategy is to examine what a person does in solving a problem and then claim that the descriptions of what is involved are not applicable to what computers do when they solve problems. We can consider this strategy via an example.

Consider what is involved in solving the following crossword clue: 'Sage involved in giving letter with distorted loops to woman' (11). The correct answer to this is 'philosopher', but what are the conditions for my knowing why it is the correct answer? I must know that 'phi' is a letter, and hence that 'letter' in the clue refers to a member of an alphabet and not to correspondence. I must know that 'distorted' functions as an instruction to distort the letters of the word 'loops', and I only know that they have been correctly distorted from the fact that the resultant whole fits the sense of the clue. I must also know that 'her' is a feminine pronoun and that 'sage' refers to a philosopher rather than a herb. In saying that I must know these things, I do not mean that I match one symbol with another. I must know what the symbols mean and what the whole thing is about. I need to know the kinds of things to which the symbols refer as this is an essential precondition of distinguishing senses of the same symbol. It is not sufficient for me to have *just* symbols. Although it can be claimed that I have used an example containing ambiguous symbols, the problem remains as to how a computer operating with unambiguous symbols *explains* what it is I do when operating with ambiguous ones.

▶ Searle and the systems reply

It has been argued by some, including John Foster in *The Immaterial Self*, that although Searle's claims regarding the man in the Chinese room seem highly plausible, something crucial has been overlooked. It is obvious that the man in the Chinese room does not know the meanings of the Chinese symbols (he does not technically know that they are symbols) . This ignorance, according to Foster, pertains to a quite different life from that to which the supporter of strong AI wishes to attribute understanding. The manipulation of Chinese symbols according to rules written in English constitutes a sub-system within the English speaking system and, according to strong AI, understanding can be attributed to this sub-system. Indeed strong AI, to be consistent, must hold this position as the sub-system has passed the Turing Test, that is, it can fool native speakers of Chinese.

There are a number of ways of answering this objection. In the first place it could be argued that the systems reply does not just create different sub-systems or levels of mentality, it also creates different levels of under-standing. Thus we have the full-blooded sense of 'understanding', the sense in which you and I understand stories in English, can make contextual inferences, have internal representations or referential knowledge of the content of the story. In other words, we know what the whole thing is about, including the fact that it is a story. There is, then, a weaker sense of 'understanding' in which we know none of these things but simply manipulate symbols that we do not even know are symbols. We take them in, match them according to shape and pass them out. The problem here is to see what these two kinds of 'understanding' have to do with each other. Strong AI was supposed to explain in computational terms what it is we do when we 'understand' in the full-blooded sense and ends up describing a case of 'understanding' that is totally different from the full-blooded sense. Even if we allow different sub-systems or levels of mentality to have this secondary kind of understanding, the difference between the two kinds of understanding re-emerges at this level and a further explanation is then needed to account for this difference in the sub-systems. It can also be argued that the term 'understanding' is now being used too loosely. Indeed, it is being used so loosely that virtually any system can be said to have it. Imagine a case where I use a waterfall as a kind of primitive calendar. The waterfall is a steady system and erodes soil and rock on a consistent basis. I can use such erosions as indices for measuring time segments. Do we really want to say that this system knows the time or understands anything? It seems rather implausible to suggest that whereas a part of it does not, when all the parts are added together it does. Examples such as this are likely to figure when the term 'understanding' is being used too loosely. If it is said that in the waterfall case, there is nothing corresponding to information, it can be argued that the prevailing weather conditions can be regarded as such and the resultant erosion can be regarded as output. Strictly speaking, the man in the Chinese room does not receive information, just a bunch of meaningless shapes. From his point of view, there is no information content in the input.

A consideration of the above leads to a second response. The man in the Chinese room passes the Turing Test and given that the Chinese sub-system can do this, that is sufficient for understanding. This, however, seems to beg the question. Searle's argument is intended to show that passing the Turing Test is not sufficient for understanding, given that the man in the Chinese room passes the test and understands nothing. In other words, the whole debate concerns the adequacy of the Turing Test as a test for understanding and it is no answer to this to say he must understand as he passes the test. If the test can be meaningfully discussed, counter-examples must at least be possible. If they are ruled out *a priori* then the status of the test seems to have been elevated to that of a necessary truth or to that of a linguistic stipulation to the effect that any system than can fool native speakers of a language is to be described as having understanding. Further, we will stick to this stipulation even when the system obviously does not understand in anything like the manner we understand when we understand stories in English. No philosophical impact whatsoever can be made via this kind of move. It is a mere statement of linguistic intentions.

A far trickier problem for Searle will become apparent in the next section. It should be realised that this is not so much a problem intrinsic to the Chinese room example, but rather, emerges when the example is taken in conjunction with another thesis of Searle's, *Biological Naturalism*. If purely syntactic systems cannot produce understanding, and the brain, a physico-chemical structure, is such a system, then it is going to follow that not only does the man in the Chinese room not understand Chinese, neither do the native speakers. We now need to clarify what Biological Naturalism is.

Biological Naturalism

This is the name Searle gives to his thesis that attempts to solve the mind-body problem. Searle sees the main objective of any attempt to solve the mind-body problem as that of squaring two conceptions: the human and the scientific. There is our ordinary way of talking about ourselves in terms of intentions, desires, hopes, fears and so on, and there is the scientific way in terms, ultimately, of physics and chemistry. The question of how the mind is related to the brain seems an incredibly difficult one.

Searle thinks one of the chief difficulties is that it is an essentially twentieth-century problem couched in seventeenth-century vocabulary. We find it very difficult to solve such a problem given our Cartesian inheritance. Traditional solutions, like materialism or behaviourism, are rejected as they end up denying the reality of the mental. There are certain features of mind that make the problem difficult, but no adequate theory can ignore them. The features are:

(1) *Consciousness*. This is a fact about the world that seems incredible. That there should be such a thing as awareness given the physical composition of the world.

(2) *Intentionality*. This concerns the directedness of mental states. As Searle says, the fact that the stuff in the skull can refer, represent, be directed at all, presents a difficult problem. The more one thinks about this, the more amazing it seems. Intentionality can range over the distant past, the present and the future.

(3) *The subjectivity of mental states*. I am aware of my own mental states in a different way from that of the mental states of others (see earlier section on Other Minds).

(4) *Mental causation*. This is essentially Descartes' problem of how the mind as cause can have physical effects. If the mind is regarded as an immaterial substance then its interaction with the physical, a different ontological type, becomes problematic.

Searle wants to make the following two claims:

(I) All mental phenomena are caused by brain processes. Thus, for example, when pain signals are transmitted to the brain, the brain conditions are sufficient for the sensation of pain.

(II) Mental phenomena are features of the brain. Searle is here questioning the standard Humean idea that there are two distinct events in causation. An example might clarify this issue. We can explain a feature of a table, such as its solidity, by appealing to the micro-elements of its molecular structure. We can make a similar appeal in explaining the realisation of liquidity in the molecular structure of water. The analogy that Searle wishes to draw is that mental states are caused by and realised in the physical structure of the brain. Thus mental states are purely natural; they are a biological function of brain states. There should not be a mind-body problem any more than there is a stomach-digestion problem. They are equally natural biological functions. Consciousness is caused by higher level brain processes. There are a number of critical points that emerge from this thesis.

(1) Biological reduction and the Chinese room
The issue here is whether biological facts are reducible to facts of physics and chemistry. If Searle thinks they are, then the simple fact of biology that brains produce minds will ultimately reduce to the fact that consciousness is caused by or is a product of physico-chemical reactions. This is surely a form of materialism and invites Galen Strawson's observation that the difficulty of the mind-body problem lies in understanding *how* such processes could give rise to and sustain a mental life. There is the added difficulty of *how* this mental life can have causal powers. This seems more like the starting point of the problem, not its solution. It will be remembered that mental causation was one of the features of mind highlighted by Searle that any theory needs to explain. If we say that, for example, my intention to have a cup of tea is caused by and realised in the brain, then presumably the subsequent bodily movements are caused by physical features of the brain. The physical movements that instantiate my intention to get a cup of tea can vary considerably depending on circumstances. I can be at home, in a hotel, in the street and so on. It is comforting to know that the brain sets in motion the right movements, without the need to postulate a pre-established harmony between mind and body.

We now need to return to the Chinese room. The brain is a purely physical system and, at the ultimate level, it operates in terms of basic physics and chemistry. Searle also holds that it produces genuine understanding. The Chinese room, however, seems to be telling us that no genuine understanding can be achieved as a result of manipulation according to physical features (no semantics from syntax). If this latter claim is right and the brain operates according to the uninterpreted movements of physical features, then it is going to follow that the native Chinese speakers do not understand Chinese. It is also going to follow that the man in the Chinese room does not understand English, and neither do you or I. This problem does not seem intrinsic to the Chinese room, but certainly emerges when that example is combined with a thesis like Biological Naturalism. It seems unlikely that this problem can be resolved by appealing to the brain-mind relation as being a causal one and the Chinese room-man one as being manipulative or computational. The problem still remains that a system with no intrinsic meaning is producing meaning.

(2) The causal problem

There is a problem with Searle's claim that mental states are caused by and realised in the structure of the brain. On standard Humean accounts of causation, there are two distinct events in causation and these events can be described independently of each other. For example, we heat a metal and it expands. The heating can be described independently of the expansion. Searle tells us that mental states are realised in the brain in a similar way to that of liquidity or solidity being realised in water and tables.

One problem is that liquidity and solidity do not seem to be separate from the water and the table. They are part of what they are. So it seems that, by analogy, Searle is saying that mental states are not separate from brain states, they are part of them. This is hard to reconcile with his claim not to be a materialist.

There are further difficulties. Causal connections are contingent. It is a contingent fact that certain electro-chemical reactions in the brain produce certain bodily movements. Thus, it would seem to be a contingent fact that my earlier intention to get a cup of tea produces the movements of switching on the kettle, rather than the movements we call packing a suitcase. It seems contingency is kind to us.

To return to the water and table analogies, liquidity and solidity are not realised in just these structures. Liquidity is realised in many different molecular structures from the Pacific Ocean to a glass of Scotch. Similar remarks apply to solidity. It is an empirical matter which structures produce these qualities and under what conditions. They are clearly multi-realisable. By analogy, the same will be true for mental states. It thus becomes a matter of empirical investigation whether trees, waterfalls, asteroid belts and so on have mental states. This is not something we could know through the use of reason alone. Searle does allow for something sufficiently similar to the human brain to have mental states, but what is meant here by 'sufficiently similar'? An alien brain with a silicon base could be very different; indeed the only similarity could be the fact that it produced mental states. We may also ask why it is necessary to have a 'sufficiently similar' qualification in the brain case and not in the supposedly analogous cases of water and tables. We do not say that only something sufficiently similar to water can realise liquidity. In what sense is water similar to nitric acid? In what sense is the molecular structure of oak similar to that of ice?

(3) The gap problem

There is a difference between consciousness and non-consciousness and, arguably, a pronounced difference. It is not at all clear how Searle is explaining such a difference. To accept it as a fact of biology that a purely physical system such as the brain causes conscious states does not explain very much. We can still complain that we have no idea as to how such a physical system creates and sustains a mental life. To say that it simply does is not particularly informative. We want to know how one kind of thing gives rise to a quite different kind of thing. To be told that they are not really different or that we no longer have a vitalism issue in biology as it is no longer seen as a problem to regard some matter as being alive is not that helpful. There are clearly differences between that which is conscious and that which is not. This is a fact about the world that needs explaining, not explaining away.

In some earlier writings, Searle attempted an explanation in terms of higher-level brain functions. This, however, leads to circularity. We cannot define 'higher level' in terms of the ability to produce consciousness, otherwise all we would be saying is that consciousness is caused by that which has the ability to cause consciousness. We need some independent account of the term 'higher level'. One is reminded here of a remark by Sir Karl Popper that one does not explain the emergence of novelty in the universe by attributing the ability to write poetry to molecules.

Searle seems to have been aware of this difficulty, as in later writings, he referred to consciousness being caused by lower-level brain functions. We are, however, owed an account of how we distinguish higher- and lower-level brain functions. The problem is that the designations 'higher' and 'lower' do not seem to be intrinsic parts of the physical system *qua* physical system. They may be conferred by us according to the values we ascribe to the accompanying mental content. If we take pure physical complexity as our criterion, that is, the complexity of the physical story involved in a particular activity, we could end up with some strange consequences. Distinguishing two similar looking bars of chocolate at a distance as being milk and plain may be a more complex *physical* affair than internalising the rules of chess.

(4) The re-emergence of property dualism

Searle, described liquidity as a feature of water, the mental as a feature of the brain. Had he used the term 'property' rather than 'feature' he would have been led to the conclusion that the mind and the brain have different properties. The road is then wide open to property dualism and the attendant difficulties of specifying the relationship between the properties. This is a thesis that Searle would want to avoid, but he cannot avoid it by the word substitution of 'feature' for 'property'.

(5) Hobbes revisited

It could be argued that when all the gloss has been stripped away, biological naturalism is just a revised form of crude sixteenth-century materialism. Thomas Hobbes once wrote that the brain secretes thought in the way the liver secretes bile. Although the language is colourful, one cannot help seeing a similarity. This is especially so given Searle's initial comparison with the stomach and digestion.

Given the difficulties we have encountered in this chapter with the attempts to solve the mind-body problem, it might be thought that the problem is insoluble. We will conclude this chapter with a brief consideration of a claim that the problem is in fact insoluble.

Colin McGinn and the CALM conjecture

McGinn has attempted to argue that the mind-body problem, together with some other central philosophical problems, the self and free-will, may be insoluble. To understand why he thinks this, a brief outline of what has influenced him should help.

The first influence is Noam Chomsky's theory of innate structures. This involves the claim that human beings have an innate capacity for grasping the grammar of languages. It is hard to explain how we can understand sentences we have never come across before without supposing that we have a built-in capacity for grasping the depth grammar of natural languages. This influence is then combined with Nagel's claim that there may well be things we can never know about the world. There may be chunks of reality that are forever closed off to us. From a knowledge point of view, perhaps there is an alien race that stands in the same relation to us as we do to animals.

McGinn has argued that we could have a certain cognitive structure that shapes our knowledge of the world and this structure breaks down when trying to deal with certain intractable issues in philosophy. We now need to understand what is meant by the CALM conjecture.

The letters of 'CALM' stand for Combinatorial Atomism and Law-like Mapping. McGinn holds that our understanding of the world consists of knowing what objects are made up of (their combination) and how they change through time (their mapping and the laws which govern it). This is held to represent our understanding of physical objects, organisms, sentences and mathematics. It is by applying CALM procedures that we render problems in these areas understandable and soluble. We have this inbuilt cognitive structure that enables us to deal with problems in this way.

The problem, however, is that CALM seems to break down when applied to the relation of consciousness to the brain. To take an example, our experience of a particular colour cannot itself be broken down into neuron firings. If it could, there simply would not be a problem. The breakdown of CALM will mean that any attempt to solve such problems is doomed to fail. Although this might seem pessimistic, that in itself is not a good reason for rejecting the conjecture. Thus psychological responses to the effect that we must keep trying make little philosophical impact.

Problems with the conjecture
One of the main difficulties concerns the independent evidence for the conjecture. There is a corresponding difficulty with Chomsky's theory of innate structures. The problem is that the evidence for them seems to be exhausted by the phenomena which they are intended to explain. The problem is essentially one of circularity. We cannot do the mind-body problem due to the restrictions of the CALM conjecture and we support the CALM conjecture by appealing to our inability to do the mind-body problem. We really need independent evidence for the existence of such cognitive structures. It may be argued that the way we solve problems in other areas may constitute such evidence. But this does not imply any innate structures; it might only imply that we use and extend methods which we have found profitable.

This leads to a further difficulty. McGinn describes one aspect of our understanding but that is not the whole story. It seems that the kind of understanding involved in grasping the meaning of a work of art does not obviously conform to the conjecture and thus the breakdown of the conjecture does not necessarily imply a failure to understand but rather a failure of a certain kind of understanding. It could, of course, be retorted that these forms of understanding are likely to be of little or no relevance in solving the philosophical issues to which McGinn refers. We are here concerned with what we might broadly call scientific understanding and this is well described by the conjecture. Again, this can be questioned. It is not immediately obvious that all general scientific theories are arrived at through elaborate decombining of objects. Newton's laws of motion or relativity theory do not seem to fit the bill in a straightforward way. The danger is that the CALM conjecture could be taken as operating at such a level of generality that virtually anything could be subsumed under it. This carries the corresponding danger of trivialising the conjecture.

There are further difficulties to which I can now only briefly allude. It is not clear that our understanding of human actions is a clear application of the conjecture and neither is it clear that scientific method is the solution to the problems of philosophy. A scientist once remarked that free will could well be possible if we could find random, unpredictable events in the brain. This seems to be completely irrelevant to our understanding of the issue. If this is the path our innate structures lead us, then perhaps we should postulate some corrective structures that enable us to see *why* it is irrelevant.

I will conclude with a reference to what I can only call 'the uneasy feeling'. In a material world considered as matter in motion there are conscious beings that realise their limitations. They can postulate that chunks of reality are inaccessible. We have a disanalogy with the rest of nature. We have no explanation of how matter, as we conceive it, can be the realising ground for this feat of awareness. (For a more accessible account, see McGinn, *The Making of a Philosopher*.)

▶ Personal identity

The problem of personal identity is concerned with just what it is that makes us the same individuals through time. We say that Mr X is the same person today as he was ten years ago. The question concerns our criteria for making identity claims through time. Philosophers have given different solutions to this question. Some have favoured physical or bodily criteria; others have favoured mental criteria, especially continuity of memory. There are traditional difficulties with either solution. People can undergo many physical changes, including radical plastic surgery, and yet we say that he/she is the same person in spite of all the physical changes. Philosophers who emphasise bodily criteria will not mean by this the same body in terms of recognition, but rather the spatio-temporal continuity of the body. We shall say more about this later.

Perhaps the best way to start the discussion is to look at two historically important and opposed approaches to the problem.

In the writings of Thomas Reid the emphasis is very much on that of an enduring mental substance. We all have thoughts, emotions, sense experiences, and these mental events are regarded as part of the history of our individual selves. They cannot exist on their own, they must *belong* to someone. What connects such a series of mental events is their belonging to the same individual. For Reid, it is the mind which binds the experiences together. There is some similarity here with Locke's theory of physical substance. It will be remembered from our discussion of Berkeley in the first chapter, that Locke had argued that sensible qualities like redness, hardness and so on, could not simply float around but had to inhere in a material substance. A physical object was substance plus attributes. Reid's point regarding personal identity is similar, namely, there is both the mental substance *and* the various experiences. It is in the mental substance that Reid wishes to locate personal identity. Consider the following well-known passage from Reid:

> My personal identity implies the continued existence of that indivisible thing which I call *myself*. Whatever this self may be, it is something which thinks, and deliberates, and resolves, and acts, and suffers. I am not thought, I am not action, I am not feeling; I am something that thinks, and acts, and suffers. My thoughts, and actions, and feelings, change every moment; and they have no continued, but a successive existence; but that *self*, or I, to which they belong, is permanent, and has the same relation to all the succeeding thoughts, actions and feelings which I call mine. Such are the notions that I have on my personal identity. (*Essay on the Intellectual Powers of Man*, III, Ch.4)

It will be realised that in the above statement of the mental substance thesis, Reid clearly distinguishes mental events or experiences from the mind which has them. It is the mind which owns or possesses them that is said to constitute personal identity. The experiences themselves continually change and thus could not be used as a criterion of identity.

Problems with the mental substance thesis

One immediate difficulty with Reid's mental substance is that it is as elusive as Locke's physical or material substance. It has the status of a 'something we know not what'. We just do not seem to have any idea of it over and above the particular experiences which it is said to possess. It might, as Reid saw, be a requirement of reason to suppose there had to be such a substance to bind the experiences together, but it is difficult to give an account of what this substance is. It, therefore, becomes extremely problematic to use such a thing as mental substance as a criterion for personal identity.

We said that it seems there has to be a something which has or owns the various mental events but this claim gives rise to a second difficulty. Some philosophers have found difficulty with the use of the concept of ownership in this context. 'Ownership' is essentially a socio-legal concept and its use is, therefore, parasitic on human conventions. However, its use in the case of the mind and its experiences has nothing to do with human conventions. In this latter case there is no connection, for example, with related social concepts like rights and obligations. It seems, therefore, that some justification of the use of the concept in Reid's sense is required. There may be some plausibility in saying that its use is more figurative than literal but this still raises the problem of whether we have a clear enough idea of what we are talking about to use it as a criterion for personal identity. We shall return to this issue at the end of the discussion.

Hume's 'Bundle of Perceptions'

Having seen some of the difficulties with an 'ownership' theory in the preceding section, we can now look at an alternative which eschews the notion of ownership. In Book I of the *Treatise,* Hume writes as follows:

> There are some philosophers who imagine we are every moment intimately conscious of what we call our *self;* that we feel its existence and its continuance in existence ... For my part, when I enter most intimately into what I call *myself* I always stumble on some particular perception or other, of heat, or cold, light or shade, love or hatred, pain or pleasure. I can never catch *myself* at any time without a perception and never can observe anything but the perception.

On this account the self is analysed into a succession of states of consciousness, or the bundle of perceptions or sensations. They are constitutive of the self. Thus on Hume's account the self considered as some kind of substance or object is replaced by the bundle of sensations. The successive states of consciousness which Reid thought could not account for the self are being used by Hume to analyse the self. Clearly a no-ownership thesis such as Hume's is going to avoid some of the objections raised against Reid. However, there are considerable difficulties of a different kind with Hume's thesis.

Problems with Hume's thesis

In the quotation from Hume that we have just considered, he uses expressions such as 'I can never catch myself' and 'when I enter ... into'. The problem though is *what* is doing the entering or looking, *what* is conducting the search? In other words to what does the 'I' refer? It cannot be the owner as Hume has rejected that. This leads to a further difficulty that without an owner what is it that leads him to say that the perceptions he finds are his? It seems perfectly natural to say that what he discovers are his *own* states of consciousness. The omission of an experiencing subject leaves us with a succession of sensations and the difficulty of saying how they can be discovered. It could be argued that the possibility of their recognition presupposes a subject who has them and who carries out Hume's search. The idea of a succession of perceptions without an owner leads to problems regarding their status. It would be odd to regard perceptions as free floating. If we regard the self as a bundle of successive perceptions, it becomes hard to understand what makes one bundle mine and another bundle yours.

Hume leaves us without a criterion for distinguishing the various bundles. There is clearly a difference between my experiences and those of someone else but this difference is hard to explain on a Humean account. It might be said in Hume's defence that the way to individuate the bundles is to assign a spatio-temporal location to the body in which they occur. Thus what makes my experiences mine is that they occur in a particular body at a particular time and location. The spatio-temporal co-ordinates will serve to distinguish this body from any other body as no two bodies can occupy the same space at the same time. There are, however, difficulties with this kind of move.

In the first place it fails to provide an adequate solution to our first problem of specifying just what it is that carries out Hume's search. It is hard to see how this can be answered in terms of spatio-temporal co-ordinates. The second difficulty is that, whereas it might have some plausibility in regard to perceptions like colour patches, it has little plausibility in regard to feelings like love or sadness. My experience of a particular colour patch may be said to be mine as my body at a particular time and location is stimulated in a certain way but to try and individuate our emotional lives in this way is difficult. It could be argued that what makes certain feelings mine, or even makes them possible, is *who* I am and not *where* I am. In other words, their very possibility presupposes identity in terms of an enduring, experiencing subject. This leads to the final problem I want to discuss in regard to Hume.

Earlier we saw that Hume had claimed that when he looked inside himself all he found were particular sensations and not something called 'I'. He then attempted to analyse the 'I' in terms of the succession of sensations. Hume's radically empiricist epistemology involved the claim that there could be no idea of something without there being a corresponding impression of that thing. So if there was no distinct impression of a self or 'I' then there is no clear idea of it either. For Hume, the only distinct impressions would be of the sensations succeeding one another. There are a number of ways of arguing against Hume's position.

The first way is to argue that the empiricist epistemology is too extreme. In order for us to have ideas it is not necessary to have such particularised, distinct impressions as Hume supposed. (His own discussion of the shades of blue example, should have alerted him to this issue, see Chapter 1.) We have ideas of things like the national economy or the balance of payments which do not obviously correspond to some particular impression or aggregate of such impressions. J. O. Urmson in his book *Berkeley* makes the same point in regard to the concept of a trump in Bridge. There is no additional impression over and above the four suits which corresponds to a trump and yet we do have such an idea.

A second line of attack is to question the claim that I am not aware of myself as a continuing entity. I do not have experiences just as experiences;

what I have are *my* experiences. The ownership aspect should be seen as an integral part of the total experience. The situation described by Hume seems to fit best with a sort of internal magic lantern show. Here the viewer sees one picture following another and stands in an external relation to the entire procedure. This sort of model does not match well with our own experiences. There is an example, from a different context, that can be used to illustrate this issue. Sartre once gave a fairly vivid account of the experience of shame. Suppose I am bent down listening at a keyhole to a conversation in the next room. Unknown to me someone has come up behind me and is observing me in the act of eavesdropping. When I discover that another is watching me, myself and my shame form an integrated whole. I do not observe the shame and neither am I just the shame. The experience is dependent on the fact that it is *me* who is caught, so how can the 'me' just be the experience(s)? The total experience is best characterised as *my shame*.

Criteria for personal identity

Bodily criteria

Clearly the appearance of our bodies is a criterion of identity in everyday life, but it does not solve the problem of personal identity. Our bodies change internally (cell renewal) and externally. We can have plastic surgery and be unrecognisable. We would, however, be the same person in spite of the bodily changes. What is far more important than the appearance or the composition of the body is its spatio-temporal continuity. Although the body changes, there are no gaps in its continuity. Imagine we see Mr A change into the Incredible Hulk – the limbs enlarge and the appearance is transformed. It is no longer the same body. There would, however, be a spatio-temporal continuity. We see the body change; there would be no gaps in its continuous existence. It could, therefore, be argued that it is the spatio-temporal continuity of the body that allows us to identify Mr A with the Hulk.

This, however, is not the complete story at all. If we are to say that Mr A and the Hulk are the same person we would want to know whether the Hulk could recount Mr A's past experiences. We would want to know whether the Hulk's memories were those of Mr A. We may also feel some hesitation in making same person attributions if the subsequent behaviour was radically different. I shall say more about this in the next section.

The appeal to the spatio-temporal continuity of the body has certain advantages. It can accommodate changes in mental characteristics and still retain the same person. It can even accommodate total amnesia and still retain the same person. Yet as we saw above, we seem to need more before being confident in our same person attributions. Perhaps the following examples will help us to understand what else is needed.

John Hick asks us to imagine the following case. Professor Smith attends a convention in New York and then suddenly disappears from everyone's view. At that very moment he appears at a convention in Australia. In this case what would be crucial in saying it was the same person would be if Professor Smith was as baffled as everyone else and could not explain or understand how he had got from one place to another, and also that he could recite his life history. Here there would be a gap in the spatio-temporal continuity of the body and yet it is the same person. It is the continuity of states of consciousness that have now taken priority in the same person attribution.

Hick then offers a variant on the example. Let us suppose that Professor Smith dies in New York, people see the corpse and there is a funeral. At the moment of death a body just like his appears in Australia, it can be recognised as such. The personality traits and memories of the newly emerged body are the same as Smith's. We now have two bodies. Nevertheless we would still identify the person who appeared in Australia as being the same as the one who died in New York. Smith himself would know if he remembered being taken ill in New York. He would know that he had survived the death of his body in New York. Hick regards these examples as logically possible and what they are intended to show is that although bodily identity is a criterion often used in everyday life, it is not the only criterion. We have now introduced the idea of mental criteria in the ascription of identity and the most important of these is memory.

Memory

One of the best known attempts to appeal to memory as an intelligible criterion of personal identity was provided by John Locke. Locke asks us to imagine that the soul of a prince, together with his memories, entered the body of a commoner after his soul had departed. In such a case Locke thought that we would regard the commoner as the same as the prince. At this point, Locke draws an important distinction between the same person and the same man (or woman). Locke agrees that we tend to use these terms interchangeably, but there is an important difference. In Locke's example, we would identify the commoner (man) as now being the prince (person). The point of the example is to demonstrate the intelligibility of conceiving of personal identity as depending on memory (psychological criteria) rather than the body. There is something immediately attractive about Locke's thesis. It would, for example, allow us to talk of Dr Jekyll and Mr Hyde as being the same man but two different persons. In the case of someone with amnesia, then, on Locke's thesis, he would continue to be the same man, but would cease to be the same person. Locke's theory seems to imply that a new person had emerged.

There is some support for Locke's thesis. The psychologist William MacDougall reported the interesting case of Mary Reynolds. On awaking from a long sleep, Reynolds suffered total amnesia, together with the loss of her skills. Mentally she differed from a baby only in the fact that she had the learning capacity of an adult. Five weeks later she awoke to her normal state. She now remembered her life up to but excluding the breakdown. Several weeks later, she again lapsed into the secondary state. This continued for several years. On Locke's thesis we would say that she remained one woman but alternated between two different persons. Further support for Locke is provided by the fact that the two states displayed different and opposite traits of character. Reynolds's normal state was bold and outgoing whereas the secondary state was dull and afraid. (The cinematic treatment of the case of the Boston Strangler explored similar issues, together with the question of responsibility.)

Cases such as these raise the issue of what happens to person A when person B is in control. If one were to follow Descartes, one would have to deny the possibility of a personality being split or fragmented. The mind was regarded as indivisible. Psychologists who treat such cases would reject the Cartesian view. They are likely to regard person B's emergence as an expression of the patient's repressed desires. It seems that the cure for this is the re-integration of a mind which has broken in two.

There have been more modern variations on Locke's theory. In an appeal to science fiction, Shoemaker invites us to suppose the possibility of a brain transplant. Two men A and B, have an operation in the same hospital at the same time. A's brain is transplanted into B's body and vice versa. A dies, but B survives with A's brain. B would remember the past experiences of A and not B's former life. Shoemaker says that in this situation, we would adopt Locke's conclusion, that is, the person in control of B's body is the A person. Shoemaker's example assumes the intelligibility of swapping bodies and also assumes that memories are stored as physical parts of the brain and will be destroyed when the brain is.

Bernard Williams has cast doubt on just how supportive of Locke these kinds of examples envisaged by Shoemaker are. Williams amends the Shoemaker example and invites us to consider the example from the point of view of the subject. In the amended example the brains of A and B are not interchanged. He invites us to suppose that scientists can extract information from the brain, and later, after storage, feed it into the brain of another. Information is extracted from A and fed into B, and from B into A. Williams uses the expression the A-body person to refer to the person who before the operation had the body called A, and the B-body person to refer to the one who had the body called B. The experimenter tells A and B that after the operation one will be tortured and the other rewarded. He asks A who he thinks should be tortured. On Locke's theory A would say torture the body I am now in (the A-body) and this seems to be the right choice but then Williams casts doubt on Locke's theory. Suppose the experimenter gives A the message in a piecemeal manner:

(1) You are going to be tortured.

(2) Don't worry; you are going to have an operation so that you will forget your past experiences. I will give you a set of different memories.

(3) The same is going to happen to B, and B's memories will be transferred to A's brain.

(4) A's memories will be transferred to B's brain.

(5) A must decide who is to be tortured.

Would A lose his fear on being told of the memory swap? Would we really have enough confidence in Locke's theory to make a decision? Have we got into a dilemma of generating two of the same person?

Examples such as these make certain assumptions. Williams assumes that memories are stored in the brain and that they are the sorts of things that can be extracted and stored. Analogies with computer 'memory' are likely to reinforce this way of thinking. There are, however, difficulties here. If this kind of operation were possible, then there would be nothing preventing the experimenter from transmitting A's memories to B *and* C. We would then have three of 'the same person'. This seems an unacceptable paradox. Neither does there appear to be any principled reason why stored memories cannot be partly transferred. Thus, A could retain some memory and receive memories from B, C and so on. The resulting situation would be hard to describe.

A supporter of Locke would want to reject the idea that memories are stored as physical parts of the brain. He might argue that memories are modifications of mind which is an immaterial substance and it is by endorsing this that we avoid the paradoxes alluded to earlier. There are, however, further difficulties with regarding memory as the sole criterion of identity.

Difficulties with the memory thesis

(1) In a famous example, Thomas Reid attempted to derive a contradiction from the memory thesis. He argued that it would imply that a man may be, and at the same time not be, the person who performed a particular action. Reid's example is as follows: a man is flogged at school for theft; he later performs heroically in battle and in later years is made a General. When he acted heroically, he remembered the flogging, and when he was made a General he remembered his heroic action, but had lost the memory of the flogging. He who was flogged at school is the same person who acted heroically and he who acted heroically is the same person as he who was made General. This is guaranteed by the memory. This logically entails that he who was flogged is the same as he who was made General: $(A = B = C$, therefore, $A = C$). However, the General lacks *this* memory, so, on the memory thesis, he is not the person who was flogged. Therefore, he is both the same person and not the same person who was flogged at school.

Proponents of the memory thesis may amend their thesis from he who has the memory to he who *could* have the memory. The identity of the person does not hinge on the possession of one memory and he can be identified by the possession of other memories. It is the possessor of these other memories who could have the memory of being flogged. This kind of move runs into difficulties in cases of total amnesia and Locke's distinction between man and person is likely to come into play here.

(2) Memory requires a subject. Remembering is an activity which requires *someone* to do the remembering, someone to perform the mental act. It is this someone who has the better claim to be the self rather than what it does. Memories, whether visual or verbal, are not a series of isolated events. They require an agent for their recall, for their contemplation. It can be argued that the occurrence of memories presupposes a self for their recall and thus they cannot be identified with that self. It can also be argued that memories are the past experiences of the self and are, thus, separate from the self that has those experiences.

(3) Some proponents of the memory thesis have claimed that memory has a unifying effect. It binds our present experience to past experience and in doing this provides the experience of personal identity. The problem with this kind of move is that it seems that there must already be personal identity before there can be any experience of it. As Butler wrote on this claim: 'And one should really think it self-evident, that consciousness of personal identity presupposes, and therefore, cannot constitute personal identity; any more than knowledge, in any other case, can constitute truth, which it presupposes' (*Of Personal Identity*).

(4) One may question just how supportive cases like the Mary Reynolds case reported earlier are to the memory thesis. When it is claimed that they demonstrate two different persons in the same body, it is not clear that they are different persons in the sense that you and I are different persons.

Concluding remarks

We have seen that it is difficult to give an adequate account of the self in terms of something else, body or memory. It may be that the 'I' cannot be analysed in terms of something more fundamental. If the self is a conceptual cornerstone of our thinking and of our experiences, it may be futile to attempt an analysis of it in terms of something else.

A further difficulty concerns what some philosophers have called the recessiveness of the 'I'. No matter what we define the self in terms of, it is always possible for the 'I' to adopt a point of view on the suggestion, or to seem to stand in an external relation to that which it is analysed into. It seems to escape us, to slide away from what it is identified with and yet non-referential theories are ultimately unsatisfying. They leave us with a feeling that *something* has been omitted.

3 The Philosophy of Religion

▶ Introductory remarks; The concept of God

In this area of philosophy we are primarily concerned with questions relating to the existence of God, the possibility of rational belief in God and problems which face a religious believer. We are not concerned with questions relating to the causes or functions of religious belief. These latter questions are the province of an appropriate social science. Our concern is with the *rationality* of such beliefs. We are concerned with the content of beliefs, the validity of arguments and the logical implications of arguments. This is an important distinction to bear in mind. To give the causes of religious belief will not answer the questions of whether such beliefs are rational or what the criteria of rationality are.

Before we can embark on our discussion, we need to get clear about the most important conceptions of God. Whenever one embarks on an enquiry it is essential to have a clear idea of the subject under discussion. In the case of the existence of God, we need a clear idea of what is meant by 'God'. There are three conceptions which are of importance to us.

The biblical concept of God

This concept of God was prevalent in Judaism and Christianity in the first and second centuries. The existence of God is taken for granted. It is neither doubted nor argued for. The discussion of God's attributes does not take the form of an abstract discussion. It is taken for granted that God has acted in history. Biblical statements about God are made in relation to His actions. It was the later theologians who took a more metaphysical view.

God is seen as the 'Sovereign Lord' whose will cannot be resisted. Nothing can be hidden from Him. He loves his people and this is a jealous love. He is capable of feeling anger. He is the judge of all men and no one can escape that judgement. No other being has comparable power and majesty. There is one and only one God. Christ gave new emphasis to the Old Testament idea of God as the Father. In the New Testament the love of God is emphasised. The accent is not so much on anger or jealousy. He is, however, still regarded as the judge of all men. In both testaments God is spoken of in personal and dynamic terms. His power is regarded as being demonstrated in human history rather than natural history. He is regarded, though, as the creator and sustainer of the physical world.

What is of extreme importance in this brief description is that God is thought of as very much a personal and living God. Such a conception needs to be distinguished from the 'remote' God of the philosophers.

The philosophical concept of God

This concept of God was prevalent in pagan circles during the middle-Platonist era (100 BC–AD 200). In presocratic philosophy the concept of God was firmly rooted in the quest for the origin of the physical universe. The Greek gods had been organised in a hierarchy. Each one was thought to have dominion over a particular phenomenon, such as the sea or love. This kind of account of how the world came to be and why it is the way that it is ceased to satisfy the first-class minds of the time. Through their dissatisfaction we have the beginnings of philosophy. Early philosophical attempts were made to provide answers.

The Milesian philosophers held that the world had come from an indefinitely large mass of eternal 'stuff'. This eternal stuff was in some sense alive and it exercised some control over the material world. It maintained a just relationship in the world. The stuff in question is a single homogeneous whole and it pervades the universe. There is no distinction drawn between mind and matter. Since operations of the stuff were large-scale and regular, and beyond the influence of human beings, the idea of divine personality diminished. It was not a requirement of the theory. As the stuff was impersonal, there would be no prayer to it and no cults. The impersonality is emphasised by the account given of how the world emerged. It is a mechanical process with no need for planning or design. Our world is regarded as being an inevitable result, given the nature of the original stuff.

Later philosophers rejected the idea of a single stuff in favour of a dualism between mind and matter. Anaxagoras is an example of such a philosopher. Matter is inert and unchanging, whereas mind is active and concerned to realise the good in matter. The middle-Platonists held that God was the Supreme Mind. It acts without itself undergoing any change. Some have regarded this religion as intellectual devotion to the supreme. The idea of divine personality was not introduced. Ideas such as prayer to a personal God or direct intervention by such a God were alien to the middle-Platonists.

In the Platonist religion there were two tiers of divinity. There were the inferior gods and the Supreme Mind with whom one would be united at death. What was the impact of the philosophical conception? Many Christians were impressed by the biblical and philosophical concepts of

God. Clement thought that Plato had some grasp of the true nature of God. Consider the following remarks of Plato's:

> It is a hard task to find the maker and father of this universe. (*Timaeus*)

> God keeps an unswerving path but has always the right to take vengeance on those who disobey the divine law. (*Laws*)

There are certainly points of similarity between the two concepts. The philosophical one speaks of a single, universal and transcendental God. In the Bible there is one God and He is totally different from what we can perceive. The philosophical conception regards God as a mind directed to the good. This is in harmony with the Christian teaching that God is a spiritual being and perfectly good.[1] Philosophers regarded God as incomprehensible, theologians referred to his hiddenness or unknowability. Some thought that these similarities were so striking that it was likely that Plato and the earlier philosophers had read the Old Testament.

In spite of these similarities, there were important differences. In philosophy the existence of God was correlated with that of matter. In presocratic philosophy the divine being was regarded as material up to the time of Anaxagoras. Even in middle-Platonism the material upon which the Supreme Mind acts pre-exists the Supreme Mind. Christian doctrine, on the other hand, speaks of a creation from nothing. God is held to have brought matter into existence through His own free decision. The middle-Platonists held that matter was eternal and limited what God could do with it. This was contradicted by Christianity.

Secondly, we have a difference concerning the idea of immutability. In philosophy God is immutable, the contents of the divine mind are fixed for ever. Although He causes motion, He does not change. The biblical God is not immutable in this sense, but rather in the sense of being eternally faithful to His own free decisions. The philosophical concept left no room for emotion in God. Immutability implied impassivity. The Bible speaks freely of emotion in God. Talk about a loving or angry God has no place in the philosophical concept.

A third difference is that immutability seemed to imply timelessness. If God does not change, then it is impossible to distinguish times in God. We could not, for example, distinguish earlier and later states of God. We could not attribute position or duration to God. In the Bible there is no concept of timelessness. The nearest concept is that of God's eternity meaning duration with neither beginning nor end, and complete and unaltered powers at any time. In philosophy immutability entails simplicity. If God were complex, then He would be immutable only if the various elements in God were held together by something external to God. (It was thought that complexes were unstable, see Plato's *Phaedo*.) If He is both complex and stable, then He must be held together by something external to Him; but then God would not be the cause of all things. In the biblical conception God's simplicity should be understood as meaning that there are no conflicts or unconnected actions. He is single-minded and wills one thing.

Finally, in philosophy one is trying to argue from features of the known world-order to the first cause. The most satisfactory outcome of such an enterprise would be to arrive at a cause that necessarily and inevitably gives rise to the known world-order. In other words, given the original cause, one could see why this world-order rather than another resulted. This would satisfy the principle of sufficient reason. Such an enterprise will succeed if and only if it picks a cause whose operations we can understand. The Bible, however, does not suffer from this limitation. It is asserted there that God created the world and the question concerns what kind of God His creation shows Him to be. It is dubious though to reason from the world to a free and transcendental creator for if He is free, then how can it show *why* He created this world and not another? The second problem here is that if He is transcendental, then how can we assume that we know enough about Him to say that creating our world is the kind of thing that He would do? We cannot argue from what God has done in the world to the kind of 'person' He must be. It is impossible to produce a satisfactory argument from the nature of the world to a free and transcendental creator. The only explanation that is possible is the mechanistic one of the Greeks to which we referred earlier.

The philosophical conception had effects on the biblical one. In the second century AD we find Irenaeus saying that God is not subject to passions. Christian theology takes from philosophy the complex ideas centring on immutability, timelessness, passivity and incomprehensibility. The adoption of these ideas poses a problem, namely, the problem of God's action in history. The incarnation says that God became man at a certain time. But if He is timeless and immutable, then how can He be said to have acted? Does not any action involve a change in the agent?

Theology took a stand against philosophy on the doctrine of creation from nothing. In spite of the teaching of Greek philosophy that nothing can come from nothing, theologians adhered to the doctrine of creation from nothing. This doctrine involves a radical difference between God and any other agent or cause.

The cross-cultivation of the philosophical and biblical conceptions resulted in the classical Christian conception.

The classical concept of God

This concept is elaborated by Thomas Aquinas and also in the Catholic and Anglican traditions of the seventeenth and eighteenth centuries. It is still accepted as orthodox. Its principal characteristics are as follows:

(1) There is one God or God is one. This can mean that there is exactly one God, or that God is undivided or non-complex.

(2) He is the creator of everything other than Himself. There was no pre-existing matter from which God created the world. The world had a beginning in time and it is sustained in existence by God. He is responsible for the universe running in a law-like way and for its intelligibility.

(3) He is self-existent. This means that God depends on nothing other than Himself. He did not come into existence because of something else, He does not remain in existence because of something else and He will not cease to exist because of something else (sometimes referred to as 'aseity').

(4) He is incorporeal. This means that God is not a material thing. He is not perceptible to the bodily senses. There is some dispute as to whether He is perceptible to another faculty. If there is direct awareness of God, then it is not of God as a material entity. God does not occupy space to the exclusion of other things. His omnipresence does not mean his occupation of space. It must be seen in relation to His omnipotence and omniscience. For any place, He knows what is happening and can affect it.

(5) He is eternal. The biblical account means infinite, unchanging duration. A more philosophical account would involve timelessness. He has neither duration nor location in time.

(6) He is immutable and impassible. He cannot change in any way. He cannot experience passions or emotions. It is difficult to reconcile this with the Bible. It is also problematic as to whether such a being could be said to understand the passions of another. The background to the ideas is important. They involve the Aristotelian idea that when things change, they are being changed by something else. If God were to change, then He would be subject to something else. He would not then be the ultimate cause. Immutability and impassibility are the consequences of two ideas, the Aristotelian and the requirement that God should be the ultimate cause.

(7) He is simple. There is a total absence of complexity or composition in God. The background to this idea is the same as that of (6). He cannot be held together by anything else. This led to some odd ideas such as God being identical with any one of His *different* properties.

(8) He is perfect and good. Perfection in this context means that for any property, God has it in the highest degree. It is inferred that He is good as perfection is taken to imply goodness. There is a problem here concerning the multiplying to infinity of certain properties. Can a being be infinitely just *and* infinitely merciful? To administer perfect justice to a wrongdoer seems to involve *some* element of

punishment. To administer perfect or complete mercy involves *no* element of punishment.

(9) He is transcendent. He is substantially distinct from the world. He can be apprehended by man but not comprehended.

▶ Arguments for the existence of God

The argument from design (the teleological argument)

This argument is the most empirical and the least technical of all the arguments for the existence of God. There are different ways of arguing for the existence of design in the world, and, hence, for the existence of a designer.

In the eighteenth and nineteenth centuries the most popular way of arguing for design was to try and show an analogy between natural production and human production. If one could demonstrate a resemblance, then, it was argued, one could, by adopting the principle of like causes produce like effects, argue that the causes of these effects resembled each other. Thus if one could show some kind of similarity between a man-made object and the natural world, and we know that the former is the product of planning, design and purpose, then we could infer that the same is true of the latter.

In Hume's *Dialogues Concerning Natural Religion,* Cleanthes, the proponent of the argument, tells us that when we think about the natural world, we find that it is a vast machine comprising infinitely many lesser machines and these in turn can be sub-divided. He continues:

> All these various machines, and even their most minute parts, are adjusted to each other... The curious adapting of means to ends, throughout all nature, resembles exactly, though it much exceeds, the productions of human contrivance; of human designs, thought, wisdom and intelligence. Since therefore the effects resemble each other, we are led to infer by all rules of analogy, that the causes also resemble; and that the Author of Nature is somewhat similar to the mind of man; though possessed of much larger faculties, proportioned to the grandeur of the work, which he has executed. By this argument *a posteriori,* and by this argument alone, do we prove at once the existence of a Deity, and his similarity to human mind and intelligence. (pp. 115/16)

Cleanthes also tells us that in works of human contrivance, we see a symmetry of parts and discover an adjustment of means to ends, and a tendency to self-preservation. This is also to be found in the natural world, so, by analogy we infer a similar cause. We can see then that it is important how parts of machines are adjusted to one another in such a way as to make the whole fit for a purpose and give it a tendency to self-preservation.[2] This is a similar style of reasoning to that which was later used by William Paley.[3]

Paley imagines himself out walking and he comes across a stone and a watch. In the case of the watch, we perceive something which we could not perceive in the case of the stone. We see that its parts are designed for a purpose and our conclusion would not be weakened if we had never seen a watch being made, or if some of its parts were not in working order, or if we did not understand the function of some of its parts. We would still know that it was the product of deliberate contrivance. Paley holds that we find comparable works in the natural world. This should force us to conclude that there is a similarity in their creators. Paley went on to discuss examples from the natural world which he thought demonstrated design. Bodies of fishes are perfectly designed for existence in water. Animals are perfectly designed to live in various environments and so on. Since Darwin's theory of evolution, however, these arguments based on features of the animal kingdom have become defunct.

Another way of arguing for design is to claim that there are phenomena in the natural world whose existence cannot be accounted for by the laws governing the behaviour of matter. Paley hints at this approach when he says that it would be preposterous to try and account for the existence of the watch by appealing to random combinations of matter which just happened to come together to form the watch.

Both Paley and Cleanthes regard the universe as a spatial arrangement displaying spatial regularities which represent an adjustment of means to ends. Another proponent of the argument from design, R. W. Swinburne, whom we shall discuss later, recognises regularities in patterns of spatial order, but emphasises regularities of succession. He argues for design on the basis that the behaviour of objects occurs in a regular manner in accordance with the laws of nature.

Some of the most important criticisms of the design argument are made in Hume's *Dialogues* and in S X1 of his *Enquiry Concerning Human Understanding*. In the *Dialogues* Philo is the fictional character who opposes the argument. As it is generally regarded that Philo's views are in fact Hume's, I shall refer to Hume as the opponent.

Hume has a general objection to comparing the universe with a human artifice and then proceeding to argue from analogy. The objection is that there is no obvious sense in which the universe is like the objects of human production. To use Hume's example, the universe is not very much like a house and certainly not sufficiently like one to permit the inference to similar causes. In order to justify such an inference we would need a strong analogy with striking similarities. The comparison of the universe and a house or watch does not provide such a justification. Indeed, it could be said that it is because the universe does *not* resemble houses or watches that we need to build and make such objects.

In response to this Cleanthes claims that such an objection involves a misunderstanding of the analogy. What the analogy shows, according to this response, is that the resemblance between the universe and human artifice lies in the display of an adjustment of means to ends, rather than in the display of physical similarities. Cleanthes is presenting his argument as an empirical or *a posteriori* one, and, to be consistent, he ought to appeal to observable features of the world. Even though these features may be ordered, they do not all display intelligent design. The generation of animals and plants would be such an example.

The comparison of the universe with the mechanisms of human production is quite arbitrary and too selective. Hume was to claim that, rather than regard the world as a machine, you could just as well regard it on the model of a gigantic floating vegetable or a large crustacean. This is a general criticism of the comparison procedure involved in the design argument. Hume has also a number of particular criticisms and it is to these that we now turn.

First, in propounding his argument, Cleanthes is saying that God created the universe with reference to a plan. The plan existed in God's mind prior to the creation. In appealing to the plan, we are thereby picking out the cause of the created universe and giving an explanation of it. Hume counters this by saying that if order in the physical world requires an explanation, then so does order in the mental world of God's mind. Abstract reason requires a cause for this mental world and we would have every reason to seek the cause of this ideal world in another ideal world and so on *ad infinitum*. This creates a regress which can be avoided. It can be avoided by simply stopping at the physical world. The order in the world is to be located in the laws governing matter and there is no need to go beyond them. There is no reason for preferring an explanation in terms of the divine mind rather than just accepting physical laws. The reader should remember that Cleanthes claims to be an empiricist, and, as an empiricist, he should hold that the mental and the physical are governed by similar laws. Thus if one allows that ideas may fall into order in the mind (that is, the plan in God's mind) without a known cause and that the physical and the mental obey similar laws, then why cannot matter fall into order without a known cause? There is no *rational* ground for not stopping at the physical.

Second, Hume claims that the argument fails to prove the infinity of any of the divine attributes. He holds as a general principle that when we are arguing from effects to causes, we should not attribute to the cause anything more than is sufficient to produce the effect. This principle is illustrated by the following example:

A body of ten ounces raised in any scale may serve as a proof that the counterbalancing weight exceeds ten ounces but can never afford a reason that it exceeds a hundred.[4]

This principle is then applied to the argument from design:

> Allowing, therefore, the gods to be the authors of the existence or order of the universe, it follows that they possess that precise degree of power, intelligence, and benevolence which appears in their workmanship, but nothing further can ever be proved.

As we shall see later, Swinburne was to attack Hume's general principle. For the present though, suffice it to remark that if we conceive of the universe along the lines of what Hume called his 'Epicurean Hypothesis', that is, as a finite arrangement of parts, then it is always possible that what we have so far discovered is not the universe in its entirety. New discoveries could force us to say that the universe was larger than we had previously thought. We could then say that God had more power than we had previously thought. Our judgement of His power will always be provisional. Although this reply to Hume does not show God's power to be infinite, it is, nevertheless, more than Hume admitted. If the universe (the effect) were discovered to be larger, then more power would be attributable to the cause. This could, in principle, continue without limitation. Hume's argument, however, points the way to a serious problem that he was to raise.

Third, the problem is that we cannot prove the perfection of God because the universe contains many faults. In examining the structural defects of the world, Hume produces a powerful argument against the legitimacy of inferring a perfect cause from the known effect. The analogy here would be that if you were to judge the merit of a workman, then your judgement would be in proportion to the quality of the work he produced. Anything short of perfect work would mean that you would not attribute perfection to the workman.

Fourth, Hume tells us that for all we know the world could be the result of trial and error.

> Many worlds might have been botched and bungled, throughout an eternity, ere this system was struck out: much labour lost: Many fruitless trials made; And a slow, but continued improvement carried on during infinite ages in the art of world-making.[5]

Clearly, it would be wrong to impute excellence or perfection to God if He had been bungling through eternity in order to create the present world. The objection, however, does not work. There is simply no evidence of earlier designs or efforts. There is, therefore, no necessity in postulating or speculating about processes of trial and error. It would mean going beyond the present evidence and this is something which Hume himself insists we should never do.

Fifth, Hume argues that our experience of the world cannot prove the unity of God. We might as well say that the world was produced by a team of Gods. It is important to note exactly what Hume is getting at here. He is not suggesting that there are signs of conflicting design in the world. His point is that if we postulate a unanimous team of gods, then we are sticking closer to our experience. To take an analogy, in order to explain the production of a house, we would refer to the various kinds of craftsmen, the builder, the architect, the joiner and so on. By parity of reasoning one would posit a division of labour in the production of the world. As Hume remarks: 'Why may not several Deities combine in contriving and framing a world? This is only so much greater similarity to human affairs.'

Sixth, Hume argues that there is nothing in our experience which permits us to exclude the sexuality and mortality of the divinity. Swinburne attempts to refute the last two arguments by arguing that God, conceived as the ultimate foundation of all causal connections, must be disembodied. We shall later examine the success or otherwise of this argument.

Hume has another general point concerning the legitimacy of any probability arguments concerning God as the designer of the world. We shall be concluding the discussion with this point.

Swinburne's argument

Swinburne distinguishes two kinds of regularity:

(a) regularities of co-presence – these are patterns of spatial order; and
(b) regularities of succession – these concern the behaviour of objects in a regular fashion in accordance with the laws of nature.

Whereas Cleanthes began his defence of the argument with co-presence, Swinburne starts from succession. He has two reasons for doing this. The first is that such regularities are all pervasive, that is, we are dealing with universal laws of nature. The second is that he regards succession as more basic than co-presence. In saying that they are more basic, he means that developments in science show that regularities of co-presence can be accounted for by supposing natural laws to have acted on an initially chaotic state. Regularities of succession are not, however, to be explained by appealing to more regularities of succession. They are, according to Swinburne, to be explained in terms of personal agency, if they are to be explained at all. He tells us that we have a choice either to accept regularities of succession, such as the basic laws of atomic physics, as unexplained brute facts, or to explain them in terms of personal and rational agency. The latter choice is to be preferred as it fits in well with regularities of succession known to have been produced by human, rational agency. Swinburne is claiming that there is a similarity between those regularities of succession known to have been created by human agency and the fundamental regularities, namely, the laws of nature. We should therefore postulate a fundamental rational agency.

Swinburne has another reason for opting for the rational agency thesis. He claims that the thesis is supported by the consideration that its acceptance would simplify all our explanations by tracing them to one principle. All our explanations would follow from this principle and this, he claims, is in line with the ultimate aim of science.

Swinburne argues that if we postulate a personal and rational agency as the fundamental explanation of regularities of succession, then such an agency must be disembodied. He argues that any body, for example, my body, is distinguished from any other part of the universe by my controlling it *directly*. This applies to anyone's body. The other parts of the universe are controlled *indirectly* by my moving my body or you moving your body. The natural laws which make this indirect control possible exist independently of me. If God had a body, then He would have to control some parts of the universe via independent natural laws. This would mean that His existence would not explain all the regularities of succession. By showing that the producer of fundamental regularities of succession must be incorporeal, Swinburne disposes of Hume's sixth objection. It does not, however, dispose of the fifth. Swinburne's proof of God's incorporeality does mean that Hume's 'team of gods' could not be distinguished by their bodies. Hume's argument, though, does not require them to have bodies. Hume could easily claim that several different intelligences working as a team can be postulated.

Another issue on which Swinburne takes Hume to task is the one we referred to earlier concerning Hume's general principle of what we can legitimately infer from a given effect. Swinburne claims that our understanding is not advanced by saying that the cause of any given effect has a characteristic exactly sufficient to produce that effect and nothing more. Thus, if you were asked what produced a particular effect, then it would be futile to reply that it was a power in the cause to produce that effect and nothing more. Such a reply would indeed be futile. The problem is that it is not Hume's reply. On Hume's account the effects can be specified and so can the character in the cause which produces the effect. There is nothing futile about such specifications. They are highly informative. It is possible to criticise Hume's principle on other grounds. He tends to overlook the fact that most of the important scientific hypotheses say more than can be actually tested. They predict more than the actual event which gave rise to the formulation of the hypotheses. Hume should be taken as making the point that when the cause is known *only* by the effect, as in the design argument, then we shall not attribute to it more than is necessary to produce that effect. Not all scientific causes are known solely by their effects.

The question of prediction is problematic. In the case of the design argument, it is not clear what we can predict with God as postulate that we cannot predict with Hume's Epicurean hypothesis. This leads to a serious problem with Swinburne. To say of some regularity of succession that it exists because God wills it does not really add to our understanding. This is markedly so if we get the same answer concerning different regularities of succession. The introduction of God's will does not afford the same kind of understanding that one is accustomed to in science.

Another difficulty with Swinburne concerns the nature of the similarity between those regularities of succession produced by human agency and the fundamental ones. It is unclear what is meant by regularities of succession produced by human agency. If, for example, he is referring to machines and the way they work, then the resemblance becomes very non-specific. The universe is not like a telephone exchange or piston engine.

The final problem with Swinburne concerns the notion that the rational agency thesis simplifies our explanations by reducing them all to one principle. We must not confuse simplification with the ideal of having one type of explanation. There is nothing contradictory in supposing that physical science could use one type of explanation and yet be extremely complex in structure.

Neither the approach of Cleanthes and Paley nor that of Swinburne provides us with a proof of a designer of the universe. There is another approach to which we referred earlier, namely, that some aspects of the universe cannot be accounted for by appealing to the properties of matter. An example of this kind of approach is the claim that there is a tendency in evolution that cannot be accounted for by classical Darwinism. The tendency in question is the emergence of self-conscious beings. We cannot here pursue this but the reader should be aware of a general difficulty with this type of argument. Even if it could be shown that there are features of the natural world that cannot be accounted for by the basic tendencies of matter, it is not clear just what would follow from this. It could be taken as an incentive to improve one's theory of matter. A guider or designer cannot be established by appealing simply to the inadequacy of current scientific theory. What needs to be shown is a purpose in the way matter behaves rather than that there are gaps in science.

Although the argument from design falls short of constituting a proof of God's existence, perhaps it at least shows that the existence of a designer is probable. Anyone who feels attracted to this suggestion must face another of Hume's challenges. In order for us to make judgements concerning causes and effects, we need to have observed the constant conjunctions of the relevant events. In order to judge the probability of a particular cause producing a particular effect, we need to know the frequency of such conjunctions in the past. This is what probability judgements have to be based on.[6] Hume is stressing the importance of experience in determining probability judgements. In the case of the design argument, we have no experience of how universes begin, and, therefore, cannot make a probability judgement concerning the universe. It is a case which Hume refers to as being single, individual, without parallel or specific resemblance.[7] He is not saying that the probability is difficult to calculate; he is making the conceptual point that the concept of probability can have no application to such a singular case.

The cosmological argument

This is an argument which is based on the observed fact of change and causal contingency and concludes with a being which is the ground or ultimate cause of these but is not itself subject to them. The classic source material for this family of arguments is Aquinas' *Summa Theologica.* In Aquinas' five ways of proving the existence of God, the first three are cosmological arguments. Let us take the first way for our model argument. It can be expressed in the following sequence:

(1) Some things are in motion. (Observed fact)
(2) Whatever is in motion is being moved by something else.
(3) This something else is either itself in motion or not in motion. (Tautology)
(4) If it is not in motion, then it is an unmoved mover.
(5) If it is in motion, then it is being moved by something else again.
(6) One cannot go back *ad infinitum* in the series of moved movers, that is, in the series of movers that cause motion by themselves being in motion.
(7) Therefore, there is an unmoved mover. (An unmoved mover causes motion without itself being in motion.)
(8) This all men think of as God.

Aquinas has the following secondary argument to prove proposition (6) above:

(i) Assume that the series of moved movers goes back *ad infinitum.*
(ii) If that is the case, then there is no prime mover.
(iii) But second movers cause motion only if they are moved by a prime mover.
(iv) Therefore, there are no second movers.
(v) Therefore, there are no movers at all.
(vi) But we know that some things are in motion.
(vii) Therefore, assumption (i) is false as it entails (v) which we know to be false.

Before embarking on a discussion of this argument, there are some preliminary remarks to be made. The term 'motion' has a technical sense here. It refers to any kind of change, whether it is in quantity or quality, as well as change in spatial position. The second point is that the conclusion, proposition (8) of the main argument, does not establish that the cause of the motion has any of the traditional attributes of God. The most it can show is that there is a first cause or prime mover. It will not necessarily follow from that that such a cause is an appropriate object of worship. We can now turn our attention to the question of whether the argument succeeds in establishing that there must be a first cause or prime mover.

There is a problem concerning proposition (iii) in the secondary argument. It is not self-evidently true to say that second movers cause motion only if they are moved by a prime mover. What is self-evident is that second movers cause motion only if they are moved by an *earlier* mover. This leaves it an open question as to whether the earlier mover is moved or not. If this weaker claim is substituted for (iii), then Aquinas cannot reach his conclusion.

Although (iii) is not self-evidently true, neither is it self-evidently false. This raises the question of how we can know whether it is true or false. Observation cannot settle the issue. We cannot settle it in this way for even if we found an unmoved mover at the end of a caused series, this would not establish the truth of the claim. The claim is in the form of a universal generalisation. It is concerned with *all* second movers and we cannot investigate all these or be sure that the ones we have investigated are all the ones that there are. The claim cannot be falsified by observation either. If we failed to find an unmoved mover at the end of a series, there would always be a further step backwards and there seems to be no theoretical end to this. A consideration of the meaning of the terms or a conceptual analysis will not settle the question of the truth or falsity of (iii). In the light of these considerations perhaps our most profitable approach is to examine the implications of retaining or rejecting (iii).

The question to ask here is why did Aquinas think that he needed (iii). We need a clear understanding of the causal series that Aquinas is talking about. Patterson Brown[8] has distinguished two kinds of causal series.

(A) *The Essentially Ordered Causal Series*
This has the following form:

> *a's* being *F* causes *b* to be *G*
> *b's* being *G* causes *c* to be *H*
> *c's* being *H* causes *d* to be *I*

The lower case letters refer to any objects and the capital letters refer to their causal properties. The essential feature of the series is that except for the first and last members, if there are any, each member is causally dependent on its predecessor for its own causal efficacy regarding its successor. Thus, for example, *b's* causal efficacy is the possession of *G* and this is acquired by *b* being changed by its predecessor, *a*. The fact that *b* becomes *G* due to *a* is not an accident. There is some necessity in the causal series.

(B) *The Accidentally Ordered Causal Series*
This has the following form:

> *a's* being *F* causes *b* to be *G*
> *b's* being *H* causes *c* to be *I*
> *c's* being *J* causes *d* to be *K*

In this series the causal efficacy of each member does not depend on the action of its predecessor. Here *b* changes *c* by virtue of being *H*, but *b's* being *H* has no connection with any effect which *a* has on *b*. This series is represented by Aquinas' remark that it is not essential for any particular hammer to act after the action of another. Similarly, it is not essential for any particular man *qua* begetter to be begotten by another man, for he begets *qua* man not *qua* son of another man. Aquinas' point is that a man begets by virtue of being a man and not by virtue of himself being begotten. The causal power of begetting is dependent upon the member of the series being a man rather than on its predecessor of the begetter himself being begotten.

Having distinguished these two kinds of causal series, we must now ask what kind of series Aquinas was working with in the first way. He uses the example of a hand moving a stone with a stick. The hand moves the stick and this in turn moves the stone. We have the simultaneous movement of the three members of the series. In this case if someone were to ask what was the immediate cause of the stone's motion, the answer would be the stick's motion. As we have seen from our setting out of the cosmological argument, Aquinas holds that whatever is in motion is being moved by something else. There is some kind of necessity in this. Aquinas regards motion as being necessarily a caused property. The above example used by Aquinas is an essentially ordered series of a special kind. We are dealing with the same property (motion) throughout and all changes are simultaneous. Aquinas believed that such a series could not go back *ad infinitum*. This would be a logical impossibility. An accidentally ordered series could, in principle, go back *ad infinitum*, though in fact Aquinas thought they all ended in a final point, God. Having established that the hand moving the stick which moves the stone is an essentially ordered series, as the stick is dependent on its predecessor in regard to its causal efficacy in moving the stone, we have to ask why such a series cannot go back for ever. The answer to this depends on Aquinas' two implicit claims:

(a) For every event it must be possible to speak of the cause of that event.
(b) The causal relationship in an essentially ordered series is transitive.

When we have an essentially ordered series, like that of hand, stick and stone, we are logically bound to say that the hand moves the stone. Combining (a) and (b) with such a series, we find that if there is no unmoved mover at the beginning of the series, then there is no such thing as the cause of a later event in the series. This is why Aquinas held that such a series could not go back *ad infinitum.*

It can, however, be objected against Aquinas that there is no real problem here as the concept of *the* cause has no application to such a series. Aquinas would regard such a claim as amounting to a denial of a first cause in the series and thus implying the non-existence of all subsequent causes in the series. This is a confusion which can be avoided. Kenny in *The Five Ways* has said that Aquinas confuses the concept of *the* cause having no application with the denial of a first cause. Let us take an example to clarify the issue.

Suppose that a tree crashes to the ground after being struck by lightning, and we know that there were no other factors present which might have caused the tree to fall. If Aquinas is right, then it would be incorrect for us to say that the lightning caused the tree to fall as the motion of electrical discharges which constitutes the lightning was itself caused, and, arguably, essentially caused. On Aquinas' account it is the cause of *this* motion which has the better claim to be called *the* cause. It is Aquinas' concept of *the* cause that implies we are wrong to call the lightning the cause. This raises a problem for him.

The concept of *the* cause which is ordinarily used is quite different from the one used by Aquinas. The reader should consider how we normally use the concept of *the* cause. In our example of the tree, we would look for a factor present when the tree fell that was not present at times when the tree was standing. The different factor was the lightning and this enables us to speak of *the* cause. When we speak of lightning as *the* cause we do not mean that the lightning was uncaused. Aquinas was misled by the example of the hand moving the stick which moved the stone. If we asked what caused the stone to move, it would be odd to say the stick's motion as a stick is inert. If there is a problem with the stone's motion, then there is the same problem with the stick's motion. We can thus identify Aquinas' error as follows: he thought that the same problem arises with the stick's motion *just because* the stick's motion is caused, thus, he continued, an explanation in terms of a caused phenomenon will not do. In our example of the tree, we know that when trees are struck by lightning they often fall. We just do not need to go on to ask what was the cause of the lightning in order to get an explanation of why the tree fell. We can allow that lightning is a caused phenomenon *and* that an appeal to it furnishes us with a satisfactory explanation.

Aquinas can therefore be charged with misunderstanding his own example and confusing satisfactory explanations and uncaused phenomena. We can end this part of the discussion by saying that the rejection of (iii) does not have any unacceptable implications.

I now want to turn to the second premiss of the main argument, 'whatever is in motion is being moved by something else'. Aquinas inherits this idea from Aristotle. The idea is that change of any kind is always the transmission of a property from one thing to another and that like causes produce like effects. Thus motion can only be caused by something in motion. This is not inevitably true. In order to see that it is not, the reader should contrast it with Newton's Law of Inertia:

> Every body perseveres in a state of rest or of uniform motion in a straight line unless compelled to change by forces impressed thereon.

If we inquire as to why something is in motion, Aquinas tells us that something else must be moving it. Newton thinks that this is a possible answer, but it is not the only answer. In accordance with the Law of Inertia, one could say that it was moving earlier, at the same speed and in the same direction, and since then, no external force has been impressed upon it. We need not appeal to anything except the moving body itself. Neither Aquinas nor Newton thinks that motion is self-explanatory. Newton, however, does not think that motion in general points to something motionless as its cause. In Newton's system motion can be explained in terms of the earlier states of some entity in conjunction with freedom from other forces.

The cosmological argument presented in Aquinas' first way does not constitute a proof. We have seen that (iii) in the secondary argument can be rejected, and hence (6) in the main argument remains unproven. We have also seen that (2) of the main argument need not be accepted.

I want to conclude our discussion with a criticism made by Hume which applies to Aquinas' first two ways. In the second way Aquinas attempts to show that although an accidentally ordered series can go back *ad infinitum*, such a series implies the existence of an essentially ordered series, which, Aquinas held, could not go back *ad infinitum*. Given the serious nature of Hume's objection to asserting the necessity of a first cause, I shall quote in full from S IX of the *Dialogues*. The argument is between Demea, its proponent, and Philo who opposes it:

> 'The argument', replied Demea, 'which I would insist on is the common one. Whatever exists must have a cause or reason of its existence; it being absolutely impossible for any thing to produce itself, or be the cause of its own existence. In mounting up, therefore from effects to causes, we must either go on in tracing an infinite succession, without any ultimate cause at all; or must at least have recourse to some ultimate cause, that is necessarily existent: Now that the first supposition is absurd may be thus proved. In the infinite chain or succession of causes and effects, each single effect is determined to exist by the power and efficacy of that cause, which immediately preceded; but the whole eternal chain or succession, taken together, is not determined or caused by any thing: and yet it is evident that it requires a cause or reason, as much as any particular object, which begins to exist in time. The question is still reasonable, why this particular succession of causes existed from eternity, and not any other succession or no succession at all.'

Demea is arguing against the supposition that the universe may have always existed. He is claiming that the universe as a whole requires an initiating cause. Philo replies:

> in tracing an eternal succession of objects, it seems absurd to inquire for a general cause or first author. How can any thing, that exists from eternity, have a cause, since that relation implies a priority in time and a beginning of existence?
>
> In such a chain too, or succession of objects, each part is caused by that which preceded it, and causes that which succeeds it. Where then is the difficulty? But the WHOLE, you say, wants a cause. I answer, that the uniting of these parts into a whole, like the uniting of several distinct counties into one kingdom, or several distinct members into one body, is performed merely by an arbitrary act of the mind, and has no influence on the nature of things. Did I show you the particular causes of each individual in a collection of twenty particles of matter, I should think it very unreasonable, should you afterwards ask me, what was the cause of the whole twenty. This is sufficiently explained in explaining the cause of the parts.

The most damaging objection made by Hume here is that thinking of the universe *as a whole* is an arbitrary act of the mind. This point can be turned against the actual example used by Aquinas in the second way. The example is that of the series of fathers and sons. The series of a man's male ancestors is a series of effects and causes. Let us assume that the series goes back *ad infinitum*. For any member of that series, we can explain his existence by referring to the next member back. If we are then asked to explain the existence of the series *as a whole,* our problem would lie in understanding what it was that needed explaining. There is no *further* explanation in addition to the explanation of the individual members.

Although it is true to say that not all cases of seeing things as wholes are arbitrary acts of the mind, we still cannot come to the aid of Demea or Aquinas. A non-arbitrary whole can be defined as something whose existence is not to be explained solely in terms of its individual parts. An arbitrary whole simply is the sum of its parts, and the universe is the sum of its parts. In the case of non-arbitrary wholes it is always possible to distinguish parts that belong to them from parts that do not. In the case of the universe such a distinction is impossible as the universe incorporates all that there is. Hume's argument is a powerful one and it is difficult to see any way of overcoming it.

The ontological argument

(a) Anselm's argument.   The most famous and historically most important version of this argument is presented by St Anselm (1033–1109). The argument has a long philosophical history. It is a unique argument in that it attempts to prove the existence of God by purely logical means. There is no

appeal to a first cause or to the way things are in the world or to religious experiences. It attempts to derive the proposition 'God exists' on conceptual grounds alone.

The first version of the argument that we are to consider is to be found in the second chapter of Anselm's *Proslogion*. Anselm takes the case of the biblical fool who says in his heart 'There is no God'.[9] In order for the fool to express his atheism, he must understand his own words. He must understand what is meant by 'God', namely, something than which nothing greater can be conceived. Given that he understands this, then something than which nothing greater can be conceived must stand in relation to his understanding (literal translation: 'is in his understanding'). It is greater to exist in reality *and* the understanding than to exist in the understanding alone. But if something than which nothing greater can be conceived existed only in the understanding, then it would be possible, by conceiving it to exist in reality, to conceive of something greater than that which nothing greater can be conceived. This would be logically impossible. So, Anselm concludes, 'something than which a greater cannot be conceived undoubtedly both stands in relation to the understanding and exists in reality'.

Anselm needs to establish that something than which nothing greater can be conceived exists in the fool's understanding. He can then go on to argue that it is greater to exist in reality than just in the understanding. If such a conception existed only in the understanding, then it would be possible to conceive of something greater. Such a conception is impossible. Therefore, something than which nothing greater can be conceived must exist in reality as well as the understanding.

There are objections to the claim that something than which nothing greater can be conceived exists in the fool's understanding. It has been argued that Anselm is misusing the following general principle:

> If one understands an expression for x, then x exists in one's understanding.

If you allow the Anselmian substitution of x and something than which nothing greater can be conceived, then you get unacceptable logical implications, such as the falsity of all generalisations.[10]

A second objection that could be made concerns the object-directedness or intentionality of 'to understand an expression for x'. It could be said that whereas the fool understands an expression for something than which nothing greater can be conceived, he does not *know* of such a thing. It is therefore not legitimate to say that it is in his understanding.

We can summarise the next stage of the argument as follows:

(1) Something than which nothing greater can be conceived exists in the understanding only.

(2)   So it can be conceived to exist in reality too.
(3)   To exist in reality is greater than to exist in the understanding only.
(4)   So it is possible to conceive of something greater.
(5)   Therefore that than which nothing greater can be conceived exists in reality as well as in the understanding.

Proposition (4) is self-contradictory, therefore (1) is false. Proposition (1) can be false for two reasons:

(a)   Something than which nothing greater can be conceived may not exist at all, or
(b)   It exists in both the understanding and in reality.

Anselm wants to exclude (a) as a way of falsifying (1). He attempts to do this by appealing to the fact that the intelligibility of the fool's words means that he has something in his understanding. Even if this is allowed, there is still a problem with (5). Anselm's concept of God is 'the unsurpassable being'. He has not established that there is anything corresponding to the concept. The expression 'the unsurpassable being' is an expression of the form 'the so and so'. This expression presupposes the existence of one being which fits the description. The argument relies on a premiss containing a definite description. A definite description is a denoting phrase containing the definite article and it presupposes the existence of something corresponding to the description. When, for example, you use expressions like 'the first man on the moon' or 'the man who stole the crown jewels', you imply, by the use of the definite article, that there is someone or something which conforms to the description. Thus for Anselm to use such an expression or its equivalent is to beg the question. He cannot prove the existence of such a being while at the same time presupposing its existence.

(b) Gaunilo's criticism of Anselm.   Gaunilo provides us with something of a send-up of Anselm's argument. Gaunilo offers us a tongue-in-cheek proof of the existence of an island known not to exist. The argument is presented in S 6 of Gaunilo's *On Behalf of the Fool*. The island in question is said to be the most excellent land and Gaunilo understands the expression 'the most excellent land'. It therefore stands in relation to his understanding. If it existed in his understanding *alone*, then it would not be the most excellent land. It must therefore exist in reality too. We can set the argument out in the following sequence:

(1)   He understands the expression 'best island'.
(2)   Therefore, the best island exists at least in his understanding.
(3)   Whatever really exists is superior to what exists in the understanding alone.
(4)   Therefore, if the best island exists in his understanding alone, then it is inferior to any existing land.

(5)   But he understands that island to be the most excellent land.
(6)   Therefore, he cannot doubt that it exists in reality as well as the understanding.

Gaunilo identifies the error for us: 'to accept that the lost island's superiority was in my understanding as something truly and indubitably existing and not as something false or uncertain'. This implies that he should not have accepted (2) above. That proposition should not be accepted until you know such an island to exist in reality. The description 'best island', where 'best' incorporates existence, cannot be applied to any place until you know that there is such a place. The analogy with Anselm is that he ought not to have accepted that something than which a greater cannot be conceived stands in relation to the fool's understanding until he knew such a being to really exist. This is a different criticism from the definite descriptions, one where presupposition of existence was the problem. Gaunilo is claiming that, where descriptions apply to real existents, they should not be used until it is known that there is something to which they apply.

J. H. Hick[11] has pointed out an important difference between Gaunilo's and Anselm's arguments. Gaunilo's argument concerns a contingent existent, namely an island, whereas Anselm's concerns God whose existence is necessary. If you incorporate 'existence' into the subject of the argument, as in the case of 'excellent island', then you can always extract 'exists' and conclude that something exists corresponding to the subject. There will be no theoretical limit to what could be proved on parallel arguments to Gaunilo's. There is, however, an important difference between the concept of God and the various possible subject-concepts of the arguments. Although existence is incorporated into the concept of God, this is not an accidental feature, as it would be, say, in the concept of an existent-lion. In this latter case the linking of the two components is contingent or external. In the case of God and perfection (from which existence is derived) the connection is internal or necessary. Perfection, which is held to entail existence, is a defining feature of God. We shall discuss the implications of this via the Cartesian reformulation of the argument.

(c) Descartes' argument.   This reformulation occurs in *Meditation* V. He tells us that existence can no more be separated from the essence of God than the fact that the sum of its angles is equal to two right-angles can be separated from the essence of a triangle. He uses another analogy, the idea of a mountain cannot be separated from the idea of a valley. You can no more conceive of God not existing than you can conceive of a mountain without a valley. He is claiming that existence is a logically necessary property of God, or 'the supreme being', in the same way that certain properties of a triangle are necessary or the connection between mountain and valley is logically necessary.

Descartes then moves on to consider a possible criticism of his argument. The objection is that granted you cannot conceive a mountain without a valley or a triangle without its logically necessary properties, it does not follow from this that there are *in fact* any mountains or triangles. So, the objection runs, although existence is part of your conception of God, it does not follow from this that there is a God corresponding to your conception. As Descartes himself remarks, 'my thought imposes no necessity on things'.

His reply to this is that although ideas of mountains and valleys cannot be separated regardless of whether such things exist, the case of God is different. He cannot be conceived without existence, therefore, existence is inseparable from Him, and therefore, He really exists. Descartes holds that the proposition 'God exists' is a necessary truth. It is analytic.

There are a number of objections that can be brought against Descartes. There is a very obvious gap in his reasoning. The reader should realise that Descartes is not claiming to have any direct experience of God. He claims to have an abstract idea of God, and the gap lies in his getting from the abstract idea to an existent being. He tells us that because he cannot conceive God except as existing, it follows that existence is inseparable from Him, and therefore, He exists. All he was entitled to say was that existence was inseparable from his *idea* of God. He has still not bridged the gap between idea and real existence.

The most important objections to Descartes were made by Kant.[12] Kant argued that proponents of the ontological argument were guilty of the logical error of treating existence as a predicate. His point is that 'existence' is not a genuine property of things akin to properties such as 'being red', 'being square', 'being soft'. The point that Kant is making is that if you list the properties of, say, a cricket ball, as being spherical, being hard, having a leather cover and so on, and go on to say that it exists, then you have not thereby added a further property akin to the other three. You are merely saying that there is something which has those properties or of which those predicates can be asserted. It is clear from our exposition of the Cartesian argument that Descartes regarded existence as being a property – a necessary property – of God. It is this which Kant is questioning. Whereas it is true that expressions like 'being red', 'being round' and so on along with 'exists' function as grammatical predicates, there is a difference. In the case of 'exists' surface grammar leads us astray. Kant holds that 'existence' differs from other grammatical predicates in that to ascribe existence to something adds nothing to the conceptual content of that thing: 'By whatever and by however many predicates we may think a thing – even if we completely determine it – we do not make the least addition to the thing when we further declare that the thing is' (*Critique* A600/B628).

Important as this Kantian criticism is with its identification of the issue of existence and predication, it requires further logical refinement. The claim that the attribution of existence adds nothing to the subject concept has drawbacks. This is a highly technical question but there is a *prima facie* case for an objector to complain that, for example, an existent Loch Ness Monster is very different from a non-existent one and to know that such a thing existed would make a real difference to our knowledge. (The technical question centres on whether this should be regarded as adding to *conceptual* content.) Kant seemed to be aware of problems like this when he conceded that a hundred real thalers would affect his financial position in a way that a hundred imaginary ones would not.

The greater logical sophistication is to be found in Russell's theory of descriptions. In Russell's technical writings on logic, one of his key notions is that of a propositional function. This is an expression which contains undetermined constituents, for example, 'n is a number', 'x is a man', 'x is a unicorn' and so on. In order to get a proposition we have to fill them in or 'determine' them. Now to say that men exist is to say that the propositional function 'x is a man' is true for some value of x. To say that unicorns do not exist is to say that the propositional function 'x is a unicorn' is false for all values of x. Russell's point is that some philosophers have treated predicates like existence as if they were properties of particular things, rather than about propositional functions. In the above examples, when you say that men exist or unicorns do not exist, you are not attributing the property of existence to men or the property of non-existence to unicorns. What you are doing is talking about the respective propositional functions and saying that the concept 'man' is instantiated, whereas the concept 'unicorn' is not. When you take a propositional function and assert that it is true for some values of its undetermined constituents, then you have arrived at the meaning of 'exists'. This is neatly expressed in the epigram, 'To be is to be the value of a propositional function'. Russell is saying that existence is not to be regarded as a property of God or of anything else. It is to be analysed in terms of the propositional function.

Kant has a second objection to the Cartesian argument (*Critique* A594–8/ B622–6). We saw that Descartes drew an analogy between the logically necessary properties of a triangle and the logically necessary properties of God. In addition to the problem of regarding existence as a predicate, there is a further objection to Descartes' procedure. Kant expresses it thus: 'the unconditional necessity of judgements is not the same as an absolute necessity of things'. What does Kant mean by this?

He is quite happy to say that we cannot admit that there are triangles and deny their logically necessary properties as that would be self-contradictory. In Kant's terms, you cannot retain the subject and deny the predicate. This does not, however, commit him to the validity of the ontological argument. You can deny subject *and* predicate without contradiction. There is no contradiction in saying that there are no triangles. Thus Descartes' analogy does not give the conclusion he wants. To say that God does not exist is to deny the existence of a supreme being together with all it predicates. This no more involves a contradiction than does the denial of the existence of triangles or mountains and valleys. Clearly, Descartes intended the proposition 'God exists' to be logically necessary or analytic. Kant considers the possible objection that there is a concept, God, whose rejection is self-contradictory. If there is, then Kant's argument above will no longer apply.

Kant's answer to this is that we cannot introduce the concept of existence, by defining it as part of perfection or by any other means, into the concept of the thing whose possibility is under discussion. If we do this, then all we succeed in doing is producing tautologies. We have included existence as a defining feature of the concept of the thing and then asserted that the thing exists. We cannot move from the concept of a supreme being to the actuality of such a being. This gap cannot be bridged by incorporating existence into the concept of the thing. Kant concludes by saying that:

> The attempt to establish the existence of a supreme being by the famous ontological argument of Descartes is therefore merely so much labour and effort lost; we can no more extend our stock of theoretical insight by mere ideas, than a merchant can better his position by adding a few noughts to his cash account. (*Critique* A602/B630)

I shall conclude our discussion of the ontological argument with a brief discussion of necessity.

(d) Necessity.   We saw in our preceding discussion that Descartes regarded the proposition 'God exists' as logically necessary. It is important to distinguish two kinds of necessity that have been used in discussions of God's existence. Failure to make this distinction can lead to faulty arguments. The kind of necessity that Descartes was using was logical necessity. This is the kind of necessity that is involved in saying that a triangle has three sides.

There is another sense of 'necessity' applied to God. This is the idea of a necessary being. Norman Malcolm[13] explains this idea by saying that it just does not make sense to regard God's existence, or any of His attributes, as being dependent upon, or conditioned by, anything else. Thus the notion of causal dependency, which is the hallmark of the world in general, can have no application to God. The kind of necessity involved here is that of God as an eternal or absolutely unlimited being. It corresponds to the attribute of aseity referred to in our discussion of the classical concept of God. Malcolm then offers the following version of the argument:

(1) God's existence is absolutely unlimited.
(2) Therefore, if God does not exist, He cannot come into existence; for if He did, He would either have been caused to come into existence, or have happened to have come into existence. Both would contradict (1).

(3) If God does exist, then He cannot have come into existence or cease to exist. This would also involve causality and contradict (1).

(4) We conclude from (2) and (3) that if God does not exist, then His existence is impossible, and, if He does exist, then His existence is necessary.

(5) Either God exists or He does not. (Tautology)

(6) Therefore, His existence is either impossible or necessary.

(7) His existence is not impossible as the concept is not self-contradictory.

(8) Therefore, God necessarily exists, that is, Necessarily God exists.

The fly in the ointment in this argument is the confusion between the two senses of 'necessary'. The type of necessity incorporated in the first premiss is that of aseity or lack of limitations. By the time we get to (6) this sense of 'necessity' has been transformed to that of logical necessity. This is how Malcolm arrives at the logical necessity of (8). We cannot, however, move from aseity as a divine attribute to the logical necessity of the existence of a being having the attribute. All we are entitled to conclude from Malcolm's argument is, '*If* God exists, then He exists eternally'. This is how (4) should be understood. The disjunction in (6) should be taken to mean that God's existence is either impossible or eternal. By excluding the first disjunct, we derive 'eternal existence' as a description of the nature of God's existence, *if* He exists. We cannot, however, derive the proposition that there is a being who has this nature. Propositions (2) and (3) unfold the meaning of aseity. It is possible for a necessary being to exist, where 'necessary' is understood in terms of aseity, but aseity does not permit the inference to actual existence.

To say that 'God exists' is logically necessary flies in the face of the empiricist tradition in philosophy. No existential statement is logically necessary. An opponent can claim that its necessity consists in the impossibility of 'God exists' being otherwise if it is true. We cannot, however, derive 'Necessarily God exists' from 'If God exists, then Necessarily God exists' without assuming the truth of the hypothetical clause.

The argument from religious experience

It is an undisputed fact that people claim to have experiences of God or experiences which are in some way revelatory. There are two central philosophical issues which arise out of such claims. The first concerns the possibility of such experiences. To raise the question of whether such experiences are possible is not to deny that people have particular experiences. It is to question whether those experiences can be described correctly as experiences of God. The problem is that if God is transcendent and timeless, then how can there be experience of Him in this world?

The second issue, and the one with which we are concerned, concerns the evidential status that these experiences can have in relation to the question of God's existence.

We need to distinguish three senses of 'vision':[14]

(1) *External visions*. What appears does so as part of the environment and may be confused as being part of the external world.
(2) *Imagined visions*. What appears does so as an object of vision but can be distinguished sharply from material objects.
(3) *Intellectual visions*. These involve a *feeling* of presence. They are religious experiences if they involve a divine person. The first two would be religious experiences if they involved seeing an angel, the Virgin Mary, etc. We are mainly concerned with (3).

The argument is normally expressed by saying that the occurrence of these intellectual visions is conclusive evidence for God's existence as the subject knows that he is being acted upon and is not just conjuring the whole thing up himself. The experience is regarded as self-authenticating. There is a difficulty with arguments of this type which has been pointed out by Flew. The authenticating characteristic of such experiences is some felt quality, let us refer to this as property F. Property F is either purely subjective or it is not. If it is purely subjective, then the statement that my experience had property F is true, if it is true, irrespective of the case in the external world. We have to explain how the occurrence of this felt quality carries some implication about the external world. It would imply something about the external world if it had already been established that God was responsible for property F. I would know through property F that God was communicating with me if I already knew that God was the cause of F. We cannot therefore begin with the experience and conclude from that that God exists. To do that would be to presuppose His existence.

There are more sophisticated versions of the argument from religious experience. H. P. Owen seeks to show an analogy between religious experience and ordinary, everyday experience of physical objects. The analogy is intended to show that religious experiences tell us that God exists in a similar way to our sense-experiences telling us that physical objects exist.

Owen invites us to consider the case in which he has an experience which he can minimally describe as seeming to see a table. The question is how does he set out to determine that the experience was neither illusory nor delusory. He suggests the following procedure:

(1) I would consider what my other experiences were on that occasion and see whether they cohered or fitted in with the questioned experience. This is an extension and correlation of experiences with a view to testing the questioned experience. At some time I am

obliged to assume that some of my experiences are veridical. This applies even when the questioned experience turns out to be illusory or delusory. (There is a similarity here with Descartes' reasoning in *Meditation* I, where he had to take something for granted.)

(2) I would ask other qualified observers what they seem to see, that is, do they seem to see a table? In this context 'qualified' means having normal vision and being in the right place at the right time. The existence of observers and things other than the table is assumed.

(3) Before the question of carrying out these tests arises, I must know that I was not dreaming or having an after-image.

What needs to be shown is that the table's presence *caused* him to see it. He wants to say that a believer can justify, in an analogous way, the claim that God caused him to have a religious experience. Let us suppose then that the experience is an intellectual vision and assume that it is given from the outside. In keeping with the analogy, we have to ask what corresponds to (1) and (2) above.

What other experiences are relevant to the validation of this religious experience? If we say other experiences of God, then we would be taking their truth for granted. We cannot do this as they are of the same character as that which is now being tested. Even if there were some justification for this (in (1) we do take for granted the existence of physical objects which are of the same character as the table) we would be taking for granted that God existed. In the case of the table we appeal to experiences with a different content, the truth of which does not involve or presuppose the existence of the table. Examples of these would be experiences of other physical objects which carry no presuppositions about the existence of the table.

On the question of qualified observers, it is difficult to say what qualifications would correspond to those in (2) above. It is difficult to specify them in a non-circular way and a way that does not immediately disqualify the experience from being a veridical one. Thus, for example, what corresponds to normal vision cannot be that they see or experience visions similar in nature to the one under investigation.

There is a further problem concerning the distribution of religious experiences. Christians will have Christian experiences, Hindus will have Hindu ones and so on. Religious systems can be incompatible – for example, monotheism and polytheism – so how can the religious experiences validate incompatible systems? It might be said that these differences are what one would expect as God manifests Himself in a way that respects the understanding and free will of man. A Hindu is aware, in a Hindu way, of the same God as the Christian is in a Christian way. This, however, changes the logic of the argument from experience. It began by arguing from experience to reality, it was then confronted with the distribution objection and conjectures are made in regard to this. But these are not based on experiences; they are made *to make* the experiences compatible with the claim that God exists. It is also very difficult to establish the criteria for saying that *different* experiences are of the *same* objective reality.

▶ Problems facing the religious believer

The possibility of a rational belief in miracles

To believe in the occurrence of at least one miracle, – the resurrection of Christ – is essential to the Christian faith. The Christian thus faces a challenge in S X of Hume's *Enquiry Concerning Human Understanding,* where the possibility of a rational belief in miracles is subjected to a number of criticisms.

Hume holds that experience can be our sole guide in reasoning concerning matters of fact. As not all effects are equally certain to follow from particular causes, there are differing degrees of assurance as to whether a particular effect will follow from a particular cause. A wise man (that is, a rational man) proportions his belief to the evidence. If our experience has shown us that events of type A and events of type B are constantly conjoined in all cases, then we have a 'full proof' that they will continue to be so conjoined in the future. If experience has shown us that events are not always so conjoined, but only sometimes are, then our judgement concerning their future conjunction involves weighing up the probabilities. If the events are more often than not so conjoined, then their future conjunction is probable.

Hume tells us that a miracle is a violation of a law of nature and that the operation of such laws has been established by firm and unalterable experience. Hume's argument is that it is never rational to believe that a miracle has occurred. The reason for this is that the rational man, in weighing up the evidence, weighs up the testimony of others (those who claim to have witnessed a miracle) against the universal experience of the invariability in the operation of laws of nature. Hume claims that it is always more credible for people to have been deceived or to deceive than for an event contrary to universal experience to occur.

On the question of the testimony of others, Hume points out that there is no necessary connection between such testimony and the events which it describes. We afford a credence to testimony because we usually find a conformity between testimony and event. The case of a miracle is, however, problematic. In this case our experiences of testimonies and natural events are at odds with each other. We can express the difficulty by saying that if testimony derives its credence and authority from a generally observed conformity to the pattern of events, then how can testimony *itself* be used as a proof that those very events are other than what has been universally experienced? In such a case we get, in Hume's words, 'a mutual destruction of belief and authority'. This is the deep point in Hume. There must, Hume says, be a uniformity of experience against every miraculous event in order for that event to warrant the title 'miracle'. This uniformity of experience is held to constitute a 'full proof' that such violations do not occur. This proof cannot, for Hume, be destroyed and neither can the miracle be rendered credible by any superior proof. In order for testimony to constitute a superior proof, then the falsity of that testimony must be more difficult to accept than the violation of the law of nature.

In the second part of S X Hume goes on to say that as a matter of fact we never have testimony which would constitute a superior proof. He claims that the number of witnesses is never so great as to constitute a superior proof. The second point he makes is the psychological one that talk about miracles engenders agreeable emotions and people are therefore too ready to affirm the miraculous. The third point is the anthropological one that accounts of miracles abound among uncivilised people, and even when civilised people assent to the miraculous, they have inherited such accounts from the barbarous. The fourth, and philosophically more important point, is that different religions have different miracles at their foundation. As such religions are contrary (Hume holds that whatever is different in religion is contrary) then in proportion that a miracle supports one system of which it is a part, it also destroys the systems of which it is not a part. In doing this it destroys the credit of testimony upon which the miracles of the other systems are built. The problem, however, is that it must rely on the credit of testimony. This is the point of Hume's remark that 'not only the miracle destroys the credit of testimony, but the testimony destroys itself'. In undermining testimony which is the foundation of other miracles – and this they are bound to do – the miracles undermine their own foundation.

Hume concludes his discussion by remarking that no testimony *has ever* amounted to a probability, let alone a proof, of a miracle. It should be noted that Hume is here presenting his conclusions as a factual matter. In earlier editions of the *Enquiry* he had made the stronger logical claim that no testimony *can ever possibly* amount to a probability or proof of a miracle. When he formulates his general maxim he reverts to the stronger claim that, 'no human testimony can have such force as to prove a miracle and make it a just foundation for any such system of religion'.[15] In the following paragraph Hume admits the possibility of miracles or violations of laws of nature which would be susceptible to proof from human testimony. This should be understood in terms of theoretical possibility. Hume's point would be that although such a violation was theoretically possible, the overwhelming evidence is against it. It cannot, therefore, *itself* have the status of evidence and stand as the foundation for a religious system. It would be logically odd to use as a foundation something whose very nature was inherently dubious. We can now move to a critical discussion of Hume's account.

When Hume says that we have a proof that certain events will continue to occur, given the occurrence of certain other events, he means that the universal experience of mankind has shown these events to be constantly conjoined. There is no necessity for Hume in the relation of cause and effect. On Hume's theory of causation there is nothing we can pick out as the causal power which necessitates the effect. Causal sequences are not known *a priori* like the truths of geometry.

Ninian Smart[16] draws two conclusions from Hume's position: (i) it is not impossible that something quite contrary to our previous experience should occur; and (ii) we have proof, in Hume's sense, that nothing contrary to our previous experience will occur. It is then claimed that Hume is involved in a paradox, 'he must fail to believe in a miracle, the violation of a law of nature, and yet on his general philosophical principles, experience being the sole guide he cannot rule out the theoretical possibility that such an event should occur'. The question for us to ask is whether Hume's position is so paradoxical.

What Hume has attempted to show is that from the outset the probabilities are always against the miraculous, and as the rational man apportions his belief according to the probabilities, it is not rational to believe in miracles. Suppose that I buy a raffle ticket in a raffle consisting of millions of tickets. It would be true to say that there is a theoretical possibility that my ticket will win, but it would be irrational of me to believe that I shall win. It would also be irrational of me to make plans for projects contingent on the eventuality of my winning. To admit a theoretical possibility does not entail that a belief in the realisation of that possibility is a rational belief. There is neither inconsistency nor paradox in saying that a miracle might occur though it is highly unlikely.

A second point to emerge here is that it is not likely to prove fruitful for the Christian to aim an attack on Hume's theory of causation and then attempt to show internal inconsistencies in Hume's position. If you substitute an account of causation in terms of natural necessity for Hume's constant conjunction thesis, then that is unlikely to be helpful to the defender of the miraculous.

There are problems with Hume's account. If he claims that testimony *can* never amount to good evidence for the occurrence of a miracle, then it is difficult to understand why he should complain that such reports emanate from too few or unreliable witnesses. If there *cannot* be such evidence, then why bother to examine what there is? It would be more consistent of Hume to claim that there could be such evidence, but, as a matter of fact, there is not. Unless we read Hume in this way, we can attach no sense to the project of examining what testimony there is.

Smart refers to another problem which Hume might have to face, namely, the evidence of one's own senses. If Hume were present at a miraculous event would he not be bound to believe the evidence of his own senses? Would he not also have to say that others to whom he related the experience are rationally bound to disbelieve him? No doubt Hume would reply that such a situation would not occur and we have no reason for believing that it could or would occur. Hume is basing his argument on universal experience and Smart is saying, 'but suppose that your experience were different'. Let us consider an example. In our experience objects do not remain suspended and unsupported in the air, they fall to the ground when dropped. If someone claimed to have dropped an apple and saw it fly toward the sun, then we would be sceptical of such a claim and this would be a rational scepticism. The question is whether it is a good *argument* against our scepticism to say, 'well suppose you saw it fly to the sun'. This would be to task us to *assume* what we have every good reason to deny.

However, it is open to the Christian to claim that these cases are not analogous. There is more than mere oddity involved in an event being classed as a miracle. It can be claimed that the Christian belief that God has caused some violations of the laws of nature, or at least violations of uniform experience, has to be seen in relation to what Christians believe that Christ did. The miraculous is not to be seen in terms of bizarre one-off events, but as a part of Christian theology. Christ was the embodiment of God's power in reversing Satan's work.[17] Christ is not to be regarded as a kind of super-magician. Rather than ask Hume to imagine himself present at an event which violates uniform experience, we must give the event an appropriate context. We could put the following question to Hume: suppose that you had seen Lazarus being raised from the dead *at Christ's command*, could you then doubt that it was Christ who had done this? Perhaps Hume's reply would be to make a counter-supposition, namely, that advocates of other religions asked him to imagine himself present at different and contrary miraculous events. What replies would he then be expected to make?

Hume's point that miracles cannot function as a foundation of religious belief is a valid one. In the Lazarus example the use of the term 'command' presupposes beliefs such as that of supernatural causation. Without presupposing such beliefs one cannot give any sense to the activity of issuing commands to the dead. Indeed, Smart himself draws such a conclusion when he says, 'that miracles by themselves could not serve as conclusive evidence of a divine revelation' (*PRT,* p. 56).

The Christian needs the idea of supernatural causation in order to distinguish a miraculous event from one which contravenes universal experience but seems quite random and to have no significance other than posing the question of how it is to be explained. This would be the case in our earlier example of the apple. Smart identifies and attempts to solve a number of problems associated with the idea of supernatural causation. He identifies the following three difficulties with the idea:

(1) There can be no comparable laws of supernature to be tested in the ways laws of nature can be tested.
(2) The cause is, in principle, unobservable.
(3) Supernatural explanations do not afford the same predictive power as natural ones.

In attempting to resolve the first problem Smart appeals to the way we explain human actions. He claims that we have an analogy in that such explanations do not appeal to laws of nature. We can, for example, explain why someone ran out of a room by saying that he had promised to be elsewhere at a certain time. In such a case we appeal to social institutions, such as promise-keeping, or to regularities in a person's behaviour, personal characteristics and so on. We can agree with Smart that this constitutes an explanation. The problem, however, is whether it constitutes an analogy. Smart wants to say that just as we can fit in the human action to be explained with known features of a person's behaviour, so we can fit in the miraculous with God's character. The trouble concerns just how comparable these cases are. Consider the case of miraculous faith-healing. Does appealing to God's character, or God's aim in reversing the work of Satan, tell us why only some are cured? Even if it were claimed that curing all would devalue the status of a miracle, we can still protest and ask why one particular person was saved rather than another. In the case of human explanations we can appeal to what we know of a person's character in order to establish, for example, who he will make promises to and who he will value so much that he will keep those promises come what may. We have knowledge of the person's character independently of the act to be explained. Such knowledge explains the *particularity* of the act. It is this specifiable particularity which is lacking in the appeal to God's character or nature. The Christian would certainly not want to say that random curing was part of the divine nature. An appeal to the mysteriousness of the divine nature can be of no use here. Such an appeal would not, by definition, have explanatory power.

The first difficulty is tied up with the third one concerning predictive power. It is not just explanations in terms of natural laws which have predictive power, but also explanations based on knowledge of a person's character. I can know how a person will behave in given circumstances without appealing to physics or chemistry. Knowledge of God's character or nature does not afford the same power of prediction in regard to miracles or anything else.

Let us now turn to the second difficulty identified by Smart. The problem here is that God, unlike the causation of natural science, is both unobservable and seems unrelated to predictive theory. Smart tells us: 'it may be absurd to try and fit all knowledge into a physical-scientific straitjacket. It is by no means obvious in advance that all knowledge must be based on public observation' (*PRT*, p. 45). There are two problems here for Smart. The first is that if 'public observation' is interpreted in a wide sense so as to include all that we see and hear in everyday life, in addition to what the scientist observes in his laboratory, then it is not clear why we should describe the derivation of knowledge from such diverse sources as constituting a 'straitjacket'. There is no absurdity in saying that all knowledge[18] is based on public observation in this wide sense. The second problem for Smart is that whereas he claims that not all knowledge is concerned with the publicly observable, or about natural processes, he also says it is clear that the more ignorant people are, the more events there will be which are inexplicable to them in terms of natural processes. There is a logical asymmetry here. On Smart's account, knowledge is not to be understood as explanatory power in terms of natural causation, yet ignorance, which is its opposite, is to be understood as the absence of explanatory power in terms of natural causation. Smart is measuring knowledge and ignorance by different yardsticks.

The idea of supernatural causation then seems fraught with difficulties. The supernatural must in some sense be understandable in order to count as an acceptable explanation. It must also remain mysterious in order to inspire awe and wonder.

The problem of evil

The problem is generated by the believer's acceptance of the following propositions: (1) God is omnipotent, (2) God is perfectly good, and (3) Evil exists. The problem is that the acceptance of any two seems to commit one to the rejection of the third. If any two are true, then the third is false.

In S X of Hume's *Dialogues* the matter is expressed by saying: Is God willing but unable to prevent evil, if so then He is impotent, if God is able to and unwilling, then He is malevolent. This is not just a problem that sceptics like Hume have raised. St Augustine remarks that either God cannot or will not abolish evil, if He cannot then He is not all powerful, if He will not then He is not all good. It might be argued that there are differing views on what counts as evil, but this will not make proposition (3) go away. It seems that no matter what conception of evil you have, that evil either has occurred or probably will occur. Augustine makes no attempt to explain away evil: 'Either that is evil which we fear, or the act of fearing is in itself evil.'[19]

In order to spell out the nature of the problem two further premisses are usually added to the three above. They are:

(A) Any good being eliminates evil as far as it can.
(B) There are no limits to what an omnipotent thing can do.

By combining (A) and (B) with (1) and (2), we would get:

(4) God eliminates evil completely.

The problem is that (4) is logically incompatible with (3). The religious critic must regard the additional premises as necessary truths. If they were just contingent, then it would be permissible for the theist to conjoin (1), (2) and (3) as a counter-example to either (A) or (B) and claim that one of them was false. The question thus becomes whether or not (A) and (B) are necessary truths. No one could argue about the necessity of (B). It is obviously necessary as it merely unfolds the meaning of 'omnipotent'. The issue will involve a discussion of the necessity of (A).

The theist needs to show that (A) is not a necessary truth. There are counter-examples which he could use to show that (A) was false. He could claim that there is no inconsistency in saying that a parent allows his/her child to get hurt in order for the child to learn not to do something which is harmful. The parent can still be a good parent. Another possible counter-example would be a doctor who allows the agony of withdrawal in order to effect a cure for drug addiction. In examples such as these, the theist brings in two evils in each. In both cases one evil is allowed to occur in order to prevent a greater one. The use of such examples implies that the toleration of an evil leads to the attainment of a good whose positive value outweighs the negative value of the evil and that the good in question can only be attained by the toleration of the evil. These would be the conditions under which people could legitimately allow evil to occur.

However, it may be argued that such conditions do not hold for an infinitely good and powerful God. It might be said that such a being could bring about the occurrence of these goods without bringing about the evils. To answer this objection the theist must claim that there are goods which *logically* entail the occurrence of some evil and that it is better for the evil and good to occur than for neither to occur. It is not a limitation on God's power to say that He cannot accomplish the logically impossible. We cannot even describe what is logically impossible. Thus if the theist can show that there are goods which logically presuppose evils and that it is better for both to occur than neither, then he can go on to claim that it is logically possible for God not to eliminate evil. He could claim that the world cannot be a better place without the occurrence of some evils as the goods which they, and only they, permit are goods of the highest sort.

This is the approach taken by Hick.[20] He considers a world without gratuitous, undeserved, destructive evils and argues that such a world would be robbed of the opportunity of true compassion, sympathy, unselfish kindness and goodwill, and these are the highest moral values. Such an approach as this can involve one in an extremely stern view of what constitutes a better world. If we are to justify the occurrence of evils by indicating their logically related goods, then we might, for example, have to say that a child struck with leukaemia has given its parents the opportunity to feel sympathy and real compassion. The difficulty is that even granting that some evils are necessary conditions for certain goods, we still do not know how much evil is necessary. There might be too much evil for there to be a good God.

Another difficulty is that some evils are necessary conditions for other evils rather than goods. Callousness would not be possible if it were not for the existence of other evils.

In amplifying the logical connections thesis, Hick refers to the fact that sometimes the direst calamities lead to graces of character that seem to make the calamity worthwhile. He admits that this may not in fact happen, but the calamity provides the opportunity for moral development or soul-making. To refer back to our example of the stricken child, it may well be the case that as a result of their terrible grief the parents develop highly desirable moral virtues or worthy souls. The calamity may bring them closer together and thus, in a sense, improve their relationship. One cannot help wondering, however, whether there are not less drastic ways of achieving such ends, and whether the value of such ends outweighs the affliction of the innocent. Again, it is not clear that the amount of these evils is the minimum necessary to achieve the good ends.

Hick remarks concerning the issue of soul-making: 'It may be that the very mysteriousness of this life is an important aspect of its character as a sphere of soul-making'.[21] When you adopt a soul-making or moral development solution to the problem of evil and are then presented with a case of a child who is deprived of the opportunity to develop, then you certainly have a mystery. It is not clear how an appeal to mysteriousness can help here. Philosophical inquiry is intended to clarify what appears mysterious and this is how our understanding is aided. Mysteriousness is the starting point of our inquiry not its terminating point. It seems necessary, as Hick says, for the Christian to believe in immortality in order to avoid instances of lives that do not have the opportunity for perfection and instances of pointless suffering. He says, 'if there are finally wasted lives and finally unredeemed sufferings, either God is not perfect in love or He is not sovereign in rule over His creation.'[22]

The idea of redemption is important to the Christian for the reasons given by Hick. Even if every evil in fact is a component of some moral good, it is surely false to say that the evil is outweighed by the goodness in all cases. Hick tells us that in the eyes of God the evil plus the redemption must be of more value than an innocence which permits neither. Hick is mainly concerned here with moral evil: 'It would be intolerable to think that God had allowed the fearful evil of sin without already having intended to bring out of it an even greater good than would have been possible if the evil had never existed.'[23] We are also told by Forsythe[24] that the justification of the process lies in its end which is redemption, 'and by this we mean that the last things shall crown the first ... the end will justify the means and the goal glorify a holy God'. Forsythe seems to be claiming that no matter what the means are in terms of evils, there can always be a justifying end. If one opts for a solution like this, then one has to include in the means cases like an unrepentant Mengele, who performed experiments on prisoners in Auschwitz concentration camp. Even granting that the redemption is not part of this world, we still have to conceive a world in which this could be justified. Mengele had a chosen means-ends project, but can we regard this as a part of some divine and infinitely good means-ends nexus? Is it the sort of thing that could ever be 'crowned'?

When presented with an example such as Mengele, the theist can argue that such evils are the outcome of people possessing free will. The free will defence might solve the problem of moral evil, but it will not solve the problem of other evils, such as natural disasters. The theist can claim that moral evils are the result of man's free decisions and it is the free choice of man that accounts for the other cases of evils not becoming a part of some good. (This latter claim presupposes knowledge of the existence of the evil.) This is to claim that in all cases of evil man is free to make the evil an opportunity for realising a greater good. In order to realise this goodness, God must leave men free. By not interfering He allows men to choose freely, and, when they choose wrongly, it is their doing and not God's. In answer to the question of why God permits evil, the theist can say that God wants man's free decision to make evils into components of some greater good. We have indicated parenthetically one obvious problem with this. Some evils occurred in such a way that no one could have turned them into greater goods.

A religious critic might also object that if these evils are so essential for the attainment of these higher goods, then why should we seek to get rid of them? Wouldn't removing such evils deprive us of the opportunities of attaining the goods which they make possible and thus reduce the total amount of good? This objection does not make much impact. The theist can reply that the lessening or eradication of an evil does not reduce the total good. It has the contrary effect of increasing it by realising the good for which that evil was a necessary condition.

There is another point which is of vital importance to the theist. He is not just saying that by realising the good, one has a better state of affairs in comparison with what existed before. He is also saying that the better state of affairs *emerged* from what had existed before. It therefore represents a moral progress. Thus the theist is not just saying that one state of affairs is better than another by comparison, he is also stressing the importance of one developing out of the other through the free choice of man. The theist can claim that the destruction of evils leads to a moral progress, and when those evils have been destroyed, moral possibilities of a different kind will be possible.

There have been a number of attacks on the free will defence. I shall mention those made by Flew[25] and Mackie.[26] Flew intends his attack to be an assault on the key position of the free will defence by showing that there is no contradiction in saying that God could have made people so that they *freely* chose what is right. If he can establish this, then he can conclude that: 'Omnipotence might have made a world inhabited by wholly virtuous people.'

Flew holds that it makes perfect sense to say that a person freely chose to do something because he was made in such a way by God. What does Flew mean by a 'free action'? He says that all human actions or decisions are determined by caused causes. An example of a caused cause which he cites is the state of one's endocrine glands. According to Flew, actions which result from such causes can be legitimately described as free. An unfree action would be one in which the agent was under pressure or duress. So if God made people in such a way that they felt no pressure in choosing what was right, their choices would be free and productive of goodness. The absence of felt pressure is not, however, a sufficient condition for an action to be described as free. People in hypnotic trances feel no pressures or constraints but we would not describe their acts as free. Flew has to add that a person could have acted otherwise. A serious difficulty now arises in his account of a free action. If all actions are determined by caused causes, then what sense can be given to the idea that a person could have acted otherwise? According to Flew a person can help doing something, for if he had chosen otherwise, he would have been able to act differently. In other words, given his capabilities and capacities, he could have acted otherwise, and yet what he does is completely determined by, or is the inevitable outcome of, caused causes. Thus on Flew's analysis of a free act a set of causal factors can exist which completely determine a person to perform an act A, and also some other act B, is a genuine alternative. Given the causal factors which completely determine that A will be done, it is possible that B and not A will be done. The argument collapses into self-contradiction.

Mackie's attack does not raise the freedom/determinism issue. His point is that if it is logically possible for a person to choose the good on some occasions, then it is logically possible for him to choose the good on all occasions. He then asks why God did not create a world in which we all freely choose the good. Such a world is a logical possibility, so why did God not bring it about? The problem here is that it is not clear how such a world would differ from a world in which it was impossible to choose evil. The difference could not be elucidated in terms of what was actually chosen as that would be the same in both worlds. An appeal to a temptation that was always overridden would not advance matters. For one thing temptation increases the likelihood of wrongdoing. Neither is it clear how any experiences in this other world could be identified as temptation. Hick has remarked, 'one who has attained to goodness by meeting and eventually mastering temptations ... is good in a richer and more valuable sense than would be one created *ab initio* in a state of innocence or virtue.'[27] A temptation that is always determined to be overridden could not give rise to the kind of goodness to which Hick is referring. No sense could be given to the notion of mastering a temptation unless there is a genuine threat of surrender. If God had made it so that the threat of surrender is always overcome, then in what sense *could* it be a genuine threat? It seems that if one adopts Mackie's position, then one has to say that a world of innocent automata is the best possible world.

If the free will defence is accepted, there is still a difficulty concerning such evils as natural disasters as they are not the outcome of the exercise of free choice. F. R. Tennant[28] has attempted to resolve this problem. Tennant holds that moral progress has displayed itself in human history on the whole and that being an example of moral progress is invaluable to some acts. Thus the extinction of *moral* evil is not essential to Tennant. The moral worth which is achieved in the stages of progress is necessarily an acquired quality and it is acquired by the person exercising his free choice. Tennant argues that such free choice can only exist within a regular order of nature. This regularity is a necessary condition for the making of predictions and probability judgements, for the having of ordered experiences and for the cultivation of habits. These are the features of life which ensure the possibility of the development of character and culture. This regular order is the condition of moral good. The regularity means, however, that it can harm sentient creatures. When faced with the problem of natural disasters, Tennant claims that they occur within the regular course of nature and such a course is necessary for the possibility of gaining moral worth. There are problems with this reply.

We cannot say with certainty that this ordered world is the one consisting in the least possibilities of evil consonant with moral development. Hick tells us that the world is not intended to be a paradise. We are meant to grow morally in an environment whose main purpose is not immediate pleasure, but the realisation of the most valuable potentialities of human personality. The problem here is that if a person created a situation in which other people would learn from their painful mistakes, or suffer pain when no mistakes are made, then we would criticise such a procedure. The theist is using two standards, one for people and another for God.

Some have claimed that God is absent from His creation.[29] This tends to arouse the sceptic into asking whether He has to be totally absent.

Divine foreknowledge and human freedom

This problem is generated through an alleged contradiction between the belief that God is omniscient and the claim that people can act freely. It has been argued that if God is omniscient, then He must know what we are going to do in advance of our doing it. We could not have acted in a way different from the one in which God knew we would act. If that is the case, then how can our acts be free acts as whatever is foreknown by God could not happen otherwise. The religious critic is trying to derive a contradiction between:

(a) God knew that X would do Y at T, and
(b) X freely chose to do Y at T.

Divine foreknowledge and human freedom are held to have contradictory implications. To say that God has foreknowledge has been taken to mean that if God knows that X will occur, then X must occur. This can be interpreted in two ways:

(1) If God knows that X will occur, then, at the time of knowing, conditions hold that make the occurrence of X inevitable.

This interpretation involves the claim that one can only be said to *know* that X will occur if conditions now hold that make X causally inevitable. It is a point about knowledge claims in general. If you adopt this view of divine foreknowledge then you are committed to saying that at any time whatsoever, and with regard to any event which is future relative to that time, conditions exist that make the future event causally inevitable.

Interpretation (1) does not seem to be in harmony with the way in which the concept of knowledge is ordinarily used. We can and do claim to know how a person will act without claiming that those actions are causally inevitable. We do not misuse the concept of knowledge if we say that we know that a person will freely choose a particular course of action. To take an example, my knowing which way my neighbour will vote in a forthcoming election does not entail that my neighbour's choice of candidate is not a free choice. By analogy, we can say that it is possible to claim that God knows how a person will act without implying that the act was causally inevitable.

(2) If God (or anyone) knows that p, then it must be the case that p.

This interpretation does not involve a specific feature of knowledge, such as the causal inevitability involved in (1), but rather a general feature thought to be essential to the application of the concept of knowledge. This interpretation itself can be understood in two ways:

(i)   Necessarily (if someone knows that p, then it is the case that p), or
(ii) If someone knows that p, then Necessarily (it is the case that p).

The first involves necessity of the *consequence*, whereas the second involves necessity of the *consequent*. The first is true, but the second is false. To see that (ii) is false, consider our earlier example of my neighbour's voting habits. The fact that I know which candidate he will vote for does not entail that it is a necessary truth that he votes in that way. Given that (ii) is false, the question is whether a contradiction can be derived from (i) concerning divine foreknowledge and human freedom.

It has been argued by J. R. Lucas[30] that such a contradiction can be derived. Proposition (i) is of the form 'Necessarily (if p then q)' or $N(p \supset q)$. What Lucas wants to derive is $N(q)$ from $N(p \supset q)$. In order to do this he requires the premiss $N(p)$. The argument would then have the form of: 1. $N(p \supset q)$, 2. $N(p) \ldots$, $\therefore$ 3. $N(q)$. The full argument is:

(1) Necessarily (if God foreknows that X will do Y, then X will do Y);
(2) Necessarily (God foreknows that X will do Y);
(3) Necessarily (X will do Y).

If (1) and (2) are correct then Lucas will establish the conclusion he wants, namely, the necessity of X's doing Y, and this would be incompatible with the claim that X might have performed some action other than Y.

The controversial aspect of this argument concerns the legitimacy of (2). Lucas is claiming that God foreknows by necessity whatever it is that He foreknows. On a strict logical interpretation of 'necessarily', it is correct to assert the necessity of a proposition if and only if the negation of that proposition entails a contradiction. The problem for Lucas is that the negation of (2) does not entail a contradiction. It can be argued that the statement that God foreknows that X will do Y is logically contingent. Its truth or falsity depends on whether, as a matter of fact, X does Y. There is, however, no independent logical necessity about X doing Y. Great care is needed in handling the modal operator 'necessarily' and one must always be clear as to how the necessity is derived.

I shall now consider briefly a different attempt at showing the incompatibility of divine foreknowledge and human freedom. N. Pike[31] has argued that if God foreknows that X will do Y and if it is also possible for X to perform some action other than Y, then it will be possible for God to hold a false belief. The belief will be rendered false if X does not perform Y. Pike wants to claim that it would be unacceptable for orthodox Christians to hold that it was possible for God to have held a false belief. The reason why he says that it would be unacceptable derives from the orthodox claim that God cannot in anything be mistaken. Pike takes this to mean, 'If any individual is God, that individual cannot hold any false beliefs.' The force of the 'cannot' is that of logical impossibility. Pike is claiming that it is logically impossible for any individual to be God and to hold a false belief. If it was in X's power to perform any act other than Y, then it would be possible for X to render false God's belief that X would Y. In saying that X

had this power, we are not saying that X has rendered false a belief held by God, but we are implying that it is logically possible for X to do this. It is in order to exclude that description of X's power that Pike needs to establish that it is logically impossible for God to hold a false belief. Pike has to regard God as *essentially* infallible. The objections against Pike will centre on this thesis of essential infallibility. They are concerned with the coherence of the notion of essential infallibility. The problem is whether it can ever be correct to say that a true statement ascribing the property of never believing anything false to an individual is a necessary truth. If it is correct to say this, then it will turn out that it is logically impossible for that individual to hold a false belief. A consequence of this that has been pointed out[32] is that any individual holding a false belief *could not* have been identical with any individual that never holds false beliefs. Assume that all of us are persons who in fact hold false beliefs. On Pike's account, it is logically impossible that any of us should have been individuals holding no false beliefs. There does not, however, appear to be a logical contradiction in supposing some of us to be such individuals. It might, of course, be highly improbable, but that is not the same as saying that it is contradictory.

Although there is a problem with essential infallibility, it could still be argued that it is precisely this concept which the orthodox have in mind when they say that God cannot hold false beliefs. Surely, the orthodox would want to say that God was incapable of error. It is possible to reply that this does not imply that it is logically impossible for God to err. It might be taken to mean[33] that God is free of those limitations that make human beings prone to error in their beliefs. The problem with this reply is that God might be regarded by the orthodox as free from *all* limitations. The orthodox will at least have to specify what limitations could apply to a being which is supposed to be able to do anything that is not contrary to the laws of logic.

There are alternative solutions to this problem which we cannot pursue. I can only suggest them. First, it might be argued that God's omniscience should not be understood in a temporal sense. He knows everything in a timeless way and not in terms of past, present and future. God might be said to be aware of the totality of events in the history of the universe in a stable and unchanging way. The problem here will concern how such knowledge could be expressed given that we have excluded past, present and future tense sentences. Some other way has to be found in which God could express His knowledge.

Second, it might be claimed that God limits His own infallible foreknowledge in order to allow us the idea of free action. He might limit Himself in order to allow in room for freedom. There are many problems with this. It might, for example, be said to change a Christian's understanding of the problem of salvation for all men. If this plan has been fixed for all eternity, then it seems that God must know infallibly that it is going to work out.

The relation between science and religion

The question that arises here is whether there are real conflicts between scientific claims and religious claims. Conflicts could arise through a direct opposition between science and religion. They could arise through misunderstanding or out of metaphysical claims founded on the practice of science. In these latter cases we would be more inclined to say that the conflicts were only apparent and not real.

Freud thought that the scientific spirit engendered an attitude to the world. The knowledge that is gained by science, and which can only be gained by science, will destroy religious belief and, ultimately, it will destroy the fundamental claims of religion. Freud regarded religion as a false science with false claims to knowledge.

There are scientists who take a quite different approach. Max Planck held that science and religion are fighting the same battle against scepticism, dogmatism, disbelief and superstition. Science and religion are not opposed; they are on the same side. If one is sympathetic to Planck's claim, then one is going to have to give some account of those cases where there have been conflicts.

It cannot be doubted that throughout the history of Christianity there have been a number of conflicts between religion and science. An obvious example would be the conflict between Galileo and the Catholic Church. The Church held that the earth was at the centre of the solar system, whereas Galileo advocated the heliocentric theory that the earth moved around the sun. The Church's opposition to heliocentricity did not rely solely on the authority of the Old Testament. Galileo's observations were amenable to a geocentric interpretation. There was also a serious theoretical shortcoming in that Galileo could not explain why objects thrown up into the air should, if the earth was moving, return to the same place. In the main, however, the opposition was due to what was regarded as a threat to the scriptures. It would be absurd to think that Galileo was shown the rack by the Inquisition simply because of deficiencies within his astronomical theory.

There was also a quarrel between Darwin and the Christian Church. Darwin's theory had destroyed Paley's argument from design based on the adaptation of creatures to their environment. Bishop Wilberforce claimed that Darwin's Principle of Natural Selection was incompatible with the will of God. If such a principle applied, then revelation as we know it was said to be an illusion. Those who wish to gloss over disputes between science and religion must take into account the historical reactions of churchmen at the time. In 1871 Darwin published *The Descent of Man* in which it was claimed that the difference between man and animal was one of degree rather than kind. If the story of Adam and Eve were taken literally, then Darwin contradicted it. Even if it is taken as a myth, Darwin's difference in degree thesis amounts to the claim that there is nothing special about man. There was some scientific criticism of Darwin. It was difficult for him to explain the pronounced difference in brain capacity between man and the other primates. At that time, however, Darwin did not have recourse to sophisticated genetic theory. The genetics of the time was pre-Mendel.

Religion lost the battles against Galileo and Darwin. It lost other battles too, such as the dispute concerning the age of the world. In regard to examples such as these, Freud's account is the more accurate. If the reader reconsiders the cases of Galileo and Darwin, he will find what we can call direct contradictions and what we can call implied contradictions. It is important to make this distinction. The *direct* contradiction in Galileo's case concerned the position of the earth. There was, of course, more to the dispute than this. The Church held that geocentricity *implied* a special status for man. We might express the matter by saying that the Church thought that the centre of the universe was the place to be. Geocentricity was held to confirm the authority of the Bible, and to deny it was to deny that authority. The geocentric theory was important because of what it was thought to imply concerning man's place in the scheme of things. Galileo's heliocentric theory was taken to imply that there was nothing special about man. The same point applies in the case of Darwin. The direct contradiction concerned the origin of human beings. The implied contradiction concerned the special status of man and the authority of the Bible.

These direct contradictions concern the same subject-matter. In both cases the battle was fought on *factual* grounds. The direct contradictions concern matters which can be settled through the application of empirical methods. It is in respect of being factual that the direct contradictions differ from the implied ones. The implied ones have an evaluative element, namely, the special status ascribed to man, and the rights and duties which follow from that status. The question now becomes whether or not science has anything to say about these implied claims.

An implied claim can no longer rest on a foundation which science has shown to be false. Science cannot, however, demonstrate the falsity of an implied claim concerning special status. Although science may remove the original base of an implied claim, there can be other ways of arguing for it. To show that the geocentric theory is false will not in itself demonstrate the falsity of the claim that man has special status. The implied claim is not made in the form: if and only if the geocentric theory is true does man have special status.

We must always be careful to distinguish what can be said within science and what cannot be. Thus, to take an example, during the last century the extermination of the North American Indians was seen by some[34] as an exemplification of the evolutionary process. The higher moral standards would make it easier for civilisation to survive. This is not, however, a scientific judgement. It is a moral one and a drastic one at that.

Disagreements concerning the status of man cannot be settled by any straightforward appeal to the facts. The implied contradictions are conflicts concerning different world views. The kind of conflict involved here cannot be characterised as a competition for the same factual ground. Direct contradictions do involve this competition.

It is not essential to religion in general that there should be such direct contradictions as it is not essential for a religion to make historical claims. Christianity, however, is a religion which does involve making a number of historical claims and whenever you have such claims, then you have the possibility of direct contradiction. On the traditional interpretation of Christianity, direct conflicts with scientific knowledge exist. It is essential to Christianity that there should be such conflicts as they are held to be manifestations of divine power. The reader should consider the case of miracles and ask just what it is that they are in conflict with.

▶ The concept of faith

The central issues with which we are concerned here are what is meant by faith, what it involves, and whether it can be a rational activity. We shall approach these issues through some of the important historical contributions to the topic.

Thomas Aquinas

Aquinas distinguishes between the virtue of faith and acts of faith. The virtue of faith is a settled disposition to act in a particular way. Human beings are born with various potentialities. The function of education and training is to bring about settled responses, for example, kindness instead of hostility, honesty instead of duplicity and so on. Faith is regarded by Aquinas as one such disposition.

Aquinas holds that acts of faith resemble: (1) acts of scientific knowing; (2) acts of belief. In regard to (1) Aristotle had distinguished scientific knowledge from intuition. To intuit is to grasp the indispensable starting points of whatever is under consideration. Scientific knowledge is the grasping of the deduced conclusions from the intuited starting points together with grasping that they are properly deduced. Aquinas makes some addition to this. In acts of intuition and scientific knowing, the intellect is moved to assent by the objects themselves. He describes intuition and scientific knowing as 'vision'. The state is determined by the objects themselves being present. It is important to grasp the point Aquinas is making here. In any form of vision the *will* of the perceiver does not enter into the matter. In intellectual vision you grasp whatever it is that you grasp as being necessarily so. Aquinas also holds that there are acts of the intellect which are subject to the will. By this he means that the object of the act does not fully determine the assent. An example of this would be acts of opinion. Thus when you inform someone of the opinion that *p* is the case, he does not technically see that *p* is the case. What he sees leaves it open as to whether *p* is the case or not. If a person accepts your opinion that *p*, then he *chooses* to come down on the side of *p* rather than not *p*. He does so hesitantly and with a certain apprehension that not *p* might be the case after all. Acts of faith bear a resemblance to acts of opinion in the sense that there is no *vision* of what is believed. It is the will which inclines the intellect to assent to the truth of what is proposed to it.

To accept something in faith involves complete certainty that what you accept is true. There is so much personal conviction that what is accepted is necessarily[35] true. Religious faith is an act of the intellect which assents to divine truth through the command of the will. In religious faith one assents to all and only those things that have been revealed by God. An act of faith, then, is an act of intellectual assent to a truth revealed by God, because it has been revealed by God, at the command of the will.

The virtue of faith, the settled disposition, is the disposition to give unconditional assent to what is revealed by God because it has been revealed by God. The question we must now ask is what does the act of faith have to do with reason? What part does reason play in this account?

If we take the paradigm of reason to be the Aristotelian states of intuition and scientific knowing, then we find that some things revealed by God could not be known by such methods. In matters relating to divine revelation, the function of reason is held to be twofold:

(a) It can show that what is proposed for belief is not impossible;
(b) It can assemble reasons that support revelatory statements (these reasons cannot, however, be conclusive for then the will would not enter into it).

Aquinas discusses the issue of whether giving reasons for acts of faith lessens the merit of faith. His problem can be posed in the form of a dilemma: either a person has sufficient reason for believing, in which case he is not free to give or withhold assent and, consequently, his assent will have no merit; or he does not have sufficient reason, in which case his assent is irrational and irresponsible and for that reason will lack merit or virtue. His reply to this dilemma is that the believer has sufficient inducement to believe. The inducement is the authority of divine doctrine confirmed by miracles and God's inner inspiration. Thus the believer does not believe lightly or irresponsibly, but his state of mind is not scientific knowledge because there is merit in the belief. Aquinas seems to escape the second horn of the dilemma but there is still a problem concerning rationality. If one follows Hume, then one should proportion one's belief to the strength of the evidence. The most we can have here is an opinion rather than the total conviction envisaged by Aquinas. There is a difficulty in saying how one is to recognise a statement as having divine authority as it cannot be a matter of faith in Aquinas' sense. If it were, then one would need a further divine authority to tell you that the first statement was divine. If one appealed to non-revelatory considerations, and these turned out to be conclusive, then one would have a demonstration and the act of will would be redundant. This would mean that the assent was without merit. A person can assent to God's existence in faith, but it is difficult to see how this faith can be religious faith given that Aquinas defined religious faith as assent on the basis of divine authority alone. How is it possible to accept the proposition 'God exists' on God's authority? In order to accept this authority one must *already* have accepted His existence.

In Aquinas the act of faith can be described as irrational in that it involves a degree of conviction unwarranted by what the mind sees. Hick[36] criticises Aquinas on this ground. He argues that Aquinas' approach to faith involves the assent to propositions for which there is insufficient evidence and this detracts from the merit of the assent.

William James

James attempted to specify the conditions, if any, in which it would be rational to assent to a proposition without sufficient evidence. His conditions are as follows:

(i) When we are confronted with a choice between two or more alternative hypotheses.
(ii) The choice must be a genuine one.
(iii) We do not have at the time evidence to decide the matter.

It is under these conditions that James says we accept the hypothesis which is most congenial to us.

What does James mean by 'genuine' in (ii)? In order for a choice to be a genuine choice, it must be living, momentous and forced. To describe a choice as 'living' means that all the options must appeal to us in some degree. For a choice to be 'momentous' means that what is at stake is important and the opportunity to choose must be a rare one. The choice must also be irreversible.[37] To say that a choice is 'forced' is to say that one has to make a choice. It must be impossible for you not to choose. The consequences of a refusal to choose must be the same as those of one of the options. Thus, to take an example, if a motorist's brakes fail on a steep hill, then he either stays in the car or jumps out. It is a momentous choice and there is no refusing to choose. There is no time to collect evidence concerning what is the best course of action. James wants to say that questions of religious belief can be like this. They satisfy the above conditions.

We might well wonder why it is a forced choice between belief and atheism. It could be claimed that a third choice is available, namely, agnosticism. James does not regard agnosticism as really constituting a third choice. It shares important consequences in common with atheism. Thus, for example, both atheism and agnosticism preclude direct religious experience. Hick has said that what would follow from James' position is the entrenchment of prejudices, we believe what we feel like believing rather than what is true. This is an unfair criticism. What James is saying is that when you are forced to make a choice without sufficient evidence either way, then accept the choice that is most congenial to you. According to James, if a person adopts an agnostic position, then that person is adopting an attitude that will make it impossible to have a direct acquaintance with God. It is important to realise that James is not suggesting that you simply believe whatever you want to. Much is going to depend on whether the times of choice are crisis moments in a person's life. James thinks that there is a time when you make a choice either for or against religion. As we have said, the choice of agnosticism precludes religious experience and James believes that such experiences are the best evidence available. He accepts that there can never be sufficient evidence either for belief or atheism. Any decision between these two goes beyond the evidence. It seems that agnosticism is the only rational alternative. Agnosticism, however, can only bring you to the conclusion that there is not sufficient evidence either way. A person who chooses agnosticism, though he does not know it, chooses to be an agnostic for the rest of his life. There is never going to be a moment of religious choice.

James' remarks about agnosticism have many interesting features. Perhaps the reader feels that there is no difficulty in sifting through the facts and deciding that for the time being suspension of judgement is the rational thing to do. This is tantamount to deciding not to decide. We should also consider what 'sifting through the facts' amounts to here. If we postpone a decision, then are we implying that a decision will be made on the discovery of some new fact? There is a deep problem involved with this. If we are doubting whether God exists, then we are doubting the legitimacy of religious concepts. The problem is how a fact, which is neutral in relation to religious concepts, *could* persuade us to adopt such concepts. If we do not regard the fact as neutral, then have we not already accepted the use of such concepts? A question which the reader might like to consider is how there could be purely factual evidence that a particular person was the Messiah.

There are two further points to be noted about James:

(1) Believers are uneasy about James' idea that when we make such a choice, we opt for what is most congenial to us.
(2) Many believers object to James' idea of a direct sensing of God in this life.

Not many believers reason: if I commit myself sufficiently strongly to religious belief, then I can expect a direct experience of God in this life.[38] James attaches a great deal of importance to this reasoning. This seems to be a distorted view of why people commit themselves to religious belief. It is possible that people commit themselves in order to have a more comprehensive or integrated view of life and the world. Expectations of direct experience need not have anything to do with it. On James' account, the man who commits himself to religious belief seems to be banking on a direct experience. Assent to religious doctrine in faith is the only way to obtain such an experience. There is too much emphasis on religious experience. Another aspect of religion is explanation and/or understanding. A reasonably complex religious system offers a particular picture of the world. Assent to religious doctrine in faith can give significance to science (a scientist might see himself as discovering God's plan) it can also provide a foundation for why there is something rather than nothing. These are possible alternatives as to why a person chooses to assent to religious doctrine.

Pascal's Wager

Pascal's famous wager can be seen as an attempt to ground faith in rationality. Suppose I gamble on the existence of the Christian God and I live my life as if there is such a God. There are two possibilities. First, I could be mistaken, and if I am, what have I lost? One life of three score years and ten. The second possibility is that it turns out that I am right and there is such a God. In this case I gain eternity.

What are three score years and ten when pitted against eternity? They are nothing of any significance. There is so much to gain and so little to lose. Therefore, the rational option is to live the life of faith. This wager has an initial appeal but there are problems with it.

The first problem concerns its claim to be the rational option. If all I have is one life and there is no God, then I have lost everything. I have gambled all that I have and some would say that that sounds more like recklessness than rationality.

Many religious believers would not be comfortable with the comparison between faith and a bet. Some have argued that this trivialises belief in God, others that it is a gross oversimplification. It could be said in mitigation that

Pascal was merely providing an easy way in to faith for the uneducated. There might be some truth in this but we cannot avoid philosophical issues by appealing to a possible social dimension.

A third difficulty is that even if we allow that faith can be a kind of bet, shouldn't the rationality of a bet be related to evidence? The promise of eternal life is the *outcome* not the evidence. The claim that the bet is rational should be based on the evidence for the outcome, not just on the outcome.

The final difficulty I shall mention is that the bet appeals to self-interest as the prime motive. Religious believers would not be satisfied with this as a motive for Christian belief. It could be argued that commitment to the Christian faith is not best characterised in terms of what the agent can get out of it *himself.* Rather, such faith involves a certain way of seeing the interests of others and of experiencing events in the world. It is not at all clear how self-interest can bring this about. It is not clear that I can simply *decide* this through a consideration of what is best for me thought of in terms of future benefits. There are also other difficulties with such a 'decision', especially regarding the subjective convictions characteristic of faith.

▶ Verification and religious language

There are a number of propositions which religious believers assent to in faith. Among these we may include 'God exists', 'God loves mankind', 'God is sovereign in rule over His creation'. The problem we are now going to discuss concerns the significance or meaning content of such propositions. Religious language has been regarded by some[39] as a species of nonsense. Obviously, the religious believer cannot accept such an account of his faith.

The verificationist critic of religious language takes his paradigm form of language to be the standard of the literary meaningful, namely, scientific language. In science, dichotomies can be made between analytic and synthetic, necessary and contingent, empirical and non-empirical, informative and uninformative, and factual and non-factual propositions. The factually significant propositions are distinguished by being empirically verifiable and falsifiable. The verification can either be actually carried out or be possible in principle to carry out. One could say what would count as a verification or a falsification. The conclusion is that any sentence or proposition is factually significant, or a genuine assertion, *if and only if,* it is empirically verifiable or falsifiable. Armed with this theory of meaning, the verificationist can issue a challenge to the religious believer. The challenge is that in respect of the non-analytic aspects of religious language what will the believer accept as a verification or falsification of the propositions which he believes? If no answer is forthcoming, then the verificationist will claim that such propositions which form the cornerstone of the believer's faith are not genuine propositions. They are pseudo-propositions masquerading in the surface grammar of genuine ones. There are two questions which arise here.

The first concerns why it should be thought that the types of observation admissible in science are the only types of respectable observations there are. The answer that will be given to this is objectivity. The assumption behind this answer is that the analysis of the meaning of words and the broadly scientific techniques of observation are the only ways of determining an objective truth-value.

Secondly, why should we suppose that the way science determines truth-values for non-analytic statements is the only way? The burden of proof that the scientific criterion is the one and only one surely rests on the verificationist. We cannot simply assume that scientific language provides the standard for judging all forms of language. The philosophically correct approach is the neutral one of examining established forms of language equally. To begin with one form, science, and apply its criteria of significance to all other forms requires a justification.

A justification that might be offered is that scientific language is the only language which corresponds to objective reality. It has been argued by Winch[40] that the idea of an appeal to objective reality in order to establish scientific language as *the* language of significance is confused. Winch has objected to the idea of an external relation between language and reality. It is the concepts of our language which determine what is real. There is no stepping outside the concepts and comparing them to something called 'reality' to which we have access independently of our conceptual systems. The verificationist is claiming that scientific language corresponds to reality, but in order to see if this is the case, we would have to conceive reality to ourselves via some means other than the language of science. The conceiving cannot be done in the language of science as that would merely result in saying that scientific language conformed to scientific language. The problem for the verificationist is that there is no language in which the question of the correspondence between scientific language and objective reality can be discussed when that correspondence is taken to be an external relation.

Those influenced by Winch hold that the concept of objective reality is *internal* to the language we use; it is given to us in that language. In scientific language, or physical object language in general, what is independently real is what is observable. To say this is to say what kind of language it is – we have specified the independent reality criterion at least in a broad sense. Even if one accepts the Winchian thesis concerning the external relation confusion, there are still the issues of how one discovers that there is a concept of objective reality in a particular language and of what the reality amounts to.

Winch holds that God's reality is independent of what any man thinks. The reality in question can only be seen in the context of religion in which the concept of God is used. It is within the religious use of language that the conception of God's reality has its place. This does not mean that God's reality is a matter of personal whim. Such a claim would be tantamount to saying that God had no reality. God has reality if and only if there are shared rules which determine what can and cannot be said about God. The rules determine truth-values about God. Thus we have a check within religious language, which although different from the observation check of scientific language, is still a check. God's reality is different from the reality of physical objects. The idea of a check against reality is thus not confined to science. Winch wants to defeat the supposition that just because statements about God are not verifiable by observation, then anything can be said about God. Such a supposition as this is obviously false for two reasons:

(1) The concept of God is a complex and analysable concept. It is possible for someone to say something about God and then be shown to be contradicting himself. We thus have a check regarding the internal conceptual content.

(2) It is also possible for a person to say something that contradicts what he has already said. We thus have a check on the external relation between the sentences.

There are, however, some problems here. If one wishes to maintain that religious language somehow lies on a level with scientific language, then we are going to have to explain how it is that scientific language contains (1) and (2) above and, in addition, a third check. There is a disparity here. The third check is, of course, observation. We would need to show that in religious language there are the analogues of the observation statements of physical object or scientific language. Let us assume that the most fundamental kind of physical object sentence is the singular sentence. It is fundamental in the sense that it is the base of what else we know to be true in that language. The truth conditions of such sentences are wholly present at the time and place of the utterance. If we transfer this to the case of religious language, we find that it is difficult to find the counterparts of such sentences. Consider the case of a singular sentence of physical object language such as, 'This is a flower', it is made true by the situation it describes being wholly present when and where it is uttered. In the case of the religious language statement, the situation is never wholly present. The statement 'Christ arose from the dead' is a statement of religious language and its truth could have been settled by observation. But its status as a truth of religious language depends upon its being an act of God[41] and this feature of religious language statements is not wholly present. Furthermore, the *religious* meaning of such statements is not exhausted by descriptions of states of affairs, no matter how detailed those descriptions might be.

4 An Introduction to Ethics

Ethics may be defined as the study of the logical status of our moral judgements. It differs from morals in that it does not involve making moral judgements. According to Ayer, the distinction is not always marked between the moralist, who sets out a moral code, and the moral philosopher whose concern is to analyse the nature of moral judgements. Ayer tells us that a strictly philosophical treatise on ethics makes no moral judgements. It analyses ethical terms showing to what linguistic categories they belong. In other words, philosophers stop philosophising and start moralising when they make moral judgements. Ayer's position is a neutral one. It should be contrasted with that of Plato and Socrates. They saw the task of the moral philosopher as discovering and describing the ideal life and the social and political institutions which are conducive to that life. Aristotle's concern was with the chief good for man.

One of Ayer's motives for making his claim is modesty. He is reacting against the view of the philosopher being an authority on moral issues. Plato thought that the philosopher was such an authority on the ground that only philosophers could have insight into the essential nature of 'the Good'. In Plato's ideal society philosophers would be kings. Nowadays, philosophers would agree in not making a claim like this. The question is whether they need go to the opposite extreme. If there is a general consensus that they should, then it becomes difficult to understand why philosophers should be appointed to government commissions on moral issues. Two recent examples of this are Bernard Williams on pornography and Mary Warnock on embryo/person research.

Ayer's approach would also exclude a number of questions which moral philosophers have concerned themselves with. Plato was concerned with the nature of the good life, Aristotle with the chief good for man, Butler and Kant with the motives from which people ought to act, Bentham and Mill with an objective principle which could test the rightness or wrongness of any proposed action, rule or law, and Sartre with the phenomenon of moral choice. Ayer does not show an interest in any of these questions. His concern is with the question: what meaning do ethical pronouncements have? The adoption of Ayer's approach would thus exclude from ethics much of what has been traditionally classified as moral philosophy.

There is certainly a distinction between morals and ethics but this distinction can be preserved without going to Ayer's extreme. It is not necessary for a work on ethics to contain any actual moral judgements as opposed to examples of such judgements, but neither is it necessary to rule them out. We should describe a book as a work of morals rather than ethics if it was devoted to recommending a certain moral code or moral reform. This does not mean, however, that it is illegitimate for a moral philosopher to defend his own convictions. Many have indeed tried to do this. Such a procedure can be justified on the ground that we expect the moral philosopher to state in detail his reason for making a particular moral judgement. Our expectation can be justified on the ground that he is the one who has reflected on the nature of morality.

▶ Plato's ethical theory

We cannot hope to understand Plato's ethical theory without understanding his theory of Forms. Plato's ethics and epistemology (theory of knowledge) are intimately connected. The connection between the two is most obvious in Plato's thesis that evil is due to lack of knowledge. For Plato, virtue is knowledge. If a man knows what is the nature of the good life, then he will act in accordance with that knowledge. It is assumed by Plato that when a man knows what is right, he will do right. The doing of evil will indicate ignorance. The questions we need to examine concern how Plato arrives at this position and the theories and arguments which support such a position.

The theory of Forms

Plato is concerned with the nature of ultimate reality and with the possibility of gaining universal knowledge. Universal knowledge refers to that knowledge which is certain for all people, in all places and at all times. This is especially so in relation to moral knowledge. For Plato, moral values will have an objectively real and absolute status. The first point that we need to get clear about is to understand why Plato thinks that knowledge, in order to be worthy of such appellation, must be of the Forms and what he means by 'Forms'.

Knowledge and belief

Knowledge and belief are distinguished by Plato in the *Republic* 475a–480. According to this distinction knowledge is infallible, whereas belief is fallible. Thus if you *know* that something is the case, then it is necessarily[1] and always the case. In contrast to this, if you *believe* that something is the case, then sometimes it is and sometimes it is not the case. In this passage Plato assumes that the fallibility of belief depends on the objects of belief. We are told that that which really exists (the existent) must be the object of knowledge. The non-existent is the object of ignorance. The objects of belief or opinion[2] are held to lie between these two extremes.

It is important to get clear at this point what Plato means by 'the existent'. He does not mean this or that particular instantiation of a quality, but rather the quality itself. If, for example, we ask what is redness, we might answer by pointing to a number of red objects and saying that redness is the one property that they all have in common. Thus a letter-box, a London bus, blood, rubies all have something in common, namely redness. They all partake in a common nature. It is this which Plato calls a Form or an Idea ('Idea' does *not* mean a mental entity). The Form of Redness is not any particular red thing but that in which all red things partake or participate. Red things are to be distinguished from Redness itself. It is the Forms which are held to be the appropriate objects of knowledge.

This conception of knowledge and how it is to be attained is manifested in the examination of the central question of the *Republic* – what is justice? In order to find out what justice really is we examine particular instances of just acts and see what they have in common. This common nature will be the Form or essence of justice. A particular just act will not give us true knowledge of what justice is because the particular can change with circumstances. Thus what presents itself as a just act under some circumstances could present itself as an unjust act under different circumstances. Similarly, what is beautiful in some conditions might appear ugly in others. This is why particular acts or things cannot qualify as justice or beauty itself. It is this possibility of variation which excludes for Plato the particular as the appropriate objects of knowledge. The particulars are the appropriate objects of belief or opinion. Someone who could recognise particular beautiful things but who had no insight into beauty itself, or the essence of beauty, would possess opinion not knowledge. The honorific title 'knowledge' can only be applied to the Forms. It is the Forms which possess pure existence or ultimate reality. If this is the case, then the Forms of moral qualities will be objective and absolute.

The Forms

We have seen that Plato regards the Forms as the only legitimate objects of knowledge. In the middle dialogues Plato uses a number of technical expressions to represent the Forms. The 'F', the 'F-itself', 'F-ness' and 'F-ness itself' all have the same meaning. The values of F are moral and aesthetic terms (for example, justice and beauty), greater and smaller, mathematical equality and inequality, health and strength, odd and even. Earlier, I gave the example of Redness and this is consistent with Socrates' remark in the *Republic*, 596a:

> We have, I believe, been in the habit of assuming the existence in each instance, of some one Form, which includes the numerous particular things to which we apply the same name.

This passage seems to mean that for every grammatical predicate there is a Form. You can substitute F in the technical expressions with any grammatical expression that can be predicated. This line of interpretation is also taken by Russell[3] who says that a universal will be anything which may be shared by many particulars and that, broadly speaking, substantives other than proper names, adjectives, prepositions and verbs stand for universals. In the *Republic* Plato speaks of the Form of a bed or a table, but it should be noted that in a later dialogue, the *Parmenides*, doubts are expressed concerning this blanket application of 'Form' to anything which can be predicated. There Socrates is asked whether dung, dirt and hair have Forms and he hesitates with his reply.

The aforementioned technical expressions appear in the early dialogues, but up to the *Hippias Major* they designate characteristics with no metaphysical background. It is in the middle dialogues that they come to designate Forms which, for Plato, are the ultimately real objects of universal knowledge.

Properties of the Forms

(1) One of the most important characteristics of the Forms is that of simplicity. Particular sensible things, like this colour or that shape, are complex and it is because of their complexity that we may say, for example, they are beautiful here but not there. This variability excludes sensible things as the objects of universal knowledge. The attribution of simplicity to the Forms means that we cannot distinguish parts within the Forms. It is only complex things that are composed of parts.

(2) The Forms are ungenerated and indestructible. The Forms do not come into being or cease to exist. These are ruled out by the attribution of simplicity. The processes of coming to be and ceasing to be can only occur by composition and decomposition. Such processes require a multiplicity of parts. As we have seen, the Forms are perfectly simple and have no parts. (See the *Timaeus*, 52A.)

(3) The Forms are immutable. The simple nature of the Forms excludes the possibility of change. In order to bring out the unchanging nature of the Forms, it is necessary to make a distinction between the accidental and essential properties of a particular thing. It is an

essential property of a triangle that it should have three sides, whereas it is an accidental property that it is blue or red. A change in the accidental properties will not alter its continuance as a thing of whatever kind it is, but a change in its essential properties will mean that it ceases to be a triangle. This distinction between essential and accidental properties applies to all sensible particulars. It does not apply to the Forms which are perfectly simple. (See the *Phaedo*, 80d and the *Cratylus*, 439c.)

(4) It is problematic whether the Forms are intended to be timeless, though they are immobile. We are told in the *Timaeus*, 37c:

> We say that eternal being was and is and shall be, but 'is' alone really belongs to it and describes it truly; 'was' and 'shall be' are properly used of becoming which proceeds in time ... for they are motions.

The point of this passage is that inasmuch as the use of past and future tenses implies changeability, then they would be inappropriately applied to the Forms which do not change. This does not, however, entitle us to infer timelessness as it would not then just be inappropriate to use past and future tenses; it would be unintelligible. The unintelligibility can be seen by substituting a genuine timeless entity. To say that the number two is at all times equal is unintelligible *because* '2' is timeless.[4] Plato does hold that at all times a Form is invariable and constant.

(5) The Forms have independent existence. This means that for a Form to have existence is not for it to be manifested in some particular thing. It exists independently of particular things. A Form is manifested itself by itself with itself (*Symposium*, 211A).

(6) The Forms are not spatially located.

We are now able to say of Plato's theory that the Forms, for example, Beauty and Justice, are immutable and exist forever. They are perfect, therefore absolute. They alone are amenable to knowledge.

The ordinary world in which we live contains many beautiful things and instances of justice and so on. But these things change, they do not exist for ever and they are neither perfect nor absolute. They do, however, have some kind of existence and thus they cannot be the objects of ignorance. Plato held them to be the objects of belief or opinion.

This part of Plato's theory is further supported by his explanation of the position of the Forms, and especially of the Form of the Good. As we shall see, Plato held that the Form of the Good is the ultimate source of all other values. This absolute value is the foundation or 'mother' of all other absolute values, such as truth, beauty and justice. The Good is their 'mother' in the sense that it is the source of their existence and absoluteness.

The way in which Plato explains this is by means of a simile between the visible world (the world we see) and the intelligible world which we may know or understand with our minds. In the world of perception, the sun is the source of growth and light. Without this source things would not be capable of being seen, nor would we be capable of seeing them. The Form of the Good, says Plato, is like the sun. Just as the sun is the source of growth and light in the perceptible world, so the Good is the source of reality and truth in the intelligible world of the Forms. It is right to think of light and growth as being like the sun, but wrong to think of them as the sun itself. Similarly, it is right to think of knowledge and truth as being like the Good, but wrong to identify them with the Good.

We can now see the importance of the Good for Plato. It is the origin of all absolute values and of the source of our ability to know and understand these values. It is also the source of Reality. Only the Forms are real and can be known. The material world, consisting of particular things, can only be the object of belief. This is why Plato's ethical theory depends on his theory of Forms.

Let us now venture further into the relation between the forms, reality and knowledge on the one hand, and the ordinary world, appearance and belief on the other. In doing so, the link between Plato's ethical theory, his theory of Forms and his epistemology should become clearer.

The allegory of the cave

The most interesting way in which Plato draws out these differences occurs at the start of Bk VII of the *Republic*. We are invited to imagine a group of men living in an underground cave. There is an open entrance so that light extends along the entire length of the cave. The group in question has been confined from childhood with their legs and necks shackled so that they are forced to sit still and look straight ahead of them. We are also asked to imagine a bright fire burning in the distance above and behind them and an elevated roadway passing between the fire and the prisoners with a low wall built along it.

Let us then suppose that a number of people are walking behind this wall and carrying statues of men, images of animals and other articles. Some of them are talking, others are silent. He then proceeds to discuss the predicament of the prisoners. They could not see anything of themselves or of each other beyond the shadows caused by the fire on that part of the cave which is directly in front of them. Similarly, their knowledge of what is being carried past them is equally limited. It is limited again to the shadows cast upon the wall. If the cave returned an echo from the part facing them whenever one of the passers by spoke, then they would attribute such sounds to the shadows before them. If one's view were restricted to the shadows, then the shadows would exhaust one's conception of reality.

There follows a description of what would happen if one of the prisoners were to be released and turned towards the light. If he is told that in his prison days he was only acquainted with shadows but was now in a position to see more clearly, then he would be baffled and likely to want to cling to his old visions. If he were compelled to gaze at the light itself, then his eyes would shrink away and return to what he could see distinctly and he would still consider them as constitutive of reality. If he were dragged up from the cave and forced into the light of the sun, he would be angry at such treatment. His eyes would be so dazzled by the glare that he would be incapable of making out any of the objects that are now called true. He might, however, be able to look at shadows and reflections and then gradually when he could see the objects in the sunlight directly, he would look at the stars and watch the changing seasons. Finally, he would be able perhaps to look directly at the sun itself. It is this which represents a vision of the Form of Good. This would correspond to a glimpse of the source of knowledge. He would be able to conclude that the sun is the ground of all things in the visible world.

There are parallels to be drawn between this allegory and the different stages of intelligence referred to in Bk VI of the *Republic*. The first stage is that of conjecture or uncertainty in which the objects we perceive are shadows or pale reflections. This state of mind is the predicament of those chained in the cave. What they are aware of are the shadows of the images being paraded along the wall. They are therefore the victims of a double deception. It is not that all they see are images, but rather all *they* see are the *shadows* of images. For Plato, this is the condition of most of mankind. They believe these shadows or appearances to constitute reality.

The second stage is where we come to feel a greater degree of certainty. The objects of our apprehension are the perceptible things of everyday life or their direct reflections, hence the reference to the actual men or their reflections in water. But even in this stage we are still in the realm of opinion or belief. We are not, for example, in a position to answer questions like 'what is beauty?' as all we are acquainted with is this or that particular beautiful thing. We cannot say why they are beautiful as we cannot give an account of beauty itself. This state of mind, though more certain and praiseworthy than the first, still has drawbacks. It is very much tied to the particular and when the particular changes with circumstances we cannot say what makes it a particular of that kind. It is in the third stage that we begin the quest for Forms. This may be loosely translated as the intellectual stage. Unlike the previous stage the sensible particulars are not treated as the ultimate reality, but rather as symbols of something insensible.

The Good

Let us now inquire a little further into what Plato meant by the Good. The traditional Greek conception of the good of any object, whether it is an artifact or a biological organism (including man), is for it to be or do what it is intended to be or do. We have to understand its function in order to understand what is the good in relation to it. All objects are complex in the sense of being composed of parts and to understand their function is to understand how the various parts cohere to the end of the whole. The end that each whole has is regarded as the good for that whole. Thus, for example, that which enables a knife to cut well contributes to the good of the knife. The end or function of a knife is that it should cut well.

In the case of organisms, this conception involves the notion of teleology, that is, the taking into account of their purpose. Thus, the good of an organism is whatever is conducive to its being an organism of that kind. It is that principle which organises its constituent parts into the unified structure which the organism is. The parts stand to the whole as an adaptation of means to ends. This same idea applies to the individual man, human society and morality. An individual action is good if it is conducive to the good of the whole person. Plato makes it clear at the start of Bk IV of the *Republic* that we cannot consider the good of individuals without considering the good of the whole of which they are a part. This whole is, of course, society. Each individual has a role to play in society according to his capacities. A good man is one who performs that role well. Hence the importance of knowledge of the good for those who rule a society.

We can draw two important and closely related implications of this conception of the good. The first is in connection with knowledge. Given the relationship between function and the good, and that we understand things inasmuch as we understand their function, we can see that, for Plato, understanding things is to see what is the good in relation to them. The second is in connection with ethics. Good actions are those actions which are in accordance with a man's function in society. The relation is that if one had perfect knowledge, then one would have perfect understanding of things and consequently of one's own function and how it contributed to the good of the whole. One would then have a perfect picture of the whole as a whole of which one was a part. If we had this knowledge, then we could not fail to act in accordance with it. As Cornford remarks, knowledge of the Good cannot fail to determine will and action.[5] This is what lies behind Plato's thesis that virtue is knowledge.

We have already seen the other aspect, the Form of the Good, namely, that it is the source of all being of the objects of the intellect. It is the cause of their being objects of knowledge; it is the cause of their property of being knowable. The Form of the Good thus becomes a kind of super-Form. It is that from which all other Forms derive their being.

Both Nettleship and Taylor[6] agree that the Form of the Good corresponds to the Christian God (*not* the god of Platonic philosophy as that would be a soul rather than a Form). Taylor writes:

> Neither Plato nor anyone else could tell another man what the Good is, because it can only be apprehended by the most incommunicable and intimate personal insight. Thus, as it seems to me, metaphysically the Form of the Good is what Christian philosophy has meant by God, and nothing else. (p. 289)

The Form of the Good is essentially unknowable, though according to Plato, the philosopher must inquire into its nature and acquire some understanding, but never complete understanding. Let us now summarise the purely philosophical nature of Plato's ethical theory.

Summary

Plato's ethical theory rests on the existence of absolute values, the Forms. According to Plato, these were derived from the highest Form of all, the Form of the Good.

These aspects of Plato's theory also provided the basis of an epistemological theory, a theory of knowledge. Plato held that the world of the Forms was reality. The physical world, although existing in a sense, could not achieve full existence or complete reality and was therefore the world of appearance. We can have knowledge of the real world, we could only have belief in regard to the world of appearance. To put this in modern terms, knowledge of the Forms, being independent of the way things are in the physical world, would correspond to *a priori* knowledge. Beliefs or opinions about the physical world is what we would refer to as empirical or *a posteriori* knowledge.

As we have seen, Plato was led to the thesis that virtue is knowledge. If a man did wrong, this was simply due to ignorance as a man could not have knowledge of the good and do wrong. A man with knowledge of the good must always do what is right. This position forms the second element of Plato's ethical theory and can be described as the practical or psychological aspect of the theory in contrast with the purely philosophical which we have been discussing.

Plato's ethics in practice

In the *Republic* Plato outlined his ideal political state. He believed that such a state should be run by philosopher kings, the Guardians. These men would have been trained from their earliest days to seek knowledge and would aspire to knowledge of the Good. They had to endure a rigorous physical training and they had to undergo a thorough training in mathematics. They were to be kept away from what Plato considered to be corrupt music and dance. Once they had acquired knowledge and had developed virtuous habits, these men would become good rulers of the state.

The ordinary mass of citizens would have neither the training, nor, Plato believed, the intellectual ability to become rulers. They must, therefore, be ruled over and in their lives they should be guided by the example of the rulers' lives which they could imitate. There would be strict censorship in the state where presumably what was censored would depend on the views of the rulers. Breeding was also carefully controlled so that the state should produce just the right number and type of citizens.

All this was designed to produce a static state. A dynamic or ever-changing society could not, in Plato's eyes, be ideal. We have already seen how, in his philosophical theory, he associated change and mutability with imperfection and belief, and immutability with perfection and knowledge.

Criticisms of Plato

First, the preceding brief outline of Plato's ethics in practice provides us with a very obvious criticism. Plato believed that there are ultimate moral standards. Some of these are presumably reflected in his blueprint for the ideal state. There can, however, be radical disagreement concerning this ideal state. Plato's vision of the Good led him to advocate censorship not free speech, elitism not democracy, and the murder of children if the state found it convenient.

Different philosophers can have very different conceptions of the good and it is not clear what rational procedure could solve such disputes. Plato's suggestion of direct apprehension of the good by vision is open to the criticism that different philosophers could have different visions. Besides, the appeal to 'visions' tends to impugn the rationality of the procedure.

Second, the position of the individual agent is precarious. If we accept Nettleship's thesis concerning knowledge of the good being related to function, we might well ask what this has to do with moral goodness as we understand it. Is the individual to be told by the rulers what his function is and have his goodness judged according to how well he fulfils that function?

Third, the thesis that virtue is knowledge is open to criticism. The thesis might be interpreted as a logical one. Plato may be saying that it is logically impossible for a man to know what is right and at the same time do wrong. He would thus be making it a condition of ethical knowledge that it involves acting rightly. If a man acts wrongly, then he cannot be said to have knowledge of the good.

Now, given the way in which Plato defines knowledge, it does become logically impossible to do wrong when one knows what is right. The problem though is that Plato can be accused of defining 'knowledge' in such a way that it alters the concept of knowledge beyond recognition. On this interpretation of Plato, if you have knowledge of the good, then you cannot make a mistake, lie or pretend. If you did any of these things, Plato would have to conclude that you did not really have knowledge.

Plato's thesis can also be given a psychological interpretation. It would then be taken as a statement about how men actually think, feel and behave. If a man knows that stealing is wrong, then, Plato holds, the man would not steal. If he did, then he would not have properly understood what was meant by saying that stealing is wrong.

This is obviously false. We can know what is right and still do wrong. We can even agree that what we have done is wrong and continue to do it. We could do it out of sheer bloody-mindedness, compulsion or weakness of the will. Thus, as a psychological theory, virtue is knowledge does not seem to hold. The reader should consult the following section on Aristotle for a further discussion of this and for criticism of the theory of Forms.

Fourth, it is not clear how Plato's theory can help in the solution of moral dilemmas. The difficulty here is whether all ethical problems can be solved by the acquisition of knowledge.

▶ Aristotle: the Nichomachean Ethics

Book I

This is an attempt to establish in outline what the supreme good for man is. It must be remembered throughout that Aristotle is speaking as a participant in the respectable morality of his time. Ethics, he says, reasons not from but to first principles. It reasons from the generally held and rather confused ideas of moral goodness that are implicit in the behaviour of people who have acquired good habits. This is why Aristotle is so ready to argue from what men do to what is best for them: he is talking about what decent men do.

Aristotle regards ethics as a branch of political science and as such not an exact science. We can only expect that degree of precision which is afforded by the nature of the subject. We cannot expect to have the exactitude of logic or physics. If we ask what the supreme good for man is, then, says Aristotle, we would get a unanimous reply, namely, happiness. All would agree that the supreme end for man is happiness. It is when we ask what happiness is that we find differences in what people think. Some identify happiness with honour, some identify it with pleasure and others with wealth. These suggestions were, however, treated by Aristotle as being too superficial. Honours can always be removed, but goodness cannot easily be taken away. Honour is also sought *for the sake of* virtue and not just for its own sake. Similarly, virtue is not just pursued for its own sake but also for the sake of happiness. We can also be virtuous and suffer misfortune and, therefore, not be completely happy. Wealth too is not sought for its own sake, but only as a means to something else. This distinction between something being pursued for its own sake and something being pursued for the sake of something else is of crucial importance in the study of Aristotle's ethics.

The opening words for the *Ethics* are: 'Every art and every inquiry, and similarly every action and pursuit, is thought to aim at some good'. Aristotle's inquiry will be into what is the highest of all goods achievable by man's action. He assumes that there is such a good, and that it is the supreme good for man. The criterion for being the supreme good for man is set out in chs 1 and 2, and also in ch. 7. When A is done *for the sake of* B (that is, when B is the end of action A) B is better than A. Thus if there is something, or perhaps several things, for the sake of which everything else is done, and is not itself done for the sake of anything else, it, or they, will be the supreme good for man, or the final end of political science.

In ch. 2 Aristotle presents an argument to show that whatever we do is done for the sake of some end for whose sake everything else is desired. If I desire A for the sake of B, and B for the sake of C, and so on *ad infinitum*, then my desire is said to be 'vain'. The implied premiss is: 'If x is desired for the sake of something else, y, then the desire is satisfied only if y is achieved; and if x is desired for the sake of y and y for the sake of z, then x is desired for the sake of z'. On this premiss, nothing that happens or is achieved will ever satisfy my desire, since my desire will always be for something else again. The most that this argument shows is that a desire is non-vain only if, in the final analysis, it is a desire for something for its own sake. It will not show that a desire is non-vain only if there is something that every desire aims at for its own sake. It does not establish that there is some *one* thing which all desire aspires to achieve. The distinction between the valid and the invalid conclusions is like that between 'Everybody loves somebody' and 'There is somebody whom everybody loves'. Aristotle's argument does not constitute a justification for the claim that there must be one supreme good for man.

Aristotle holds that happiness is the only thing which is desired for its own sake and not for the sake of something else. This is held to be the supreme good attainable by action. The word translated as happiness is *eudaimonia* which means a state of general well being rather than a feeling or state of euphoria. The fact that *eudaimonia* does not simply mean a state of euphoria is obvious from Aristotle's remarks in ch. 4 to which we referred earlier. When people dispute as to whether happiness is honour, wealth, pleasure and so on they are obviously disputing about what it is to live well rather than about what it is to feel euphoric.

In ch. 7 Aristotle introduces a third kind of good. Hitherto he had talked about things that are desired and thought good merely as means or instruments for the attainment, ultimately, of things that are desired as good for their own sakes. He now introduces the idea of things that are desired and valued *both* for their own sakes *and* for the sake of something else. Examples of these are honour, pleasure, reason, the virtues and sight. That they are valued for the sake of something else is shown by the fact we choose them for the sake of happiness. We judge that by means of them we shall be happy. That they are valued for their own sakes is shown by the fact that we would choose them even if nothing resulted from them, or that we choose them even when they are isolated goods. In one sense they are final ends, but in another sense they are not as *the* final end cannot be desired for the sake of anything else. Happiness is the only thing which fits this absolute criterion of never being desired for the sake of anything else. Happiness is chosen for itself, whereas the virtues are chosen for themselves *and* for the sake of happiness. Happiness is therefore regarded as more ultimate than the virtues. Aristotle makes an odd remark at 1097^b, 'Happiness is not chosen for the sake of virtues nor in general for anything other than itself.' To be consistent Aristotle should not have said 'in general'; he should have said that happiness is *never* chosen for the sake of anything else. Aristotle also makes the point that by itself happiness makes life desirable and lacking in nothing. This is what is meant by saying that happiness is self-sufficient. In Aristotle's account a man's final good includes that of his family and friends, and also his fellow citizens. To be truly happy it is necessary not just for a man in isolation to be living well, but also those related to him must be living well. Happiness is very much a social phenomenon. We have followed Aristotle in laying down the conditions which the final good for man must satisfy. Before we proceed to a more definite account of what this good is, we need to note Aristotle's rejection of Plato's universal good or Form of the Good. The cluster of arguments which constitute this rejection occurs in ch. 6. The arguments are as follows.

First, Aristotle tells us that the proponents of the theory of Forms did not postulate Forms of classes in which they recognised priority and posteriority. The term 'good', however, is used in the category of substance (that is, the category of individual things upon which the existence of qualities and relations depends; such individuals are the ultimate subjects of predication) and in the posterior or dependent categories of quality and relation. Therefore, there cannot be one Form which accommodates these different goods. Thus if the class of good things were to be included under one Form, then there should be no prior/posterior distinction in the uses of 'good' as there is no such distinction in the classes of which Forms are posited. But, Aristotle points out, there is such a distinction with 'good', namely, 'good' used in the category of substance and 'good' used in the categories of quality and relation. Some commentators have taken Aristotle to be saying that there is no prior/posterior distinction within the realm of the Forms, rather than within the classes which answer to a Form and have then adapted the argument accordingly. I have not chosen this interpretation for two reasons: (a) Plato did afford priority to the Form of the Good, and even when specific references to this Form became muted, he still spoke of a supreme Form, (b) the analogy with number at 1096ᵃ of the *Ethics* is better preserved by talking of classes. Platonists did not posit a Form embracing the class of numbers as some members of the class would be prior to others. They could be prior either in the sense that numbers constitute a series or in the sense that numbers are generated through the operation of addition on unity.[7] Plato did posit Forms for particular numbers. The number two and the number three are used in the *Phaedo* to exemplify Forms. The Forms of particular numbers can be said to constitute a continuum rather than a series.

Second, there are so many different uses of 'good' that it is implausible to claim that there is one Form in which they all participate. The dissimilarities in the various uses of 'good' (its use in different categories) are too pronounced to allow talk about a common 'good' or one Form of Good. Aristotle does not here discuss the possibility of investigating systematic resemblances among the uses of the term.

Third, as there are distinct fields of study of the things falling under each Form, then one would expect there to be one field of study of all the diverse goods. There are, however, many fields of study of the diverse goods rather than one for all things called good.

Fourth, in so far as goodness is concerned, there is no difference between 'Goodness' itself and particular things which are good. They are both good. Eternal existence, a property of the Forms, will not make the thing itself (the Form) any more good than the particular goods. Aristotle contrasts this with the case of whiteness. The Form of Whiteness will not be any whiter through existing eternally than particular white things will be through existing for a limited period. The reader should note that eternal existence is not the only attribute of the Forms and should consider whether the other attributes make a difference. Plato held that particular goods are good under certain circumstances, whereas Goodness itself is not subject to any qualifications. It could not be anything other than good whatever the circumstances. It is immutable.

Fifth, there will still be a problem even if the Platonists distinguish those things good as ends from those which are good as means and claim that, whereas the latter are good only in a secondary sense, the former ones do participate in a common Form. The problem is that if we examine those things thought to be good in themselves, such as honour, pleasure and wisdom, we find diverse accounts of what their goodness consists rather than some common good in which they all participate.

Sixth, even if there is *one* Good it could not be achieved by man. If it is unattainable, then it cannot be the end of political science. Aristotle goes on to consider the claim that even if the Good cannot be achieved, knowledge of it might, nevertheless, be useful as a kind of guiding light. He deals with this by doubting the utility of such knowledge (i.e. of the universal) and proceeds to emphasise the utility of knowledge of particulars by analogy with other subjects.

We can now proceed to Aristotle's account of the chief good for man. This is outlined in the second half of ch. 7. Aristotle's reasoning is as follows:

(1) If *x* has a function, then its goodness resides in the function. That is to say, if *x* has a function, then the question, 'Is *x* good?' means 'Does *x* perform its function well?'.

(2) If man has a function, then the question, 'Is that man good?' means 'Does he perform his function well?'. We are of course, talking about his function *as a man*. (He may be a teacher but the question is 'Is he a good man?' not 'Is he a good teacher?'.)

(3) As each of his bodily parts has a function, so does man similarly have a function.

(4) This function is the life that is peculiar to man as such. What is this life? The soul is divided into a rational and an irrational element. That part of the irrational element which is concerned with nutrition and growth, or perception (sensation) is not peculiar to man as such and can therefore be excluded. The life peculiar to man is the active life of the element in man that has a rational principle. Of this element one part has a rational principle in the sense that it obeys a rational principle, whereas the other part has such a principle in the sense that it exercises thought.[8] The life peculiar to man is activity that follows or implies a rational principle.

(5) Consequently, the chief good for man is activity of soul in accordance with virtue (*aretê*), or with the best and most complete virtue, throughout his adult life. The reader should note that good functioning is an activity and not a state of mind.

'Virtue' is the accepted translation of *aretê*. It can also be translated as 'excellence'. To have *aretê* is to perform one's function well. Thus Aristotle's conclusion in (5) above is that man's chief good (happiness) is good functioning of that element of his soul that is peculiar to man as such. To be a man is to be capable of certain sorts of activity, namely, activity following or implying a rational principle, that is, rational activity. This is the function of man and to be a good man is to perform this function well.

How do 'virtuous' activities relate to happiness? Happiness is a quality of complete lives. To ask whether a man is happy is to ask a question that involves considering his whole life, how it has been, is and will be (see chs 9 and 10). The happiness of a life depends on two main factors: being successfully virtuous, and being fortunate. In order to enjoy happiness a man must meet with success in the projects he undertakes as a rational creature and also meet with good fortune in those matters which are not under his control. Under the first heading would come such things as good birth and good health (see ch. 8).

Virtue by itself is not a sufficient condition of a happy or blessed life. A virtuous man can be so beset with misfortunes that lie outside his control that his life cannot be called truly happy. This is the case even though his actions in the midst of misfortune are entirely such as a rational agent would undertake, and even though they succeed. In such a case the life would be regarded as noble and not miserable or pitiful.

Since happiness is a quality of an entire life, there is a sense in which it cannot be an end of action. It is not within our power at a given time to make our own lives, or indeed those of anyone else, happy ones. Nor is happiness related to virtuous actions as their consequence, since happiness cannot be said to exist independently of virtuous activity. On the other hand happiness is not identical with some sufficient preponderance of virtuous activity in a man's whole life. Although leading a happy life is better than leading just a virtuous life, this does not mean that virtue is less worthwhile. For Aristotle, the idea of a happy life is the idea of a life that contains all human goods, and more of them than of anything else. Virtuous activity is also a human good and one that is sought for its own sake. But being virtuous under certain sorts of circumstances is more of a human good than being virtuous under other sorts of circumstances, although, given either, to be virtuous is the best course of action. To be virtuous in adverse circumstances is less of a human good than being virtuous in favourable and stable circumstances, although being virtuous is the best course in either. Happiness involves the idea that part of the highest good for man is the practice of virtue within a flourishing, successful and well-favoured life.

When Aristotle says that the good man performs certain properly human activities well, does he mean that the good man is one who is good at reasoning, and acts on that reasoning, where appropriate? It can be argued that such a man would be a fine specimen of a man, in that he exhibited to the highest degree the kind of behaviour that distinguishes man from other living things, and thus satisfied perfectly the definition of his kind; but what has this got to do with *moral* goodness? It has no more to do with moral goodness than does being a fine specimen of a racehorse. Moral goodness has to do much more with the sorts of things that one does and with one's reasons for doing them than with the subtleties, complexities and length of one's reasoning. These can be exercised to the highest degree by an evil man. There is no guarantee that Aristotle's good man will be a good man.

Even if Aristotle includes in his account of practical reasoning (see below) some reference to an ability to grasp moral facts (so that one whose view of a situation is morally wrong is somehow defectively rational), the fact remains that persons are also distinguishable from animals by their ability to act on wrong principles. The distinction is not between acting on right principle and not acting on principle at all, following right reason or not following right reason at all; but between acting on principle, whether right or wrong, and not acting on principle.

There are other problems which emerge from Book I of the *Ethics*. We saw that the soul was to be divided into a rational and an irrational element. This division is reflected in Aristotle's account of the virtues. There is a split between the intellectual and the moral. Philosophical or theoretical wisdom (*sophia*) and practical wisdom (*phronesis*) or reasoning with a view to act, are the virtues of the intellect. The moral virtues include such things as temperance and liberality. These are to do with a man's character rather than his intellect. There is a problem here concerning the extent to which reason is to be excluded from the exercise of moral virtue. Aristotle, as we shall see, tends to identify moral virtue with acquiring good habits. One may well question whether what we mean by 'morality' is adequately captured in the concept of a good habit. The acquisition of such habits tends to fit better with what we mean by etiquette rather than morality. Aristotle does, however, have more to say about such habits in Book II. There are related issues which the reader should bear in mind as we approach Book II. First, can we solve our moral dilemmas through the acquisition of good or better habits? Secondly, the exercise of moral virtue is supposed to be pleasurable, but as habitual behaviour is an automatic process one may wonder about the kind of pleasure that could be involved in this.

Book II

Aristotle begins with the distinction between intellectual and moral virtue. The former is acquired through being taught and the latter through habit. No moral virtue is acquired through nature. What is derived from nature is the *capacity* for moral virtue. The virtues themselves are cultivated and developed through habit. All nature does is enable us to receive them. Aristotle tells us that it is through performing virtuous acts that we become virtuous. It is by performing acts of type *x* that we develop the *x* state of character. It is therefore of crucial importance to form the right habits as these are what make our states of character what they are. As Aristotle is concerned with *how* we are to become good, we shall need to examine the nature of action. He is concerned with 'doing' as it is what we do that determines what we are, that is, our states of character. The account he is going to give will, he says, be rough, as that is in accordance with the nature of the subject. Matters relating to conduct are not fixed and exact. Much will depend on individual situations.

What does Aristotle mean when he says that it is through being virtuous that we become virtuous? The meaning of this becomes clearer when we consider the analogies he uses. At 1104^a we are told that it is by becoming temperate that we are most able to do temperate things. This is contrasted with physical strength. Once you are strong, you are thereby better equipped to do those things which make you strong, such as physical exercise, and it is through performing such exercises that you become strong. Virtuous acts must not, however, be a matter of chance. They must proceed from knowledge within the agent. This is the point of the analogy with the grammarian at 1105^a. In addition to the agent's knowledge, there are two further conditions for virtuous acts:

(1) The agent must *choose* the acts for their own sake.
(2) The action must proceed from a firm and unchangeable character.

These extra conditions are held to distinguish virtuous acts from the case of arts and crafts and it is the former which are by far the most important. Not only must virtuous activity be done in order to be virtuous, but also it must be done *in the way* the virtuous do it.

These considerations suggest that being virtuous amounts to more than acquiring good habits. If one still wants to claim that the above is a matter of habit, then one would be altering our concept of habit beyond recognition. It can, of course, be the case that once we have become virtuous, then we perform virtuous acts automatically where 'automatically' is understood in terms of flowing naturally from our characters. Even so, the preconditions of such habitual or automatic actions are not *themselves* just a matter of acquiring habits.

Aristotle then proceeds to a discussion of what virtue is. Virtue must be an aspect of the soul. The contents of the soul are listed as follows: (1) passions (feelings); (2) faculties (that which enables us to have the passions); and (3) states of character (the way we bear the passions). Aristotle dismisses the idea of identifying virtue with the passions as it is not the passions *per se* which are the appropriate objects of praise and blame. Passions do not involve choice in the sense that, for example, we do not choose to be afraid. Similar considerations rule out the identification of the faculties with virtue. So, by process of elimination, virtue must be states of character. The next question is what sort of state.

It is that state which enables a man to be good in himself and to do his work well, that is, fulfil his function as a man well. In discussing how this state is to be brought about, we are introduced to Aristotle's doctrine of the mean. The first reference to this thesis occurs at 1104[a] where we are told that things are destroyed by excess and deficiency. Thus, for example, bravery is destroyed by excess (rashness or foolhardiness) and by deficiency (cowardice). The virtue of bravery is the mean between rashness and cowardice. Similarly with temperance, it is said to be the mean between self-indulgence and insensibility. Whenever we act we can always choose the more, the less or the equal in an absolute or relative sense. In any art one chooses the intermediate relative to the agent. We avoid excess and defect, and this is how every art fulfils its function or does its work well. Virtue too must therefore aim at the intermediate (the mean) in relation to actions and passions. They admit of degrees and, therefore, of an intermediate. In both passions and actions there are excess, defect and intermediate. Virtue is said to be a kind of mean, that is, aiming at what is intermediate. There are many ways of going wrong but only one of being good, namely, the mean relative to us. When Aristotle talks of the mean relative to us, he means that what is a mean for us depends upon the kind of person we are. Thus, for example, what would be an intermediate amount of food for a wrestler would not be an intermediate for a sprinter. It would be an excess relative to the sprinter, and the sprinter's food would be a deficiency relative to the wrestler. This is obviously unsatisfactory as it stands. We do not know what kind, or how much, of a particular virtue any given person should aim for as this is relative to him. Aristotle tells us that the mean relative to us – our target – is determined by a rational principle, 'and by that principle by which the man of practical wisdom would determine it'. The reader can see from this the importance of practical wisdom in Aristotle's system. It is through practical wisdom that we select the right means to achieve our ends *and* acquire knowledge of what those ends are. There is, however, a problem here. Aristotle is saying that the good life for particular people can vary from individual to individual, we aim for the mean relative to us. But he also seems to be saying that a life of moderation is right for everyone. What is a moderate life for one person may be immoderate for another and nothing particularly informative seems to have been said concerning the actual content of such lives. The appeal to practical wisdom hardly advances matters.

Having put forward the doctrine of the mean as the important way to develop a virtuous character, Aristotle (1107[a]) then lists important exceptions to the doctrine. Some things are bad in themselves, 'however they are done they are wrong'. Similar exceptions are admitted in the realm of the passions; spite and envy, for example, are wrong in themselves. It is not, therefore, correct to say that all vice is either excess or deficiency.

Aristotle then switches to talk about individual cases. The emphasis on the particular has more practical importance than talk about the general. He gives particular examples of the excess/deficiency/mean analysis in practice. Liberality is a mean which lies between prodigality and meanness. There are also some rather contrived examples where it is necessary for Aristotle to invent names for vices in order to make the analysis seem plausible. There are other problems with the doctrine.

Consider his account of the truthful person. He is said to lie between the boaster and the mock-modest. This might be an adequate account of modesty, but it will not do as an account of truthfulness where that is taken to mean 'honesty'. Honesty is not a mean between lying and something else; it is the *opposite* of lying.

Another problem can be brought out by considering his claim that the wit lies between the buffoon and the boor. Although these are not intended to be points on the same scale, there is still a problem in that there is neither psychological nor conceptual connection between, say, the wit and the clown. Furthermore, Aristotle tells us that the mean is closer to the extremes than the extremes are to each other, but in what sense is a buffoon *closer* to a wit than he is to a boor?

We might also wonder how the doctrine of the mean will help us choose the right course of action in a particular case bearing in mind that the kind of person we are may itself be a reason as to why we are having moral difficulties. In such a case as this we are not so much concerned with what is right relative to us, but with the kind of person we ought to be.

Finally, Aristotle regards hitting the mean as a difficult task. When we cannot hit the mean, then we should opt for whichever extreme is the lesser evil. Blame is to be proportioned to the amount of deviation from the mean, so, presumably, there is to be considerable uniformity in what counts as the mean in various cases. This must be the case as we blame people for what they do not for what they do relative to themselves. Aristotle admits a difficulty in specifying the degree to which one can deviate from the mean as he allows for much variation in individual cases. He concludes with what many would take to be an unenlightening remark, 'the decision rests with perception' (1109^b).

Book III

Aristotle is here concerned with the nature of voluntary action and with that of choice. We saw at the start of Book II that the nature of action is an important issue for Aristotle. Let us then turn to Aristotle's account of voluntary action.

It is important to distinguish voluntary from involuntary action for the purposes of legislation and for judging the appropriateness of praise and blame. Involuntary acts are done either through compulsion or ignorance. In the case of acts performed through compulsion, Aristotle says that the principle of the action lies outside the agent. This means that the agent does not contribute anything to the act. The act is entirely caused by events external to the agent. A voluntary act would, by contrast, be one where the principle of the action lies inside the agent. He is the initiator of the act and thus contributes to it. There are, of course, borderline cases which share features in common with the voluntary and the involuntary. This is because they are worthy of choice at the appropriate time and because the context of the choice is to be taken into account, 'the terms voluntary and involuntary must be used with reference to the moment of action'. Borderline cases are voluntary given the context, they are not said to be voluntary in the abstract. This means that the actions in question are worthy of choice given the situation, but they would not be chosen in and for themselves. Such actions are the appropriate objects of praise and blame. Sometimes such acts are pardoned. Thus if the external pressures on the agent are so great, then his subsequent act might be pardoned. There are also some things which we should never do *irrespective* of the pressure upon us. The reader might like to apply this to the case of Nazi war criminals who claimed that they *had* to obey orders.

In addition to involuntary acts performed under compulsion, there are also involuntary acts performed through ignorance. Aristotle divides the acts performed through ignorance into the not-voluntary and the involuntary. Acts which are not-voluntary are not followed by repentance. If acts performed through ignorance are followed by repentance and pain in the agent, then the acts are described as involuntary. The kind of ignorance which is relevant to the 'involuntary' ascription is when the agent is ignorant of the particular circumstances of the act. This is the kind of ignorance that can be pitied or pardoned. Ignorance of the purposes we should have is not excusable. In the case of voluntary action the agent is aware of the particular circumstances of the act and the moving principle of the act lies within himself.

Anger and appetite do not entail involuntariness as any creature which acts just from these (such as children and animals) could then never be said to have acted voluntarily and this would be an inappropriate way of talking. It would also mean that if the right thing was done from such a cause, then it would be involuntarily done as it is absurd to say that only the ignoble acts which proceed from anger and appetite are involuntary. Not all things done from appetite are regarded as painful, whereas involuntary acts are followed by pain. We can now move to Aristotle's account of choice.

Choice is intimately connected with virtue and character assessment. Aristotle distinguishes chosen acts from voluntary acts. Chosen acts constitute a narrower category than voluntary ones. Children and animals act voluntarily but do not participate in choice. An examination of what Aristotle means by choice should go some way to clarifying Aristotle's earlier claim about children, namely, that they act solely from appetite (and anger). What is choice?

Choice is not to be confused with appetite or anything else which is common to irrational creatures. It is not to be confused with wish as you can wish for the impossible (for example, immortality) but you cannot choose the impossible. It is a logical property of the objects of choice that they are things which the agent *thinks* can be brought about by his own efforts. This is a logical point which contains a psychological reference rather than a psychological point. Aristotle is elucidating the *concept* of choice. His own remark, however, '*in general* choice *seems* to relate to things that are in our power' (my italics), is a bit weak for a logical point. If he had intended this as a generalisation from experience, then he ought to have told us what would count as an exception. He also rules out the identification of choice with opinion. Truth or falsity is predicated of opinion, whereas good or bad is predicated of choice. He also distinguishes choice from opinion on the grounds that choice is relevant to character determination, whereas opinion is not. What you think to be the case or not the case in matters related to what we would loosely describe as scientific fact is not a determinant of character. What Aristotle is attempting to do here is to delineate that aspect of voluntary action which can be identified as choice. At 1112^a we begin to get a more positive account. Aristotle asks:

> Is it, then, what has been decided on by previous deliberation? ... Choice involves a rational principle and thought. Even the name seems to suggest that it is what is chosen before other things.

(The reason why Aristotle makes a philological appeal is that the literal meaning of the Greek word for choice is 'preferential choice.')

The next question concerns what it is that we can be said to deliberate about. What are the appropriate objects of deliberation? We can only deliberate about those things that can be brought about by our own efforts. Things which happen through nature, necessity or chance are not the objects of deliberation. Deliberation is also said to concern the *means* and not the *ends*. Thus when we deliberate, we are working out which is the best of all the means available for achieving the *assumed* end. The reader should be familiar with the Aristotelian reasoning which lies behind this from his study of Book I. Aristotle holds that the end cannot be the subject of deliberation, because 'deliberation is about the things to be done by the agent himself, and actions are for the sake of things other than themselves'. If the end were also a matter of deliberation, then that would be for the sake of something else and so on. The object of choice is that which has been decided upon as a result of deliberation. 'Choice will be the deliberate desire of things in our own power' (1113^a).

There is an obvious problem here. From what Aristotle has said about choice it is difficult to see why choice is morally important. If choice is always about means, then wrong choices will always be a species of miscalculation (deliberation = calculation; see 1139^a). To choose wrongly will be to work things out incorrectly. The problem here is that in morality it is the ends which are all important. It is odd to suggest that choice has nothing to do with ends. Aristotle holds that it is 'wish' that is concerned with ends. The end is *wished* for and the means *chosen*.

Given that the means are objects of choice and therefore voluntary, it follows that actions performed which concern means will also be voluntary. Now Aristotle holds that the virtues are concerned with means, so, he argues, the virtues (and vices) will be voluntary and lie within our power. Being good or being bad is understood in terms of practising virtue or vice, therefore, being good and being bad lie within our power. In contrast with Plato, Aristotle holds that wickedness is voluntary and this, he thinks, is assumed in our notion of deserts.

Aristotle holds that men are responsible for their characters as activities are chosen and it is the activities we choose that determine our character. They are the same. It might be argued that each man desires what is apparently good to him but he has no control over what appears to him to be apparently good. Aristotle's answer to this is as follows. If what we wish or desire is the apparent good, and our state of character determines what the apparent good is, then, given that we are responsible for our state of character, it follows that we shall be responsible for what appears to be good to us. Even if the end appears to us as a matter of heredity, and thus we are not responsible for it, there will still be something dependent on us. This will be the means of bringing it about. Virtue and vice will then still be voluntary. There are difficulties with this. We do not blame people (or praise them) just for the ways in which they attempt to bring something about; we also blame them for *what* they are trying to bring about. But if this end can be dictated by heredity or nature, then where do praise and blame come in? A further problem which the reader should consider in Aristotle's account of responsibility and voluntariness concerns his example of the man who has sunk to such depths of decadence that he no longer has the power to act virtuously, even if he wanted to.

Book VII

The first part of Book VII is concerned with the problem of whether it is possible for a person to know what is right or good and yet do what is wrong or bad. Plato had held that this was impossible. According to Plato, no one could knowingly act in a way that was contrary to the good. All wrongdoing arises through ignorance of the good.

Aristotle charges Plato with asserting what is contrary to fact. On Aristotle's account it is possible to know what is good and yet not act in accordance with it. He cites the example of the weak-willed person in order to support this. A weak-willed or uncontrolled person knows what is right, and, up to the point of action, thinks that he should act accordingly. This distinguishes him from the merely licentious person who simply thinks that the pleasure of the moment should always be pursued. The problem for Aristotle is to give a logically coherent account of this example so that the weak-willed person can be said to know good and do bad.

Some followers of Plato had maintained that if a man acts wrongly, then he had opinion and not knowledge. Aristotle dismisses this by appealing to the psychological state of such an individual. People who believe their opinions to be true act *as if* they constituted knowledge. From the point of view of action there is no difference and, therefore, the claim is irrelevant to the present discussion.

Aristotle wants to say that a weak-willed or incontinent person can be said to have knowledge but not to be using it. He thinks that there is nothing odd in saying that a person has knowledge but fails to use it. He offers examples where this would be permissible.

First, in knowledge there are two kinds of premisses. There is knowledge of the universal (All As are B) and knowledge of the particular (This is A). Aristotle argues that it is quite possible for a person to have knowledge of the universal and of the particular and still act in a way contrary to that knowledge. In such a case the knowledge of the particular is not being used. It might, for example, be at the back of his mind. Aristotle needs an account of what it is to know something 'at the back of one's mind', and the reader needs to consider whether this could be of moral interest. It should also be noted that knowledge is not present at the time of action. At 1147^a Aristotle says of the incontinent man in relation to knowledge of particulars, 'the incontinent man either has not or is not exercising the knowledge'. In the case of his not having knowledge of particulars, as opposed to his having it and not using it, he is, of course, deficient in knowledge. (See also 1147^b.)

Secondly, there is another sense in which it can be said that a person has knowledge but fails to use it. This is the sense in which people who are asleep, drunk or mad can be said to have knowledge. They are said to have it in a sense and yet not to have it. Aristotle goes on to contrast such cases with cases of men who are under the influence of their passions. He claims that there is a similarity between the incontinent and those who are asleep, mad or drunk. This is an interesting line of thought, but one which needs to be approached with care. The case of madness, for example, is not a clearcut case of someone having knowledge and not using it or not having it in some other sense. It can be the case that a failure to display particular kinds of knowledge is a criterion for saying that someone is mad. The fact that he had such knowledge in the past will not entitle us to say that *now* he has it and does not have it.

Thirdly, a person can behave incontinently as a result of appetite being contrary to the right rule. Thus you can know that all Xs are bad for you and that this (some perceptible object) is X, and still pursue X. You are moved by appetite and by opinion (Aristotle does not refer to this as 'knowledge') that X is pleasant. One is moved by appetite to pursue what is harmful even though one knows that it is harmful. Aristotle claims that this is a fact of human nature. He is undoubtedly correct in making this claim. The case of addiction would fit this account as would cravings in general. In the case of moral evil, however, it should be noted that it always makes sense to say that any appetite can be overcome by a stronger one. Hopefully, the reader will ponder this rhetorical statement.

Aristotle's use of the concept of weakness of will does not eliminate all the problems surrounding the question of whether it is logically possible to choose to do what you regard as evil. The reader should consider Sidgwick's remark that 'Aristotle's vicious man must aim at what then appears to him good'.

Pleasure (Books VII and X)

The importance of a study of pleasure and pain is recognised early in the *Ethics*. In Book II we are told that the virtuous man derives pleasure from doing those things which are virtuous. It is therefore important that the right education will teach us to derive pleasure from the right things and to feel pain at doing the wrong things, 'moral excellence is concerned with pleasures and pains' (1104^b). The connection between the virtues and pleasure and pain is so intimate that the whole enquiry must concern pleasure and pain.

Aristotle's view of pleasure is that it is *a* good, but not *the* good. Pleasure is not the sole good. Some things are pursued for their own sake rather than for any accompanying pleasure. In Book VII Aristotle considers and rejects the traditional arguments that attempt to show that pleasure is not a good. Indeed, he claims that such arguments do not even show that pleasure is not the supreme good. It is in Book X that we get a positive account of the kind of thing that pleasure is.

At 1174^a Aristotle claims that there is an analogy between pleasure and seeing. The point of this comparison is that at any moment seeing is complete. It is not completed by having something added to it at a later stage. Pleasure is said to be like this. It is a complete whole which is not made complete by any subsequent additions. Thus it is not movement as movements are incomplete. They are completed by later additions. Movements are *for* something, as in the case of fitting stones together which will *later* be a temple, or *to* something, as in the case of walking.

All the senses are said to exercise their activity on what is sensed. Perfect activity is that which is exercised by a sense in good condition on the finest object that can come under its jurisdiction. This activity will be the most complete and pleasant. What Aristotle means here is that pleasure completes the activity. It is an external sign of the goodness of the activity. It is not a factor which makes it perfect. We must not think of the activity as a means to the attainment of pleasure. When a faculty is performing its function well on the best of its possible objects, then pleasure will be involved in the activity. It is said to complete the activity.

There are, of course, different types of pleasure. As there are different activities, then the pleasures which accompany such activities will also be different. Given that activities can be good or bad, some worthy of choice and others not, the same will be true of the corresponding pleasures. There is an intrinsic relation between pleasure and activity, though the relation is not that of identity. The pleasure belonging to a worthy activity is good, to an unworthy one, bad. As there is a superiority of activities, so too there will be a superiority of pleasures. Aristotle held that the most superior activity was thought. He did not, however, decry bodily pleasures. If bodily pleasures were not good, then it would be difficult to understand why their contrary, bodily pain, was regarded as bad. Aristotle held that it was not the pursuance of bodily pleasures that made the bad man bad, but rather the pursuance of an excess of them.

▶ Utilitarianism

Introduction

I want to approach this ethical theory via a consideration of one of the most important motives of its proponents. Consider the difference between a moral dispute and a factual dispute. A factual dispute is always, in principle, soluble. To take a simple example, if there is a dispute as to whether there are books in the cupboard, then we know how to solve it. We open the cupboard and look. Many factual disputes are, of course, more complicated than this. A dispute about prehistorical facts or a dispute about the composition of an astronomical body many light years away may be virtually impossible to solve. They are, however, *in principle* soluble. That is to say, if we had more data or more sophisticated technology, then we would know how to solve them. The difficulties we have in solving them are of a *practical* kind.

The kind of examples above can be contrasted with a moral dispute. Suppose two people disagree as to whether they should tell a third that his wife is unfaithful. They know that this man lives solely for his wife and that such news would cause him anguish. On the other hand, they know that she is unfaithful and that she is using him. They feel that the truth should be told. One thinks that the truth is more important than causing distress, whereas the other thinks that in this case not causing distress is more important than truth or honesty. In such a case as this we have a clash between our moral principles, namely, that we should be honest and that we should not cause pain to others. An appeal to either principle cannot solve the dispute. It is because they regard both principles as important that they feel the weight of the dilemma. When they have decided to act on one or other of these principles, they may still wonder whether they have done the right thing.

The utilitarians were concerned that apparently there are some moral disputes that cannot be solved. They were suspicious of this as the notion of insoluble disputes tends to make morality an arbitrary affair. What was required was an objective principle for deciding questions of right and wrong, good and bad. In the first chapter of *Utilitarianism* J. S. Mill regards the foundation of morality as the main problem for speculative thought. He tells us that: 'a test of right and wrong must be the means ... of ascertaining what is right and wrong'.

It is important to place the utilitarians in their historical context. Many were concerned with legal and social reform. This is especially true of Bentham, J. S. Mill and Austin. Bentham in fact uses the law as the first analogy with morality. If you have a conflict between two legal principles, then there is a court available to provide an objective judgement on the matter. Thus if I think that I should be allowed to play my stereo late at night on the grounds that I can do what I like in my own home, and my neighbour objects on the grounds that it constitutes a nuisance, then the court will decide which principle is to be upheld. Both parties are prepared to accept the court's decision. Without this the law becomes senseless. The court decides in an independent and non-arbitrary manner. The point of the legal analogy is that the utilitarians are looking for some system to solve moral disputes in the same independent, non-arbitrary way as the courts do in legal disputes.

Bentham is an example of a philosopher who attempts to derive his ethical theory from a theory of human nature. His fundamental principle of human nature is that pleasure and pain are the realities underlying and determining human action:

> Nature has placed mankind under the governance of two sovereign masters, pain and pleasure. It is for them alone to point out what we ought to do as well as to determine what we shall do. On the one hand the standard of right and wrong, on the other the chain of causes and effects, are fastened to their throne. They govern us in all we do, in all we say, in all we think ...[9]

Man continually pursues his own pleasures or happiness and retreats from pain. Given this conception of human nature, it follows that his ethical theory is going to be based on the motives of pursuance of pleasure and avoidance of pain. Thus the central tenet of his ethical theory is that those acts which increase the happiness of people are right and those which decrease it are wrong. Since a particular act may please some people and harm others, he added that '[t]he greatest good of the greatest number is the measure of right and wrong'. This is the proposed test of rightness and wrongness.

Bentham's objective was to measure the values of various pleasures and pains. It was towards this end that he developed his felecific or hedonic calculus. He tells us at the start of the fourth chapter of *The Principles* that pleasure and the avoidance of pain are the ends which the legislator has in view: he should therefore understand their value. Bentham is here using 'value' in an arithmetical sense. He intends to provide a method for measuring the value of various pleasures and pains, and hence the value of actions involving those pleasures and pains. The measurement depends on a number of objective factors which are: (1) Intensity; (2) Duration; (3) Certainty or Uncertainty; (4) Propinquity or Remoteness; (5) Fecundity, that is, the tendency to produce other pleasures or pains; (6) Purity, that is, the chance it has of not being followed by sensations of the opposite kind; (7) Extent, that is, the number of persons affected by it.

The calculus operates along the following lines. To assess the general tendency of any proposed act we begin with the person most directly affected by it, and take into account the value of each of the distinguishable pleasures and pains which appear to be produced by it in the first instance. This value is determined by the first four factors in the calculus. We then consider the value of each pleasure and pain which appears to be produced by it *after* the first, (5) and (6) in the calculus. We then make out a kind of moral balance sheet. On the one side we calculate the sum of the pleasures, and on the other, the sum of the pains. When we have done this we compare the totals to see which is the larger. If the pleasure side is the larger, then this will give the *good* tendency of the act upon the whole, with respect to the interests of that individual person. If the pain side is the larger, then that will point to the *bad* tendency.

The next step is to take into account the number of persons whose interests appear to be concerned, (7) in the calculus. The process is then repeated with respect to each. We then:

> Sum up the numbers expressive of the degrees of *good* tendency, which the act has, with respect to each individual, in regard to whom the tendency of it is *good* upon the whole: do this again with respect to each individual, in regard to whom the tendency of it is *bad* upon the whole. Take the *balance:* which if on the side of pleasure, will give the general *good tendency* of the act with respect to the total number or community of individuals concerned; if on the side of pain, the general *evil tendency*, with respect to the same community. (*Principles,* ch. IV)

This is how Bentham calculates the greatest good of the greatest number. With this method we are held not only to obtain the value of an act, but are also able to assess the objective goodness or rightness of two opposing courses of conduct. The calculus was given a practical use by some. At that time there was a question of whether it was right to require vaccination against smallpox. Since some children died as a result of the vaccination, the procedure was not a universally approved one. The proponents of vaccination argued that if 10 per cent of those inoculated died from the inoculation, whereas 50 per cent of the group would otherwise die from the disease, then the inoculations were justified. They were justified with the proviso that the survival of the larger number would be a good for all of society. The reader should try changing the figures and the disease and consider this in the light of the recent controversy over whooping-cough vaccine. It is obvious from examples such as these just how much practical importance a philosophical theory can have. The practical implications concern life and death. It should also be realised that according to the Benthamite procedure saving lives is contingent on the fact that it increases the greatest happiness. It *just so happens* that saving lives is conducive to procuring that benefit. The reader might like to consider how the case of an over-populated country would be dealt with on these principles.

One very obvious problem with Bentham's procedure is the idea of quantifying pleasure. There are no units of measurement. Bentham was aware of this problem but adopted a somewhat cavalier attitude by remarking that, 'strict logicians are licensed visionaries'.

Bentham, Austin and James Mill (J. S. Mill's father) thought that activities were only worthwhile if they were pleasure-producing. They were in favour of legal, social and penal reform, and in favour of increased individual liberty. But, like the example of saving lives, these only had the status of contingency. It just so happens that they produce more 'units' of pleasure than their alternatives. If it could be shown that a big brother society involving deprivation of liberty produced more units of pleasure on Bentham's calculus than a society which takes certain risks by allowing freedom to its citizens, then Bentham and his followers would be forced to say that deprivation of liberty was a good thing. This consequence is due to the fact that Bentham does not distinguish quality and quantity of pleasure. In a famous remark he said that quantity of pleasure being equal, push-pin is as good as poetry. J. S. Mill did distinguish pleasures in regard to their quality. He would have held that the *kind* of pleasure obtained from living in a big brother society would not be worth having. If you believe in liberty then the pleasures of oppression ought to be excluded. As all Bentham takes into account are quantities of pleasure, then he has to consider the pleasure that some would gain out of oppressing others.

I shall conclude this discussion of Bentham by indicating a serious problem underlying the whole idea of calculation in morality. The question that needs examining is whether it is necessary to quantify our moral notions in order for us to have rational discourse and argument on moral issues. The obvious answer is 'no', as we already have such discussions without quantification. The question then becomes whether it would give them added precision if we could use such quantifying techniques. Would it not be preferable to equate arithmetical value (assuming the intelligibility of talk about units of pleasure) with moral value? Whatever has the higher arithmetical value of pleasure units over pain units would, by virtue of its higher arithmetical value, have a higher moral value. If this were adopted as a thesis concerning the *meaning* of moral terms, then arithmetical value would become synonymous with moral value. The reader should try the following thought experiment. Consider Oscar Wilde's definition of a cynic as a person who knows the price of everything and the value of nothing. If we think that the Benthamite procedure is a viable one, then we could rephrase Wilde's definition along the following lines: a cynic is a person who has performed one set of calculations (monetary) but not another (hedonic). Do you think that this adequately captures the sense of 'value' which Wilde intended in the original definition? If you do not think that it does, then ask yourself why not. Is it because something is omitted? If you think this is the case, do you mean that the calculus is incomplete, that there is another factor to be added to the seven listed by Bentham, or do you mean that the idea of quantification is misplaced in morality?

J. S. Mill

Mill wanted a principle for testing the rightness or wrongness of action and thus providing the means of ascertaining what is right or wrong. In ch. I of *Utilitarianism* he dismisses the idea of a moral faculty fulfilling this function as it does not discern what is right or wrong in a particular case in the way that our senses inform us of sights and sounds in a particular case. A 'moral sense' then would not be like our other senses. On the subject of traditional ethics, Mill tells us that the intuitionists hold the principles of morals to be evident or *a priori*, whereas the inductivists hold that issues of right and wrong are questions of observation and experience. Mill's complaint is that although both of these schools of thought hold equally that morality must be deduced from first principles, and that there is such a thing as a science of morals, they seldom attempt to make out a list of the principles. They hardly ever make an effort to reduce the various principles to 'one first principle or common ground of obligation'.

Mill's first principle is the greatest happiness principle or the principle of utility. This states that actions are right in the proportion that they tend to produce the greatest happiness of the greatest number. Men's sentiments, both of favour and aversion, are greatly influenced, he says, by what they suppose to be the effects of things upon their happiness. Mill is here claiming that it is the *consequences* of actions which are the most important consideration in matters relating to the morality of action.

Mill does not think that the greatest happiness principle is susceptible of proof in the usual sense of the word, but neither does he think that this detracts from its validity. Whatever can be proved to be good must be so by being shown to be a means to something admitted to be good without proof. The point that he is making is that unless you hold something to be good without reason, then you cannot accept anything. To use his own example, if you believe that health is good, then you can see why medicine is important. But how would you set about showing that health was good? It is *because you* regard health as good that you are able to appreciate the value of medicine.

In the second chapter we get a positive account of Mill's utilitarianism. Utilitarianism holds that actions are right in proportion as they tend to promote pleasure or happiness, wrong as they tend to promote the reverse of happiness. Happiness is defined as pleasure and the absence of pain, unhappiness as pain and the privation of pleasure. Mill holds that pleasure and freedom from pain are the only things desirable as ends. All desirable things are desirable either for the pleasure inherent in themselves or as a means to the promotion of pleasure and the prevention of pain. Mill is not saying that it is only *one's own* pleasure that can be desired. He is saying that pleasure and absence of pain are the only things valuable as ends. This thesis is known as Hedonism and is to be distinguished from Psychological Hedonism which asserts that an individual can only seek his own pleasure. Bentham held this latter thesis.

Mill's next contention marked another important divergence from Bentham. He says that it is quite compatible with the principle of utility to recognise the fact that some kinds of pleasure are more desirable and more valuable than others. Mill is introducing a quality consideration in addition to the purely quantitive considerations of Bentham's calculus. Mill wants to distinguish two kinds of pleasure, the higher, such as the arts, and the lower, such as eating. According to Mill those who have experienced both will say that the higher are the most important. Mill is here comparing two kinds of life, that of Socrates and that of a fool. He wants to point out a lack of symmetry between the two. Mill's point is that Socrates will experience both kinds of pleasure, whereas the fool will be ignorant of the higher pleasures. There are activities, such as mathematics or art appreciation, which you cannot enjoy or even understand unless you have already learnt something about them. On the other hand you do not have to learn to appreciate food in order to understand hunger. The higher pleasures are therefore dependent on other things being learnt. Socrates would thus be in a better position to judge the relative merits of the pleasures. This is the point of Mill's famous remark that it is better to be a human dissatisfied than a pig satisfied.

He then admits exceptions to the rule that the higher pleasures are always chosen by those who know both sides of the issue. He mentions the pursuance of sensual indulgence to the injury of health, and youthful enthusiasm sinking to indolence and selfishness in later life. He does not believe, however, that the inferior pleasures are voluntarily chosen in preference to the higher ones. On the question of which is the more valuable of two pleasures, we rely on the judgement of those who are qualified by knowledge. If the competent judges disagree, then, according to Mill, voting will settle the issue.

Later in the second chapter Mill refers to an objection against utilitarianism and his answer to this objection casts light on his conception of the relationship between the greatest happiness principle and other moral rules. The objection is that there is no time before a proposed action to calculate and weigh up the effects of any line of conduct on the general happiness. Mill's answer to this is that there has been ample time, namely, the whole past duration of the human species. We have learned from experience what the tendencies of actions are. He says that mankind must have acquired positive beliefs as to the effects of some actions on their happiness. The beliefs which have thus come down are the rules of morality for the multitude, though we still have much to learn concerning the effects of actions on the general happiness:

> to consider the rules of morality as improvable is one thing; to pass over the intermediate generalizations entirely, and endeavour to test each individual action directly by the first principle [i.e. the greatest happiness principle] is another.

Mill is here saying that whatever principle we adopt as the fundamental principle of morality, we require subordinate principles to apply it by. No system can do without them.

It is only in cases of conflict between these subordinate principles that the first principle should be appealed to. Mill's position is known as rule-utilitarianism not act-utilitarianism. The latter thesis asserts that a person ought to perform whichever of the actions open to him will maximise the general happiness in the circumstances. The thesis implies that moral rules are, in principle, superfluous, and may be treated as rules of thumb which have a useful function in cases where one does not have the time to assess the results of actions. Mill is not claiming that all our individual actions should involve appeals to the greatest happiness principle. It is only in cases of conflict between our secondary or subordinate principles – for example, it is wrong to lie can conflict with the principle that we ought to act benevolently – that we need to make this appeal.

Mill also asserts that there is no case of moral obligation in which some secondary principle is not involved. By combining this with the previous point, he avoids a traditional objection against act-utilitarianism, namely, that actions which are morally irrelevant will involve an appeal to the greatest happiness principle. Mill is saying that unless some secondary principle is involved, you do not have a moral question and it is only via the secondary principles that we appeal to the first principle. Therefore, it is only morally relevant actions which can involve such an appeal. Mill is, of course, a rule-utilitarian and we shall discuss this thesis in more detail later. It is important to grasp at this stage that when Mill says actions are right if they promote the general happiness, he is referring to *classes* or *types* of actions. In considering an individual action we do not usually appeal to the greatest happiness principle. If the proposed act is a member of a class of actions which experience has taught us is conducive to the greatest happiness, then there is no need to make a direct appeal.

Finally, in the exposition of Mill's thesis, I want to say something about Mill's 'proof' of the principle of utility. This has given rise to much philosophical controversy. Mill reminds us of his earlier observation that questions of ultimate ends do not admit of proof in the usual sense of the word. Questions about ends, he says, are questions about what things are desirable. He then expounds the utilitarian thesis as holding, 'that happiness is desirable, and the only thing desirable as an end; all other things being only desirable as a means to an end'. Mill claims that there is an analogy between 'visible' and 'desirable' in the sense that the only proof one can give to show that an object is visible is the fact that it is seen, and, similarly, the only proof one can give that an object is desirable is the fact that it is desired. He continues by saying that no reason can be given as to why the general happiness is desirable, except that each person, so far as he believes it to be attainable, desires his own happiness. This, according to Mill, is all the proof that is possible and necessary to show that happiness is a good; that each person's happiness is a good to that person and the general happiness, therefore, a good to the aggregate of all persons. He considers the objection that people desire other things besides happiness, such as virtue. Mill argues that it is quite consistent with utilitarianism to hold that people desire virtue as an end in itself and not just as a means. The justification he offers for this is that virtue is *part* of happiness or at least capable of becoming so:

> in those who love it disinterestedly it has become so, and is desired and cherished, not as a means to happiness, but as part of their happiness.

He does not regard happiness as an abstract idea, but as a concrete whole of which virtue is a part. He gives other examples of parts of this concrete whole: love of music, health and money. A part such as virtue is distinguished from a part such as money on the ground that the utilitarian standard tolerates and approves those other acquired desires only up to the point, after which, they become injurious to the general happiness. Virtue is to be cultivated to the greatest possible strength.

As a result of those considerations he says that, in reality, there is nothing desired except happiness. Those who desire virtue for its own sake, desire it because the consciousness of being without it is a pain, and with it, a pleasure. He then claims that we have an answer to the question of what kind of proof is available:

> If the opinion which I have now stated is psychologically true, if human nature is so constituted as to desire nothing which is not either a part of happiness or a means of happiness, we can have no other proof that these are the only things desirable.

Mill asks the question whether mankind desires anything for itself except that which is a pleasure, or of which the absence is a pain. He regards this as a factual question. The sources of evidence will declare that desiring a thing and finding it pleasant, aversion to it and finding it painful, are phenomena entirely inseparable, or rather two parts of the same phenomenon. They are two ways of regarding the same psychological fact. Mill is saying that to think of an object as desirable (unless for the sake of its consequences) and to think of it as pleasant are one and the same thing. He concludes by saying that to desire anything, except in proportion as the idea of it is pleasant, is a physical and metaphysical (that is, logical) impossibility.

Criticisms

Mill can be criticised for equating happiness with pleasure and absence of pain. He treats pleasure and pain as opposites. A powerful case against this has been made by Ryle. Ryle points out conceptual differences between them. Thus, for example, one can locate pains in a way that one cannot locate pleasures. They are not mutually exclusive as it can be asserted intelligibly that one derives pleasure from pain. There is no contradiction involved in saying that a person was happy through a period of time, even though he suffered pain during that period. It is to be granted that this is not the case for all pains, for as Hume remarked, it would be absurd to say that a man enduring agony on the rack was happy. The above considerations do, however, suggest that the terms 'pleasure' and 'pain' are not contraries. In view of this, and of some considerations to be discussed later, it could be said that it is preferable to interpret the principle of utility in a negative rather than a positive way. The main thrust of the principle would then be the mitigation of pain rather than the pursuance of pleasure.

We saw that Mill rejected Bentham's hedonic calculus on the grounds that differences in the quality of pleasure are important enough to outweigh differences in quantity. Mill tends to exploit the ambiguity of the word 'quality'. It can be used to refer to kinds of pleasure, but it would be trivial to say that different pleasures were of different kinds. The word 'quality' can also be used in an evaluative sense. The criticism to be made against Mill here is that if we adopt the thesis of hedonism, then we have no right to legislate that some pleasures are superior as pleasures to other ones. John

Plamenatz in *The English Utilitarians* has criticised Mill on this point. Most people derive pleasure from those things for which they have an aptitude. Plato, for example, had an aptitude for rhetoric, and he derived more pleasure from this than he did from games. Does this entitle him to say that his pleasures are superior as pleasures to those of the athlete? If one rejects hedonism, then one can argue that intellectual activity is, or its product is, intrinsically valuable. If one holds, however, that pleasure is the *only* criterion of value, then one cannot treat one's own personal pleasure as the supreme good. Thus, in our imaginary example, if Plato were to argue that his pleasure was the supreme good, the athlete would be equally entitled to say that his pleasure was the supreme good. An appeal to the verdict of fellow intellectuals would not advance matters as the athlete could appeal to the verdict of fellow athletes. Mill's argument that people change from mental to physical pleasure because they have lost the capacity for the former can be met by the athlete. He could argue that people change from physical pleasures to mental ones because they have lost the capacity to pursue strenuous activities. It seems that in order to be consistent a hedonist must say that each person is an authority on what gives him pleasure.

We can certainly accept Mill's point that those who have experienced both kinds of pleasure (higher and lower) are in the best position to pass judgements on their worth, but his claim that all those who have experienced both will always choose the higher is unfounded. The problem, though, is what if they do not? We can grant Mill's lack of symmetry between the fool and Socrates, but the problem is that if the fool cannot understand the higher pleasures, then he will treat them as unimportant or illusory. Furthermore, Socrates is not going to convince him otherwise. Mill suggests that competent judges could decide the issue, but he also allows for disagreement here, hence the need for voting. This is hardly satisfactory as it is tantamount to admitting the kind of irresolvable dispute that the utilitarian thesis sought to remove.

The next difficulty I want to discuss concerns Mill's 'proof' of the principle of utility. Mill wants to show that some things are good and others bad by appealing to the principle of utility which is the ultimate principle, i.e. the terminating point of all chains of reasoning in morality. He says that he can show that we all accept such a principle. The argument is as follows. People already accept (1): Happiness alone is desired by the individual. This leads to (2): The greater happiness is desired, from which he infers (3): The greatest happiness is desirable.

Mill is equivocal as to the status of (1). As we saw earlier, he claimed that it was a physical *and* metaphysical impossibility to desire anything except in proportion to the idea of its being pleasant. There is a problem in saying that it is both. If something is logically impossible, then the question of its factual possibility cannot arise. It seems, however, that Mill intended it to be a factual question as he talks of 'the sources of evidence'. If it is a factual question, and (1) is a factual answer, then (1) must be informative. Let us then inquire into its informative content.

In considering this we should remember that the utilitarians wanted to be able to resolve disputes between people who wanted different things. In order to do this, they claim that there is something similar about all our desires. Thus, for example, the desire for freedom and the desire for security have something in common, that is, pleasure. They are desired as a means to happiness or as a part of happiness. Having found something in common (pleasure) you can then calculate which desire, when realised, will produce the most pleasure. The problem though is that what the utilitarians mean by 'pleasure' is 'anything that may satisfy a desire'. This does not establish that there is some *one* thing which we all desire. They cannot *mean* by 'pleasure' some particular thing like money or the love of music, to use Mill's examples. The problem here is that if the *meaning* of pleasure is equated with some particular(s), then anyone not desiring the thing(s) in question would *ipso facto* not be desiring pleasure, and (1) would have been empirically falsified. Given this difficulty of defining pleasure in terms of any particulars, 'pleasure' comes to represent anything that may satisfy desire. It is of no help here to regard happiness or pleasure as a concrete whole for which we all aim. We get exactly the same problem with 'the concrete whole' as we did with 'pleasure'. To say that we all desire concrete wholes and concrete wholes are what satisfy our desires is hardly informative. This does not establish any particular concrete whole which we all desire. It could be said in criticism of Mill that his argument amounts to no more than the following: what we all want is the satisfaction of desire, and what we all desire is satisfaction. If this is Mill's argument, then it involves what is known as the fallacy of composition. The following argument would involve the same fallacy and would be equally uninformative: whatever the parts of a physical object are, the object is always composed of parts, therefore, all physical objects are made of the same things, namely, parts.

The aim of the utilitarians is the production of the greatest happiness, but given the way Mill uses the term 'happiness', there does not seem to be a particular procedure to engage in. The nineteenth-century utilitarians had a fair idea of what they meant by 'happiness', for example, social reform, so there was an agreed criterion. The problem is that when 'happiness' becomes a blanket term that covers 'anything which may satisfy a desire', the agreed criteria become difficult to state. This is because in the field of morality Mill has not established any one thing which we all desire.

The next problem with Mill's proof concerns the validity of the move from propositions (2) to (3). Mill does not seem to think that there is any problem involved in moving from 'desired' to 'desirable'. He is claiming that if something is desired, then that thing is desirable. In other words, what is desirable is what is desired. A powerful case against this move has been made by G. E. Moore.

In *Principia Ethica* Moore accuses Mill of committing a logical error – the fallacy of the ambiguous middle term. Moore takes Mill to task for claiming that there is an analogy between 'visible' and 'desirable'. It does follow from the fact that something is seen that it is visible because 'visible' *means* 'able to be seen'. If Mill's analogy were correct, then 'desirable' would mean 'able to be desired'. It would follow from this that 'undesirable' would mean 'unable to be desired'. Moore points out that 'desirable' means 'what *ought* to be desired' or 'what *deserves* to be desired'.

> 'Desirable' does indeed mean 'what it is good to desire'; but when this is understood, it is no longer plausible to say that our only test of *that*, is what is actually desired. Is it a mere tautology when the Prayer Book talks of *good* desires? Are not bad desires also possible?[10]

Moore's argument has been criticised by Mary Warnock. She takes the view that all you can go on is what people think worth desiring and this is the test for what is desirable. Warnock argues that Mill was trying to show that people think that happiness is good and this is proved by people desiring happiness. Thus what people desire is the test for what is good. The determinant of desirability is what is desired. Warnock thinks this is a good test and supports her argument with an appeal to the practice of estate agency. When an estate agent says that a house is desirable, the test is that it is desired. It would be a lie if no one desired it. Her example, however, raises no *moral* issues and this constitutes an important difference. If I tell someone that it is desirable to adopt a code of honesty in his dealings with others, then I imply that he *ought* to behave honestly. But if an estate agent tells us that a house is desirable, this does not carry the implication that we ought to want it or that we are obliged to buy it. The kind of house that we should buy, assuming that we should buy one, is contingent upon many extraneous factors such as income, security, family size and number of cars. It would be absurd to suggest that our moral conduct should be determined by factors of this kind. Moore can be taken as saying that what is appropriate in the field of estate agency is inappropriate in the field of morality. Mill thinks that the final test of what is desirable is what is actually desired, whereas Moore is pointing out that you can object to, and judge, desires. If Mill were correct, then how could this be so? On Mill's account anything that is desired is, *ipso facto,* desirable. One would expect a utilitarian to condemn bad desires as those desires which are not conducive to the greatest happiness. If one adopts this position, then some other way has to be found for moving from (2) to (3).

I mentioned earlier that there were two main versions of utilitarianism, namely, act- and rule-utilitarianism. We saw some of the difficulties with act-utilitarianism and Mill seemed aware of these. Just to re-cap, act-utilitarianism is the thesis that a person ought to perform whichever of the actions open to him will maximise happiness in the circumstances. This implies that moral rules are rules of thumb, a useful guide perhaps in a case where you do not have enough time to assess the results of your conduct. How should rule-utilitarianism be defined?

It is something equated with the theory which Urmson attributes to Mill, namely, the acceptance of the following four propositions:

(A) A particular action is shown to be right (or wrong) by showing that it is in accord with (or transgresses) some moral rule.

(B) A moral rule is shown to be correct by showing that recognition of that rule promotes the ultimate end.

(C) Moral rules can be justified only in regard to matters in which the general welfare is more than negligibly affected.

(D) Where no moral rule is applicable, the question of the rightness or wrongness of particular acts does not arise.

If rule-utilitarianism is defined thus, then it is not Mill's theory and, furthermore, it is an inadequate theory. First, it is incomplete as there is no mention of resolving conflicts between moral rules by appealing to the greatest happiness principle. One of the main merits of utilitarianism is that it is supposed to provide such a criterion. Secondly, and more seriously, it is incoherent. Urmson's (A) implies that in any case of conflicting duties, whichever of the conflicting rules is obeyed, the action will be both right and wrong. This can be illustrated with an example. If the duty of truth-telling were to conflict with the duty to act benevolently, then, in telling the truth, you have acted correctly (that is, in accordance with the moral rule not to lie) and incorrectly (that is, by transgressing the moral rule to act benevolently).

A more adequate version of Mill's rule-utilitarianism would be the following:

(1) A moral rule is justified if and only if more happiness will result from the general adoption of the rule than from the general adoption of another rule, or from having no rule.

(2) In most cases an individual action is right if it conforms with, and wrong if it violates, a moral rule.

(3) When two accepted moral rules conflict, the conflict should be resolved by appealing to the greatest happiness principle.

(4) In cases where no specific rule is called for, the agent is under no moral obligation.

In order to provide an adequate account of rule-utilitarianism, one would need to add Urmson's proposition (C). Mill does not mention it but it seems essential. It also seems to be the case that Mill had not fully realised the implications of rule-utilitarianism. He tells us that it is always wrong to lie. Lying would weaken the reliance that each of us has on the words of others and this would be a bad precedent. This exposes Mill to the reply that such a consideration would not be relevant if the lie went undetected, or more generally, where one violates any moral rule without being detected. The reader should note the consequentialist element here. It is not so much what is involved in lying that is of importance, but rather the effects it has.

Mill should not have said that it is *always* wrong to lie. The position suggested by this claim is known as restricted utilitarianism. This is a version of rule-utilitarianism which regards moral rules as being akin to laws, that is, they should never be broken. Mill need not have said that it is always wrong to lie. He could have said that we all ought to accept the moral rules of our society, and only in cases of conflict should we apply the greatest happiness principle. Thus, in the case of lying, we could justify telling a lie if telling the truth conflicted with some other moral rule and the observance of this other rule in a particular case leads to the promotion of the greatest happiness. This position is known as extreme utilitarianism and is one that should be attributed to Mill, that is, propositions (1) to (4) plus Urmson's (C). Mill does actually say that there cannot be a rule of thumb to which there are no exceptions.

I now want to consider the application of these two versions of rule-utilitarianism (restricted and extreme) to a moral example. The example comes from Dostoevsky's *Crime and Punishment*. The central character, Raskolnikov, is led to the conclusion that in a particular case murder is justifiable. The money he obtains by robbing and killing the pawnbroker would help himself, his sister, the pawnbroker's sister and all the debtors. All round, her death would serve the greatest happiness. He therefore kills her.

According to extreme utilitarianism he would be right. He has found an exception to proposition (2) which stated in *most* cases an act is wrong if it violates a moral rule. He has engaged in the procedure advocated in (3) and found that the greatest happiness is served by committing the murder. He could argue that, in this particular case, an exception to the general rule that murder is wrong has been found.

The restricted utilitarian would say that, generally speaking, the greatest happiness is not served by murder and therefore he should not commit murder. (Although if he came across enough cases where it was, then he might try to alter the rule.) It might be claimed that he ought not to commit the murder as he knows with certainty that in general murder will not increase the general happiness, but does not know with certainty that it will in a particular case. The problem with this is that in our example, he would, as a matter of fact, know with certainty that it will. There would be something odd in saying that you can have certain and general knowledge of the consequences of murder, but yet cannot know in a particular case. It is odd because in order to know general consequences we must already know *some* particular ones.

There is a general problem which emerges here. In both of the above replies appeals are made to consequences. Raskolnikov also appeals to consequences. Surely what has been omitted is that the murder of an individual has not been adequately represented as a wrong against *the individual*. It has only been considered a wrong inasmuch as the generalised effects of such a practice would cause misery *to others*.

Conclusions

I shall end the discussion by saying that any version of utilitarianism has two implicit claims:

(1) The rightness/wrongness of actions depends solely on their results.
(2) The hedonist thesis that nothing but pleasure (happiness) is intrinsically valuable.

The first is consequentialism and this can be accepted without accepting hedonism. Historically, it is correct to define utilitarianism as necessarily involving hedonism. Philosophers in the eighteenth and nineteenth centuries commonly regarded hedonism as self-evident. Nowadays, it is legitimate to use the term 'utilitarianism' as a way of referring to consequentialism.

Mill held both (1) and (2). In regard to consequentialism, Mill held that a person's motives for performing an action had nothing to do with the morality of the action, but rather, with the worth of the agent. It is the results of actions (the effect on the greatest happiness) which determine the objective rightness or wrongness of actions. The motives of the agent determine whether he is to be praised or blamed. This seems a legitimate distinction to draw but Mill's use of the term 'morality of action' is ambiguous. He uses it to mean objective rightness, but in practice it can be used to apply to either of the features which Mill distinguishes. If motives were quite irrelevant to the morality of action, then it would be difficult to account for our attitudes towards the hypocrite. The question of what matters morally is, of course, a central question for ethics.

If utilitarianism is equated with consequentialism (that is, without hedonism) then it will not provide the complete ethical theory for which Mill was looking. Without the thesis of hedonism consequentialism does not provide a criterion for testing moral judgements. I shall leave the reader to consider the adequacy of the proposed criterion.

▶ Deontological ethics

I now want to examine an ethical system which is very much opposed to consequentialism. The type of system in question is best exemplified by Kant's *Groundwork*. Kant opens Section I by making a sweeping claim. He tells us that it is impossible to conceive anything good without qualification except a good will. He is using the expression 'good will' in a semi-technical sense. He says that a benevolent action motivated by love or affection has no moral worth. What he means by 'good will' is the will of a person who has respect for what he regards as a morally right principle. The simplest interpretation of 'good without qualification' is the distinction between good as an end and good as a means, good for its own sake or good for the sake of its results, intrinsically or instrumentally good. He tells us that:

> A good will is good not because of what it performs or effects, not by its aptness for the attainment of some proposed end, but simply by virtue of the volition – that is, it is good in itself. (p. 12)

It would follow from this that good will – and only good will – was intrinsically good. Anything else that was valued would have to be valued as a means to the only good end, namely, good will. We may well wonder whether Kant could have meant this. Let us consider some of the examples he gives of things which he holds are not good without qualification. He lists virtue, courage and happiness. Could he have believed that, for example, people value courage and happiness only as a means? If he did, then he was mistaken. The common view is that happiness and so on are intrinsically valuable. He does not, however, necessarily mean to imply that happiness and so on are only pursued as a means. His reason for saying that courage is not good without qualification is that it might be harmful as in, say, the case of a villain. Similarly, happiness is said to be not good without qualification because the person enjoying it may not deserve it. The question is how acceptable this is. How is a good will supposed to differ from a virtue like courage? It seems that we would distinguish the virtue of courage from a particular virtuous act. What Kant says is true of a courageous act, its value will depend on other factors. The same can be said though of an action motivated by good will. It could be harmful if, for example, the agent is a fool or a fanatic. One would need to show that it was logically impossible for a fool or a fanatic to be motivated solely by a good will. Kant would, presumably, claim that when he says that a good will is the only thing good without qualification, he is considering only the motive in abstraction from all other factors in the situation. It is this motive which is always valuable. The problem with this reply is that it does not provide a ground for distinguishing a good will from virtues like courage. If we adopt this interpretation, then Kant has not provided a reason for saying that a good will alone deserves the title of good without qualification.

Kant certainly wanted to make the following claims:

(1) In assessing the moral worth of a person or action, a good will is the most important consideration.
(2) Good will is more valuable than anything else in the world. It is more valuable than any good state of affairs which may be produced as a result of our actions.

If these are all that Kant wished to claim, then he has expressed himself unclearly. He ought to have made it clear from the start, as he does make clear in paragraph 7, that 'Goodwill is the supreme good but not the only good or complete good'. This amounts to the claim that the will of a conscientious man is more valuable than anything else in the world. Even in this passage he adds the surprising statement that a good will is the condition of every other good including the desire for happiness. (The latter clause probably means 'deserving happiness'.)

Kant regarded reason as the instrument for achieving a good will. He did not regard the function of reason to be that of promoting happiness or pleasure. Kant argues for this on the teleological assumption that each of our faculties must be perfectly adapted to achieve some specific purpose. The function of reason, he claims, cannot be the promotion of human happiness because reason is an inefficient instrument for the purpose. Our happiness would be more efficiently promoted if all our actions had been promoted by instinct. He concludes that the purpose for which we have been endowed with reason was something different from that of maximising happiness. The purpose is that of achieving a good will. This is hardly a plausible argument. One could challenge the teleological assumption that faculties are properly adapted to achieve some purpose. The assumption could only be defended on the basis of religious beliefs and Kant did not want to bring religion into ethics. He talks of 'Nature' rather than 'God'. One could also challenge the view that reason was less efficient than instinct by appealing to the achievements of medicine. An interesting feature of this passage is the light it throws on Kant's view of human happiness as a basis for morality. Kant was hostile to hedonism.

I shall conclude our all too brief discussion of Kant with the following remarks. A consequentialist would criticise Kant on the ground that he has no criterion to decide which duty is to be followed in the case of conflicting duties. The problem of conflicting duties is an acute one for Kant. He says that a Categorical Imperative is an unconditional duty. The word 'unconditional' means a duty that it is never right to disobey. The problem arises when we have a situation in which two moral rules conflict and when each one is a Categorical Imperative. Suppose that you can only fulfil one by ignoring the other? Kant in a later essay offered a partial solution to this. He distinguished perfect duties (for example, truthtelling) from imperfect ones (for example, benevolence) and said that in the case of conflict the perfect duty always takes priority over the imperfect one. This would be plausible as long as we are to consider benevolence in terms of charitable acts, but Kant treats the duty to protect another's life as the duty of benevolence and thus as an imperfect duty. It is wrong to treat saving another's life as this type of benevolence. The duty to prevent another's death is a perfect duty. If Kant had recognised this, then he would have seen that duties of the same class can conflict. It may, for example, be necessary to lie in order to save the life of another.

Kant assumes that whenever a person is confronted with a moral problem, then he is in doubt as to his immediate duty. The test procedure is to ask whether the corresponding maxim can be universalised or whether he can will its universalisation. The difficulties here are that in many of Kant's examples he appeals to the consequences of universalisation rather than showing how universalisation leads to formal contradiction. It is also the case that a maxim involves describing an action in general terms and it is not clear as to why Kant should assume that there is only one general description which is relevant. There are cases where the proposed action has many different moral features and can be described differently by different people.

Philosophers other than utilitarians or consequentialists have offered strong criticisms of Kant. Bradley in *Ethical Studies* accuses Kant of making the opposite mistake to the utilitarians. The utilitarians held that consequences alone had moral worth, whereas Kant claimed that nothing but the motive has moral worth. It is one of the characteristics of Kant's 'good will' that it is formal. That is to say, it is the *form* of lying that is wrong and not the consequences of lying. Duty is thus separated from empirical considerations and thus the nature of morality is divorced from empirical considerations. Bradley has argued that no moral principle can be explained in purely formal terms. That charity or generosity are moral values is connected with human life. It is not a purely formal matter.

In opposition to Kant's duty for duty's sake, Bradley attacks Kant's idea of a being whose whole activity lies in rationality as a false abstraction. The social background must, to some extent, determine what is morally possible. It determines what you *can will*. Bradley is attacking a concept of duty which is divorced from what makes it coherent or gives it its sense. We cannot see our duties as irksome or as being imposed from outside. If we do, then the situation which produced them collapses. It would lose its meaning. There is no sense of duty *in vacuo*. The reader will find similar arguments in Ms Anscombe's *Modern Moral Philosophy*.

▶ The emotive theory of ethics

Historical background

The emotive theory of ethics is logically distinct from the theories of hedonistic utilitarianism which we have been discussing. Hume held both theses, but he did not develop the emotive theory in much detail. It is fair to say that Hume adopted the emotive theory in so far as he thought that moral terms should be defined in terms of certain emotional attitudes, namely, approval and disapproval. Hume's position is to define 'virtue' as meaning whatever action or quality gives to the spectator the pleasing sentiment of approbation. Broad in *Five Types of Ethical Theory* has said that according to Hume, 'the good' means approved by all or most men. But this is to read into Hume more than he actually says. It is a difficult point of interpretation as Hume is not very clear on this. Hume speaks as if his thesis is that when a person makes a moral judgement he is expressing or reporting his own approval or disapproval. The word 'good' (virtuous) means approved by a disinterested spectator. This might be taken to suggest that Hume took it for granted that all spectators would feel the same moral sentiment towards an action, provided that they were all disinterested.

It is, however, with the twentieth century that the theory of emotivism is more usually associated. The first explicit formulation of the theory was by Ogden and Richards in *The Meaning of Meaning* and it was later worked out in greater detail by C. L. Stevenson in *Ethics and Language* and in a paper 'Emotive Meaning and Persuasive Definitions'. The most famous statement of the position is given in ch. 6 of A. J. Ayer's classic work, *Language, Truth and Logic.* It is to this that we now turn.

Ayer's emotivism

The emotive theory is a theory of value judgements in general. What applies to ethical judgements will apply *mutatis mutandis* to aesthetic judgements. Ayer draws strict limits to what he means by a value judgement. He tells us that in 'the ordinary system of ethics' there are four different types of judgement:

(1) Propositions which express the definition of an ethical term. These are analytic as they are definitions.
(2) Propositions expressing the phenomena of moral experiences and their causes. These are synthetic, empirical judgements and the subject of an appropriate science.
(3) Exhortations to moral virtue, for example, love thy neighbour as thy self. Ayer does not regard these as genuine propositions as they

cannot be true or false. He regards them as ejaculations or commands intended to provoke a certain activity.

(4) Expressions of actual ethical judgements, for example, Murder is wrong.

Ayer claims that propositions belonging to the fourth category are meaningless or nonsensical. They have no truth-value and are akin to expressions such as 'boo' or 'hurrah'. There is a connection between Positivism and Emotivism. The Logical Positivists wanted to exclude religious and metaphysical propositions from the field of meaningful discourse. Ayer uses the example 'time is unreal' to serve as a typical metaphysical judgement. Such a proposition is not analytic, that is, it is not part of the meaning of 'time' that it is unreal. It cannot be verified or falsified by observation, so, according to the verification principle, it is meaningless.

Given this theory of meaning (the meaning of a proposition is its method of verification) the propositions of ethics had to be analytic, synthetic or meaningless. If they are to be regarded as meaningless, then the positivists have to give an account of why people use them and think that they have a meaning.

It should be realised that not all positivists were emotivists. Moritz Schlick was a notable exception. The emotive theory is not a necessary consequence of positivism. Some philosophers have detected too close a connection between the two. Thus, for example, Sir David Ross has said that Ayer discredited ethical terms *because* of his positivism. Ayer was not *logically* committed to the emotive theory as a result of his holding a positivist position. Ayer could still have discredited ethical judgements without holding the emotive theory.

Ross has objected to Ayer's thesis on epistemological grounds. Ayer does not give actual examples of ethical judgements. He uses expressions like 'X is good', which is a substitute for an ethical judgement, rather than an example of such a judgement. Ayer does use the example 'Murder is wrong', but this seems somewhat artificial. He does not use examples from contexts in which they are likely to occur, for example, the justification of murder in particular circumstances, such as the bomb attack on Hitler organised by his generals, and the subsequent moral judgements. In Stevenson's exposition of the theory we do find actual examples but they are sparse. At this point we should note a difference in approach between Stevenson and Ayer. After examining ethical judgements, Stevenson thought that the emotive theory fitted them best. Ayer begins by saying that some theories must be wrong and all that is left is emotivism. Let us now examine Ayer's thesis in detail.

It can be argued that ethical judgements are not analytic, that is, they do not simply unfold the meaning of words. Could they be synthetic, empirical judgements? Ayer argues against this on epistemological grounds. He agrees that some of the words used in moral discourse, such as 'good', do occur in genuine empirical judgements. At this point Ayer wants to make a distinction. He says that there is a danger of confusing moral judgements with empirical ones. The distinction that he has in mind is this: we can say in an evaluative way, 'that's a good film', whereas we can also say 'that's a good film' and mean that other people evaluate it in this way. The latter usage is a statement of fact concerning what other people say. The word 'good' can also be applied to functional objects. To say of a knife that it was a good knife would mean that it cuts well, that is, it performs its function well. These last two senses of 'good', the statement concerning what others say and the functional sense, occur in propositions which are empirically verifiable and falsifiable. It is a matter of fact what people say about a film and it is also a matter of fact whether a knife cuts well.

Ayer could have taken a subjectivist view and said 'this is good' means I approve of it. This would be a factual matter as my approval is a factual matter. The statement that I approve of something is verified by whether I do or do not approve of it. Alternatively, he could have said that 'X is good' means X leads to the greatest happiness, or a certain group of people approve of X. These too would be factual matters. In rejecting these options Ayer makes use of an argument of G. E. Moore's.

In *Principia Ethica* Moore regarded the utilitarians as saying that 'good' was equivalent in meaning to 'productive of the greatest happiness'. Therefore, the proposition 'it is good to produce the greatest happiness' is a tautology and says nothing to people who understand the words. Given the tautological nature of the proposition, it cannot be significantly asked whether it is true or not. But, Moore argues, the question, 'Is it good to produce the greatest happiness?' can be and is significantly asked. Therefore, the initial definition cannot be right. This is almost the same argument as Ayer's. Ayer argues that if 'X is good' were equivalent in meaning to 'I approve of X' or 'X leads to the greatest happiness', then it would be self-contradictory to say, for example, that you approved of something bad. It is not self-contradictory, therefore, the initial definition must be wrong. This can be denied without self-contradiction. Ayer uses denial where Moore uses question, otherwise it is the same argument. This forces Ayer to claim that ethical judgements are nonsensical.

Moore had ended up with Intuitionism. He said that 'good' refers to a property of a non-empirical kind. Goodness is a property which actions or states of affairs have, but it is discovered by intuition rather than sense-experience. A thesis such as this would be incompatible with Positivism and Ayer shows no sympathy for it. He argues that what is intuitively certain to one person is not necessarily intuitively certain to another. It follows that some criterion other than the intuitions is required. This seems a good argument against intuition being self-validating.

Alternatively, Ayer could argue that because ethical judgements are not empirically verifiable, then, according to Logical Positivism, they must be meaningless. This would be a bad argument as ethical judgements should be treated as *counter-examples* to the thesis that all propositions are analytic, empirically verifiable or meaningless. To refuse to treat them as counter-examples involves arguing in a circle. Their being empirically unverifiable does not entail that they are meaningless, unless you hold that any such proposition is meaningless. It is precisely this that he is trying to prove.

Ayer holds that ethical concepts are pseudo-concepts and that moral judgements are just expressions of feeling. He realises that this is inadequate for he has ignored their dynamic effect. He compensates for this by saying that moral judgements are more like words of command, which, for Ayer, are also unverifiable. He says that they are calculated to arouse feelings or provoke responses. Ayer thinks of these as being a secondary function of moral judgements. The primary function is to express feeling.

There are a number of ways of attacking this theory. The assumption that there is only one kind of meaning, factual meaning, can be attacked. According to Ayer all propositions which have meaning are either factually meaningful or analytic. One could argue that whereas ethical judgements do not have factual meaning, this does not entail that they have no meaning. An attack such as this would be an attack on Positivism and would involve an examination of the ways in which language is actually used.

The theory can also be attacked internally. Let us start with Ayer's claim that moral judgements express or evince feelings. It could be argued that this does not distinguish them from factual judgements. The statement 'I am bored' expresses feeling and it is also factual and non-evaluative. Ayer is aware of this and that is why he says that moral judgements are expressions of feeling which do not necessarily involve making an assertion. Neither will saying that moral judgements arouse people to action or provoke responses distinguish them from factual judgements. The statement 'the house is on fire' is factual *and* it arouses action. The emotivists need to claim that moral judgements, or value judgements in general, do not have any descriptive content. As we shall see shortly, this claim is questionable, but even if we accept it, there are still problems. The military command 'charge!' can express or arouse feeling, it can provoke a response and it is non-assertoric; it does not, however, become a value judgement for all that.

The assumption that there is a radical distinction between a factual and an evaluative statement can be questioned. The assumption is that there is on the one hand the purely factual untouched by evaluation, and on the other, pure evaluation without any descriptive content. Consider, however, the statement 'It is dainty'. This is evaluative but it also contains a descriptive element. The distinction between a factual statement and an expression of feeling is also doubtful. What is meant by feeling? The following are all expressions of feeling: (1) 'Ugh!'; (2) 'I can never forgive myself for doing that'; (3) 'She's an extravagant woman'. If we consider expressions of the first category, such as 'ugh!' or 'ow!', we find that we can feel the kind of disgust or pain represented by these expressions irrespective of what factual beliefs we have. This is the model of 'feeling' that Ayer is working with. Expressions of remorse, however, depend on our having a factual belief. The feelings logically entail a factual belief and this distinguishes them from the kind of feeling which belongs to the first category. Some propositions express feeling *and* a factual judgement and there is no clear distinction to be drawn. Ayer thinks that there are many things which are expressions of feeling and thus come under the first category. John Wisdom has highlighted this difficulty with Ayer's position. Wisdom invites us to consider a question such as, 'What was the comedy like?'. He lists the following possible answers: (A) Everyone laughed a lot (factual); (B) It was very funny (evaluative); (C) Ha Ha Ha (just laughter). Ayer is assimilating (B) to (C).

There is another important criticism to be made. G. E. Moore criticised subjectivism on the ground that if it were true, then it would be impossible to have disagreement in ethics. The force of this criticism is that if ethical judgements are analysed into the individual's approval or disapproval, then it is difficult to see how there can be any moral disagreement. *My* saying that I approve of something does not contradict *your* saying that you disapprove of something. This same argument can be used against Ayer. If I evince my feelings and you evince yours, then how can there be disagreement? Ayer accepts this and says that there can be no such thing as a moral argument. According to Ayer, disputes are always about matters of fact and not value. He does not offer an argument for this but issues a challenge to identify such an argument. This claim of Ayer's is surely wrong. The statement 'abortion is murder' is not a plain matter of fact and when people dispute the issue, which they do, their argument does not reduce to a factual argument. Indeed, in cases such as this, it is one's value system which may determine how the facts are to be classified or even what is to count as a fact. It may be impossible to give an account of what the facts are which is neutral in relation to value systems. There are other ways of meeting Ayer's challenge which we cannot pursue here. I shall mention two.

(1) Even when all the facts are agreed on, there can still be disagreement concerning what ought to be done. This disagreement will not necessarily be resolved by discovering any new facts and is not itself about what the facts are.

(2) People can come to see things differently and change their views morally without there being any corresponding change in the facts of the situation.

I shall conclude by remarking that in the introduction to later editions of *Language, Truth and Logic,* Ayer claims that not all disagreements can be expressed in the form of a contradiction. He claims this in order to try and avoid Moore's objection to subjectivism. But he also holds that the only genuine disagreements are factual ones. This is glaringly inconsistent. If you and I disagree on a factual matter, then we *do* contradict each other. If you assert that something is the case and I disagree, then I must be understood as saying that it is not the case and that is as plain a contradiction as you can have. It cannot be consistently maintained that all arguments are factual, all factual arguments are expressible in the form of a contradiction, and not all arguments are expressible in the form of a contradiction.

▶ Richard Hare and prescriptivism

The problem of facts and values

In our preceding discussion we came across the idea that there was a radical distinction between evaluative and descriptive language. We must now pursue this matter in some detail. The idea that judgements about what one ought to do, or about what is good or right, can be deduced or derived from statements of fact (empirical judgements) has been a matter of much philosophical controversy. The claim that such a derivation is logically illegitimate is generally regarded as dating back to Hume. Statements concerning what is or is not the case are factual or descriptive, whereas statements concerning what we ought or ought not to do, or about what is good, are prescriptive or evaluative. The problem that Hume posed was that from any factual statement, or set of factual statements, no evaluative conclusion can logically be derived. In *A Treatise of Human Nature* Bk III, pt i, 5 1, Hume writes:

> For, as this *ought* or *ought not,* expresses some new relation or affirmation, it is necessary that it should be observed and explained; and at the same time that a reason should be given, for what seems altogether inconceivable, how this new relation can be a deduction from others which are entirely different from it.

Hume can be taken as saying that no set of non-moral premises can entail a moral conclusion. In other words, value judgements cannot be deduced from factual statements. An 'is' statement cannot entail an 'ought' statement. It is this alleged logical gap that is referred to by philosophers as the fact-value distinction or the is-ought problem.

The maintenance of such a distinction has important implications. Thus, for example, the statement 'he stabbed the child' (factual) will not entail 'he ought to be punished' (evaluative). Hume's distinction is, of course, socially and politically neutral. Thus from the factual statements that many people are homeless or are hungry we cannot deduce any evaluative conclusions concerning what ought to be done. Some social scientists have ignored the problem of the fact-value gap and have attempted to derive evaluative conclusions from purely factual premises. An example of this occurred in the USA in the early 1960s where some psychologists attempted to derive statements about how negroes ought to be treated (evaluative) from alleged factual statements concerning IQ levels. Those who doubt the practical importance of ethics would do well to ponder this example.

The fact-value distinction creates obvious problems for any ethical theories which attempt to derive conclusions about the good or about our duty from premises which assert facts, or at least make factual claims, about human nature. If the fact-value distinction is upheld, then all such theories are going to contain a logical gap. Consider the implication this has for utilitarianism. From the premiss 'X leads to the great happiness' (factual) you cannot deduce 'I ought to do X' (evaluative).

Ethical theories which attempt to derive moral obligation from factual premisses are known as naturalistic theories. The attempt to move from the factual to the evaluative has become known as committing the naturalistic fallacy. Briefly, this term was coined by G. E. Moore who used it to describe any attempt to define 'good'. Moore held that 'good' referred to something simple and unanalysable. It refers to a non-complex object in the sense that it cannot be broken down into simpler parts. In this respect it would be like the concept 'red'. Moore accused some philosophers of trying to define a simple, non-natural object, goodness, in terms of something natural and complex such as pleasure or the greatest happiness. Moore held that the naturalistic fallacy consisted in the attempt to define the indefinable. He had thought that Mill had wanted to define 'good' as 'whatever is conducive to the greatest happiness'. According to Moore, this would confuse a non-natural object (goodness) with a natural one (happiness). Moore's argument would apply equally to any attempt to define 'good' in terms of any metaphysical or non-sensible object. Moore was not just saying that 'good' could not be defined in terms of the factual, he was saying that it cannot be defined in terms of anything. As a matter of historical interest, it should be realised that Moore was not distinguishing facts and values; he was marking off indefinables.

Richard Hare

The fact-value gap is discussed in ch. 5 of Hare's *The Language of Morals*. This has been a most influential work on recent ethics and it is to this that we shall now turn. The central problem for Hare is that you cannot move from factual statements to evaluative ones. If that is the case, then what account can be given of reasoning in morality?

In ch. 5 of the book Hare asks us to imagine that there is a picture hanging on the wall and we are discussing whether to assent or dissent from the judgement 'p is a good picture'. It must be understood from the context that what we mean by 'good picture' is not 'good likeness' but 'good work of art'. He then tells us that there is a very important peculiarity in the word 'good' as used in the sentence, 'p is a good picture'. The peculiarity can be brought out by supposing that there is another picture, q, standing next to p, and either p is a replica of q or q is a replica of p – we do not know which. We do know that both were painted by the same artist in the same period. Now there is one thing that we cannot say, namely, that p is exactly like q in all respects save this one, that p is a good picture and q is not. This is intended to show that goodness is not to be thought of as a constituent in a list of properties such as rectangular, hazy purple, signed and so on. Two pictures could differ in respect of one of these properties and be the same in all other respects, but the difference could not consist solely in one being good and the other not. There must be some further difference to account for the one being good and the other not being. The goodness would be a consequence of this further property. This is why Hare refers to goodness as being a 'consequentialist' or 'supervenient' characteristic.

When we judge something to be good we have criteria for making the judgement. We must not think, however, that any set of factual statements *entails* the value judgement that it is good and neither must we confuse the *meaning* of 'good' with the *criteria* of goodness. As there is a fact-value gap, we must not regard 'good' as equivalent in meaning to our criteria for saying that something is good. Hare adapts Moore's open question argument here. If we defined 'good picture' as 'a picture admired by members of the RA', then we could not say something which we might want to say and which could be intelligibly asserted, namely, that members of the RA admired good pictures. This would reduce to saying that members of the RA admire pictures which are admired by members of the RA. No matter what criteria or characteristics you use for 'good picture', if you attempt a definition in terms of them, then the same problem always arises: 'whatever defining characteristics we choose, this objection arises, that we can no longer commend an object for possessing those characteristics' (p. 85). If 'good' meant some set of characteristics, then in calling an object 'good', all we would succeed in doing would be to say that it had those characteristics. It omits the commendatory function of 'good'. Commending an object for possessing those characteristics is something that we might want to do. In the above example we wanted to commend pictures admired by the RA but the definition prevented this. Therefore, the definition is wrong. All our definition permitted was the tautology that the RA admire those pictures which they admire. According to Hare, what all naturalistic theories of ethics omit is the commendatory or *prescriptive* function of 'good'.

The word 'good' has a descriptive meaning, as in good cricket bat, good radio and so on, but it also has an evaluative meaning and this cannot be elucidated just by listing the criteria of goodness. For Hare, the primary function of 'good' is to prescribe or commend. This evaluative aspect is fundamental and remains constant, whereas the descriptive element will vary depending on what we are talking about. Thus the descriptive meaning of 'good' in 'good cricket bat' will differ from the descriptive meaning of 'good' in 'good radio'.

If the relation between goodness and its criteria is not one of entailment or identity of meaning, then what is it? Hare gives examples where we can use the word 'good' without knowing what the criteria of application are. If a person were the sole owner of a cactus, and his friend on seeing it decided to buy one, then either of them could go on to say that his cactus was the better of the two. They could do this even though they had never learnt to apply the word 'good' to cacti. The word 'good' could be used in the absence of agreed criteria of goodness. They could set up their own standards of goodness for cacti. There is, however, a problem here concerning how far this kind of example can be extended to cover morality. In morality it seems strange to say that you choose your reasons for saying that something is good, and even stranger to say that you invent them as you go on as in the cacti case. The problem which the reader should note at this stage is that the cacti example does not take into account the social background which is essential to morality.

Hare makes much of the notion of commending. It is the essential and primary function of 'good'. By inquiring into what is meant by 'commending' we get a picture of the type of reasoning Hare wants for morality.

Commending and choice

To say of something that it is good (that is, to commend it) is related to choosing. We would only call something good if the occasion could arise in which that thing was chosen. This applies to all things – lug-worms, sunsets, snooker cues and, of course, men. We would not speak of 'good men' unless we had the choice of what sort of men to become. Sunsets are only described as good because we choose to look at some of them and so on. The point to grasp here is that, for Hare, to commend is to guide choices. He tells us: 'Now for guiding a particular choice we have a linguistic instrument which is not that of commendation, namely, the singular imperative' (p. 129). Hare holds that moral judgements entail imperatives. What is good is, other things being equal, what one chooses. To say that x is good will entail imperatives on oneself and others, for example, 'choose x'. 'I ought to do *x*' will entail 'Let me do *x*'. This latter example of a self-addressed imperative though sounds more like a request or a wish than a command.

Part One of *The Language of Morals* is devoted to establishing the possibility of imperative deduction. It is possible to have argument forms along the lines of the syllogism which contain imperative sentences. Imperatives can have logical relations, such as contradiction. (The command 'open the door' contradicts the command 'close the door'.) Thus, to take an example of Hare's, we can have imperative deduction along these lines:

> (1) Take all the boxes to the station. (Major imperative premiss)
> (2) This is one of the boxes. (Minor factual premiss)
> Therefore (3) Take this to the station. (Conclusion)

Hare tells us that there are two rules governing the deduction:

(A) No indicative conclusion can be validly drawn from a set of premisses which cannot be validly drawn from the indicatives among them alone.
(B) No imperative conclusion can be validly drawn from a set of premisses which does not contain at least one imperative.

If we transfer this to moral reasoning, we get, for example:

> (1) One ought never to say what is false. (Major moral premiss)
> (2) *x* is false. (Minor factual premiss)
> Therefore (3) You should not say *x*. (Moral conclusion)

The moral conclusion (3) will entail the imperative 'Don't say *x*'. By analogy with the case of imperative deduction the rules governing moral and factual statements are the same as those governing imperative and indicative statements. This is the account Hare wants to give of moral reasoning. The fact-value gap is brought out by the indicative-imperative distinction. We apply the above rules to argument forms containing a mixture of imperatives and indicatives, and, as moral judgements entail imperatives, this is the form of reasoning deemed to be appropriate in morality.

This account of moral reasoning is meant to elucidate the connection between morality and action, or goodness and choice, as it is sometimes called. Hare argues that if moral judgements were purely descriptive, then there would be no such connection. This was a problem which had bedevilled the intuitionists who held that moral judgements describe. Hare asks what is it that has a connection with action and answers imperatives, therefore, in order to be action-guiding, moral judgements must entail imperatives. If they were merely descriptive, then they could not be action-guiding which they obviously are. Moral judgements, or value judgements in general, are held to be prescriptive not descriptive.

Universalisability

Hare then considers a possible objection to his thesis. The objection is that he is in danger of assimilating moral judgements to ordinary imperatives. Thus, to take his example, a moral judgement like 'You ought not to smoke in this compartment' is not the same as the imperative 'No Smoking' (a sign in a railway carriage) even though both will, on Hare's thesis, entail the singular imperative, 'Don't Smoke'. So how does Hare distinguish moral judgements from ordinary imperatives?

His answer is that if we hold something as a genuine moral principle, then we must be able to apply it to all in like circumstances. In other words, it must be universalisable. Ordinary imperatives are not really universal in character. They are tied specifically to individual cases. The sign in the carriage refers to *that* carriage. Ordinary imperatives are not instances of universal principles, whereas moral judgements are.

The central point about universalisability is consistency of application. We must be able to apply it to all in similar circumstances. Moral judgements are thus isolated as universalisable prescriptions. Having established the possibility of imperative deduction, he can go on to establish moral reasoning as syllogistic inferences between imperatives which are entailed by moral judgements. If we say to someone that he ought to pursue a certain course of action, then the reasoning involved would be:

(1) All men in situation x ought to do y.
(2) You are a man in situation x.
Therefore (3) Do y.

The imperative conclusion is held to provide the connection between morality and action.

Criticisms of Hare

First, in an important paper, 'Moral Beliefs', Philippa Foot[11] objects to the idea that there is something called 'evaluative meaning' which can be separated off and treated independently of its objects. She agrees that 'good' has a commendatory function, but she does not think that just anything can be the object of commendation. Foot argues that this is part of a more general mistake of thinking that we can adopt whatever attitude we like to anything. We cannot. She gives the example that it is not possible to feel proud of the sky. If the evaluative meaning of 'good' could be separated off and attached to virtually anything, then there are going to be no limits to what can count as a moral principle. There will be all kinds of things that a moral eccentric will be able to put in here. When Hare is confronted with the objection that he allows rubbish to count as moral principles, he replies that it is not rubbish – it is just unusual. This criticism of Hare is a result of his inability to restrict the possible objects of commendation. Hare's account does not seem to do justice to a distinction which we would legitimately want to make. The distinction is that between what I do not see as a moral consideration but could understand how others could, and, on the other hand, what I do not see as a moral consideration and *cannot* understand how anyone could.

Second, if we look at the prescriptivist or emotivist accounts of value judgements, we find that there is no problem in understanding moralities different from one's own. This is because they hold that you can specify what it is to have a moral attitude or viewpoint *independently* of the content of such viewpoints or attitudes. This is known as adopting a purely formal approach to ethics. For Hare, we are said to understand moral viewpoints independently of their actual content. This aspect of Hare's position is strikingly brought out by his remarks on p. 148 of *The Language of Morals*. He imagines the case of a missionary armed with a grammar book landing on a cannibal island. The vocabulary of his grammar book gives him the equivalent cannibals' word of the English word 'good'. By a strange coincidence their word is also 'good'. As long as he uses the word evaluatively and not descriptively, then he can communicate with them quite happily about morals. The only thing that either party will find odd is that different things are commended. Thus, for example, the missionary will find it odd that they commend scalps, whereas the cannibals will find it odd that he commends pieces of paper bound in leather (the Bible). There is no problem in their understanding his morality or his understanding theirs as the moral viewpoint (evaluative meaning) common to both can be specified independently of any content. The implication of this is that he can understand their morality without knowing what relation the objects of commendation have to their lives and vice versa.

Third, the previous difficulty recurs in Hare's account of why we feel the way we do about moral goodness. Depth of feeling about what is good or right is accounted for by appeal to the likelihood of our being in the situations in question. Thus, for example, we do not feel too deeply about Agamemnon's sacrifice of Iphegenia because we are not likely to be in Agamemnon's position. There is a problem here. The barrier to feeling in the Agamemnon case is not just a contingent fact that we are unlikely to be in his position. The barrier to feeling lies in imagining what his position was. We are dealing with a cultural remoteness. The trouble here is the problem endemic in Hare's approach, namely, that you can specify moral attitudes independently of what they are attitudes about. The difficulty with the Agamemnon case lies in understanding a form of life in which human sacrifice plays a part. Thus it is not just a question of the probabilities of our being placed in his position being slim, but rather understanding what that position was. On Hare's formal approach there would be no such problem of understanding as you can specify Agamemnon's moral attitude independently of the life in which it is rooted.

Fourth, Hare's universalisability thesis can be criticised. The reader should remember what Hare said concerning the two pictures. If you apply a word to something, then you have to apply it to anything else which is like it in the relevant respects. Hare thinks that this is interesting when applied to moral judgements. It would be useful in some arguments. If a nazi claimed that all Jews should be exterminated, then he could be asked to suppose that he were a Jew. If he replied that that would be different, then he would not be universalising the judgement and, for Hare, this would mean that he was not holding it as a genuine moral principle. If the nazi replied that he should be killed, then he would have universalised the judgement and thus be holding it as a genuine moral principle. It is here that argument would fail and Hare calls such a person a fanatic. But all universalisability has given us so far is a method for weeding out hypocrites and special pleaders.

The claim that you must apply the same word to an object as you apply to another object similar to it in the relevant respects is trivial when taken descriptively. If I describe one plump and juicy strawberry as good, then I call others which are like it good. When we apply this to value judgements we run into problems. Consider the case of two actions. If we say that one is good or right, then we must say that the other also is, provided that the actions are alike in the relevant respects. It should be noted that Hare does not say that the actions must be exactly alike. If he had said this, then he would have been open to the objection that no two actions are exactly alike. So the question becomes what are the 'relevant respects' in regard to actions? Could two different people be a relevant difference? If Hare claims that it is not and there must be some further difference, then he is wrong. If you say of two similar acts that one is right and the other wrong, then there must be some relevant difference in the situation to account for this. This prompts the question of whether the agent is part of the situation. If he is, then a difference here would mean a difference in the situation. It would then be a relevant difference. There are occasions where it certainly can be. To see that this is the case, let us contrast a case where it is not with one where it obviously is.

Suppose that nurses wonder whether it would ever be right for them to go on strike. This is not just a problem for an individual nurse; it would be a problem for all nurses. In this case the difference in the individuality of the agent would not be a relevant difference. But not all moral problems are like this. Consider now Gauguin's problem of whether to leave his family in order to fulfil himself as an artist. This was essentially a problem for himself and not a problem for all painters. In a case such as this it is not at all clear how universalising can help – besides what sense could we make of the notion 'all men in his position'? Suppose that your position is unique or the problem is unique. It is not difficult to establish this uniqueness given the uniqueness of the individuals involved and the possible detail with which situations can be described. The reader might like to consider what would count as 'relevant respects' in Eden's Suez problem.

It seems that the way a person sees a situation can also be a relevant difference. There are occasions when I might not have acted in the way another did and yet I would not want to say that what he had done was wrong. Thus universalisability, which Hare thinks essential to a moral judgement, does not seem to be either a necessary or a sufficient condition for calling something a moral principle.

Fifth, if we say sincerely that *x* is a good man, then on Hare's account we mean by 'good' in this context 'man to try and become like'. But surely I can say sincerely that Mother Theresa was a saint but I could not have been like her. The judgement that she was a saint can be sincere *without* entailing a self-addressed imperative. We can add to this the problem there would be in admiring *different* kinds of person, for example, Lenin and Gandhi, Churchill and Christ. It would not be possible to try and become like both of a very different pair, yet we can admire different lives and make favourable moral judgements about them.

Sixth, according to Hare the function of moral judgements is to guide choices. There are counter-examples to this. We can pass a moral judgement on a world leader who is in the process of turning the world into radioactive waste even though no further human choices will be possible. Some moral judgements passed on oneself are not directed towards future choices, for example, remorse. I do not feel remorse *in order* to prevent myself from performing similar acts in the future. Hare is in danger of assimilating moral judgement to practical censuring.

Seventh, Hare's attempt to connect morality and action via imperatives can be criticised. It could be argued that moral judgements should not be assimilated to imperatives, but rather, they should be distinguished from imperatives along the following lines. Imperatives or commands are not normally required to be supported by reasons, whereas moral judgements are. The reader should note the difference between 'Don't do that' and 'You ought not to do that'. The first does not imply a reason in the way the second does. If, in the second case, no reason was forthcoming, we would conclude that it was a mere whim or an order, and consequently a misuse of 'ought'. We would not, however, speak of misusing a command if no reason were given. In making a moral judgement that something *ought* to be done, then you must have some reason for making such judgements otherwise it would be a misuse of 'ought'. In contrast to this, commands have the opposite characteristic – they say in effect, 'don't ask for a reason just do it!'. Interestingly, Hare (p. 176) says that if we make a moral judgement, then we can always be asked to support it with reasons. The disadvantage for Hare though is that all that can be offered in the way of reasons for a particular judgement is the universalised form of that judgement. On Hare's account the giving of reasons for moral judgements amounts to no more than the subsumption of the particular judgement under the universalised form of the principle and there does not seem to be any rational procedure governing the content of these principles.

Attempts to bridge the fact-value gap

(a) Philippa Foot. I now want to return to Foot's criticism of Hare (see above) and consider some of her own suggestions that arise from her rejection of Hare's position. She pointed out, correctly, that there was a problem with the idea that just anything could be the object of commendation. She makes an excellent point against what may be described as the 'free-floating' view of attitudes and feelings. Such a view holds that attitudes and feelings can be attached to anything in the way a coat can be tagged on to any peg in a cloakroom. She shows, for example, that you cannot be proud of just anything or be indignant towards just anything.

However, what she has not yet shown is that there are conceptual limitations concerning what a person may hold as a moral principle: Foot thinks that if you could show that there were such limitations, then anything lying beyond those limits could not be a moral principle. Your account would then have something that Hare's lacks, namely, a way of excluding rubbish. What Foot wants is a clear line of demarcation so she can say that what lies on one side are moral principles and what lies on the other are not. She thinks that in order to make distinctions like this you need a clear line with rigid boundaries.

Foot claims that there is a feature that moral principles must have. Moral virtues are connected with human good and harm and not just anything can be thought of as human good and harm. She lists the cardinal virtues of prudence, temperance, courage and justice, and says that these qualities must benefit their possessor. In the case of courage she says that when we describe an act as courageous, there is no further question of whether we commend it. She is objecting to the idea that to say of a courageous act that it is good is to go beyond the facts. In other words, when we know what courage is, then there is no gap between facts and values. When we know that someone has acted courageously, given the facts of the case, there is no further question of whether we commend or how we evaluate. There is no additional factor of commendation or evaluation to be considered after the factual circumstances of a courageous act are known.

The problem though lies in this notion of being a benefit that she sees as a kind of end result which being virtuous brings about. She anticipates an objection to this, namely, that courage may harm someone and thus not be a benefit. She dismisses this on the ground that it can only harm when some incidental harm arises, like an unforeseen circumstance or underestimated risk, which does not jeopardise the status of courage as a virtue. The difficulty though is that if we make the virtuous status of courage dependent on its producing an end result which benefits its possessor, then what are we going to say of cases where courage kills its possessor? It is hard to see how this can be described as a *benefit* to the dead person. To take an example, the end result of defending the Alamo was death for all the defenders and their deaths were not the result of unforeseen circumstances. It is true that their courage was a benefit to others, but it is difficult to make any sense out of the idea that it was a benefit to *them*. Foot does not consider cases where courage kills its possessor.

There is also a problem with the virtue of justice. Foot claims that, if in giving an account of why you acted or refrained from acting in a certain way, you say 'because it's just' or 'because it's unjust', then that will only count as a reason if the nature of justice can be shown to be such that it is necessarily connected with what a man wants. Thus the question of why I should or should not do something would not be fully answered by saying that it is just or unjust. The chain of reasons cannot end in an appeal to justice unless it is established that justice is necessarily connected with what a man wants thought of in terms of some benefit or end result. She considers Thrasymachus' challenge to Socrates in Book I of the *Republic*. The challenge is 'why should I be just?'. Isn't injustice more of a benefit if you are strong, a good liar and a good actor? Foot's solution to this is unsatisfactory. She says that keeping up such a pretence would be difficult and that a man has a need for justice in his dealing with other men. She concludes by saying that Thrasymachus' assumption that injustice is the more profitable is dubious. It *might* be dubious, but what follows if the assumption is right?

Her claim that keeping up a pretence is difficult may well be true if we are considering the acts of an individual who is under scrutiny but injustice need not be carried out in this way. Suppose that injustice is perpetrated by the powerful who have elaborate methods of covering up. It seems wrong to make the reprehensibility of injustice dependent on the contingent fact that people would find it difficult to sustain over a period of time. What if they could? She needs to show some *logical* impossibility here and I do not think that she achieves this or even comes near. There is no logical impossibility in imagining that the Marcos regime could have remained in power in the Philippines in the 1980s. What made it impossible was that he lost the support of the armed forces and this loss of support had very little to do with being caught perpetrating unjust acts. We should also add that it is unsatisfactory to attempt to make the virtuous status of courage dependent on its social utility.

The main problem with Foot is her idea that the chain of reasons adduced for why you performed an act cannot end in an appeal to justice unless you can further show that justice itself must serve some end which is necessarily wanted. The idea behind this is that if, for example, you said that something produced pain, or caused you discomfort or boredom, then you would not be expected to give a further reason for not doing it. She allows these to be terminating points in chains of reasons, but will not allow justice or injustice to be regarded as terminating points. They have to be further questioned until something self-evident like pain or happiness emerges as the final point in the chain of reasons. It seems that the correct answer here is that justice can be a terminating point for some but not for others. Foot cannot accept this as she wants to show that it must apply to all in the sense that appeals to pain or boredom apply to all. They are terminating points of chains of reasons for all of us. When we say that something is painful there is no gap between the description and the evaluation, between facts and values.

The important point here is that acting unjustly is painful for the just man but we cannot specify the nature of this pain *independently* of the concept of justice. The person who feels no such pain may well not understand its nature. If this is the case, then it will not be painful in the sense that we talk of physical pains. The kind of pain felt will be internal to the moral framework. We shall not be surprised to find that someone standing outside that framework will find the pain of being without justice hard to understand. J. S. Mill remarked about virtue in general that to those who pursue it disinterestedly the consciousness of being without it is painful. This illustrates the point that needs to be made. We cannot say what the pain of being without virtue is independently of virtue or of what pursuing virtue involves. We cannot point to something *external* to virtue and say, look *that* is what it achieves. What worries Foot is the idea that the pain of acting unjustly is not felt by all, so she feels that some knockdown reason has to be found that will apply to all. The charge she would level against me would be that I cannot give a compelling reason why a person should be just. The answer to this charge is that justice can itself be a reason for some but it need not be. The debate between a man of justice and an unjust man can always break down. If you consider what is involved in such a debate, then you will find that this is so. The unjust man knows what justice is (fair play, the notion of rewards and so on) and then asks why he should bother about it. In asking this question he places an unbridgeable gap between himself and the just man. Foot wants to find some compelling way of bridging that gap but there are some gaps that can never be bridged.

We might also ask of what value it would be if the unjust man came to act justly as a result of being convinced that justice pays off. This would have to be thought of in terms of being profitable to him rather than in terms of producing a state of moral goodness. Foot can hardly regard the beneficial effect as an end result of moral goodness as a man who knew what justice was and asked why he should be just is going to ask exactly the same question about moral goodness. He is going to want to know why he should bother about it. Sooner or later Foot is going to have to offer a non-moral consideration as to why one should be moral. Once you set off on that road you end up with a corrupt account of morality.

I shall conclude Foot's account of justice with one further remark. She accuses philosophers of assuming that an unjust man could hide himself from others. This she finds dubious. But this is not what matters. What matters here is that the unjust man *feels* no need to hide from himself.

Foot sees the danger of Hare's position, namely, that anything can be commended and no facts commit one to commending. It follows that a moral eccentric could commend just about anything or withhold his commendation from virtues such as courage or justice. She sees the problem of a rigid distinction between facts and values – no facts can commit one to the evaluation and the evaluations can be tagged on to any facts – and in order to avoid this she wants rigid limits to mark off moral principles. Thus if we are able to distinguish genuine moral principles from spurious ones, we must have a clear line of demarcation which will serve us in all cases. Her fear is that without such a line we will be pushed into a position like Hare's. This is, however, a false dichotomy. With the use of any concept there can be borderline cases, but the existence of such cases does not show that we never know what lies on either side. Indeed, the recognition of dubious cases only becomes possible if we already know in *some* cases what lies on either side.

(b) The 'social fact' argument.   There have been other attempts to bridge the fact-value gap which we cannot pursue at any length. Basically, they involve attempting to deduce moral conclusions from factual premisses concerning social institutions in which we partake. The premisses are sometimes said to refer to 'social facts'. Two of the most well-known attempts are those of Searle and Ms Anscombe. Searle attempts it with the institution of promising and Anscombe with that of debts. Let us take Anscombe's argument first.

From the facts that I bought potatoes and the grocer delivered them, I owe him for them. I have a debt to him. She thinks that this shows that it is wrong to think that there is a dichotomy between facts and values. So what has led philosophers to make such a dichotomy? She thinks that they have had a misconception of what a fact is. She holds that it is false to say that there is one block of statements which is factual and another which is evaluative and that there is a rigid distinction between them. Anscombe holds that the notion of a 'fact' is a relative term. What does she mean by this? Consider the following:

(1) You owe the grocer for potatoes.
(2) You ordered potatoes and the grocer delivered them.

The first will follow from the second and the second will be the matter of fact *relative* to the first. For Anscombe, what follows from (1) and (2) is action. Failure to act would be irrational. Suppose, however, that you needed every penny to pay for your child's operation. There can be disagreement concerning where your obligations lie. She does not discuss moral dilemmas and that is the problem here. Even though we partake in social institutions, there is still room for much diversity and disagreement about what we ought to do. This is why our duties are not entailed by factual descriptions.

Searle holds that from the factual statements that I uttered certain words at a particular time (for example, 'I promise that . . .') it follows that I *ought* to do whatever I promised to do. Thus the statements recording the sounds I made would be factual and from them we would be able to draw a moral conclusion concerning what I ought to do. We would be deriving an 'ought' from an 'is'. In addition to the above point concerning moral dilemmas, we need to note Hare's reply.[12] Hare maintains that we cannot move from factual premisses to a moral conclusion. We need at least one moral premiss in order to get a moral conclusion. Now for Searle, the *fact* that a person has uttered a certain phonetic sequence entails the institutional fact that he has made a promise. This in turn entails that he ought to do whatever he has promised. On this argument then, we would be deriving a moral conclusion, 'You ought to do x' from the factual premisses, 'You uttered phonetic sequence y' and 'Phonetic sequence y is the promise to do x'. Hare's reply is that the conclusion 'You ought to do x' can only be legitimately derived with the addition of a moral premiss, 'One ought to keep one's promises'. Thus on Hare's account the argument would be:

(1) One ought to keep one's promises. (Moral premiss)
(2) You promised to do x. (Factual premiss)
Therefore (3) You ought to do x. (Moral conclusion)

This account of moral obligation and social or institutional facts retains the fact-value gap. According to Hare, we can derive the moral conclusion if and only if we accept the principle that one ought to keep one's promises. We can only be participants in such institutions if we accept the appropriate major moral premiss such as (1) above.

Concluding remarks on facts and values

Factual matters are related to statements about what we ought to do, but we have seen the problems that arise if we regard this relation as one of entailment. The problems occur when we regard facts and values as completely separate. We cannot put them together and derive the evaluative from the factual. What can be attacked is the idea that there is a purely factual realm and a purely evaluative one.

Consider the concept 'father' – is this purely factual? If we say that it is, then we face the problem of saying how the biological fact of paternity can be a basis for moral obligation. We get the fact-value gap. However, some of the concepts we learn already have moral significance. We do not learn what 'father' is in purely factual terms and *later* tag on evaluations. If we consider concepts such as 'rape' or 'torture', we find that we do not learn what they mean independently of moral considerations. The fact-value gap is not as clearcut as some have thought. This is the line taken by Melden in *Rights and Right Conduct*.

If we saw everything in purely factual terms, then nothing could move us to moral conclusions. We cannot move from pure facts to values. That is why the psychologists referred to at the outset cannot derive statements about how people ought to be treated from what are supposed to be factual premises whose factual status is supposed to be strengthened by the use of rigorous scientific definitions. All such arguments achieve is to highlight a gap in one's reasoning which Hume had indicated some 200 years previously. The point we must bear in mind is that some of the terms we use are not purely factual. The reader should think back to the beginning of our discussion and to some of the examples there. We do not, for example, learn concepts like 'child' or 'homeless' in purely factual terms. These concepts have moral import and thus when they figure in moral arguments, one is not moving from purely factual descriptions to evaluative conclusions. Melden adopts the strong thesis that there are concepts which cannot be learnt without moral considerations. This is dubious, but it is not necessary when arguing against someone like Hare. It is sufficient to show that many of the concepts we learn already have moral significance.

▶ Moral principles and behaviour

As we have seen in our discussion of Hare, moral judgements are regarded as prescriptive and not descriptive. At the start of *The Language of Morals* Hare tells us that a man's moral principles are revealed by his behaviour rather than by what he professes in his conversation.

> If we were to ask of a person 'what are his moral principles?' the way in which we could be most sure of a true answer would be by studying what he did. (p. 1)

This is one account given by Hare of the relation between moral judgement and action. We have seen in our preceding discussion that he also says moral judgements are action-guiding and entail imperatives on oneself and others. These two theses can be treated separately. We have already discussed the imperative/action connection. I now want to concentrate on the thesis that moral principles are revealed through behaviour.

Hare seems to waver between two positions here depending on what is understood by 'behaviour'. We shall see that one position is true but trivial, whereas the other is interesting but false. 'Behaviour' can be interpreted in a strong or weak sense. The strong sense of 'behaviour' would mean only overt actions, that is, publicly observable action. This sense of 'behaviour' would exclude such things as what a person thinks, says, the way he says things and feelings such as remorse. It is this sense of 'behaviour' which gives us Hare's strong thesis. On this account if a man says that honesty is important but does not act on it, then he does not really believe that honesty is important. Hare claims, that as a matter of logic, if one believes that one ought to do *x*, then one will do *x* unless it is physically or psychologically impossible.

This account runs into a major *difficulty*. It denies the possibility of weakness of the will. If Hare is to sustain this thesis using the strong sense of 'behaviour', then he will have to deny the existence of any cases of weakness of the will. Alternatively, he will have to say that they are incorrectly described as a person believing in a principle and not acting upon it. Let us consider an actual example to see what is involved here.

Suppose a man says 'I ought to treat my wife better' but does not do so. According to Hare, if he does not actually do so, then he simply does not believe that he ought to. Hare has three options for denying that this is a case of believing something and not acting on it. They are:

(1) When the man says 'I ought to treat her better', he is using the inverted comma sense of 'ought', meaning this is what other people say one should do though he does not believe it himself.
(2) It is physically impossible for him to treat her better.
(3) It is psychologically impossible for him to treat her better.

We can exclude (2) as irrelevant to the discussion. (1) need not be the case as he may really believe that he ought to treat her better. He might, for example, feel remorse at not treating her better and still not treat her better. We are thus left with (3), psychological impossibility. It is not clear how far Hare is willing to extend this notion of psychological impossibility. There are cases which are legitimately described as cases of psychological impossibility. A soldier on a battlefield allows his position to be overrun even though he could have mowed down the enemy. When asked afterwards why he did not open fire, he might say that he froze – he found it impossible to press the trigger even though he was not physically prevented from doing so and felt that he ought to have done so in order to save his comrades from death or capture. He might suffer great anguish at not doing so. Another possible example of psychological impossibility would be the case of the compulsive gambler who stakes everything he owns on the roll of a dice. In such a case rational considerations play no part. A borderline case would be that of emotional blackmail. Cases like these have to be distinguished from cases in which one has a very strong desire. A desire of any strength can be overcome by a stronger desire. Hare cannot allow strong desires to count as psychological impossibilities. If he did then he would just be *re-christening* or *calling* weakness of the will 'psychological impossibility'. His three options just do not cover all cases of weakness of the will.

Imagine the case of a man who loses his temper easily and ends up striking anyone who annoys him, but also thinks that it is wrong to do this. He is not physically forced to hit people, so, according to Hare, he must be either psychologically compelled to do so or be insincere when he says that he thinks he has acted wrongly. We can tell whether he is sincere or not by whether he feels remorse or shame. If he does feel this, then Hare would have to say that it was psychologically impossible for him to stop hitting people. It must be an irrational compulsion like that of the gambler. But why *must* it? It may be just a strong desire or frustration or exasperation. These are things which could be overcome by rational considerations.

We noted earlier that there was a weak sense of 'behaviour'. If Hare weakened 'behaviour' from overt actions to mean everything that a man says, thinks, argues for, his facial expressions, the nuances of all aspects of what he says or does, then of course it is true that we know what his moral beliefs are by observing his behaviour. This is, however, a trivial truth as 'behaviour' has now become so exhaustive that there is nothing else to go on. This weak sense of 'behaviour' would not serve to distinguish moral beliefs from other beliefs as this is how we determine *any* and *all* beliefs that a person might have. As I said at the start, there are two possible interpretations of 'behaviour'. The strong one gives us the false thesis which fails to account for weakness of the will, whereas the weak one gives us the trivial thesis above.

It is not clear which sense of 'behaviour' Hare has in mind. He tells us that we discover a man's principles by seeing what he actually does, but later on in *The Language of Morals* he says that when we say that St Francis was a 'good' man, the judgement is based on the whole life of the subject, 'inner' and overt (p. 145).

▶ Jean-Paul Sartre and existentialism

Probably the most central claim of any existentialist philosophy is the claim that existence precedes essence. This claim is elaborated at some length by Sartre in *Existentialism and Humanism*. A good way of getting to grips with this claim is to contrast it with other philosophical positions to which it is opposed.

There are ethical theories which hold that it is possible to specify in advance what a person's moral purpose ought to be no matter who he is. Sartre remarks on p. 27 of the essay that the idea that essence precedes existence is to be found in many places, including Kant's theory. Diverse sorts of individual man are held to have the same fundamental nature or essence. This is the kind of doctrine which Sartre is opposing.

There have been many philosophers who have formulated theories of human nature. Thomas Hobbes would be an example of this. In the case of Hobbes, fear and pride were taken as fundamental. Moral rules are then worked out from this in order to mitigate the disastrous effects and preserve the good ones of such a conception. On such a theory as this we have an essentially determined human nature. There are other philosophers, such as the British Idealists, who hold that moral values are known *a priori*. They are held to be self-evident and valid for all. The values upon which you ought to act are thus pre-determined for you.

The utilitarians would also hold that it is possible to specify in advance what a person's moral purposes are. For the utilitarians there is no question of *choosing* the ultimate goal of morality. This is known in advance and moral choice is a matter of calculating whatever is conducive to the greatest happiness. Sartre is setting out a position diametrically opposed to the above.

He tells us that there are two kinds of existentialist, the christian and the atheist. What they have in common is the view that existence precedes essence. In his major philosophical work, *Being and Nothingness*, Sartre defines 'existence' as meaning simply concrete, individual being, here and now. It also has a subjective quality when applied to human reality and this distinguishes people from material objects or such things as moss and so on. When applied to people, existence always precedes essence, and to see what Sartre means by this we can consider his example.

We are invited to consider an article of manufacture, a paper-knife. Such an object can be seen to have been made by an artisan who must have had a conception of it prior to its being made. He tells us that the knife is at the same time an article producible in a certain manner and, also, one which serves a definite and pre-determined purpose. We could not suppose that a man would produce a paper-knife without knowing what it was for. He says that its essence, by which he means the sum of the formulae and the qualities which made its production and definition possible, precedes its existence. On such a conception as this, we are viewing the world from a technical standpoint, and if we view man in this way as having his essence precede his existence, then we would be viewing man from the technical standpoint. Sartre then speaks of the anthropomorphic conception of God in which God is regarded as a supernal artisan (as when we think of God as the creator). Whatever religious doctrine we are considering, we always imply that the will follows from the understanding. In other words, when God creates something (wills it) then he knows (understands) what he is creating. Sartre then compares the conception of man in the eyes of God (that is, created and creator) with the knife in the eyes of the artisan. He says:

> God makes man according to a procedure and a conception exactly as the artisan manufactures a paper-knife, following a definition and a formula.

The conclusion Sartre draws from this is that if you have this conception of God, then each individual person is the realisation of a certain conception that dwells in the divine understanding. Thus his essence precedes his existence as the essence of man (the conception of what he is) would be in the divine understanding prior to the actual existence of man.

There are difficulties with this conception of God, notably the problem of evil. If you bought a faulty knife, then you would blame the craftsman. There are some men who are bad, therefore, if God stands in the same relation to the men he creates as the artisan does to the knife, then God would have to be blamed for the faulty product. It might be possible for the craftsman to blame his tools or materials, but, as God is omnipotent, He could have no such excuse.

Sartre then proceeds to a discussion of human nature. He is talking about human nature as that conception of human being that is found in every man. Even if the idea of God is suppressed, he says, we still find those who want to say that each man is a particular instance of a universal conception, and thus again essence would precede existence. For Sartre, however, the idea of a human nature is very much bound up with the idea of God. He says:

> if God does not exist there is at least one being whose existence comes before its essence, a being which exists before it can be defined by any conception of it.

Thus if there is no God, then there cannot be a human nature as God would be a necessary prerequisite of such a thing as human nature. That is to say, God would have to have a conception of human nature prior to the creation in order for there to be a human nature.

Sartre's thesis is that man first of all exists; he is something that propels itself towards a future and is aware that he is doing so. This awareness is an important aspect of what Sartre means by 'subjectivity'. If we draw out the consequences of the claim that existence precedes essence, we are supposed to be left in possession of ourselves. On the atheistic standpoint which Sartre is arguing from, there is no God to have a conception of human nature and, therefore, no human nature to take as fundamental or foundational. Owing to God's absence, our moral values have to be created by ourselves. This is what is meant by our being left in possession of ourselves. Since there is no pre-established pattern for human nature, each man creates his own essence (what he is) as he lives. What is of crucial importance in Sartre is that man is totally responsible for what he creates. Man is totally free to create his values. Sartre tells us that, 'Man is condemned to be free'. He is 'condemned' because he did not create himself and not only is he free to choose, but he *must* choose. Even a refusal to choose is still a choice.

Sartre refers to a number of criticisms that have been brought against existentialism. One of them is that if you deny the existence of God, then everything is permitted – it does not matter what you do. This criticism does not bring out Sartre's position clearly. Sartre means that you *do* have to think about morality. There is nothing laid down or pre-determined for you. Thus the problem is not that of living up to values, but of deciding them. It is here that an awesome sense of responsibility comes in. We are responsible for what we decide. We are free in the sense that we determine what we want. He says that whether an object is a starting point, an obstacle, matter of indifference or opportunity depends upon my free projects. To be in a situation, which is the meaning of human presence in the world, is to be responsible for one's manner of being. He declares that he is strongly opposed to a certain type of secular moralism which seeks to suppress God at the least possible expense. What Sartre is getting at here is that if God, the lawgiver, existed, then there would be no problem concerning which values were to be taken seriously. But when God is swept under the carpet there are some who claim that those values have an *a priori* status attached to them and that they exist somewhere in an intelligible heaven. Sartre's claim, however, is that once God has gone there also vanishes with Him any possibility of finding any values in an intelligible heaven. This is why Sartre says that for the existentialist it is extremely embarrassing that God does not exist. There can no longer be any *a priori* values as there is no infinite and perfect consciousness to think them, 'it is nowhere written that the good exists'.

If it is correct to say that existence precedes essence, then one will never be able to explain or justify one's actions by reference to any given and specific human nature. In this part of the text he draws out the full consequences of his atheistic position. He says that if God does not exist, then we are not provided with any values or commands that could legitimise our behaviour. There are no excuses, not even the power of passion as each man is responsible for his passion. He quotes approvingly from Ponge, 'Man is the future of man'. This means that there is only man, and if there were a predetermined future laid up in heaven, then that would not constitute a genuine future. Sartre is thinking of a virgin future and to say that such a future was pre-determined, or had already been decided on, would be contradictory.

This total freedom which is central to Sartre's thesis carries with it the most awesome responsibility. It is what Sartre means by 'anguish'. It is in anguish that one tastes this absolute freedom; it is revealed to us through anguish. If you experience anguish, then you are in a state of abandonment. You are thrown into this world without reason or justification. You must create through your choices and bear total responsibility for those choices. He claims that this responsibility does not just apply to oneself but to all men. When you choose, you choose for all men. In choosing you choose an image of man and you are responsible for the creation of this image. You create an image of man as you believe he ought to be. He goes on to say that to choose between this or that is at the same time to affirm the value of that which is chosen. What we choose is always the better as it derives its value from being chosen. He goes on to claim that nothing can be better for us unless it is better for all. 'If... existence precedes essence and we will to exist at the same time as we fashion our image, that image is valid for all and for the entire epoch in which we find ourselves.' Sartre illustrates this principle with the example of marriage. If I choose to marry, then I commit the whole of humanity to the practice of monogamy. This seems to exclude the possibility of my saying that some course of action is right for me but not for someone else.

In using this notion of deciding for the whole of mankind, Sartre intends to show the depth of our responsibility and to give a rebuff to those who accuse existentialism of irresponsibility. The point of the marriage example and the claim that in fashioning myself I fashion man, is to bring out the fearsome responsibility involved in moral choice. It is through such awesome responsibility that anguish is created. It is important to realise here that Sartre is saying that you do not choose some image or whatever because it is good, but rather, it is good *because* it is chosen. As we have remarked, it is the fact that it is chosen which gives it value. The only restriction he seems to place on a chosen image having value is that it should be chosen freely. This has the implication that fascism would be valuable if it were chosen freely. Presumably, the answer that Sartre would give here is that fascism or nazism are not the kinds of thing that could be freely chosen given what they involve. He might, for example, claim that commitments to such images necessarily involve an act of bad faith. He does say in another context in the essay that those who claim that their existence is necessary he will call scum. We all exist accidentally. Sartre might be taken as saying that certain political-racial ideologies involve or imply that the existence of some groups of people is necessary and this would involve an act of bad faith. They would be fleeing from the accidental nature of their appearance on earth. Even if this interpretation is correct, it is by no means clear that all brands of fascism must suffer from *this* defect – and what if they do not?

I now want to take a closer look at Sartre's notion of freedom via an example he offers. The example concerns a student in war-time France who approaches him seeking moral advice. The student faces a moral dilemma. His brother has been killed in the German offensive, his father is a collaborator and his mother is left alone. She lives solely for the one remaining son. The dilemma is that of a conflict of duty. Should he stay with his mother and fulfil the happiness of one individual or does he join the resistance, avenge his brother and fight for a greater though more ambiguous cause? At the end of the essay Sartre is reproached for not giving the student an answer. He says that what the student was looking for was freedom so he let him decide for himself. In using this example Sartre is attempting to show that there are no moral formulae which work for everyone. Moral problems have to be worked out by the individual.

Given that we have to work out moral problems for ourselves, how can there be such a thing as moral advice? Sartre's answer to this appears early in the essay. He refers to the anguish of Abraham. There are no signs vouchsafed for us; it is we who must interpret the signs. In the case of Abraham receiving advice or instruction, it is he who must interpret that it is an angel that is talking to him and that it is to him that the angel is talking. He goes on to tell us that there is not much point in seeking advice for in seeking the adviser you have already chosen the type of advice that will be given. This implies that you cannot get unexpected advice.

In addition to anguish and abandonment, Sartre refers to bad faith. This notion too is intimately connected with freedom. Bad faith is a term Sartre uses to refer to the ways in which people deceive themselves into thinking that they are not free when they are inescapably free. This can be contrasted with Freud who was concerned with the ways in which people may think they are free when they are not. Sartre's concept of bad faith is the exact opposite of this.

The reason people pretend not to be free is to avoid the responsibility that total freedom involves. To return to the example of the paper-knife, any fault in the knife is not the fault *of* the knife. Bad faith can be understood as the project of persuading ourselves that we are like paper-knives. To express it in more metaphysical terms, it is the attempt to assimilate the ontological status of our being to that of the being of material objects – we, along with our properties and qualities, are simply given rather than self-created. In *Being and Nothingness* Sartre gives striking examples of this phenomenon. One concerns a girl who goes out with a man and on their first romantic encounter he takes her hand. She 'does not notice' that he has taken her hand. If she leaves her hand there, then she commits herself to a flirtation. If she withdraws it, then she will upset the harmony of the moment. She leaves it there but *does not notice* that she has: 'the separation of soul and body is achieved. Her hand rests passively in the hot hands of her companion, neither consenting nor resisting: a thing'. As the hand has been disowned, she is no longer responsible for what happens to it. This pattern of bad faith is characterised as trying to become thing-like. The girl is pretending that her hand is just an object in the world and she is no more responsible for what happens to it than she is for what happens to the table upon which it is resting. It is simply there like other objects.

The second kind of bad faith is that of playing a part or role-playing. In *Being and Nothingness* Sartre gives an example of a waiter who performs all the actions that are expected of a waiter. The man is trying to lose himself in being a waiter; he is trying to become a waiter in the sense that, for example, an inkwell simply is an inkwell:

> A grocer who indulges in day-dreams is offensive to the customer because he is no longer wholly a grocer, courtesy requires him to contain himself within his function as a grocer, like the soldier at attention who makes himself into a soldier-thing, by his direct and unseeing gaze which is no longer even intended to see, since it is the regulation and not the interest of the moment which determines the point on which his eye should rest.

Sartre is saying that we absorb ourselves in various social roles, and we allow the expectations of the roles to determine what we do. We justify our behaviour by appealing to what is involved in such roles. Such a project is doomed to fail as the roles are 'representations' for ourselves and others and if I have to represent the role to myself, then there must always be a sense in which I am not it. At best I can play at the role but I can never fully realise it – there is always a sense in which it escapes me. I cannot simply be what others define me as.

The notion of bad faith or a flight from freedom is important in Sartre's answer to a second objection to existentialism. (The first is that it does not matter what you do.) The second objection is that you cannot judge others. Sartre claims that this objection is true in one sense and false in another. It is true in the sense that whenever a man chooses his purpose and commitment in all clearness and in all sincerity, then whatever that purpose might be, it is impossible to prefer another for him. Thus again we are confronted with the idea of free decision as the sole criterion for judging moral value. There is, however, a sense in which we can judge. It is possible, he says, to judge a man whose decisions are made in bad faith. He tells us that perhaps such a judgement is not a value judgement or a moral pronouncement, but rather a logical judgement to the effect that the choice or decision is based on error. He says:

> One can judge a man by saying that he deceives himself. Since we have defined the situation of man as one of free choice, without excuse or help, any man who takes refuge behind the excuse of his passions, or by inventing some deterministic doctrine is a self-deceiver.

If asked what is wrong with self-deception, Sartre replies that it is not for him to judge the man morally, but as self-deception (bad faith) is defined as an error, one cannot avoid making a judgement of truth. Having said this, he then goes on to say (p. 52) that he can make a moral judgement. This is because freedom can have no other aim and end except itself; and when a man has seen that values depend upon himself, he can will only one thing and that is freedom as the foundation of all values.

There is a problem here. If he *can* will only freedom, then what does it mean to say that he could be criticised for not doing so? If he has not realised that freedom is the only foundation of value, then in what sense can he be said to be deceiving himself? In *Being and Nothingness* Sartre observes a difficulty in the idea of self-deception. The main problem is that it is not straightforward like lying. Sartre begins there by talking about lying. The liar does not hide the fact of his lying from himself. A difficulty arises when we compare lying with self-deception. If a person *knows* that he is lying, then he cannot deceive himself and if he does not know, then his state is one of ignorance rather than self-deception.

There can, however, be an alternative to knowledge and ignorance which would be a corruption of both these states. Thus a characteristic of self-deception would be the evasion of any of the checks which would normally be carried out to ascertain the truth. In such a case one would normally be corrupting the standards of truth. An example of this would be the case of a man who is reluctant to believe tales of the infidelity of his wife. The reluctance could shade into bad faith if he shrank away from the ways of ascertaining the truth. There are two reasons why we would do this: (a) our desires interfere with the usual standards of truth; (b) the abandonment of our responsibility. Barriers are erected which restrict the individual's freedom by deception. Sartre refers to three possible barriers:

(1) The idea that social role determines a person's actions. In such a case the person adopts a role and this disguises the fact, or is intended to disguise the fact, that the role has been chosen.
(2) Pre-determined values. This is the idea that the values in one's life are already laid down and are thus not the result of *our* choice.
(3) The idea that your character determines your actions. The deception here lies in the idea that your character is simply given and that your actions just flow from it in an automatic fashion.

Sartre objects to (3) on the ground that it involves arguing in a circle. A person's character, or what he is, is nothing more than the sum total of his actions. He gives examples of this. The genius of Proust simply is the totality of Proust's works and nothing more. A person's capacity for love simply is the sum total of loving acts manifested in his lifetime. If character simply is what we do (we are what we do) then it cannot be identified as a separated cause which determines what we do. For Sartre, character is *itself* explained in terms of action and, therefore, it cannot be used to excuse or explain actions. As we are responsible for our actions, then we are responsible for our character. They are the same.

Such a thesis as this is diametrically opposed to the view that we are born with a certain kind of character and there is nothing that can be done about it. This is what Sartre is getting at with his comments about Zola (pp. 42–3). At the end of the passage Sartre tells us that what counts is 'total commitment'. It is not by one act that a hero or coward turns himself irrevocably into a hero or coward; he can always change.

Sartre does not think that there is a definitive set of examples of bad faith. He thinks that it is a dominant and consistent part of human behaviour. Whenever you have desire, then you have the possibility of bad faith. It might be objected against Sartre here that this sounds suspiciously like a facet of human nature which would be the very thing that his theory should not contain. Sartre could reply that he is merely pointing out the possibilities which emerge from an ontological analysis. He is not making naturalistic discoveries or pointing out a necessary pattern of events. Such deceptions might occur but we are free to unmask them and to avoid them. He would say that our freedom is a necessary condition for their possibility.

Later in the essay (pp. 45–7) he remarks that whereas there is no human nature, there is nevertheless a 'human universality of condition'. Sartre is here talking about what it means to be 'man in the world', that is, what is necessarily involved in the human situation or predicament. He is not accounting for historical similarities by appealing to a fixed and unchanging nature, but by appealing to the basic similarity of the 'human situation'. There are certain limitations that confront us all no matter who we are, for example, to work, to survive and to die. Many human projects in different historical epochs can be seen as ways of coming to terms with these fundamental limitations. They go to make up what it is to be man in the world. This is what is meant by saying that they define his situation.

Criticisms

Mary Warnock has offered a criticism of Sartre. She says that bad faith does not really matter. She takes the example of the waiter from *Being and Nothingness* and says that good may emerge from those who play at social roles, for example, the soldier or the judge. She also says that Sartre is confused in thinking that all immorality reduces to bad faith. Thus Warnock wants to say that self-deception is not that important and that good can come from it. It may well be the case that good can come from self-deception, but that does not mean that the deception does not matter. It would be preferable to achieve a similar end without deceiving oneself. Sartre in all his writings gives striking examples, but the real problem is that he thinks they show more than they actually do. The waiter pretends that his job is not the result of choice; he has tried to turn himself into a kind of object before others by acting out a role. He is said to be playing with his situation in order to realise it. It does not follow from this, however, that everyone who is a waiter is play-acting, and it certainly does not follow that everyone who has a social role is trying to absorb himself in it and disguise the fact of choice from himself.

We now come to a major difficulty with Sartre. In the case of the student who thinks that his mother and country are important, his deliberation is about two values which he has accepted. It is because he holds these values to be important that he has to make an agonising choice. Sartre tells us that these values are the result of a more fundamental choice. It seems, however, that we hold values which have not been decided on in the sense that the student has to make a decision. Thus, for example, we do not arrive at a *decision* that murder and torture are wrong. Sartre rejects the idea that anyone decides our values for us. There is no God and no *a priori* values; there are just ourselves with each of us making a fundamental decision as to what is important. Much criticism has been directed at this notion of a fundamental decision. Any fundamental decision like this is bound to be somewhat arbitrary as it cannot rest on a reason. It is by definition prior to any reason. Sartre's reply to this would probably be to say that that is just too bad, it is the way things are. Sartre cannot, though, shrug off the objection we alluded to previously. Consider a statement such as 'theft is wrong', we teach words like 'right' and 'wrong' by application. If they were used independently or abstractly, then they would have no meaning. They only have a meaning in application. Sartre says that the whole of morality is decision-making, but the difficulty is that our ability to make decisions about right and wrong presupposes that we have been taught those words in connection with something. How could *that* be a matter of decision-making? It cannot be in the sense that Sartre's student must make a decision. Sartre recognises the decision-making element in morality but goes on to say that *all* morality is decision-making. As we have seen, this causes problems for him.

There are other problems which the reader should note. Need determinists believe in God? Surely not, scientific determinism is quite independent of any religious beliefs. Sartre's attitude to scientific determinism is dubious. He seems to rule it all out. It is unclear what his attitude is towards what it is theoretically possible for a science such as genetics to discover.

The example of the student is also problematic. We are told that value lies in action, the student, however, feels the weight of two values *prior* to action. This is why the student has a dilemma. It would seem that action itself is not sufficient to reveal all values.

5 Social and Political Philosophy

▶ **Introduction to social and political philosophy**

In this chapter we are going to examine the nature of political obligation and the origin of the state. We are going to ask why there should be laws and why they should be obeyed. We shall also examine different images of society to see what light they cast on the concepts of freedom and authority.

Political obligation and the origin of the state

Scholastic philosophers of the Middle Ages claimed that the authority of the sovereign was derived from the consent of the people rather than from God. The sovereign does not rule by divine right. According to the divine right theory, it does not matter how bad a ruler a sovereign might be, the subjects are still duty-bound to obey. The sovereign rules by consent of God. It was this theory that was coming under challenge. The scholastic philosophers were saying that if a ruler became a tyrant or failed in his duties as a ruler, then he could be justly overthrown. He would no longer have the consent of the people to rule.

Prior to the writings of famous political philosophers, such as Hobbes, Rousseau and Locke, there were important debates in the area of political obligation and the origin of the state. In 1599 Juan de Mariana published *On the King and His Education*. In this work Mariana refers to a state of nature existing before social organisation. In such a state men were completely free. It was not, however, a desirable kind of freedom. Men lived like beasts. There were no laws, no institutions, no private property – in short there was neither civilisation nor culture. This natural state is fraught with danger. The only rule is that of force and all human action is governed by instinct. In order to counter this undesirable state of affairs, men organised themselves along social lines. The members of any particular group either openly or tacitly entered into a contract whereby the members of a group agreed to delegate their power or authority as a group to a leader. The people were to check this delegated authority. The authority lay ultimately in their hands. Some sort of assembly would check this authority and make laws.

The leader would be limited by these laws together with religious and moral constraints. In the event of the leader becoming a tyrant, the people would have a perfect right to depose him.

For Mariana, the best form of government is an hereditary limited monarchy. Facts about human nature are said to exclude the possibility of democracy. People are not equally endowed with intelligence and other abilities. The reader may wonder how a people deemed unfit to vote can legitimately and justly overthrow a ruler. Mariana holds that such a decision must not be taken just by a majority, but by 'the public voice of the people' which includes the learned and serious men. If the monarch's rule becomes tyrannically unendurable, then not only can he be deposed, he can also be killed justly and with praise and glory. It is not clear how often this would occur given the virtual total consent of the people required by Mariana. What is important though is the break with divine right and the reference to a social contract.

In opposition to Mariana's limited monarchy, Bodin's *La République* (1576) proposes the idea of an unlimited monarchy. In Bodin there is no talk of a social contract or any general agreement. Such a concept might be applicable to the case of small-scale communities, but is thought quite inappropriate in elucidating the origin of the state. Bodin holds that the origin of the state is a matter of conquest. One group conquers another by force and the leader of the victors assumes ultimate authority. In the same way that it is natural for a father to be responsible for the maintenance of order in a family, so it is natural for the unlimited, absolute ruler to maintain order in the state. The will or consensus of the people does not enter into it. The backing for the law is not consent but the organised force of the ruling power. Bodin takes a dim view of democracy:

> In every popular assembly the votes are counted without weighing them; and always the number of the foolish, the wicked and the ignorant is a thousand times greater than the men of worth.[1]

To enforce his naturalistic thesis, Bodin tells us that monarchies have the more permanent backing of history. In this they are likened to the patriarchal family. They are regarded as natural states of affairs.

One rather obvious problem with Bodin's view is that if the ruler's conception of order is total obedience to all his whims and any dissent is unceremoniously crushed, then rather than having a paternal figure as their leader, the people will have a tyrant. As long as he has the requisite force it is difficult to see how there can be justified resistance by the subjects. To have the right to resist and protest would be to impose limitations on that which Bodin holds must be unlimited in order to fulfil its function.

Tyrannical rule is a corruption of the governmental function and such a possibility is endemic in absolute and unlimited rule. Bodin realised this and thought there had to be a way of meeting such an eventuality. He thus allows the right of the subjects to resist and even kill the ruler. The philosophical difficulty here is to see how, on his own premisses, he *can* allow for such safety valves. The authority of the ruler was never based on consent, only on force.

There are other problems with Bodin's view. It is unclear just how far the paternal analogy can be pushed in order to justify the kind of unlimited power Bodin was talking about. The family father, unless he is a mafia godfather, does not have power in this sense and we would not think much of a father who justified tyrannical rule on the grounds that he had the physical force to implement it. For Bodin, the family is the base of morality, but morality cannot be reduced to the exercise of unlimited power. Bodin tried to justify the supremacy of the father with the use of some dubious psychological premisses concerning the natural mental weakness of women.

This was the historical background to the more important political philosophers and social theorists. The germs of many of their ideas are to be found in this background. Let us now move on to a discussion of some of the important ideas that were to follow.

Thomas Hobbes

Hobbes offered a theory of moral and political obligation which was independent of revealed religion. His most influential work, *Leviathan*, was published in 1651. In the eleven years prior to this, Hobbes had been in self-imposed exile in France. He was afraid that his first book, *Elements of Law*, might lead to his imprisonment or death. He had defended the view that the sovereign had absolute power. In 1640 Parliament had asserted its authority by imprisoning Laud and Strafford, both of whom were later executed. This undoubtedly frightened Hobbes.

It is important to realise that Hobbes' view concerning the absolute power of the sovereign was not held as a result of the English Civil War. He had held this view for a long time. Indeed, he had thought that it might prevent civil war by depicting the horrors of anarchy which he thought inevitable if Charles I was overthrown.

Hobbes' method of philosophical argument is to give definitions of his key terms and then make deductions from those definitions. What goes into those definitions is therefore of crucial importance. He presents his moral and political conclusions as following necessarily from his account of human nature. We need to say something about this.

Hobbes held that a person's desire must always be directed to one of the following: (a) self-preservation; (b) power; or (c) pleasure or contentment for oneself. All men's motives are selfish. Even actions which we describe as performed out of love or pity are regarded by Hobbes as emanating from a desire to purchase friendship or peace, or from a desire to exercise one's own power. Clearly, if you hold a theory of human nature such as this, it is going to carry important implications for your political theory. We shall come to that shortly. It should be realised that Hobbes claims to make these naturalistic discoveries by introspection. He takes it for granted that all people are alike in their passions. He can be criticised for making a sweeping generalisation from a single case.

According to Hobbes, all men are competitive and antisocial. He believed that there are three main causes of quarrels. They can be summarised as follows:

(1) Competition for the means of satisfying desires leads to violence.
(2) Diffidence, that is, fear or mistrust makes people attack others out of the fear of being attacked.
(3) Glory, the feeling of contemplating one's own power.

He says that a state of affairs in which there is no sovereign power is war. It is all against all. There is no industry because no one is sure of enjoying the fruits of his labour. There is continual fear and danger. In the state of nature life is nasty, brutish and short.

Hobbes made use of the social contract theory which was regarded as historically true. This states that each man gives up his freedom to rob, kill, rape and so on, if others do the same. Each man agrees to obey those elected by the majority. This theory was used by others to show that the powers of the sovereign were not absolute. It was accepted that the sovereign was a party to the contract as he had promised to exercise his power for certain purposes. If he failed to fulfil his promises, then the contract was null and void.

What was novel about Hobbes was that he gave the social contract theory a new twist. He used it to justify absolute power for the sovereign. We can see strands of both Mariana and Bodin here. According to Hobbes, the sovereign was not a party to the contract. He has made no promises and he uses his power as he thinks expedient. Hobbes concludes that there can be no breach by the sovereign. No one is in a position to arbitrate between sovereign and subjects, no one has the power to force the sovereign to do anything.

An obvious problem with a view such as this is that a contract which no one can enforce is vacuous. The sovereign is above the law. Hobbes defines the term 'law' as a command by the sovereign backed by a threat of punishment. On this account it would be meaningless to accuse the sovereign of acting unjustly. What is unjust is what is contrary to law, and law is made by the sovereign who is free to make any law he wishes.

In ch. XVIII of *Leviathan* Hobbes argues that the sovereign cannot be said to injure any of his subjects. This is because each citizen has transferred his right to govern himself to the sovereign. Therefore, each citizen is the author of what the sovereign does. An odd implication of this is that if an innocent man were to go to prison, then he would be imprisoning himself!

He argues that the sovereign must have the right to censor anything he thinks may cause dissent. Hobbes argues that there can be no universal church; it must depend on the government of the state in which it exists. The sovereign would be the head and he would decide what beliefs were to count as true religion and which were to be regarded as superstition. There should be no division of power between the sovereign and other institutions, such as the church or the press. Hobbes used this theory to justify dictatorship. The sovereign should have the right to appoint his own heir or assembly. When the social contract is made the minority can be justly liquidated if they refuse to comply with the wishes of the majority.

In ch. XX of *Leviathan* he argues that there is no difference in principle between a society that has been instituted voluntarily or one in which the sovereign power is acquired by conquest. Even when a country has been subjugated by force, there is no right to rebel but only a duty to obey. The duty is derived from an implicit promise to obey. The conquerors could have killed the conquered but they have refrained because the conquered have promised to obey. The act of laying down their arms contains an implicit promise of obedience in the future. For Hobbes, this would still be government by consent. The reader might well think that Hobbes is corrupting the concept of consent beyond all recognition. We may also wonder about the moral status of the so called 'promise' to obey given the conditions under which it was obtained.

As we have seen, Hobbes thought that all of the sovereign's rights could be acquired by conquest. This undermines his case for saying that rebellion is unjustified. If the rebellion is successful, then the rebels acquire the rights of the sovereign. *How* the rights are acquired makes no difference to the rights. All Hobbes is entitled to say is that unsuccessful rebellions are unjustified.

In ch. XXI he discusses the liberty of the subject. There are only two circumstances in which the subject can disobey:

(1) If the subject has been condemned to death, then he has a right to resist arrest and/or try to escape.
(2) If the sovereign orders the subject to risk his life by fighting for his country, then, if he could possibly avoid conscription, he should do so.

The reader can see how these exceptions fit Hobbes' theory of human nature. Indeed, on that theory the above exceptions follow as a matter of natural necessity. If the theory is right, then these exceptions state what will be done as a *matter of fact*. All other liberties depend on the silence of the law. Hobbes makes one further qualification. The obligation to obey the sovereign lasts as long as the sovereign is able to protect the lives of his subjects. If he becomes too weak, then he can be opposed. These exceptions to the duty of obedience are based on the principle of preserving one's own life. This is the motive which compelled men to enter into the social contract. In the state of nature there are no moral obligations. Moral obligations only come into being after the social contract has been enacted. Until such a contract has been enacted no individual can rely on others to reciprocate.

Hobbes holds that the only alternatives are the authoritarian state with absolute power or the state of nature. A division of power would lead eventually to a state of nature. He assumed that a sovereign with absolute power would enforce moral rules. What right had he to be so optimistic? In ch. XIX he recognises, briefly, an implication of his own premises. If there is a conflict between the private interests of the sovereign and the interests of his subjects, then the sovereign will pursue his own interests. Hobbes glosses over this by saying that the interests will coincide. This is surely an error on Hobbes' part. The sovereign's love of glory may lead him to wage imperial wars and treat his subjects as cannon fodder. A sovereign in wishing to flatter or impress may deprive another of all his possessions. This was just an inconvenience for Hobbes. The citizen would just have to put up with it. It is the price he must pay for general stability.

To re-cap, Hobbes holds that a person's duties are laid down by the state. If there is no government to enforce performance of the duties, then the 'duties' are not binding. There is a difficulty here for Hobbes. We know that different states enforce different laws. If the governments of these states were equally strong, then Hobbes would not be entitled to say that one country's laws were better or worse than those of another. Many would want to say, however, that in spite of considerations of efficiency, the systems of racial segregation in nazi Germany and apartheid in South Africa were unjust. It is very difficult to see how Hobbes could distinguish legal duties from moral ones. He seems committed to saying that no one has the right to resist the sovereign in the defence of an innocent man. This would clash with the principle that we have a duty to protect the innocent. At the Nuremberg trials the nazi defence of 'obeying orders' failed because it was held that they had such a moral duty.

A further implication of Hobbes' theory is that if the sovereign is above the law, then no one has the power to punish him except God. It follows that governments of different countries in relation to each other are in the state of nature. His theory implies that different states could acquire binding obligations to each other if and only if there was world government to enforce international law. He never envisaged this possibility. He thought that it was inevitable for sovereign states to struggle for power, to fight and deceive each other. I shall leave the reader to consider whether such a gloomy outlook has the support of modern history.

The Hobbesian picture of the natural state of man is non-moral and unregulated. This implies that there is something unnatural about life in a civilised society. Given that the term 'unnatural' conveys a pejorative flavour, it is not surprising that many people were outraged by such a theory. Hobbes' theory was provocative and stimulated ethics and political theory for many years.

Jean Jacques Rousseau

Rousseau's version of the social contract is very different from that of Hobbes. Here the notion of consent, understood in its normal sense, is paramount. Consent is held to be the only possible base for authority in society. We have seen the notion of force play an important part in the work of Bodin and Hobbes. Rousseau attacks the thesis of might is right. He allows that force can confer power but denies that it can confer authority. What he is getting at here is that moral obligations cannot arise out of a relationship of forced submission. Although those who have forced us into submission (Hobbes' 'conquest') have power over us, they have not thereby created rights to obedience. No amount of force can achieve this. We may obey out of fear, but this must be distinguished from obeying because we are morally obliged to do so. He is using the term 'authority' in the way we would use the term 'legitimate authority'.

In the writings of Rousseau we find explicit criticisms of Hobbes. If man were such a creature as Hobbes described, full of ferocity, dangerous tendencies and so on, then would this not perpetually erupt within a society and how could society survive? Creatures with such a nature as this would find such passions as sympathy and sacrifice quite alien. As Rousseau says, pity and sympathy would come to be regarded as the signs of a monster, 'we should be by nature all that our depraved surroundings can even now hardly force us to become.'[2]

A related criticism to this is whether such creatures, constantly at loggerheads, with no conception of morality, right or wrong, could suddenly embark upon the practice of entering into binding agreements or covenants. How could they become bound by duty to obey their pledges and receive peace in return? Rousseau makes a very interesting conceptual point when he questions whether such a group of unpleasant natures *could* form a community. He held that such a collection would not be a community; it would be a mere aggregate.[3]

There is, of course, a very different theory of human nature to be found in Rousseau. We cannot here pursue these differences. We can, however, remark that Rousseau did not regard man as inherently bad or disposed to wickedness. Sympathy is regarded as being as natural as self-preservation. Due attention is given to conscience, and to its guide, reason. In Rousseau, we have all the natural tendencies to be good. The fundamental meaning of his social contract theory is best expressed in the following words: 'Each of us gives his person and his total power to the common cause, under the supreme authority of the general will, and we receive every member as an integral part of our group.'[4] The power that makes the law is sovereign in the state. Ideally, that power will be what he calls 'the general will'. The reader should realise that when Rousseau refers to the law-making power, he is not referring to any particular legislative assembly. It is the nature of the authority that lies behind it that is important. The assembly itself is merely an agent of that power. For Rousseau, all authority must rest on the agreement of the people. A sovereign power could be overthrown when the sovereign failed to act in accordance with the general will. It is in the general will that ultimate sovereignty lies. The reader can see from this just how important the concept of a general will is to Rousseau's thought. It occurs in the statement of what the social contract is, it is the seat of sovereignty and it is the criterion for measuring the adequacy of the ruler. It is also one of the most problematic of Rousseau's ideas.

The general will means something different from rule by all the people. When we examine what people actually want we shall find that there are conflicting purposes, or conflicting wills. The general will cannot mean the sum total of individual wills. The only case where it could mean this would be the extremely rare one of complete unanimity among all the people. So how can we clarify what is meant by a general will? In order to arrive at the general will we must omit the purely personal aims of the individuals. By 'purely personal aims' is meant those aims that cannot be of public importance without sketching in a special background whereby they acquire such importance. Having eschewed the purely personal aims, we are left with the individuals' ideas concerning what is best for the community. These too can conflict. These conflicts are to be removed so that a common. element is revealed. The common element would be the dominant, overriding purpose. It is the purpose of the general will. The conditions necessary to create a general will can be summarised as follows:

(1) the will must take into account the voice of all individuals;
(2) all are obligated equally under the general will;
(3) the will is only concerned with the common cause, not private interest;
(4) the will can be perfect only if the concern of each one is the public good.

There are some very obvious problems with this. First, it is not clear that the separation of private interest from public interest can always be achieved that easily. There can be borderline cases and we cannot use the idea of a general will or common cause to settle them as it is only *after* they have been settled that we shall know what the common cause is.

Secondly, it is by no means obvious that it makes sense to talk about some residual element which remains after individual conflicts over what the public good is have been resolved. It might well be that there is no such element, or at least its content would be so vacuous that it could hardly serve as the base of the state's authority. We have, of course, assumed that conflicts over the purpose of the community can be resolved. This is a very risky assumption and seems to deny the possibility of irresolvable conflicts. Why does there have to be *one* purpose behind such conflicts?

When we look at the conditions of the general will, we find a serious problem with (4). If this is supposed to be an ideal of how people should vote, then one might claim that it is so unrealistic as to render talk of the perfect general will pointless.

We are also told that the general will is infallible in the sense that it cannot but desire the common good. Rousseau, however, allows for the possibility that it can be mistaken. Given that he allows for this, we ought to say that it desires what it perceives as the common good. There is a *difficulty* here in understanding how such an abstract concept can be thought of as having moral perceptions and of pursuing them. We can understand how individual wills can be talked of in this way, but it is not clear that such talk can simply be transferred to something as elusive as the general will. There is a further difficulty with infallibility. To say that the general *will cannot* but desire the common good looks very like a conceptual point. That is to say, desiring the common good is part of what is *meant* by 'a general will'. We are also told that it *naturally* seeks the common good.

The notion of a general will plays an important part in Rousseau's theory of law. A law, properly called, can only be enacted by the general will. It might be the case that this is intended to have greater application to constitutional laws than to the civil or criminal law. If it has application to the latter, then this will raise the issue of whether it is ever possible for an individual to disobey such a law out of conscience.

We have discussed briefly the social contract theory as an account of how the state originated and as forming a base for our obedience to the law. We must now move on to criticisms of the social contract theory and alternative answers.

Utilitarian theories of government

One difficulty with the social contract theory is that of historical inaccuracy. Bentham, in a footnote to ch. I of his *Fragment on Government* (1776), tells us that he has always been taught the doctrine of the original contract. It had given strong support to monarchic government and emphasised passive obedience. The contract was seen by lawyers, 'as a recipe of sovereign efficacy for reconciling the accidental necessity of resistance with the general duty of submission'.

Bentham tells us how he came to revolt against such an idea. No page in history can be indicated which records the 'solemnization of this important contract'. The point he is making is that such a notion is a fiction and a fiction cannot lie at the foundation of something so important as political obligation. You cannot prove the consensus to be governed by appealing to an event which is admittedly a fiction. 'Indulge yourselves in the licence of supposing that to be true which is not, and as well may you suppose that proposition itself to be true which you wish to prove, as the other by which you wish to prove it.'

There is a possible reply to Bentham's criticism. A contract theorist may claim that even though his doctrine is historically false, the state of nature can be seen as a hypothesis. It can be seen as an attempt to theorise as to what life *would* be like if it were not for socialisation. It should be seen as a way of pointing out the advantages of civil life and the disadvantages of freedom without restriction. Indeed, it seems that the social contract theory must be taken in this way. If it is not, then one faces a further argument against it as an explanation of the origin of the state. The argument is that you cannot use contract theory to account for the origin of the state because the concept of 'contractual obligation' presupposes the state and some form of socio-legal backing as a matter of logic. This is a conceptual point, Bentham's is an historical one.

J. S. Mill points out in his *Essay on Bentham* that Bentham should not be thought of as a negative philosopher. He was not just a critic of what existed. He was positive in the sense of proposing alternatives. In Bentham's theory of law the principle of utility is paramount. Thus he says in ch. 1 of his *Principle of Morals and Legislation* that an action of government is in conformity with this principle in proportion to its tendency to promote the happiness of the community rather than to diminish it. It should be pointed out that, for Bentham, 'the community' is a fiction. It is simply the collection of the individuals who comprise it. To talk of the interests of the community is just to talk of the interests of the members.

In a footnote (p. 37) he considers the claim that the principle of utility is a dangerous one. Bentham agrees that it is! But it is only dangerous to a government whose objective is the greatest happiness of some particular person or group, rather than the members of the entire community. The source of political obligation lies in the principle of utility and the justification of government is that such an organisation is conducive to the general happiness. This is the justification for laws. Laws are regarded as commands supported by sanctions. The political sanction is the judicial infliction of punishment. To the question of why we should obey the law, Bentham's answer is that, generally speaking, such obedience is conducive to the greatest happiness.

Bentham's fundamental position is that we are said to have a duty to act in accordance with the principle of utility and to forbear from action which is contrary to it. However, as Mary Warnock[5] has pointed out, Bentham, in ch. 5 of the *Fragment on Government*, claims that he is duty-bound to perform any act if its non-performance carries the sanction of legal punishment and this is the proper sense of the word 'duty'. The problem that arises here is that if obeying a law in a particular case is not conducive to the promotion of the greatest happiness, then it seems we have a duty to perform the act (as it is a legal requirement) and not to perform it (as it reduces happiness in the particular case). A duty is entailed by the existence of a sanction and yet prohibited by the utility principle. To avoid this would be, as Warnock says, to see Bentham's legal codification enterprise as ensuring that only those laws which are conducive to the greatest happiness are enacted. Thus our duty to obey is not just derived from the fact that laws carry sanctions, but also that those sanctions are necessary and justifiable in terms of ensuring the greatest happiness. In an ideal system of correct laws there would be a coincidence of the two kinds of duty.

Warnock offers a kind interpretation of Bentham but it poses other problems. Mill tells us that: 'The doctrine of codification, as the word imports, relates to the form only of the laws, not their substance; it does not concern itself with what the laws should be, but declares that whatever they are, they ought to be systematically arranged and fixed down to a determinate form of words.'[6] Mill is here answering a possible objection against Bentham, namely, that one particular set of laws is applicable to all people at all times. Mill is claiming that as Bentham was not concerned to lay down the substance of the law, then he avoids the criticism. His only universal point is that all laws are to be consistent, clear and systematically formalised. This answer of Mill's creates a problem for Warnock's account. The formal characteristics of a legal system are not sufficient to guarantee the compatibility of that system with the greatest happiness principle. Even if all these formal conditions are satisfied, we could still have a bad system as a whole because the content of the laws produced misery rather than happiness. The legal system of Draco is criticised for its severity not its ambiguity. In order for Bentham to establish a duty to obey laws in the utility sense, it is necessary to take account of the content as well as the form. We need to have *some* content. The content cannot just be whatever produces the greatest happiness on pain of having a vacuous theory.

Mill identifies three important questions in political philosophy,[7]

(1) To what authority is it for the good of the people that they should be subject?
(2) How are they to be induced to obey that authority?
(3) By what means are the abuses of that authority to be checked?

It is the third question which Mill regards Bentham as addressing himself to. The answer is, in Mill's words:

responsibility to persons whose interest … accords with the end in view – good government. This being granted, it is next to be asked, in what body of persons this identity of interest with good government, that is with the whole community is to be found? In nothing less, says Bentham, than the numerical majority: no, say we, even in the numerical majority itself; of no portion of the community less than all, will the interest coincide, at all times and in all respects, with the interest of all. But, since power given to all, by a representative government, is in fact given to a majority: we are obliged to fall back upon the first of our three questions, namely, under what authority is it for the good of the people that they be placed? And if to this the answer be, under that of a majority among themselves, Bentham's system cannot be questioned.[8]

The only danger that Mill sees in Bentham's system is that of the majority consisting of one class and this one class, no matter which, might stifle opposition from minority groups. It might be quite impervious to their requests or advice if it rules in an absolute manner. Mill tells us that wherever all the forces of society act in one single direction, the just claims of the individual are in extreme peril. An interesting philosophical point to emerge from this remark of Mill's is that he does not see the just claims of the individual as being exhausted by the direction of the prevailing social forces. We shall discuss this when we come to Mill's *On Liberty.*

An important point which we can extract from our preceding discussion is that it is permissible to break a law when such a transgression is conducive to promoting the greatest happiness. This is a common strand in utilitarian political philosophy. Austin in his second lecture on jurisprudence allows for there to be such cases. Laws are not inflexible. They can be broken in particular cases although, in general, they are good laws. The utilitarians' calculation procedure (see previous chapter) is supposed to tell us what are the exceptional cases. It is here that problems emerge. There can be real disagreement on what is to count as an exceptional case. Consider the position of those who protest at the presence of nuclear weapons bases in the UK. The protest is carried out in the name of conscience not calculation. They see breaking the criminal damage law or infringing the civil law of trespass as being quite justified given the principle that is involved. They would object to the description 'vandalism' being applied to their activities given the context in which they are performed. The problem here for a utilitarian theory is the notion of acting out of conscience. People can and do object in principle to certain methods of achieving the greatest happiness and an appeal to that principle is not going to solve the problem. There is, of course, another side to this question. Protesters of conscience may say that they do not care *how* their ends are achieved as long as they are achieved. Such a line of reasoning as this runs counter to democratic principles and the rule of law. It would have disastrous consequences if applied by all. A distinction would be required here between the person of conscience and the fanatic.

Let us turn from the question of disobedience in a particular case to the larger issue of whether it can ever be legitimate to overthrow a government. Austin argues that to disobey an established government is in itself evil. This is the case even when you have a bad government because the damage done by such a government is not as bad as the damage brought about by anarchy. Government *per se* is useful as it affords security. Government is thus justified by appeal to the principle of utility. Austin does, however, allow for resistance to an established government. Resistance to a bad government can be justified if it would lead to a good one. The intervening anarchy would be a short-lived necessary evil in bringing about a good end. The weakness of the utilitarian thesis is obvious when one considers how all this calculating is to be done. Austin admits that such a calculation is beset with problems and that wise, good and brave people might be divided and perplexed. Now the principle of utility and the objective calculation procedure were supposed to provide a method for *solving* perplexities. It now turns out that the method *itself* is a source of perplexity.

J. R. Lucas on authority and the state

A more recent attempt to clarify the relationship between authority and the state has been made by Lucas.[9] Lucas argues that we all accept various kinds of authority, for example, legal, biblical, historical or the word of another. It is perfectly rational for us to do this given that we are fallible and that we are imperfectly informed. We need authority and the wholesale rejection of it would be irrational.

Lucas holds that it is in our interest to obey authority. Even if one were omniscient and infallible, one should still be guided by the expressed wishes of others if one cares for them or has respect for their status as 'independent centres of value'. He holds that any authority which exists is, in the main, self-justifying. Lucas does not see the problem of political theory as justifying such authority, but as taming it. Once an authority has been established, it has a claim on our allegiance. This claim 'will continue, in the absence of powerful considerations to the contrary, for no other reason than it is established' (p. 53). Lucas remarks that political philosophy has for too long taken the sceptic too seriously. We cannot give logically rigorous arguments as to why the law should be obeyed. Instead, humbler though sound ones (that is, limited ones) can be given. An example of such an argument would be: authority exists *de facto* and therefore it acquires a *de jure* legitimacy. 'We start from the fact that there is an authority and I obey it, and from this incline towards the conclusion that I not only do obey it, but should' (p. 56).

Lucas allows that this conclusion does not follow logically. In order to achieve that, we should have to argue:

(1)   Whatever authority has *de facto* existence now ought to be obeyed.
(2)   This authority has *de facto* existence now.
(3)   I ought to obey this authority.

In order to get the value judgement in (3), we need an 'ought' in one of the premisses. Once we cast the argument in this form, we get a problem. The argument is now identical in form to that used by the defenders of the Nazis at Nuremberg. Lucas realised that this problem existed for he tells us that we cannot know that whatever is, is right. The preceding argument could be used to justify any and every form of despotism by simply asserting its factual existence and subsuming that under the major moral premiss (1). It is not at all clear that the sceptic or the rebel is likely to be impressed by this or by the argument in its limited form. He might, for example, want to know the conditions under which the limited form operates. It is, of course, no answer to the sceptic to refuse to take him seriously.

The sceptic is even less likely to be impressed by Lucas' next move. This consists in arguing that, in the case of the UK, I cannot prove that the Queen is always entitled to my obedience, but I can argue:

(1)   I ought to obey some authority.
(2)   The Queen is the acknowledged authority.
(3)   I ought to obey the Queen.

The apparent reasonableness of this argument stems from certain constitutional facts concerning *how* the Queen is the authority and from certain democratic principles concerning how laws are passed in the name of the Queen. We may also add that governmental authority in the UK is not tyrannical or intolerable. It is only when you sketch in this background that the argument is reasonable. It is in this background that the respect for democratic institutions is incorporated. To see that this is the case, the reader should try to forget this background and recast Lucas' argument using names like Hitler or Idi Amin instead of that of the Queen. It would be monstrous to claim that as such a creature as Amin was the acknowledged authority in a state, it followed that the citizens had a moral duty to obey him. There has to be some reference to how the authority was acquired and what it is being used for. Lucas pointed out at the start that we all accept certain sorts of authority; he should have added that the acceptance is not blind. The difficulty we have come across here then is that even if we grant that we should obey some authority, it does not follow that the existing authority is the one we ought to obey. It could be a bad authority even if it is the only one.

We can agree with Lucas that it would be irrational to reject all authority out of hand, but it is not clear how far this takes us. It might rebut the anarchist, but not the revolutionary. The revolutionary is not claiming that *all* authority should be rejected. He is claiming that a certain kind should be and that it should be replaced with his own brand. Although Lucas puts much emphasis on *de facto* authority, he does not rule out revolution. He sees that we are, generally speaking and by comparison, fortunate in the UK in not needing to rebel. He tells us, however, that we must not assume that there could never be circumstances in which it would be right to rebel. Well, what are these circumstances?

In answering this, Lucas adopts a line which will be by now familiar. There has to be a weighing up of pros and cons. We have to consider whether the alternative would be worse. He cites the French and Russian revolutions as examples of even worse consequences following from the revolution. These examples might be too selective in that we can also think of revolutions that produced results better than what went before them. He remarks that revolutions are permissible only if they can be relied on not to go too far and to observe the rules of civilised behaviour. This remark is not very illuminating as it applies to any form of authority, revolutionary or non-revolutionary. It seems that what he is saying is that a revolution must not go as far down the road of tyranny and should break fewer rules of civilised behaviour than the regime it replaces. So we are left with a kind of calculating procedure. It is not enough for the *de facto* regime under which we live to be intolerable, we (fallible creatures) must work out what the effects of an alternative would be. A point which Lucas does not make is that the situation under a *de facto* authority can be so intolerable that we cannot conceive of anything worse, let alone ponder the lessons of history. I would suggest that this was true of the Jews in Hitler's Germany. It is their lack of power to rebel that has now made *them* a lesson of history.

Perhaps Lucas could have given more specific criteria for justifying rebellion if he had developed his earlier remark concerning the regarding of others as independent centres of value. Any authority which offends against this conception is to be resisted. We do, of course, require a full conceptual analysis of what it is to be an independent centre of value. There is scope for much important and original work to be done in this area.

► Images of society

The conservative image

I shall use Edmund Burke as our guide through what can broadly be described as a conservative image of society. Burke, writing at the end of the eighteenth century, saw that the French Revolution had changed the world for ever. The traditional bases of authority had been destroyed. Tradition, the monarchy, the church and the aristocracy had been replaced by the authority of the people.

Burke thought that the French people had been led astray. He thought that society must be based on an authority which is hallowed by tradition. Order could only be based on respect and a consensus of feelings which bind people together. Revolution is disastrous because it is based on the wrong kinds of things, namely, egotism, vanity and conceit. He regarded the revolution as marking the end of chivalry, obedience, honour and freedom.

In Burke there is a longing for what is known as a closed society. Such a society is essentially authoritarian and hierarchical. Agreed status is afforded to the various members of the society. What is important is the notion that there is agreement that the authority is legitimate. Some philosophers have described such a society as one in which there is no gap between facts and values. Your obligations follow from your agreed status; they are not questioned. Such societies are stable and static. This is, of course, an idealised type. It should be contrasted with the open or pluralist society. An open society is not hallmarked with authoritarianism. It attempts to justify its power, and, more importantly, its members think that power or authority is something that requires justification. It is open in the sense that it accepts change and even regards change as desirable in itself. The open society is not elitist and does not justify itself by appeal to tradition. Events in such a society are not so predictable and there are many conflicting interests.

In the closed society Burke saw security. Man ought to feel secure and in return for security and protection he gives loyalty and confidence. It should not be necessary for man to ponder about what is right and wrong. It should be clear. There should be no fact-value gap. When we lose this certainty we move into a vacuum. We are thrown upon our own resources. The result is individualism in which each man has to calculate. Burke regarded the new age as being one of sophisters, economists and calculators.

A central theme of Burke's conservative political philosophy is the organic view of society. It is a living thing which changes slowly. It has a history which gives it an identity and from which society inherits its customs which provide stability and order. We inherit authority and some institutions have legitimised authority, the monarchy, aristocracy and church. For Burke, there is no freedom without the law. The anarchist is constantly in peril for in the state of anarchy, authority resides with those who have the greatest physical strength. When we have historical traditions and institutions sanctioned by long usage, the power has been tamed and moderated. There are built-in controls which prevent the resort to naked force. Man must have roots and a sense of belonging.

In his *Reflections on the French Revolution*, Burke directs his attack against the radical philosophers who want to restructure society by changing the old order. With the dawning of what is called 'the age of reason' the intellectuals turned their backs on authority based on tradition. Justifications were sought in terms of utility or social function.

Behind his mistrust of the age of reason, and what he called 'the mechanical philosophers' lies a deep pessimism concerning human nature. Man is frail, corruptible, fallible. He is susceptible to violence and incapable of the intellectual objectivity necessary for the criticism of our social institutions. Man is a creature governed by instinct and emotion, not reason. It is an error to put your faith in reason. The institutions we attack in the name of change and progress are the very ones that protect us from ourselves. Such institutions have stood the test of time. Experience has shown them to be sound and it is through experience or practical reason that we learn, not through theoretical reason.

Burke was opposed to the introduction of alien standards into a society. When controls are swept away the result will be anarchy. He had no sympathy for the 1789 declaration of the doctrine of natural rights. Burke regarded such a conception as an intellectual fiction. For Burke, the only rights a man can have are those which are developed in society. There are no universal rights applying to all men, in all places and at all times. As each society constitutes a separate organism, so too the nature of rights will be relative. The rights of each individual are relative to the society of which he is a member.

In Burke there is a strong undercurrent of anti-individualism. This is clearly shown in his attack on the theory of the social contract. The dissolution of the monarchy on the grounds that it had not fulfilled its part of a bargain was anathema to him. Although of a very different political type to Bentham, Burke asks a similar question of the social contract, namely, what contract? There is no contract to be construed along the lines of a business partnership. The partnership is in science, art, morality; it is a partnership with the dead, the living and those yet to be born. What we have inherited is a system based on leadership and this is held to justify the hierarchical system of monarchy and aristocracy. Burke accepts the basis of a class system. On this theory man is seen as a product of his culture and by attacking that culture, he would be attacking himself.

There is no sympathy with the ideal of equality. It is an ideal which involves going against nature. Those who try to level never equalise. He accuses the levellers of perverting the natural order of things.

Burke allows that there are conflicts within a stable and continuous order, but they are held to be only surface conflicts. Underneath there lie three fundamental harmonies: (1) integration of personalities; (2) harmony of different sections of society in which man fulfils himself by fulfilling the needs and ends of his society; and (3) harmony of history and providence. The religious sense provides one with a faith in which the mysteries of evil, pain and death can be understood. The state is divinely ordained.

There are a number of points which we need to make about this kind of thesis. A very general criticism that can be offered concerns the disparaging view of theoretical reason taken by Burke. He has a point in accusing intellectuals of oversimplifying situations in their pursuit of rational thought and answers, but Burke too is a theorist. It takes a fair amount of theoretical reasoning to give oligarchy a religious justification. Burke, given his commitment to the maintenance of society based on property, does this. In theorising we are trying to understand, to systematise and to clarify. Reason is the tool for the job. There is something very odd in holding a *theory* which attempts to undermine theoretical reasoning. It cuts away its own foundation. To renounce reason is to turn one's back on truth and yet the whole point of theorising is to get at the truth. There is a hefty quota of theory in Burke and he attempts to reveal the ultimate truth about the nature of society. In performing this task, he must use theoretical reasoning. This leads to a second problem.

When we get widespread discontent in a once stable society, the instability does not arise *because* of the theorists. It may arise out of the ill treatment of some individuals or class, through corruption and so on. The theorist records such problems and tries to explain how they occurred, but he does not create them. Such evils are not to be blamed on the use of reason. Hopefully, the use of reason will lie in solving them and in order to do this we must first of all understand them.

The sort of theory Burke is propounding tends to assimilate good institutions with the length of their usage. There is, however, no inconsistency in saying that an authority, although long established, is a bad one. The Inquisition was an established institution exercising considerable authority. But the appeal to established usage in no way assuages our doubts concerning its goodness. The notion of gradual or evolutionary change is inapplicable to examples like this. Surely it is better to get rid of such institutions as soon as possible. The general point here is that cruel and wicked practices can have histories, and long ones at that, simply through their ability to inspire fear. We object to them because of what they involve no matter how long they have been in existence or by whom they are sanctioned. Although Burke would not have wanted to justify such institutions, we need to go beyond the custom/tradition thesis in order to question them. We feel that it would be in order to make moral objections, but, for Burke, morality is solely a matter of inherited tradition and custom.

We saw that on Burke's conception of a closed society our obligations were mapped out clearly for us. We referred to this kind of society as not having a fact-value gap. There can, however, be moral conflicts within a tradition. There could, for example, be conflicting obligations arising out of an individual's relations with his family and his relations with the church. When conflicts arise within a tradition, it is not clear how an appeal to tradition can solve them. Burke, of course, claims that the closed society incorporates moral certainty. As we have indicated, however, conflicts of duty can arise and these need not be superficial. Circumstances can sometimes force us into uncharted territory and those who are accustomed to total reliance on a map may well come to grief. The choice is not so stark as that between man having every moral answer he needs guaranteed by tradition and that of man as isolated individual perplexed about all his future actions.

Burke spoke of a partnership between the different aspects of a culture. There can be conflicts here and this points the way to another problem with the closed society. Suppose there is conflict between the church and science. Now we have a conflict between the guarantor of moral certainty and the pursuers of truth about the natural world. The problem here is that if the moral certainty is to be preserved, then it may well be at the cost of truth. This raises serious questions concerning the availability of free inquiry in a closed society.

Another difficulty with the inherited tradition view is the claim concerning rulers being born to rule. It is as obvious to us now as it was to the radical philosophers of Burke's time that some of these leaders have turned out to be the most dreadful specimens of the human race.

Burke makes use of a conception of human nature involving man as governed by emotion and instinct. The reader is advised to adopt a questioning attitude to theories based on human nature which attempt to establish conclusions concerning the way things ought to be politically. First, there is the technical philosophical problem of arguing from alleged facts concerning the nature of man to value-laden conclusions. Such arguments often take the form: If we want security, stability, well-being and so on, then given the way we are, we ought to do so and so. Problems are inherent in setting up the first premiss. People can differ widely in their ideas of security, well-being and so on, and also in the price to be paid.

Secondly, there is a problem in setting up the second premiss. There are differing conceptions of human nature (Hobbes and Rousseau) and thus different conclusions will be drawn. It is not obvious how such conceptions are to be verified. It is certainly not a matter of observing behaviour and forming a theory based on those observations. Frequently, the type of theory that is held on human nature will determine the way observations are described rather than the other way round.

The liberal image

J. S. Mill's *On Liberty*[10] is to be our guide here. It will be remembered from our discussion of utilitarian theories of government that Mill regarded Bentham's thesis of authority lying with the majority as being correct. He did, however, have a reservation concerning the possible abuse of that authority. This reservation raises fundamental issues concerning the relationship of the individual to society. We are now going to examine how Mill deals with these issues and we shall see what kind of image of society emerges from what he says.

Mill's concern is with civil or social liberty. He is concerned with the nature and limits of the power which can be legitimately exercised by society over the individual. Even in the case of an elected government, this is a vital question. Safeguards are needed to ensure that the majority does not oppress the minority. The question is where to draw the line between the justifiable interference of collective opinion and individual independence.

Mill grants that it is necessary to have restraints on conduct, but what are these restraints to be? From our previous discussion the reader will know that Burke's answer would be custom and tradition. In a closed society they answer questions for you, indeed, the questions may not even arise. Mill makes a number of disparaging remarks about the ability of custom to arbitrate. Custom breeds an unthinking attitude. Mill holds that unless an opinion on conduct is supported by reasons, it is nothing more than a personal preference. If the attempt to give reasons results in an appeal to the preferences of others, then you are still in the realm of preference and not that of reason. Mill is saying that this is what, in effect, all appeals to custom amount to. He is also complaining that such appeals are far too common. If appeals to custom are dismissed, then we find that there is no recognised principle by which the legitimacy of government interference can be tested. Mill then offers us a principle for settling the question of the justification of interference with, and control of, the individual: 'the sole end for which mankind are warranted, individually or collectively, in interfering with the liberty of action of any of their members, is self-protection' (p. 135). An individual can only have his liberty curtailed if the exercise of that liberty would cause harm to others.

In an extremely important passage Mill says that the agent's own physical or moral good is not a sufficient condition for interference. We can neither force to act nor prevent from action on the grounds that, 'it will be better for him to do so because it will make him happier; because in the opinions of others, to do so would be wise, or even right'. It has to be shown that harm will result to another in order to justify interference. If the conduct concerns him alone, then his right to independence is absolute. The individualism of Mill's essay is well brought out in the claim that over himself, over his body and mind, the individual is sovereign. Mill excludes children from this on the grounds that he is assuming a maturity of faculties. (Some have argued that the mature/immature distinction is dubious. There can be borderline cases but we can and do distinguish between a child putting its hand into the fire and, say, Archbishop Cramner doing it in a gesture of defiance. It may be difficult to draw a rigid boundary but there will still be many distinguishable cases.)

Mill tells us that he is not arguing for his principle of liberty independently of considerations of utility as he regards the latter as the ultimate appeal on all ethical questions. The utility in question is, however, that of utility in its largest sense which is 'grounded on the permanent interests of a man as a progressive being' (p. 136).

The sphere of action identified by Mill as the appropriate one for liberty is that of conduct not affecting others. Its direct effects are on the agent himself. Having identified the sphere of liberty, he then particularises the following freedoms:

(1) Freedom of thought and sentiment on all subjects, including freedom of expression and publication.
(2) Freedom of tastes and pursuits as long as no harm to others accrues. The fact that others disapprove is not sufficient to warrant interference.
(3) Freedom of individuals to unite as long as the resulting union does not harm others. There must be no coercion or deception in the union.

These liberties are the hallmark of a free society.

Mill's second chapter discusses the issue of freedom of thought and discussion. On no account can a government of any kind have the right to suppress opinion. One of Mill's most famous statements follows this assertion:

> If all mankind minus one were of one opinion, and only one person were of the contrary opinion, mankind would be no more justified in silencing that one person, than he, if he had the power, would be justified in silencing mankind. (p. 142)[11]

Mill has a number of reasons for insisting that there can never be a legitimate power to suppress opinion. First, it is always possible that the opinion to be suppressed is true. If you refuse a hearing you are thereby assuming absolute certainty. You are assuming infallibility, be it your own or that of the prevailing authority. Mill considers an objection to this. It is the duty of governments and individuals to arrive at a true opinion but when they are sure that they have attained the truth are they not thereby justified in imposing this on others and prohibiting deviations from the truth they have attained? The false opinions could also be dangerous. This would not amount to an assumption of absolute certainty, but just that degree of assurance that is reasonable and sufficient for guiding our lives. Mill's answer to this is that it is only by allowing liberty of discussion that we are justified in assuming opinion to be true for the purposes of life. Discussion is necessary to elicit truth and such discussion involves listening to both sides. He considers the supposition that a belief should not be attacked if it is useful to society. A similar argument to this is used by Socrates to justify censorship in Plato's *Republic*. We thus have a distinction between truth and utility. Mill claims that such an argument does not avoid his infallibility objection. The utility of an opinion is itself a matter of opinion and therefore an appropriate object of discussion. The judgement that some opinions were so useful as to exempt them from attack would require an infallible judge. He also regards the distinction between truth and utility as inherently dubious. The truth of an opinion is said to be part of its utility and cannot be divorced from it.

Mill makes it clear (p. 149) that it is not the psychological feeling of certainty which amounts to the assumption of infallibility, but rather taking it upon oneself to decide the question *for others* in advance of any discussions. This applies equally to the truth or utility of beliefs. Such prohibitions are not just bad for the dissenters from received and accepted opinion, but also for the receivers. In fact it is worse for them as it hampers their mental development and would not be in keeping with Mill's conception of man as a progressive being. His remarks on p. 161 can be seen as a striking contrast with Burke's longing for a closed society. Here Mill tells us that where there is a tacit convention that principles and fundamental questions are not to be discussed, you have mental despotism and not freedom.

Second, even if we admit that the received opinion is the truth, it still requires open discussion otherwise it will assume the status of dead dogma. You must know the grounds of the truths especially in the case of morality and religion.

Third, discussion is needed when received opinions are partly true but need supplementing with grains of truth from heretical opinion. Even when heretical opinion is mainly false, it might contain some truth and thus we should be able to discuss it.

The next stage in Mill's argument is to move from a discussion of freedom of opinion to a discussion of freedom of action. In this case the freedom of the individual has to be limited so as not to cause nuisance to others. He can translate his opinions into action at his own cost, but must not harm others. The assertion of individuality is the main ingredient of individual and social progress. The problem is that it is hardly recognised as having intrinsic value. Most are content with custom. Mill recognises two extremes. There is total imitation calling for no individual judgement and there is the idea that nothing has been learned from experience. He tells us that there can still be individualism in matters learned from experience as we must interpret this experience in our own way. We learn for ourselves how applicable it is to our situations. Blind obedience to custom, though, requires no choice. It is vital in the development of the individual that our desires and impulses should be our own and not just inherited. They can be shaped by culture, but not blindly imprinted. The enemy here for Mill is blind conformity. On p. 190 he says that it is not that they choose the customary in preference to their own inclinations, but rather what their inclinations are as opposed to custom simply does not occur to them. In cases like this, 'the mind itself is bowed to the yoke'. Burke would no doubt describe this as a harmony – the people's inclinations and the social customs are at one. Mill also complains about the shunning of peculiarity of taste and eccentricity of conduct. At this point Mill seems to be equating individuality with oddity.

There are limits of tolerance to be applied to individual action. We begin to get some idea about these limits of tolerance when Mill tells us that incurring the displeasure of others is not sufficient grounds for applying restraint. The development of our nature requires that different people be allowed to lead different lives as long as no harm is done to others and 'harm' must mean more than arousing 'mere displeasure'.

There are reasons for supposing that permitting liberty will be of benefit even for those who cannot see the role it plays in individual development. Mill is here saying that, even if you cannot see its intrinsic value, liberty has good effects. In a free environment genius, originality and initiative can flourish.

He goes on to stress the value of non-conformity and on p. 196 he seems to be condoning eccentricity for its own sake. Eccentric behaviour does not have to be an improvement; it is sufficient that it is different. Non-conformist conduct is not confined to the exceptional few. We can all opt for unusual lifestyles as long as we possess a tolerable amount of common sense and experience. We are told, very strangely within a utilitarian context, that the actions chosen do not have to be the best in themselves, but they are the best because they have been chosen. For Mill, the differences of individuality are worth having even if they are not for the better.

Given this conception of individuality, the next question for Mill to discuss is the legitimate amount of sovereignty to be exercised by the individual and by the state over the individual. He rejects the idea of a social contract. However, as we all receive protection from society, we are, in return for this, bound to observe certain rules of conduct in our dealings with others. We are, for example, bound to observe the rights of others. It is legitimate for government to enforce this. Opinion can be used as a punishment in cases where a *legal* wrong has not been committed. The general principle he draws is: 'As soon as any part of a person's conduct affects prejudicially the interests of others, society has jurisdiction over it' (p. 205). There should be no interference in cases where the conduct affects no one except the individuals or others by consent. There is no justification in preventing a mature person choosing his own life. He is the final judge. After all advice has been given, it is the individual who has the greater knowledge of his own feelings and circumstances. Individual action which is foolish or depraved should not, for all that, attract penalties. The person in question is, however, rightly viewed as distasteful or contemptible. Such a person can be shunned and others warned about him. The reader might well think that this involves a very subtle distinction with moral disapprobation. The reason Mill does not regard this as a matter of moral disapprobation is because no breach of duty to others is involved in such actions.

Let us now turn to the distinction between acts affecting oneself and acts affecting others. If John Donne's claim that no man is an island is true, then is this distinction not difficult to operate? Mill addresses himself to this (p. 211 ff.) and allows that exercises of liberty, although only involving the individual in one sense, are problematic in that they can affect the ability to discharge duties to others. Such actions can cause indirect harm and set a bad example. If experience has shown such conduct to be without use, then should not the forces of law and order clamp down?

Mill holds that if the act involves a violation of a definite obligation, then the case cannot be regarded as one of pure individuality. It falls under the heading of 'social acts'. The risk of harm to others is sufficient to remove the act from the realm of individuality, otherwise society tolerates the act for the sake of the greater good of freedom. Mill thinks that the most powerful argument against interference in personal conduct is that such interference is likely to be done wrongly and in the wrong place.

Mill makes it clear that having a distaste for a mode of conduct is not sufficient to establish that one has been injured. To think that it was would pave the way for despotism and would justify sanctions against others merely for thinking or acting differently. There is no right which can be claimed by an individual which entails that others should act or think in the way deemed right such that a failure to so act would constitute a breach of that right (p. 211). At the end of ch. 4 Mill broadens the discussion from the national to the international with his defence of the Mormons' right to practise polygamy and claims that no community has a right to force another to be civilised.

Critical discussion

There can be no doubt that Mill's thinking has been influential. It was uppermost in the minds of the legislators in the 1960s. The legalisation of homosexuality between consenting adults, relaxation of the betting and gaming laws and the availability of abortions are examples of Mill's principles being put into practice.

A criticism often levelled against Mill is that society is far more interdependent than he allows. This was the point of our earlier reference to Donne's remark that no man is an island. Mill's individualism might be so individualistic as to be unrealistic.

A point made in Mill's own time was that his libertarianism could confer unfair advantages, such as that of rich over poor, articulate over inarticulate. There needs to be a connection between morality and the law. Thus, it could be argued, there are cases where the law can intervene even though on Mill's libertarian principle it should not be allowed to. Following the Wolfenden Report in 1959, Lord Justice Devlin argued that there were two points in the report and in Mill's theory of liberty which go against the grain of English law. On Mill's principle if free consent and privacy obtain, then an act is to be tolerated. There are, however, acts which would not be tolerated even if these conditions were satisfied, for example, euthanasia and incest. Devlin holds that laws must reflect the moral views of the citizens. It is as much the business of the law to suppress vice as it is to suppress subversion. On Mill's thesis we could only legitimately suppress vice if it could be shown that the individual's practice of it resulted in harm to others.

This principle has been defended by Hart in *The Concept of Law*. Hart argues that if an act is to be suppressed, then a group of experts must show that it is dangerous. The law should not prohibit an act because the community regards it as immoral. There must be a demonstration of actual harm resulting from the individual's performance of that act. The reader should note the trust that is placed in the experts. The danger inherent in this is that of elitist opinions on moral matters which can result in various kinds of paternalism.

Much is going to turn on the meaning of 'harm'. There can be no doubt about what is meant by harm in cases of physical harm like assault and battery. There are also clearcut cases of doing harm which do not involve physical damage. There are, however, more difficult cases to handle, namely, those involving 'psychological harm'. What counts as psychological harm? Consider the case of whether violent or pornographic material should be shown on television. On Mill's principle, prohibition could only be justified if harm results. If a person buys his own 'video nasties' and watches them in the privacy of his home, then, even if psychological harm is done to the individual, he cannot be prevented from acting. If the individual wishes to inflict psychological harm upon himself, then that is his own affair provided that no harm to others results. The problem, though, is that we are not clear about 'psychological harm'. The very fact that someone should *want* to watch certain sorts of material can be taken by some to show that he is psychologically damaged in some way. There is a danger here, though, in the use of quasi-medical terminology to describe something of which we morally disapprove. The case which is of greater public interest is that of whether such material should be shown on the public media. Here the legislators are not so much concerned with psychological harm *per se*, but with how such harm might be translated into offences against others. The problem then becomes how such connections are to be established.

Another criticism of Mill concerns the cases of suicide and drug addiction. Liberty consists in doing what one desires, and if no one else is affected by the act, then it must be allowed. The case of suicide is the more difficult for a supporter of Mill to deal with. If a person freely chooses suicide, then we have no right to prevent him. If, however, we could save an attempted suicide by administering the kiss of life, would we not do so? In such a case as this it is not plausible to say that we do so in order for him to fulfil his obligations to others, we do it to save his life even though he freely chose to end it and even though he has sovereignty over his own body and mind. Mill could try and accommodate the example of the drug addict by saying that the libertarian principle presupposes a level of rationality on the part of the agent before it can get off the ground (this would be similar to his maturity requirement). It could then be argued that a person torn apart by such addiction would be defectively rational. Mill can also argue that society is adversely affected by such addictions. We should not, however, make the evil of drug addiction dependent on harm done to others.

Mill's 'assumption of infallibility' argument has been criticised by Gibbs.[12] We saw that Mill held that to suppress opinion was to assume infallibility. Gibbs has claimed that Mill's assertion is plainly false: 'A ruler might silence an opinion without assuming himself to be infallible, without even assuming that he knows this particular opinion to be false. He might know it to be true, and silence it because it is dangerous.' We can come to Mill's assistance here. Mill's point is not that as a matter of *psychology* the ruler *thinks* that he is infallible, but rather that the act of silencing, and hence deciding for others, *logically* amounts to such an assumption. Gibbs' appeal to the danger of an opinion known to be true is well catered for by Mill. The judgement that it is dangerous is *itself* an opinion and if the ruler prohibits any discussion of the question, then he is saying in advance of discussion that discussion is dangerous. This looks very like an assumption of infallibility.

Gibbs also sees a problem with the importance Mill assigns to truth. Gibbs agrees that truth is a great good but says that it is not the greatest. He attempts to justify this by saying that it must not take precedence over everything else:

> One would obviously have the right and duty to interrupt a seminar thus interfering with the process of inquiry, in order to warn the participants that the building was on fire. There are limits to the methods that may justifiably be used in seeking the truth.[13]

The seminar example is unfortunate as the interruption would only be justifiable if it is *true* that the building was on fire. The example tends to reinforce rather than detract from the value of truth.

The limitations of method argument need not embarrass Mill. It does not just show that truth is not the most important value, it shows that there cannot be any ultimate values in that sense. One can always think of circumstances in which the pursuit of what we ordinarily value would conflict with something else we value.

The real problem for Mill is that he holds utility to be the ultimate moral principle and in *On Liberty* he argues for a connection between utility and truth. The problem is that knowing the truth can cause more misery than happiness in particular cases and it seems that Mill should have to appeal to his calculating procedure to settle this. There is a serious strain in Mill regarding the principle of utility and the principle of liberty. If the spreading of dangerous opinions can detract from the greatest happiness, then do we not have to weigh up the cost of toleration? The problem for Mill is to cope with two absolute principles which can conflict. If utility includes liberty, then we do not need the separate principle. If it does not, then how is liberty and the pursuit of truth to be justified on purely utilitarian grounds?

Democracy and free discussion

On this issue of the supposed utility of suppressing dangerous opinions we should note that if the opinions are false, then free discussion can show why they are false. If a received opinion has a firm base, then it should have nothing to fear. If, on the other hand, the opinion regarded as dangerous is true, then we ought to ask ourselves how it is that we are in a position whereby the truth is a threat to us.

In the cases Mill was most concerned with – religion, politics and morality, in which people in general have an interest – it is not clear that suppression can be reconciled with the concept of a democratic society. We assume a background of rationality and sanity in order to justify the democratic procedure. People vote on law and order, economic policy, matters of political principle and so on. Their collective vote is the ultimate justification of the leader's mandate. It seems very odd then to turn this assumption on its head and say that the people who had sufficient knowledge to select a government on complex issues should be deprived of the opportunity to discuss opinions. Indeed, what we ought to say here is that the more opportunity a people has to engage in free discussion, the more able they are to partake in the democratic process. It is a two-way process. There are freedoms which are essential to a democracy and which distinguish democracies from other forms of governments. The freedom to choose between competing parties with different policies is one of them.

Free discussion is essential to our ability to choose. Gibbs tells us that a society which is obsessive about its freedom is likely to lose it and he approvingly quotes Plato on this. There is, however, another side to this: a society that is not concerned with the issue of freedom has probably already lost it.

The revolutionary image

We shall here look at the main strands of Karl Marx's thought. Marx, in his philosophically formative years, was much influenced by the work of Hegel. Perhaps the most important influence on Marx was Hegel's belief in laws of history. This is something which lies at the heart of Marxism.

Marx was to differ from Hegel on the nature of these laws. Hegel regarded them as spiritual, Marx regarded them as material. Marx had what is known as a materialist conception of history. The source of this divergence from Hegel was Feuerbach. The spiritual realm is seen by Feuerbach as a myth created by man. In explaining why such myths arise, Feuerbach was to provide what was to become a centrally important Marxist concept. The myths arise out of man's alienation. Man is deeply dissatisfied with his actual condition, hence the need to believe in something else. There will be an improvement in some other world.

The nature of the material laws of history is, for Marx, economic. Alienation is itself a socio-economic phenomenon. Under a capitalist system a worker's own labour is in a sense alien to him. It is something he has to sell to the capitalist. The products of his labour are also alien in that they are owned by the capitalist in the form of private property. It is important to realise that Marx is not saying that there is anything wrong with work; what is wrong is the way it is organised under the present system.

Marx believed that society is organised around two pivots, (a) property, and (b) power. The owners of property and power are not going to give them up. To think that change can come about as a result of moral reasoned argument is to be guilty of what Marx called 'utopianism'. Change can come about by force and force alone. He charges the utopians with not having a scientific understanding of society. They commit the fallacy of thinking that men are motivated by ideas. Their theories are described as ideologies; they are not scientific. Marx held that the only way to get at the facts of society is to have a scientific understanding of it, where 'scientific' should be understood along the lines of natural science. Marx stresses the principle of cause and effect. It is only by analysing the causes of a phenomenon that we can truly understand it and be able to predict the future.

What is of vital importance in Marx is his claim that we should interfere with those causes. We must not just explain the world, we must also change it. This is the point behind his famous remark that philosophers have only interpreted the world, his purpose is to change it. Marx is thus a political activist not just a theorist.

Marx and Engels believed that they had found the correct scientific analysis for revealing the structure of society. The two cornerstones of this position are the materialist conception of history, whereby the development of history is seen as being determined by inexorable laws, and the thesis that the determining laws are economic in nature. Marx believed that each historical period gives rise to the next out of a natural necessity. The economic nature of the laws is brought out by his remark that: 'the mode of production of material life determines the general character of the social, political and spiritual processes of life,[14] It is the economic structure of a society that determines what happens in that society. Substructure determines superstructure. We can illustrate this as follows:

Society and social change are determined by technological changes. Man is a toolmaker, intelligent, inventive, adaptable and creative. By improving tools and production techniques he masters his environment. He is driven by biological needs to improve his comforts. If we examine the structure of society and penetrate it, we find that the distribution of economic goods determines everything, including social relations. He tells us in his Theses on Feuerbach that man is the totality of his social relations. The ruling ideas of any age are the ideas of the ruling class. This is why Marx thinks that it is so important to discover who dominates a society. He thinks in dynamic terms. Society is never entirely stable. There always comes a stage where the production relations no longer correspond to the technological changes. Marx refers to such stages as modal points. It is at such stages that a new social structure emerges. When the new structure emerges a new ideology will come with it.

Let us now try to understand Marx's method and how it actually applies to history. Marx applies what is known as the method of dialectic. It is a method he inherited from Hegel. We qualify and modify through the process of Thesis–Antithesis–Synthesis which, for Hegel, was dialectic. This is the concept Marx applied to history. History has evolved with its own kind of dialectic. Hegel's purely logical technique for ascertaining truth was applied to history. It has been said that, for Marx, logic becomes ontology. Marx thought that each historical period was a phase in a necessary evolution.

We can look at the past in terms of four great changes. We start with the nomadic and the pastoral in which possessions were shared. The modal point (point of economic/technological change) is the discovery of soil cultivation and the training of domestic animals. The change gives rise to the second period, the classical period of slavery, wealth-owners and those who owned only their own bodies. The latter class were used to produce surplus wealth for a standing army. It was a period of high achievement in the arts and of political oppression. The modal point was the coming of the barbarians and the incapacity of the social structure to administer a widely dispersed empire. The city-states of Greece and Rome reverted to a more decentralised social system. This was the third period, namely, feudalism. This, however, also had to change. A new kind of city-state emerged. This is capitalism based on technological discoveries and the need to concentrate production in urban centres. It is here that we have the rebellion of the bourgeoisie against the aristocracy.

Liberalism, the bourgeois ideology, becomes the dominant political belief. Democracy becomes the means by which the bourgeoisie tame the aristocracy and exploit the proletariat. According to Marx, the proletariat will become conscious of this exploitation and they in turn will revolt, giving birth to a new socialist society. This is the pattern by which history is said to evolve. It evolves through a process of creating a social system and that system generating upheavals or contradictions within it. In time they become intolerable and a new system takes over.

The way men think and feel is dependent on the way they act. Practice determines theory. Ideas are just reflections of economic interests. Ideas are part of the means by which the ruling classes consolidate their power. Victorian morality suited the early stages of industrial society. Utilitarianism is an expression of bourgeois morality. The kind of freedom espoused by such morality was essentially economic freedom. It is the freedom to buy in the cheap market and sell in the dear one. The fine-sounding accounts of freedom are useless to the army of workers who have only their bodies to sell. To them 'freedom' is an empty word. The situation of a free society is to polarise into two classes, the owners of capital (the means of production) and the workers. The workers can be duped into accepting an ideology which runs counter to their interests. When they realise what is in their interest they will rebel against capitalism and the result will be a classless society, 'the state will wither away'.

Criticisms.   Much criticism has centred on Marx's notion of laws of history. In a very important work Sir Karl Popper[15] has argued that laws have to be universal in form. The history of society is limited to the events on one planet and thus the term 'law' has been deemed inappropriate. Popper has claimed that history reveals trends rather than laws. Trends can change; whereas laws cannot.[16] It is a mistake to think that we can discover laws which state how history *must* occur.

A second criticism concerns why Marx's own theory should not be regarded as ideology. If social theories are generated by underlying economic causes, then why is Marx's theory not generated in this way? It seems that he must, in some sense, be standing outside his own all-embracing theoretical assumptions. Marx would of course claim that his own theory was scientific and value-free. The claim to be value-free is difficult to justify. There are clear indications in Marx that the world should be changed for the *better*. He has a conception of what kind of existence is *best* for man. He also talks of accelerating the downfall of capitalism by direct action, and yet he also holds that capitalism will fall through the operation of laws of history.

Third, there are problems with the notion of duping people into holding ideals. The main difficulty here is how we can tell whether a belief held by someone is an example of false consciousness. It might be said that if the belief is against his economic interest, then it is such an example. This reply would create problems for it seems that we can hold beliefs which are contrary to our short-term or long-term economic interests without having been duped into believing them. It just is not good enough to say that a worker who professes to hold an ideal of liberal and democratic freedom *must* have been elaborately tricked into holding such a belief. Why must he? Because the theory says so. We need good independent grounds for saying this. We must also ensure that there is not a level of description at which the holding of a liberal, democratic principle can always be described as against the believer's economic interest.

Fourth, the concept of alienation is very important in Marx's account of what is wrong with society. Marx refers to man as being alienated from himself and from nature. It is not clear what it is to be alienated from oneself. Neither is it clear what role the concept of nature is playing here. Marx might be claiming that there is something unnatural, in a pejorative sense, about capitalist society. A critic might reply that it is perfectly natural for people to behave in this way. After all, have they not done so for many years? It is not clear to what extent Marx blames private property for alienation. He says that to abolish private property would be to abolish alienation[17] but he also describes private property as a consequence rather than a cause of alienation. Perhaps the best way to understand what is meant by alienation is that man at work in a capitalist society cannot see himself as contributing to a recognisable community interest. He is, therefore, not part of a genuine community. He is treated as a means to an economic end. This is something that would have been true of the nineteenth-century industrial society. It is not obvious that it applies today. Even if there is no genuine 'community as a whole' interest, there are certainly other group interests. There is, however, a point which Marx made that none of us should lose sight of, 'industry is for man, not man for industry'.

Fifth, Marx saw the solution to the problem of alienation as lying in the complete overthrow of the system. The revolution had to be total; cosmetic changes will not do. Changes cannot be accomplished through existing institutions as they are part of the superstructure of capitalism. They are products of the system and would be impotent as weapons for the wholesale changes that are required. It would be wrong though to think that the changes which have occurred from the 1850s have only been cosmetic. Evolutionary change has had considerable effect.

Sixth, Marx is not too specific on how the change will come about. He talks of an intermediate stage consisting in a dictatorship of the working class. What guarantee is there that this would not be the start of more problems? Should a student of history not also learn the lessons of past dictatorship?

Finally, Marx's predictions concerning change in Western capitalist societies have not been fulfilled. It is, of course, true that a theorist can always appeal to hidden factors to explain why a prediction has not materialised, but there has to be some theoretical end to this.

6 The Philosophy of Science

▶ Introduction

What is science? What does it aim to do? These are probably two of the most important general questions that can be asked about science. It is in attempting to formulate answers to these questions that many detailed discussions in this area of philosophy arise.

It would, however, be misleading to say that all the detailed discussions or particular problems in the philosophy of science stem from attempts to answer general questions such as those referred to here. Frequently in the development of science, philosophical problems, or at least problems which required philosophical clarification, have resulted from the practice of science. In the twentieth century this was especially so in relativity theory and quantum theory where it might appear that some of our most important concepts were in need of revision. In addition to trying to give answers to general questions, it is in cases such as this that the philosopher of science has a role to play and his skills, together with those of the scientist can complement one another. Here we might say that the skills of the philosopher of science lie in the area of achieving conceptual clarity and in the removal of conceptual paradoxes which might seem to emerge from a particular scientific theory.

Perhaps an example will help to illuminate this point. Many strange ideas have emanated from misunderstandings of the theory of relativity. Some of these are straightforward scientific misunderstandings, whereas others are better made explicit by spelling out their conceptual implications. If these turn out to be absurd, then we know that something has gone wrong. When we realise this, our understanding of the theory should improve. Thus understanding a scientific theory and conceptual clarity go together and perhaps they are impossible to separate.

The example I have chosen is taken from Morris Kline's *Mathematics in Western Culture* (pp. 502–3). Kline sees relativity theory as implying the revision of one of the most fundamental philosophical presuppositions of science, namely, the relationship of cause and effect. Kant had argued (*Critique of Pure Reason, Second Analogy*) that the cause of an effect must precede that effect. Any adequate account of causation has to afford temporal priority to the cause over the effect. Kline's claim is that with the acceptance of relativity theory, the order of two events is no longer to be regarded as an absolute affair. This is derived from the relativistic notion that two observers moving relative to each other can legitimately disagree on the simultaneity of two events. That is to say the order of two events depends on the position of the observer. One observer might see A following B and the other see B following A. If the two events, A and B, are normally regarded as a causal sequence (for example, A causes B) then it is possible for some observers to observe B preceding A in which case the effect would precede the cause. As there is no absolute vantage point, why should priority be given to the claim that A is the cause of B rather than B the cause of A? According to Kline revision of the concept of 'cause' is in order.

Unfortunately, no revision of the concept is going to cater for the kind of situation envisaged by Kline which belies a misunderstanding. To see why this is so let us tease out some conceptual implications of what he has said. Let us suppose that the two events are an act of wrongdoing by a child and an act of chastisement by its parent. Now on Kline's account it would be theoretically possible for the act of punishment (the effect) to occur before the wrongdoing (the cause). But such a situation would not just be odd and requiring some conceptual revision, it would be *logically* impossible. We cannot *describe* an act as an act of punishment unless it is a response to, and hence follows, an act of wrongdoing. No sense can be attached to the notion of a punishment preceding that at which it is necessarily directed. One would discover similar logical problems with other series of events, for example, the events involved in the course of making an utterance. The important point to emerge from this is that these are not merely practical problems which we have no means at present for solving, rather they are conceptual impossibilities which on Kline's interpretation of relativity would be possible occurrences. This tells us that there must be something wrong with that interpretation. What is wrong with it is that Kline allows there to be disagreement concerning the ordering or timing of events which are in close proximity. This is a misunderstanding of the theory of relativity and of its philosophical implications. There can only be disagreement concerning the timing of events that are widely separated in space. This does not necessitate any revision of our notion of causal precedence. The examination of the conceptual implications of Kline's interpretation affords us a clearer understanding of the theory itself. Philosophical techniques, therefore, go hand in hand with the clarification of what the theory means and what its implications are. In the light of this example, the reader might like to consider a second claim of Kline's, namely, that the question of whether people possess free will must be reconsidered in the light of the theory of relativity (p.503).

Another area in which philosophers have been active is that of the methodology of the social sciences. Much discussion has centred on the issue of whether the social sciences can, or should, adopt the same methods as the natural sciences. If we say that the social sciences aim to provide a scientific understanding of human beings and their institutions, we are led to ask just what it is to have a scientific understanding. This in turn leads us back to the general questions posed at the beginning of this chapter. We must now get clear about the scientific enterprise in general. So let us return to our general questions.

A preliminary answer to the question of what science aims to achieve could be that it is the aim of science to explain things. However, not all explanations are scientific so we are led to ask: what is it to give an explanation of why something occurs? One possible answer to this suggested by Bridgman (*The Logic of Modern Physics*) is that to explain an event is to show that it is a member of a class of events with which we are already familiar. Bridgman holds that all explanations take the form of reducing the unfamiliar to the familiar. We are disposed to accept the familiar without further question and, therefore, our curiosity rests. Einstein has said, concerning this view, that we enjoy comprehending, we reduce phenomena by process of logic to what is already known. There are three objections that can be made to this conception of what it is to offer an explanation.

(1) Scientists can, and do seek explanations of phenomena and events with which we are most familiar. As Harré (*Philosophies of Science*, p. 115) has pointed out, we are interested in seeking out the causes of the most run-of-the-mill things. Any adequate astronomical theory of our solar system must account for events with which we are familiar such as the rising and setting of the sun, the luminosity of the moon and so on. It might well be true to say that we are more curious about the unfamiliar but this does not mean that no explanations are sought of the familiar.

(2) Explanations themselves may be given in terms that are not familiar. We might, for example, be quite familiar with the symptoms of a particular disease but the scientific explanation of its causes could take us into territory where familiarity is the last thing we feel. The familiar can, therefore, be reduced to the unfamiliar during the course of scientific explanation.

(3) Familiarity is a subjective matter, but explanation has to be objective in that it holds for everyone. Scientific explanations demand a rational or logical connection *not* a psychological one. Familiarity is not a consideration; what has been held to be important is that the scientist should be able to subsume the phenomena to be explained under a true law.

This latter aspect of a scientific explanation introduces the important notion of a law of nature. It might be thought that a law of nature describes or refers to any uniformity of nature but on reflection we see that this will not suffice. The reason it will not suffice is that not all uniformities of nature are laws and not all laws of nature describe uniformities, if, by 'uniformities' we mean invariable sequences. In the former category we would place accidental generalisations such as an increase in sunspot activity and an increase in the number of Great Crested Grebe nesting on the banks of the Rhine. In the latter category we would place statistical or probabilistic laws. Such laws as these do not provide us with statements of what invariably happens, but with statements of what will most probably happen. Let us consider an example of a statistical law. Suppose we know that 80% of persons who come into contact with a particular virus will develop symptoms of the associated disease. Now normally scientists would not be content to leave the matter at the level of the statistical. They would want to know *why* the figure is 80% and a scientific explanation should show why 20% remain unaffected. The implication here is that you can ask for an explanation of the statistical in terms of some higher level non-statistical law. In our example, if we explain why 20% are unaffected by reference to strength of resistance, then we would have to say what we meant by 'strength of resistance' other than just the fact that the disease does not develop. We would be looking for some physiological account of what it is to have resistance to that virus. This higher level law would explain why the statistics are the way they are. In this case, the statistical law is the outcome of, and can be subsumed under, some higher level non-statistical law.

However, not all statistical laws approximate to our example of the virus. Some statistical laws appear to be irreducibly statistical in nature. That is to say, there is just no appeal to the non-statistical in order to subsume them in the way in which we have been discussing. In cases of irreducible statistical laws, the statistical laws themselves constitute the higher level laws. The most famous example of this comes from quantum physics. Here it is argued that the laws are irreducibly statistical. Heisenberg's principle of indeterminacy states that if you specify where a particle is at a given instant you cannot then go on to attribute a specific speed or direction to it. On the other hand, if you do attribute specific speed or direction, you cannot then say where its starting point or finishing point is, that is, you cannot say with certainty where it is. The most you can give is the probability. In this case there is no appeal beyond the probabilistic laws. Sub-atomic events cannot be described with certainty but only with the measure of probability made possible by the use of Planck's constant.

Another example of a statistical law is Boltzmann's interpretation of entropy. The running down of energy is explained by the atoms becoming more and more disorderly. Entropy is the measure of this disorder. Although Boltzmann provided an actual formula to measure disorder the law is still a statistical or probabilistic law. Orderly states do not *always* run down into disorder, but *in the main* they will. The *probabilities* are on the side of disorderly states. This is the form that statistical laws take. They describe what will happen on most cases and ideally will provide a precise measure of probability for such cases.

In scientific explanations then we appeal to laws of nature. Some have argued that this is the model upon which all explanations are based. Thus, for example, a purposive explanation such as 'I eat wholemeal bread because I want to be healthier' could be regarded as making an appeal to a law. In such cases as this the law would, of course, be a low level law. That is to say, the purposive behaviour being explained would be subsumed under a low level law which could in turn be subsumed under higher level laws. In our example the low level law would be something like: eating wholemeal bread is more conducive to good health than the alternatives and people normally do what they want. The low level law concerning the bread could be subsumed under a higher level law concerning high fibre diets and the physiological needs of the human digestive system. We would say that people *normally* do what they want in order to avoid the charge that 'people do what they want' is a tautology rather than an empirical law. Although purposive explanations are amenable to the model of subsumption under a law, the laws are very low level and perhaps in some cases, so low level that application of the term 'low' would be inappropriate.

There is a further significant difference between purposive explanations and those normally associated with the natural sciences, namely, in the case of scientific explanations the law appealed to must be a true law otherwise you will not have a true explanation. In the case of the purposive explanation, such as my eating wholemeal bread because of the beliefs I hold concerning its connection with a healthy diet, it is not the truth of the law which explains my behaviour, but rather that I *believe* the law to be true. My belief that the law is true explains why I behave in a particular way but does not in any way determine the truth-value of the law itself. It should be pointed out here that in purposive explanations we make reference to various *intentional* terms such as belief, knowledge, value which we do not have in natural science explanations. Whether this difference constitutes a radical distinction in kind between the subject matter of a methodology of the natural and social sciences is one of the trickiest problems in the philosophy of social science. It is a problem which was discussed in Chapter 2.

▶ Deducibility

Having said that scientific explanations involve an appeal to laws of nature, the next question I want to discuss is whether it is necessary and/or sufficient for explanations to be deductive in nature. That is say, whether it is necessary and/or sufficient for us to be able to deduce what is explained from the explanation. Consider the following example:

All metals expand when heated.
This bar is made of metal.
This bar expands when heated.

This example is deductive in nature. The explanandum (that is, what is to be explained) follows deductively from the explanans (that is, the propositions which constitute the explanation). The question is whether all scientific explanations have to be of this sort. There is a thorough discussion of this in Hempel's *Philosophy of Natural Science* and it is to this that I now want to turn.

Hempel discusses an experiment in which mercury in a barometer decreases at a higher altitude. He expresses the explanation in the following four propositions:

A   At any location the pressure of the mercury column in the closed branch of the apparatus exerts pressure on the mercury below which equals the pressure exerted on the mercury's surface in the open vessel by the column of air above it.
B   The pressures exerted by the columns of air and mercury are proportionate to their weights, and the shorter the columns, the smaller their weights.
C   As the apparatus was carried upwards, the column of air above the open vessel became steadily shorter.
D   Therefore, the mercury column became steadily shorter during the ascent.

In Hempel's example D, the explanandum follows deductively from A, B and C, the explanans. Within the explanans it is possible to distinguish between two kinds of propositions. A and B are *general* laws which express uniform empirical connections. On the other hand, C describes a *particular* fact. In this case it describes the particular fact of what was actually done with the apparatus. This kind of explanation fits the phenomena into a pattern of uniformities. Explanations of this kind may be conceived along the lines of deductive arguments. Hempel's schematic account of the deductive argument form is:

$$L^1\ L^2\ L^3 \ldots Lr$$
$$\left.\vphantom{\begin{array}{c}a\\b\end{array}}\right\} \text{Explanans sentences}$$
$$C^1\ C^2\ C^3 \ldots Ck$$

$$\overline{E} \quad \text{Explanandum sentence}$$

The above is a schema of the form that a large class of explanations take. Hempel refers to them as explanations by deductive subsumptions under general laws of Deductive-Nomological Explanations (DNEs). In such explanations as these the explanans sentences logically entail the explanandum. $L^1 \ldots Lr$ are the covering laws, $C^1 \ldots Ck$ are the statements of particular facts and E follows deductively from their conjunction. This type of explanation does not just cover explanations of particular phenomena such as the decrease of mercury in the Torricelli barometer, DNEs also explain many regularities found in nature. If the explanandum sentence E, is itself a law, then $L^1 \ldots Lr$ will have to be higher level laws. In cases such as these, a law E, will be deducible from higher laws $L^1 \ldots Lr$. Thus, for example, to explain Galileo's law of freefall (E) you would appeal to Newton's law of gravity (L^1). Boyle's law, $PV = K$, can be deduced from the laws of the kinetic theory of gases. In some cases an appeal is made to a law relating to the internal structure of the phenomena as in the case of the kinetic theory of gases where the inner structure of gases is described and the explanandum is derived deductively from this description.

We must now turn to the case of probabilistic or statistical explanations and ask how they fit into Hempel's model for scientific explanation. They are very similar in form to DNEs but with one important difference. The difference is that the explanans sentences do not entail the explanandum sentence. In the following example a double line is used to show that the relationship is not one of strict entailment:

(1) The probability of a heavy smoker developing respiratory disease is high
(2) John is a heavy smoker

---

(3) John developed respiratory disease

The entailment difference amounts to this: in the case of a DNE if the premises are true, then the explanandum *must* be true as a matter of logic. In the case of a probabilistic argument it is theoretically possible for the premises to be true and the explanandum false. There is a high probability that John will develop respiratory disease but there is a chance that he will not. In the case of probabilistic explanations we do not have the strict deductive relationship which is characteristic of the DNE. The probabilistic argument is similar to a DNE with the one exception that we have mentioned. Both DNEs and probabilistic explanations take the deductive form but probabilistic explanations do not have the relationship of entailment.

Given that Hempel wishes to cast explanations in the deductive mould, we must now ask: how important is deducibility? We asked earlier whether deducibility was a necessary and/or sufficient condition for the character-isation of an explanation. It may well be the case that deducibility is a necessary condition of explanation, but it is not a sufficient condition. Consider the following explanations of why a telephone will not work:

A   Telephones won't work when there are gremlins on the lines
B   Gremlins are now on the lines

_____

C   The telephone will not work now

Or

A   Whatever fate has decreed will happen
B   Fate has decreed this telephone will not work

_____

C   This telephone will not work

Or

A   Everything that happens does so in accordance with God's will
B   God wills this telephone not to work

_____

C   This telephone will not work

All three of the above are DNEs. However, none of them constitutes an adequate explanation even though they are deductively sound. Deduction in itself is not a sufficient condition for the characterisation of an explanation. A further necessary condition is added by Hempel, namely, that the explanans sentences must be true. False statements cannot form any part of a true or genuine explanation. This further necessary condition is implicit in that one of the premisses is a statement of law. Hempel concedes that there is a minor problem here.

The problem is that we can and do get respectable explanations and yet the laws are not, strictly speaking, true. The laws of Galileo, Kepler and Boyle are not completely accurate. They are subject to revision and this is characteristic of scientific laws. We do not mean that such laws are false, but rather that they are approximate. Let us take Kepler's laws as an example. Kepler's laws were obtained by fitting formulae to data. Many different curves were fitted to the orbit of Mars before Kepler settled for the ellipse. Deductions could certainly be made from this and they were useful and respectable but even so the orbit of Mars is not perfectly elliptical. We now know that the orbit is distorted by the attraction of the other planets. Thus one of the premises would not be strictly true and yet we would not want to preclude it from the explanans. Given that scientific laws are subject to revision and are, therefore, not completely accurate, it might seem a good idea to say that they should be good approximations to the truth. This would raise two difficulties. First, there would be a problem in saying how good an approximation something was *independently* of its explanatory use. In other words we would be judging its proximity to the truth in terms of explanatory usage and justifying its explanatory usage by appealing to its being a good approximation to the truth. Secondly, if we admit degrees of truth, how can we lay down in advance of any field of study just what degree is acceptable for a statement to be admitted into an explanans in that field? Leaving aside this problem with the notion of true laws, it must be pointed out that even if you can get over this difficulty there will still be a problem. Truth and the deductive relation are still not sufficient for the characterisation of an explanation. What has been omitted from the concept of scientific explanation is the important and controversial idea of causal necessity. That is to say, the necessity by which some things rather than others must happen given their causal antecedents. We shall say more about this notion later. Explaining in science is not just a matter of subsuming phenomena or low level laws under true laws or true higher level laws. Although you would in such cases have both deducibility and truth you could still have unsatisfactory explanations. It may well be true to say that everything happens according to the will of God, but even if it is true it cannot figure in scientific explanations. To say that something happened because God willed it does not tell us why that and not something else happened. This is a task that an adequate explanation must accomplish. The theological explanation could be invoked to explain any occurrence and something which explains everything and rules nothing out has no explanatory power. In order to avoid the indiscriminate nature of such explanations, Hempel adds the requirement of testability to that of truth. This means that the premises of the explanation have to be statements that are capable of being tested empirically. You cannot test what God wills or what fate decrees and thus the requirement of testability will exclude such vacuous explanations. Any hypothesis which is not amenable to empirical testing – has no relevance to empirical findings (has no possible empirical content) – is regarded as not constituting a genuine hypothesis; it is a pseudo-hypothesis.

Hempel has a further condition to add before we have sufficient conditions for an explanation. This is the condition of explanatory relevance. This means that the facts appealed to must afford some reason for expecting the phenomena to occur. On Hempel's account of scientific explanation then, we must have a deductive relationship between explanans and explanandum; the explanans must be true and testable. They must also be relevant to the explanation. When these are taken together you have necessary and sufficient conditions for characterising an explanation. Having set up the DNE as the ideal to which scientific explanations aspire, it might be objected that as a matter of fact this is not the way in which science proceeds. Harré has pointed out that very often in science one proceeds with an analogy. By an analogy, Harré means 'a relationship between two entities, processes … which allows inferences to be made about one of the things, usually that about which we know best, on the basis of what we know about the other' (*Philosophies of Science*, p. 172). This statement of the scientist's procedure is no doubt accurate, but the dichotomy between the use of analogy and of the deductive model is not a mutually exclusive one. (Harré sees analogy as lying at the heart of science (pp. 168 and 171) – the basis of explanation. But there are dangers, for example, collaboration and committees of cells.)

Harré's point about the use of analogy is a valid one and shows that there is more to scientific method than observation and induction. However, the use of analogy is only for the purpose of setting up the premise; the deductive method is still employed after the premise has been set up. Thus the use of analogy and the use of the DNE model can, and do, go together.

There is, however, a drawback with the proclaimed value of the deductive form. It has the unfortunate consequence of assimilating scientific explanation to a matter of logic. Consider the following examples:

A (1) All tigers are striped
   (2) Ben is a tiger
   _____
   (3) Ben is striped

B (1) At constant temperature $PV = K$ (Boyle's law)
   (2) Volume of gas at $t°K$ at $t^1 = 2$ cm^3 and pressure $= 2$ dynes/cm^2
   (3) Volume is increased at t^2 to 4cm^3
   _____
   (4) Pressure at $t° K = 1$ dyne/cm^2

In each of these examples the conclusions, A (3) and B (4), follow logically from the premises. However, we would want to say that there was a difference between them, namely, that B is not just a matter of logic. Some philosophers would want to express the difference by saying that Boyle's Law states a principle of necessitation (W. Kneale) or a necessity of nature. To put it another way, given the nature of the causal mechanisms things could not be otherwise. This brings us back to a matter which we referred to earlier, namely, that scientific explanations appeal to laws of nature. We must now look at the idea of a law of nature in more detail.

► Laws of nature and accidental generalisations

The laws which are required to serve in the explanans of a DNE are statements of universal form. They assert a uniform connection between different empirical phenomena or different aspects of empirical phenomena. They are of the form: when conditions 'f' occur, conditions 'g' also occur. However, not all statements of this form, even when true, are laws of nature. If I say truthfully that all the men in the next room are bald, we would have a true statement of universal form: f (men in the next room) g (are bald), but we would not have a law. It is simply an assertion of what happens to be the case at a particular time, an accidental juxtaposition.

Such a state of affairs as that envisaged above or that referred to earlier (all Crested Grebe on the Rhine nest during periods of increased sunspot activity) are known as accidental generalisations. Similarly, with one of Hempel's examples, 'all bodies of pure gold have a mass of less than 100,000 kgs', represents an accidental generalisation. There is nothing in the laws of nature to say that such states of affairs must be the way they happen to be. That a statement should be true and of universal form is a necessary condition for its being a law of nature, but it is not a sufficient condition. If they were sufficient conditions, then we would have to admit accidental generalisations as laws of nature. We must now discuss how we are to distinguish laws of nature from accidental generalisations.

One traditional way of doing this, the way Hempel attributes to Goodman, is to point out that a law of nature can – whereas accidental generalisations cannot – support counterfactual conditionals. Let us take an example in order to see what this means. In the statement, 'if you had dropped those eggs, they would have broken', the 'if' clause (that is, the hypothetical) implies that the condition does not hold. It implies that you did not actually drop the eggs. This is an example of a counterfactual statement. In the counterfactual, 'if I had subjected this gold ring to a temperature of 2000°C, then it would have melted', we see that it can be supported by appeal to the law that all gold bodies have a melting point slightly in excess of 1000°C. Similarly, in saying that if a particle is fired towards the sun from the earth it will take at least 8 minutes (approximately) to reach its destination, I can appeal to laws concerning the speed of light, namely, that it travels at 186,000 miles per second and that nothing can travel faster than light (the laws are, of course, taken in conjunction with particular facts such as those concerning the actual distance of the sun and the composition of the particle). The laws then support the claims made by counterfactuals. An accidental generalisation such as 'all men in the next room are bald' cannot be used to support a counterfactual claim such as 'if John had been in the next room, then he would have been bald'. On the other hand we could say, for example, that if that ring in the jeweller's or that gold ingot were subjected to a temperature of 2000°C, then they would become liquid. The essential point to note is that laws of nature will support counterfactual conditionals, and accidental generalisations will not. Thus we find that the same remarks apply to other conditionals such as subjunctive conditionals. These are of the form: 'if A comes to pass, then so will B'. The reader can easily make the appropriate substitutions for A and B and see that this is the case.

This difference is related to another which we have been discussing. A law is also to be distinguished from an accidental generalisation on the ground that a law can serve as the basis for an explanation (as in our examples of DNE's) whereas an accidental generalisation cannot. The melting of the gold ring can be explained by the law that any gold body will melt at temperatures slightly in excess of 1000°C. We could not, however, say that a particular man in the next room was bald because all the men in the next room are bald. The accidental generalisation cannot itself[1] stand as a basis for explaining anything.

▶ Natural necessity

Having made this distinction in terms of explanatory power, we must now ask why it is that laws of nature can be used to explain, whereas accidental generalisations cannot be so used. One important answer that has been given to this question involves an appeal to the notion of natural necessity. That is to say, laws of nature express naturally necessary uniformities in the way the world works and this is held to show how they lend support to counterfactual propositions. To see why natural necessity has been such an important concept to many philosophers, we need to consider a rather technical issue in order to bring out just how this concept can be of value.

The problem concerns the correct logical analysis of subjunctive (and counterfactual) conditionals. The truth-functional analysis of '$p \supset q$' (p implies q) is 'not both p and not q' or $-(p - q)$. That is to say, if $p \supset q$ is true, then the truth value 'true' cannot be applied to both p and $-q$. According to this analysis, the truth of our previous example of a conditional 'if he had dropped the eggs, then they would have broken' would follow from 'he did not drop the eggs' and 'they were broken'. Indeed, this has the effect of making all counterfactuals true, for the first part always states not p (the unfulfilled hypothetical).

Even opposed pairs of counterfactuals will consist of two truths. This is known as the paradox of material implication. Consider statements of the 'because' form. On this analysis they will all turn out to be true. Thus, for example, in 'he broke his leg because he fell', you would not state the consequent (he fell) unless it was true, and so if the consequent is true, then the statement is true. A way of avoiding these difficulties has been to claim that what we have omitted to mention in our analysis of counterfactuals is a reference to some kind of non-logical connection between antecedent and consequent. It is here that the idea of a necessary connection comes in. It has been argued by C. I. Lewis that the correct rendering of the form of a conditional ($p \supset q$) is 'It is not possible that both p and not q'. To transfer this to our example, the conditional 'if you had dropped the eggs, then they would have broken' would be rendered as 'it is not possible that he should have dropped the eggs and not broken them'. It must be realised that the type of necessity referred to here is natural or factual necessity *not* logical necessity. It is this factual necessity that is held to belong to laws of nature and to be absent from accidental generalisations in terms of natural necessity and we have seen an argument to show that counterfactuals which are supported by appeals to laws of nature should be analysed with a reference to some connection between antecedent and consequent and that connection is held to be factual or natural necessity. We must now inquire closer into what is meant by natural necessity.

Earlier we referred to two examples where laws could be appealed to in order to support counterfactuals. The examples were the melting point of gold and the speed of light. There is a difference in these two cases concerning necessity. We seem to have no problem in saying it is a matter of necessity that there cannot be an increase in the speed of light. Einstein once referred to the idea that there could be such an increase as constituting an enigma of nature. If we were asked what we meant by necessity in this case, we could say that it was necessary in the strongest sense. It would be impossible to conceive its implications; we would be led into a mass of contradictions. This is why we want to say that the principle is a necessary one. In saying that the principle is necessary, we can also say that any particular statements derived from it, such as the minimum time it would take for a particle to travel to the sun, are also necessary. Their necessity can be traced back to the necessity of the principle from which they can be derived. However, our other example is not quite like this. In the case of melting the gold ring, we would say that there is a sense in which the ring *must* melt if subjected to a temperature of 2000°C. But what do we mean by 'must' here? The force of the 'must' is not logical as we do not involve analyses in either contradictions or conceptual paradoxes by supposing that the ring of gold will not melt or that the melting point of gold is other than what we have stated. We are referring to what has been termed 'factual' necessity. In our example of the gold, if you could find something in the nature of gold which causes it to have a relatively low melting point for metals, then you would have found support in the form of a connection for the conditional that if you subject it to that temperature, then it will melt. Laws of nature can thus be distinguished from accidental generalisations in terms of this element of factual or natural necessity. That is to say, factual necessity is present in the former but not in the latter.

In order to try and get clearer about what philosophers mean by factual necessity, the reader might find it helpful to consider a law-like phenomenon such as Boyle's Law. If we want to know why a particular gas behaves in the way it does, then it is not sufficient to simply answer: because it conforms to Boyle's Law. When we want to know about the pressure of the gas we want to know more than that it conforms to Boyle's Law. Consider the case of the relation between a certain kind of food intake and heart disease. Even if we can express this relation in precise mathematical terms, it still would not be sufficient to say of any particular case of heart disease that it was in conformity with the mathematical formula. If actual laws were discovered by which it could be said or deduced that, given a certain kind of diet, then heart disease must occur, this would constitute an improvement on bare conformity to a formula but it still would not be wholly satisfactory. What is required is an account of *why* such laws of correlation hold. The ideal would be to identify some property of the food (for example, cholesterol and its composition), the causal effects of which would explain the mechanics of some forms of heart disease. We are looking for what caused the heart disease to occur. This would tell us why correlated laws should be regarded as laws and not as generalisations. It is this element of necessity which allows us to say that a scientific explanation consists in showing how an event had to happen, given the existence of certain conditions. Explaining is, or course, the goal of science, and, as Harré says, scientists tell us why things are the way they are rather than some other way and why some things happen and not others (*Philosophies of Science*, p. 23).

Having stated a case for admitting the notion of natural necessity into the philosophy of science, we must now consider philosophies of science which do not make such an admission. The reader can then decide between them. We have stated a case in favour of the notion of natural necessity; we must now look at one of the philosophically famous objections to the notion.

▶ Hume on necessary connection

In section VII of the *Enquiry concerning Human Understanding*, Hume is specifically concerned with the origin of our idea of necessary connection. He starts by making a comparison between the mathematical sciences and the moral sciences (the sciences of human nature). The advantage of the mathematical sciences lies in the lack of ambiguity in their terms. In other words, their terms are clearly defined. When it comes to the moral sciences, however, we find ambiguity in their terms. Although such sciences have the advantage of simpler inferences, the lack of precision in their terms is a major disadvantage and it inhibits real progress. The terms singled out by Hume as the main culprits are 'power', 'force', 'energy' or 'necessary connection'. He wants to pinpoint their exact meaning. Failure to do so is the source of much philosophical confusion.

In following Hume in tracking down their meaning, we must remember his epistemological thesis that nothing can occur as an idea without there being an antecedent impression of that thing. Thus if we want to get clear about the meaning of an idea, then we must trace it back to its corresponding impression. If it is a complex idea, then it can be divided into its simpler ideas (for example, 'mermaid' into 'girl' and 'fish') and these can be traced back to their corresponding impressions. There is, of course, no ambiguity in Hume's impressions, they are immediately known. It is this method which he applies to the idea of necessary connection.

When we look at a single instance of cause and effect, all we find is one event following another; we do not find any quality which binds them together or which necessitates the occurrence of the effect. For Hume, all we find is that as a matter of fact, one follows the other. There is no impression that corresponds to the power in the cause or any principle of necessitation between the two objects or events. Billiard ball A hits ball B, and B moves – that is all you see. Therefore, the idea of necessary connection cannot have its foundation in an impression of sensation. We do not get it from our impressions of objects or events in the world as they simply follow each other. There is no further impression in addition to the sequence of objects and events.

It if is not an impression of sensation, could it be one of reflection? Hume considers the case for saying that perhaps we arrive at it through a consideration of reflecting on the operations of our will in controlling bodily movements. This, however, is also rejected. Even here we are not aware of any power apart from the act of the will and the subsequent bodily movement. We do not know *how* the will achieves this movement. If we were acquainted with this power, then we would know how the will produces its effects. If we were aware of such a connection, then we would be able to say why we could move some parts of our bodies but not others, that is, we could give an account of why some parts of our body are subordinate to our will and others not. We cannot do this. We learn the influence of the will purely from experience, and all experience teaches us is that one event constantly follows another. It does not instruct us in the secret connection which binds them together. So the idea of power or necessary connection is not traceable to any impression of power within or outside ourselves.

We make no progress either by suggesting that we are conscious of a power within our own minds when we call up or reject ideas. Again, all we are aware of are the act of willing and the subsequent ideas. We are not aware of any power or any notion of how the process works. This is why it is only through experience that we learn the limitations of the mind, for example, our command over our emotions.

Hume concludes that we are not aware of any connections between objects but only of constant conjunctions. Even those who argue that God is responsible for things behaving in the way they do, that is to say, those who believe that He causes things to happen in accordance with His laws of nature, are equally ignorant of the manner of force or any power here. So Hume has exhausted the possible sources of the idea and all that has been found are conjunctions, not connections. Are we to conclude that as there is no antecedent impression of either the internal or external senses to serve as the foundation for the idea of necessary connection, the term 'necessary connection' is, therefore, meaningless?

Hume's solution

Hume suggests a possible escape from the above conclusion. The alternative is this: when we experience a series of constant conjunctions to which there are no exceptions, as opposed to a single instance, we call one object the cause and the other the effect. We suppose that there is some power in the cause to produce the effect. When we get a *repetition* of constant conjunctions we *feel* a connection in the mind. This feeling comes about as a result of the repetitions. We do not get such a feeling from the single instance. It is this feeling that is held by Hume to be the sensation or impression upon which the idea of necessary connection is based. On observing a single instance, all you would have is a conjunction. After several instances, you would *say* they were connected. It is important to realise that for Hume the transition from conjunction to connection is not made on the basis of any new sense impression. It's just that after several instances, we feel them to be connected.

Hume went on to offer two definitions of 'cause':

(1) an object followed by another, and where all the objects, similar to the first, are followed by objects similar to the second;
(2) an object followed by another, and whose appearance always conveys the thought to that other.

These two definitions do not have the same meaning and that is a major difficulty if Hume is defining the same thing. The first definition should be taken as a philosophical analysis of causation, that is, what it means to say that one thing is the cause of another. The second definition is perhaps better regarded as an attempt to give a law of psychology, that is, it is concerned with how, as a matter of fact, we happen to think. Having set out Hume's position on necessary connection and his reasons for holding it, we can now move on to a critical discussion.

Assessment of Hume's position

There are a number of traditional problems with Hume's account:

(1) We think that causal sequences are necessary, at least some of us do. If you drop a stone, then it *must* fall. Hume can find nothing corresponding to this 'must' except the feeling which we acquire through the repetition of constant conjunctions. It has been thought that this emphasis on feeling tends to impugn the rationality of asserting causal connections, and hence, the rationality of science which is very much concerned with discovering such connections.

Hume can reply that he has shown that scientists deal with conjunctions and if there were any sign that nature were to change, past experience would count for nothing. On Hume's account, the only necessity is logical necessity. Such a view was echoed by Wittgenstein when he declared that belief in the causal nexus was superstition.

(2) There are problems with Hume's two definitions of 'cause'. They do not have the same meaning, and examples like night and day seem to fit both without being an example of causation. Another difficulty with the definitions is that the second one could be said to presuppose causation. The expressions 'always conveys the thought' looks suspiciously like an alternative expression for 'causes'.

(3) On Hume's account there will be a difficulty in distinguishing laws of nature from accidental generalisations. All Hume requires for a law is regularity but this is not a sufficient condition. I believe that there is a perfect correlation between an increase in sunspot activity and the nesting habits of the Crested Grebe on the banks of the Rhine. This correlation, however, is certainly not sufficient for saying that some law-like relation holds between the phenomena. Another way of bringing this difficulty out is to say that genuine scientific laws support counterfactuals, whereas accidents, even on a cosmic scale, do not. Thus, we would say confidently that if you heat that bar of gold, it will expand. We could not say with any confidence that if there is a further increase in sunspots next year, there will be more Grebe nesting on the Rhine. The problem for Hume is to explain this difference when they both exhibit the regularity which he finds crucial.

(4) As we have indicated, regularity or repetition is crucial to Hume's analysis but their importance can be questioned. It is possible to infer a causal connection from a single instance such as a one-off experiment. We may also appeal to connections made in astronomy where the objects may appear very infrequently. Hume did acknowledge this problem in the *Treatise*.

(5) There is a difficulty with the notion of simultaneous causation. How do we know which is the cause and which is the effect if the account of B's *following* A was an exhaustive account of causation? If A and B occur at the same time, and our account of causality only permits us to say that A is the cause of B if B follows A, then what right have we to say that A is the cause of B? There are examples of simultaneous causation: a high wind and rough sea, for example, but it is not clear what right we would have, on Hume's account, to say that the wind caused the waves rather than the waves causing the wind. We do, of course, know which the cause is; the problem for Hume is to say *how* it is we know.

(6) Hume's account of our recognition of causal sequences in terms of constant conjunction seems to be over-reliant on his copy principle. It will be remembered that Hume's central epistemological thesis was that there could be no ideas without impressions. The impressions that regularly go together and imprint themselves on the mind lead the mind to associate them and feel that they are connected. The issue here concerns whether this account does justice to the rational and inquiring mind which organises data and formulates hypotheses. Organisational features of mind are not well catered for on Hume's account. If we think of Darwin's observations on the Galapagos Islands, the way data were interpreted and the general conclusions drawn, it becomes difficult to account for them in terms of the copy principle and regularly conjoined impressions. The ability to generalise is also hard to account for in terms of 'similarity'. Any attempt to do so immediately poses the question of what is meant by 'similarity'. This in turn raises the difficulty that some similarity judgements can be based on objects having similar causal powers. It then becomes difficult to understand how similarity is always prior to our 'feeling' of a causal connection.

For a further discussion of some of these issues, the reader should refer to the section on Science and Conjecture, especially that part dealing with Popper.

▶ Hume's problem of induction

In the fourth *Enquiry* Hume had argued that all our reasoning concerning matters of fact is based on the relation of cause and effect. If we ask what that relation is based on, the answer is experience and not *a priori* reasoning. All conclusions from experience are based on the relation of cause and effect; they are not based on any purely rational process. Nature does not provide us with insight into secret or hidden causes and powers. All it gives us are the various constant conjunctions between objects. We do not know that particular causes have particular effects as a result of our having access to the intrinsic nature of things.

Suppose we now say that our conclusions from cause to effect are based on past experience, we will see how the problem of induction arises. Hume tells us that past experience is exactly what its name suggests, namely, experience of the past. The problem that Hume is getting at here is by what kind of inference does the mind conclude that because some things were constantly conjoined in the past, they will continue to be so in the future. Consider the two propositions Hume refers to:

(1) I have found that such an object has always been attended with such an effect

(2) I foresee that other objects which are in appearance similar will be attended with similar effects.

Hume points out that (1) and (2) are not identical in meaning, so what is the relation between them? He does not deny that as a matter of fact we infer (2) from (1), but his challenge is for us to produce the reasoning whereby (2) is shown to be a legitimate inference from (1).

There are two ways in which a proposition can be true. It is either logically true, in which case its negation is self-contradictory, or it is true by experience. Let us apply these two possibilities to proposition (2). We can see that it is not logically true as its negation is not self-contradictory. In other words, its negation is conceivable by the mind. This leaves us with the second way (true by experience) of confirming that the future will resemble the past. There are difficulties with this. We cannot show that (2) is true by experience as all arguments from experience rely on the relation of cause and effect and is thus based on the very supposition that we are seeking to prove. Thus any such attempt to prove it true by experience will be circular. As Hume says, to attempt to prove this supposition by using probability arguments, or arguments regarding experience, must involve circularity. Hume mentions probability arguments only to point out that they, too, rest on experience and involve the same problems of circularity.

It must be realised that Hume was not saying that as a *practical* principle the inductive principle should be given up. What he is saying, is that in his capacity as a philosopher he can seek out the reasons, if any, upon which the inference is based. His claim is that the enquiry reveals that such inferences are not based on any process or reason and neither can such inferences be justified by appeals to experience as these would beg the question. Any inference we make from experience will suppose, as its foundation, that the future will resemble the past.

▶ Science and discovery

Butterfield has said that advances in science do not result just from the mere accumulations of observational data, and neither is it a matter of just improving observational instruments. The above are certainly important in the progress of science but they do not constitute an exhaustive account of such progress. Butterfield claims that the most important aspect is what he calls 'transpositions in the mind of the scientist'. Perhaps an example will help to clarify what Butterfield means by this expression. In Aristotelian science, the notion of teleological explanation is crucial. In physics, his theory of motion was permeated with the idea of bodies 'wishing' to return to their natural place and being held back. This was certainly an attempt by Aristotle to explain the facts of motion. It was an attempt to explain some natural phenomena via a particular set of concepts. In Newtonian science concepts are changed and refined. Abstract concepts such as mass, force and momentum are used. These are theoretical concepts which one could not have an idea of without some understanding of the science of mechanics. Newton's laws of motion are also abstract. Consider the law of inertia. It cannot be regarded as a generalisation about the world arrived at by enumerating many instances, as no such conditions as it envisaged could ever hold in the world. There could never be motion without forces. The change from the conceptual system of Aristotle to that of Newton can, to some extent,[2] be used to illustrate what Butterfield calls a transposition in the mind of the scientist. It is like viewing the phenomena through different spectacles where the spectacles represent a conceptual system. The importance of these conjectures has not always been recognised. Many scientists and philosophers had neglected this feature of science in favour of induction. They believed that what happens in science is that one carefully or systematically observes a large number of instances of a particular phenomenon and on this basis alone, arrives at a general law about the phenomenon.

This was the view taken by Sir Francis Bacon and J. S. Mill. It was a view which had considerable influence on the presentation of scientific papers. Such papers tended to be set out in the form of observations and with an inductive conclusion drawn from the observations. Bacon is usually regarded as the founder of the inductive method in science. He tried to find a superior form of induction than induction by simple enumeration. We can illustrate Bacon's inductive scientific method by considering the phenomenon of heat. His method was to compile a list of hot bodies, cold bodies and those of varying degrees in between. Thus, he would have a list of bodies where heat is present (for example, sun rays, boiling liquids), and a list of bodies where heat is absent (for example, moon rays, liquids in their natural state). The idea is that you would find a characteristic present in hot bodies, absent in cold ones and present in varying degrees in the others. By partaking in this procedure we would arrive at laws of low generality. The various laws could be compared and we would then arrive at laws of higher generality.

Bacon gave an explanation of the property of whiteness along these lines. He thought that whiteness was produced by a mixture of air and water. This corresponded to a law of low generality. In order to arrive at a law of higher generality, he disregarded the contingencies of air and water (that is, features such as transparency which played no part in the production of whiteness) and formulated a general law to the effect that all bodies or parts which unequal equally and are in simple proportion represent whiteness.

One should test the law and he believed that his method could be formalised and systematised, and once it had been learned all men's wits would be levelled as far as science was concerned. Imagination or judgement would not be essential. He tells us that 'our method of discovery in science is to level the wit and intellect as in the drawing of a straight line with the hand. When the ruler and compass are used there is nothing left in regard to steadiness and practice, so it is with our method.' However, this view of science gives rise to grave difficulties. Although it may provide an accurate description of much of the routine work of science, it cannot provide an exhaustive account of the practice of the scientific enterprise as a whole. It gives an immensely important aspect of science, namely, the imagination involved in the theories of the great scientists.

▶ Mill's canons of inductive inference

In his *System of Logic* (Bk III, Ch. 8), Mill sets out five methods which are to be applied by scientists for discovering the causes of phenomena. They are as follows:

The method of agreement

To see how this method is intended to work, it is best to consider its use in a particular case. Suppose we were investigating the cause of an outbreak of food poisoning, we would, in applying this method, look for a common feature of the food intake of those suffering from food poisoning. If we found that there was only one common element (for example, sausages) then that would be identified as the cause. Mill expresses the matter as follows: 'If two or more instances of the phenomena have only one circumstance in common, the circumstance in which above all the instances agree is the cause (or effect) of the given phenomenon'. To put it schematically:

$$A\ B\ C\ D \rightarrow a\ b\ c\ d$$
$$A\ E\ F\ G \rightarrow a\ e\ f\ g$$
_____

A would be the cause of a.

The method of difference

Mill expresses this method in the following terms: 'If an instance in which the phenomenon under investigation occurs, and an instance in which it does not occur, have every circumstance in common save one, that one occurring only in the former, the circumstance in which alone they differ is the effect or cause or the indispensable part of the cause of the phenomenon'. Thus, for example a smoker and a non-smoker may have everything in common except chronic bronchitis which is present in the smoker. By applying this method we would conclude that chronic bronchitis is the effect of smoking and that smoking was at least an indispensable part of the cause of this case of respiratory disease. Schematically, the method can be represented thus:

A B C D → a b c d (smoker)
  B C D → b c d (non-smoker)

A is the cause (effect) of a.

The joint method of agreement and difference

In the application of this method, Mill tells us that: 'If two or more instances of which a phenomenon occurs have only one circumstance in common, while two or more instances in which it does not occur have nothing in common expect the absence of the circumstance, then the circumstance in which they differ is the cause or effect or indispensable part of the cause of the phenomenon'. We can represent this schematically as follows:

A B C → a b c   X Y → x y
A D E → a d e   U V → u v

A is the cause (effect) of a.[3]

The method of residues

Here, the method is to: 'Subduct from any phenomena such parts known by previous inductions to be the effect of certain antecedents and the residue of the phenomena is the effect of the remaining antecedents'. The schematic representation of this would be:

A B C → a b c
B is known to be the cause of b
C is known to be the cause of c

A is the cause of a.

To illustrate this with a simple example, let us suppose that the total phenomenon is my rowing down a river at 10 mph. We know that my ability as an oarsman permits only 5 mph. and that wind assistance permits 2 mph. The factor we have left out of account is the current of the river, so this would be the cause of the extra 3 mph. The residual factor must be responsible for the extra speed.

The method of concomitant variation

Mill expresses this method as follows: 'Whatever phenomenon varies in any manner whenever another phenomenon varies in the same particular manner is either cause or an effect of that phenomenon or is connected with it through some fact of causation'. The schematic representation of this is:

$$A \quad B\,C \rightarrow a \quad b \quad c$$
$$A + B\,C \rightarrow a + b \quad c$$
$$A - B\,C \rightarrow a - b \quad c$$

A is the cause (effect) or is causally connected to a.

The advantage of this method is that it does not depend on the ability to eliminate circumstances; it is concerned with the manipulation of circumstances and this can have important practical consequences. The fifth method provides for both quantitative and qualitative relations.

Criticisms of Mill

(1) An amusing objection has been made by Copi *(Introduction to Logic)*. He invites us to consider the case of the scientific drinker. Let us suppose that a scientist gets drunk every night and sets out to discover the cause of his intoxication. In accord with Mill's methodology, he draws up the following schedule of antecedents to his drunken state:

    1.   Monday – Scotch and soda
    2.   Tuesday – Brandy and soda
    3.   Wednesday – Rum and soda
    4.   Thursday – Gin and soda
    5.   Friday – Bourbon and soda

By sifting out the common ingredient our scientist resolves never to touch soda again. Clearly, something is wrong here, yet our scientist has followed Mill's methodology. What this shows us is that an analysis of the phenomena and the circumstances is of crucial importance. If the liquors had been analysed, we would have found that all the instances had alcohol present and the method of difference could then have been used to eliminate soda. However, this analysis is independent of the method advocated by Mill. The methods *themselves* will not provide you with this analysis. Thus we can say that Mill's methods presuppose for their efficacy a prior correct analysis of the phenomena and situations. This is related to a point made by Harré *(Philosophies of Science*, p. 40) where we are told that the information which Mill's canons yield will depend at least as much on the theory held by the investigating scientist as it will on what he observes experimentally. Connecting this up to our previous point, we can say that the prior analysis of situations to which we referred involves the scientist partaking in some form of theorising in advance of the application of the canons. Harré has concluded that the function of the canons is to serve as a preliminary to the deeper studies of the scientist. He assigns to them a negative role of eliminating possibilities rather than the positive one envisaged by Mill of actually proving causal connections.

(2) There is a criticism that can be levelled against the method of difference, namely, no two situations are ever as alike as that method implies. In order for that method to be foolproof, you would need examples of situations which had every relevant circumstance in common except one. The problem is that circumstances are not labelled relevant or irrelevant. In order to know which are relevant and which are not we would need to have a prior knowledge of causal relations. Again, we are faced with the need to know the answers to some questions before the method can be applied. The method itself is not sufficient and there is the same difficulty with the method of agreement.

(3) Let us consider the method of concomitant variation. The problem here is that there is simply no way of being sure that what you have is a correlation or a constant conjunction. Two phenomena may well vary concomitantly – see the earlier example of the Grebe and sunspots – but this just goes to show how misleading a correlation can be. It is, of course, true that the greater the number of observed instances of phenomena being correlated, the higher the probability will be that the correlation is lawful rather than accidental. We must, however, bear in mind that the strict application of Mill's fifth method would lead us to think that there were causal connections where there were not in fact any.

These are criticisms of Mill's methods only if they are taken to constitute an exhaustive account of what science is. Mill was inclined to adopt this attitude towards his methods. If we resist this claim for the reasons given, we can still regard Mill's canons as being important tools in the practice of science without regarding them as constituting science. One must under-stand that Mill's methods can only be used in conjunction with the hypothesis or theory that the circumstances in question are the relevant ones. Indeed, this is the starting point for any attempt to specify causes of a given phenomenon. If we investigate the cause of *a*, we have to begin with the hypotheses that circumstances A–G are the only relevant ones and hence one of *them* must be the cause. Thus to take Mill's method of agreement, we start with the hypothesis that circumstances A–G are the relevant ones we then proceed; A B C D–a b c d, A E F G–a e f g. These two instances will only yield the inductive conclusion that A is the cause of a when the initial hypothesis concerning relevant circumstances in taken as our starting point. We have to hypothesise that if G is the cause of a, then a cannot occur in the absence of G and so on for all the relevant circumstances. Our grounds for making the hypothesis though cannot themselves be Mill's methods. His methods should be understood as instruments for testing hypotheses. He describes the process and procedure of controlled experiment, but this is not to be taken as an exhaustive account of the content of science. There must be hypotheses before experiments can proceed.[4]

▶ Science and conjecture

The notion of conjecture is central to one important theory of science, namely the thesis of Sir Karl Popper in *Conjectures and Refutations* and *The Logic of Scientific Discovery*. The central idea is that science proceeds by making conjectures and attempting to refute them via the hypothetico-deductive method.[5] We have seen some of the shortcomings of attempting to define science in terms of the inductive method as Mill was inclined to do. The next issue is to examine Popper's account and to look at some other alternatives. Let us sketch out the ground.

Those philosophers known as the 'scientific realists' would want to reject a definition of science as either inductive method or hypothetico-deductive method. They would want to locate the real nature of science as being the discovery of how the world works. There are yet other philosophers who take the position that it is the imaginative leap of the scientist that constitutes the essential nature of science. T. S. Kuhn's *The Structure of Scientific Revolutions* is a major example of this position. Kuhn sees the history of science as being a succession of what he calls 'paradigms'. Paradigms are imposed upon nature by scientists and they are interspersed by revolutions. Thus, for example, the paradigm constituted by Newton's mechanics was replaced by the one constituted by Einstein's theories. According to Kuhn, scientific revolutions, that is, changes in paradigms, are due to the increasing complexities or anomalies of a previous paradigm. Scientists become impatient with such complexities and anomalies and the paradigm which has given rise to them is then abandoned. We shall see later a clash between this view and that of the realist philosopher of science who wants to say that old theories are given up because they are seen to be inadequate descriptions of the way the world works. The realist will not be satisfied with the idea that paradigms are abandoned due to complexities or anomalies; he will want to say that their abandonment is due to their incompatibility with new facts that have been discovered. This particular dispute goes to the very heart of the nature of science and is the cause of much controversy in this area.

An aspect of Kuhn's philosophy of science which would be repugnant to the realist philosopher of science is the idea that the various paradigms are neither objectively right nor wrong. Many realists would take this to imply that there was no such thing as truth in science. This is somewhat unfair to Kuhn and many of these influenced by him. Many of them would want to say that truth and falsity have a place *within* particular paradigms, but the paradigms themselves are not amenable to the true/false dichotomy. This might prove to be a difficult claim to sustain as it will involve distinguishing particular statements (which can be true or false) within a paradigm from the paradigm itself which cannot be. A discussion of this is too complex for our present purpose but it should be noted that there is a real issue here.

There is a major difference between Kuhn's view of science and that of Popper. Popper cannot be interpreted as saying that there is no such thing as truth in science. He is saying that the way science proceeds is by making conjectures and trying to refute them. For Popper, the method of science is that of criticism. He says that we prefer non-falsified theories to falsified ones because we want the truth.

Popper is opposed to Mill's doctrine that the essence of science lies in induction. This opposition raises the age-old philosophical problem of induction. As we have seen, Hume insisted that there cannot be a logical justification for the inductive procedure. Just to remind you, Hume's point was that if some objects are constantly conjoined, then although that will give us a natural disposition to believe that they will continue to be, it affords no *rational* justification for believing that they will. What is of crucial importance in Hume's writings for our discussion of scientific method is the anti-inductivist implication that theories cannot be inferred from observational statements. This is Hume's problem of induction. In the main, Popper finds Hume to be convincing. However, as we saw earlier, there are some aspects of Hume that Popper finds less satisfactory.

Hume had claimed that there was no rational justification for holding, for example, that the fire which had burned us in the past will continue to do so or that the food that had nourished us in the past will continue to do so. The constant conjunctions merely form a disposition in our minds to pass from one object to another. Our belief in laws of nature is a product of this disposition. The connection is made by our minds. In examining Hume's claim, Popper posed the question of just how it is that we move from particular instances of observation to a general law. That is to say, how we derive the general law that, for example, all fires will burn us from singular instances of a fire burning us. Hume's central idea for explaining this is repetition based on resemblances. As we have mentioned earlier, Popper finds difficulty with this claim of Hume's. He thinks that Hume is using the notion of repetition in an uncritical fashion. Popper's complaint against Hume is that Hume fails to make explicit that repetition is only repetition for us which can be allowed to have an effect on us. Repetition alone or in itself will have no effect. In other words, we must respond to situations *as if* they were equivalent; we must interpret them as repetitions. If we react to the sight of the fire by withdrawing our fingers, then we do so because we expect to be burnt. The situation is a repetition for us of a previous situation because of our anticipation that it will be similar to the previous situation. Now the kind of repetition referred to by Hume cannot be a perfect repetition as no two states of affairs are perfectly alike, so it has to be a matter of similarity. Popper holds that we can only make similarity judgements from a particular viewpoint. Popper's point is that the present is not just a repetition of the past or of previous cases. What is important is that we have to be disposed to regard it as such but this can only happen when we do so from a certain point of view. One way of putting this would be to say that what has a repetition effect on us, might not have a repetition effect on other creatures such as insects.

The important point to grasp is that before there can be a repetition effect, there must for Popper, as a matter of logic, always be a point of view. And by a point of view, is meant a system of expectations, anticipations, interest. This is held to be a logical prerequisite of repetition effects. Now given that the notions of repetition or similarity presuppose such points of view or systems of expectation, it follows that the points of view *themselves* cannot in consequence be merely the result of repetition. The Popperian claim is that before you notice the repetitions, you have to have some kind of anticipation. Even the first repetition for us must be based on some expectation or anticipation and so it would be circular to attempt to explain our anticipations and expectations in terms of repetition. This is what Popper sees as an important defect in Hume's account. We shall not notice what the similarities are unless we have a point of view.

Popper's point is a logical one that has some psychological content. The psychological content lies in the appeal to our interests. The interests that are a necessary prerequisite to the seeing of similarities and hence to the discovery of laws of nature, might well be instinctual. That is to say, it might well be part of our nature to look for similarities and to interpret them in terms of the theories we formulate. If one were to take an extreme line here, one might say that before any similarity was noted, some low-level theorising was a necessary precondition. Whatever view one takes on this, it emerges from what Popper has said that scientists do not just wait passively for repetitions to impose laws on them. Popper lays great emphasis on the scientist making imaginative 'conjectures'. Without waiting to gather a set of premises which entail a particular conclusion, scientists work by jumping to conclusions and then they attempt to refute or falsify such conclusions.

(This does not mean that scientists jump to conclusions in an intellectual void, the process takes place *within* a corpus of established scientific knowledge).

The next question to address is: why do scientists attempt to refute or falsify their conjectures rather than to confirm them? Falsifiability is, for Popper, the hallmark of scientific hypotheses. It is their susceptibility to falsification which distinguishes them from metaphysical statements or theories. In order to understand why Popper holds this thesis we need to examine the alternatives to falsifiability that Popper considers. The alternatives to saying that a conjecture is scientific if it is falsifiable are:

(1) It is scientific if it is highly probable.
(2) It is scientific if it explains or purports to explain every contingency that might occur.
(3) It is scientific if it can be confirmed.

Popper excludes the second alternative on the ground that if a hypothesis does explain anything which happens, then it explains nothing. It would be an empty hypothesis as far as the carrying of scientific import is concerned. It might, of course, have some significance for its proponents but that is not the issue here. In order for a hypothesis to be scientific there must be some observation or set of observations with which it is incompatible. This is crucial to Popper's philosophy of science and is the cornerstone of his claim that neither Marxism nor Freudianism constitute scientific hypotheses. Popper's claim is that in order for the Marxist theory of history to be scientific then there must be some possibilities which it excludes. That is to say, if it predicts a certain course of history and some other course transpires, then the theory is either to be abandoned as false or, if it is retained, its status as a scientific theory is abandoned. It is of course, possible for a hypothesis to say that under certain conditions, certain events will occur whilst also allowing for the possibility that there can be changes in the initial conditions. It would, however, to pass the test of scientific hypothesis, have to be able to state what changes in initial conditions might occur and hence what further changes could occur. And again, this would not be compatible with just *anything* happening.[6] The essential point is that when you make a scientific hypothesis, there must be some observation with which that hypothesis is incompatible. This must apply equally to changes in conditions. You cannot just go on postulating changes in conditions in order to explain away observations which are incompatible with the hypothesis. The application of this procedure is discussed in the chapter on the philosophy of mind. We can note here though, that the criticism to be levelled by Popper is, for example, what observations would be incompatible with the phenomenon of the repression of wishes? If there are no specifiable observations and there is no evidence in support of the hypothesis that there are such repressions other than any and every aspect of human behaviour, then it is written off as unscientific. It would also be possible to bring this Popperian objection against Chomsky's theory of language acquisition in terms of innate structures if no independent evidence were available for the existence of such structures.

There is a problem here with Popper, namely, that it is not always a straightforward matter to distinguish falsifiable and unfalsifiable theories. In the natural sciences there are developments which resemble the problematic developments in Marx and Freud. There are, what are seen as basic laws such as those of Newton which seem to have been refuted and yet they are retained. Newton's laws were incompatible with perturbations in the orbit of Uranus, and as a result of this a new planet was postulated as the cause of those perturbations thus making the seeming incompatibility fit in with the accepted theory. There was, however, in this case, independent evidence available for the existence of Neptune. It is also the case that given Newton's law of gravitation as an central postulate, perturbations in the orbit of a planet are just what you would expect if another planet were present. In other words, the theory contained the necessary factual import to enable one to be specific. The postulation of Neptune was not an *ad hoc* postulation. Besides, when many aspects of Newtonian theory were superseded by Einstein's work, one was able to specify the greater accuracy and economy that was available. Although it might be said that it was somewhat fortuitous that an observational check concerning the planet Mercury was available, it is nevertheless true to say that the new theory committed itself within a specified and accepted margin of error to compatibility with a particular observation and hence to incompatibility to some other observation lying outside the margin of error.

One cannot argue analogously that Marx made predictions which were to be regarded as falsified within such an acceptable margin of error. What was the margin of error? As for the first alternative, all that is needed to achieve a highly probable hypothesis is to make a trivial or vacuous suggestion such as: the video will not work because it is broken, or, John is coughing because he is ill. Those kinds of suggestion are highly probable but they lack scientific value. Indeed, one can say that there is a sense in which the scientist looks for improbable hypotheses rather than the highly probable. He certainly looks for hypotheses that commit him to having specific or definite expectations. The hypothesis that John is ill would not commit the scientist to the *specific* expectation that John will cough.

This would leave us with the third alternative, namely, that a hypothesis is scientific if it can be confirmed. The problem with the alternative is that one can find confirmation of hypotheses which are not scientifically valuable. To take an example, there are levels of description at which astrological hypotheses can be confirmed. That is to say, if interpreted in a wide enough way, they can have confirmation instances. The problem with such hypotheses is that the astrologer does not submit them to the possibility of refutation. He does not say what states of affairs would count *against* the truth of the hypothesis. This is why Popper holds that the test of refutation is the real test of scientific status. To simply confirm a hypothesis in a given number of cases is not sufficient for ensuring scientific status for that hypothesis. By rejecting the three alternatives we have referred to, Popper comes to regard refutability or falsifiability as the distinguishing feature of scientific hypotheses.

Some logical positivists saw Popper's thesis as constituting an improvement on their formulation of the verification principle. The need for an improvement on 'a proposition is meaningful if and only if it can be verified by observation' arose because of the case of general law propositions. It would be impossible to conclusively verify 'all iron rusts' unless you tested all the iron that there was and also you knew that what you had tested was all that there was. Clearly, the logical positivists did not want to say that such general propositions were meaningless so they reformulated their principle of meaning thus: 'a proposition is meaningful if it is possible to refute it', or, 'a proposition is meaningful if one could specify what state of affairs would count against it'. But to interpret Popper in this way would be to read far more into his thesis than he actually says. The logical positivists were concerned with formulating a principle of *meaning*. This principle was to have an across-the-board application. Propositions of metaphysics, ethics, aesthetics, and theology were to be regarded as pseudo-propositions: they lacked significance when 'significance' is understood as being capable of conveying meaning or having a truth-value. Popper, in formulating the falsifiability thesis, was not proposing a theory of meaning in general; what he was doing was proposing a method by which scientific hypotheses or propositions could be distinguished from those that were not. The status of the latter category need not be condemned as nonsense or mere noise. Rather than interpreting Popper as offering a principle of meaning in general, we should interpret him as offering a principle of *scientific* meaning or, if you like, a principle of demarcation between science and metaphysics.

The falsifiability thesis has not been without its critics. Ayer in *Language, Truth and Logic* (p. 51) argues that those who adopt such a thesis as Popper's assume that:

> although no finite series of observations is ever sufficient to establish the truth of a hypothesis beyond all possibility of doubt, there are crucial cases in which a single observation, or series of observations, can definitely confute it. But this assumption is false. A hypothesis cannot be conclusively refuted any more than it can be conclusively verified. For when we take the occurrence of certain observations as proof that a given hypothesis is false, we presuppose the existence of certain conditions. And though, in any given case it may be improbably that this assumption is false, it is not logically impossible. We shall see that there need be no self-

contradiction in holding that some of the relevant circumstances are other than we have taken them to be and consequently the hypothesis has not really broken down.[7]

Popper's reply to this is his proposal that the scientific or empirical method is to be characterised:

as a method that excludes precisely those ways of evading falsification which are logically possible ... what characterises the empirical method is its manner of exposing to falsification, in every conceivable way, the system to be tested. Its aim is not to save the lives of untenable systems but, on the contrary to select the one which is by comparison the fittest, by exposing them all to the fiercest struggle for survival. (*The Logic of Scientific Discovery*, p. 42)

Popper can be understood as saying that his account of scientific method is designed to specifically exclude the kind of procedure envisaged by Ayer. A very similar point to Ayer's is made by Harré (*Philosophies of Science*, p. 52) where he argues against Popper in the following way, in the main 'the proper move to make when faced with contrary evidence to some hypothesis is to reinterpret it as favourable evidence by developing the relevant theory, so that the awkward facts are now seen as being in accordance with the theory'. Harré goes on to add that it is only in rare cases that unfavourable evidence results in the abandonment of a theory. There are two points that a defender of Popper can make in reply to Harré. The first is that you must at least be prepared to say what would count against a theory. Not all counter-evidence can be treated in the way Harré suggests. The second point is that, as a matter of fact, theories are given up in the light of counter-evidence. To take a simple example from zoology, there have been many theories covering the whereabouts of giant turtles in the first year of their lives. When the actual whereabouts were discovered, all other theories were unceremoniously abandoned. There can, of course, be good and bad reasons for the reluctance to abandon a theory.

However, Harré goes on to raise a more serious objection to Popper. It is an objection that Popper himself was aware of and which he draws attention to in *The Logic of Scientific Discovery*, pp. 69–70. The objection concerns Popper's account of existential propositions. These are propositions which take the form of asserting that at least one thing of a particular class exists. Examples of these would be 'there are atoms', 'there are unicorns', 'there are pulsars'. The problem for Popper is that as no proposition describing a particular observed event can contradict an existential proposition,[8] it is going to follow that such existential propositions are unfalsifiable. Now, as we have seen, Popper was not offering a theory of meaning with his thesis of falsifiability so at least he cannot be convicted of implying that existential propositions are meaningless. However, he was putting forward a principle of demarcation for science and metaphysics and what is going to follow is that such existential propositions will be clarified as metaphysical rather than scientific. The problem highlighted by Harré is that existential propositions are extremely important in the development of science as they serve as a foundation for much of the theorising that occurs and it would, therefore, be disastrous to remove them *en masse* from science. Without entering into the technical discussion of probability statements, let us just remark here that Popper would obviously want to retain some existential statements within science and one option would be to argue against Harré that isolated or highly individual existential propositions are not of value to science. What is of value is the occurrence of the existential proposition *within* the context of a hypothesis, the resulting whole would be amenable to testability and thus would secure scientific status for its parts. One of the parts would, of course, be the existential proposition (see first footnote to p. 70, *The Logic of Scientific Discovery*). It does, however, seem to claim that propositions such as 'there are tigers' only have empirical content within the context of a hypothesis or theory. If we say that such singular utterances are at least part of some low-level hypothesis, then there is a danger of counting virtually anything as a hypothesis. (In the case of the curies singular observations came first and what is regarded as the important theory came later).

In proposing the thesis of falsifiability as the essence of science, Popper naturally lays great stress on the idea of adopting a critical attitude in science. Scientists are said to be attempting to falsify their hypotheses. One can question just how far or to what extent this is true. It is an extremely important notion in Popper's account of science. In distinguishing science from mythology or the pre-scientific tradition, Popper holds that two layers can be identified within the scientific tradition. The two layers are: (1) it passes on its theories; (2) it adopts a critical attitude toward its theories. It is this second layer that is of importance in distinguishing science from pre-science. But as we have indicated, there is a question concerning how far this is true or how far it has to be true. The problem concerns just how essential it is to adopt a critical attitude to the theory which is passed on in order for that theory to be designated scientific. If there is nothing self-contradictory about a fully satisfactory law, then why must a critical attitude be the central attitude to adopt towards it? It is, of course, *logically* possible that a theory might be revised, but logical possibility does not imply that one has to actively adopt a critical attitude. It is not necessary for us to say that one *must* remain critical towards a given theory in order for that theory to retain its place within the domain of science. It might be said that adopting a critical attitude is to be understood in terms of being prepared to abandon a theory. The problem though, is that they just do not mean the same thing. The fact that I am prepared under certain circumstances to abandon a particular belief or theory does not imply that

I am actively critical of that belief or theory. What it implies is that I am prepared to be. There does, then, appear to be a problem in locating the rationality of the scientific enterprise in the adoption of a critical attitude. Popper holds in common with Hume that scientific theories cannot be deductively inferred from observations but he dissents from the Humean view that such theories are irrational or arational. He attempts to locate their rationality in the adoption of the critical attitude. We propose theories and then do our best to refute them. Popper's method for science is that of conjecture and refutation. It is rational for us to accept a theory that stands up to all conceivable tests but there is always an air of the tentative in this acceptance due to the permanence of the critical attitude. It is essential to note that on Popper's account a theory is *not* inferred from observations. There is no logic of scientific discovery.

We have looked at some influential theories concerning the nature of science and the way science proceeds. I now want to look briefly at one further thesis concerning scientific method before moving to a discussion of the status of the data which science is concerned with. The theory in question is operationism.

Operationism as a method in science may be seen as an attempt to delineate in a precise way what are scientific concepts and what are not. It is an attempt to control rigorously what kind of concepts can appear in scientific theories. The thesis proposed that only those terms which are explicable in terms of specific experimental operations can legitimately appear within a scientific theory. Thus, if you are going to use a particular term in science you must be prepared to give the definition of that term in terms of experimental operations. If you cannot determine the concept in terms of such operations, then it is to be banished from the realm of science. Perhaps an example would clarify the envisaged procedure of the operationist. Hempel (*Philosophy of Natural Science*, p. 89) considers the example of the concept 'magnet'. In order to legitimize the use of this concept one would have to provide an operational definition in terms of experimental method. In this case, Hempel's suggested operational definition is: 'to find out whether the term 'magnet' applies to a given iron or steel bar, put iron filings close to it. If the filings are attracted by the ends of the bar and cling to them, the bar is a magnet'. What follows from this is that the term 'magnet' applies to the bar. You can see from Hempel's example that specifiable experimental procedures can be laid down in order to test the applicability of the concept 'magnet'. If certain operational conditions are satisfied, then the term applies. If no specified operational conditions can be given, then the term is scientifically useless. This was a theory that had much appeal in behaviourist psychology and could plausibly be used to show that many other branches of psychology, for example, those of Jung utilising concepts such as the collective uncon-scious, or Freud utilising concepts such as the Id, did not come up to the required standard of rigour. It would be very difficult to provide operational definitions of such concepts.

One advantage which the operationists hoped to achieve for their method was to secure a firm body of concepts which had been operationally defined. In the face of changing theories there would remain a bedrock of established concepts. However, there are difficulties with operationism.

First, consider the aspiration that such a method would provide us with a bedrock of scientific knowledge and consider it in relation to Hempel's operational definition of 'magnet'. Not only will 'magnet' require an operational definition, but so will all the other terms which form part of its definition. It must be remembered that for *any* term to have a legitimate scientific usage, then it must be possible to define it operationally. It is not clear how operational definition can be an endless process. One must stop somewhere. It might be argued that the point at which you stop is the point where it is possible to provide ostensive definition, that is, you pick things out by pointing at them. If you feel attracted to this solution, then you must bear in mind that the bedrock of concepts, that is, the irreducible body of scientific knowledge, will now consist of what can be ostensively defined rather than operationally defined. They would constitute the base upon which our operational definitions were constructed. This raises the further difficulty that our criterion for saying that some term or concept is a basic one is the actual role it plays in a particular theory. It is somewhat misleading to suggest that it is the things we can point to that are the basic elements of a scientific theory. They may form the base of *why* we theorise, but that is not the same as saying that they are the basic concepts of the theories we formulate. That question can only be answered by examining individual theories such as those of genetics, light and so on.

Secondly, the plausibility of providing an operational definition for a term like 'magnet' might derive from the simplicity of the example rather than from the viability of operationism in general. Readers might like to try an experiment of their own in which operational definitions are provided for more complex scientific terms. An interesting candidate for such a definition could be taken from modern particle physics, the gluon. It is so named as it is held to be the 'glue' that binds other elementary particles called quarks together. There are theoretical grounds for saying that quarks cannot exist in isolation, so a top and bottom quark are postulated and gluons are also postulated to bind such combinations. But it is not obvious what operational definition could be given for gluons and yet they seem to play a scientifically respectable role in particle physics. There may well be strong theoretical grounds for formulating a concept even though no specific operation can be set up to validate them. Do such terms remain scientifically meaningless until such a time as a technique is established? This would also leave it somewhat mysterious as to what people were doing when they were searching for a technique. Until the technique is found, the term has no more significance than a mere noise.

A third problem arises when you consider the possibility of operationally defining a term in *different* ways. To take a simple example, not only is it possible to operationally define 'magnet' in the way Hempel suggests, it is also possible to operationally define it in terms of the displacement of a compass needle. The problem is that, if a term can be operationally defined in a number of ways, it seems to follow that that term has a number of different meanings. Indeed, this must follow if what we are doing is providing *definitions*. Such a procedure as this can be accused of confusing the meaning of a term with the effects that a thing designated by the term has.[9] This is related to a difficulty raised by Hempel, namely, that as theories progress, different techniques are developed. Thus, for example, techniques for measuring distance or speed can change, become more refined, and so on. If we allowed every change in technique to determine a *different* concept, there would be no end to the number of concepts in science and this would conflict with the scientific ideal of simplicity.

The final problem is one made much of by Harré. We have seen that operationism could lead to the indefinite multiplication of concepts to be used in science and we remarked that this would conflict with the ideal of simplicity. There is an additional problem though, for any set of operations, irrespective of their scientific value will lead to the formation of an empirical concept as long as we can specify what the operations are.

As long as there is a level of description at which we can be said to be operating some apparatus and achieving some result, then we shall have generated an empirical concept. The point is, that if all you have to go on are the operative techniques, then there is no *independent* check concerning the theoretical importance of the concepts we generate.

▶ Realist and non-realist theories of science

I now want to move on to consider a central controversy among philosophers, namely that concerning the nature and subject matter of science. Realist philosophers of science hold that it is the business of science to explain the way the world works and to describe what there is in the world. Some would hold that it is the business of science to furnish a complete explanation and description of the world. What is essential to the realist thesis is that the terms which figure in scientific laws and explanations actually refer to parts of the world or to parts of its structure. They incorporate facts about what the world is really like and it is also by knowing such facts that we can be said to have a real understanding of the workings of the world.

A non-realist theory of science can take a number of forms. It can take the form of instrumentalism which holds that the ultimate data of science are the actual readings on various scientific equipment. What are of interest to the instrumentalist in the final analysis are the various sequences of statistics obtained from the readings of instruments. On the other hand it can take the form of phenomenalism which holds that the ultimate data of scientific enquiry are our own sense-data or sensations and that the business of scientific theory is to predict what sense-data would occur under various conditions. On a thoroughgoing phenomenalism the various conditions would of course be rendered in terms of possible or actual sense-experience.

The issue which I want to examine in some detail is the conflicting accounts given by realist and non-realist theorists concerning various scientific theories. There is fundamental disagreement concerning the nature and status of many concepts which appear in scientific theories and hence disagreement concerning the nature of the theories themselves. On the realist thesis, scientific concepts and terms describe and refer to actual items in the world. On the non-realist thesis, the function of such concepts is that of providing a method of calculation; they are convenient fictions which enable us to carry out various calculations. Their function is not to directly refer or to state facts. This is the crucial point of difference. The best way to understand what is at issue here is to examine some actual scientific theories to see how each philosophical thesis works out in practice. Let us begin by considering Newton's mechanics, and in particular the first law of motion: every body perseveres in a state of rest or uniform motion unless acted upon by external force. The non-realist philosopher of science will point out the abstract nature of this law and of the concepts utilised by Newton, such as force and momentum. He can claim that the first law should not be understood as a generalisation about the world based on a number of particular instances. His reason for saying this would be that the conditions referred to in the law could not hold. We just could not have motion without forces. When this is taken together with the abstract nature of the concepts and the fact that some would hold that Newton's laws of motion are definitions, then there is a case for saying that Newtonian mechanics is not to be seen as an actual description of what there is or what goes on in the world, but rather as a convenient device, understood in terms of theoretical fictions, for making calculations of what goes on in the world. A term such as 'force', for example, is a theoretical convenience rather than a directly referring term. If this account is generalised to cover the whole of science, then you will get a non-realist, phenomenalistic account of the nature of scientific theory. Some philosophers would claim that realism was appropriate for some theories and non-realism for others.

In *Matter and Method*, Harré draws a distinction in the realm of scientific theories between what he calls reticular theories and explanatory theories. Reticular theories are theories which connect up sets of facts all of the same kind or status. Explanatory theories, on the other hand, are said to explain one set of facts by making an appeal in the explanation to some other and distinct set of facts. An example of a genuine explanatory theory would be the medical theory whereby symptoms of a disease which constitute one set of facts are explained by reference to another set of facts, namely, those concerning viruses. The propositions referring to micro-organisms would be descriptive of items in the world. Their subject terms would have direct reference. Let us contrast this with an example of what Harré holds to be a reticular theory. Newton's dynamics is an example of this. Newton's difficulty was to connect up all the facts of motion. His method was to introduce the concept 'force' which would accomplish this connecting-up function. What is important to grasp is the role which Harré assigns to force in Newtonian theory and what Harré is prepared to admit as a fact of dynamics. The numerical value of force for a moving body can be calculated, but, according to Harré, to say that the force has the value we calculate is *not* to say that some fact is instantiated. His reason for saying this is that although we can measure force, we cannot observe it. There is nothing in any physical interchange that we can point to and identify as force. It is because you cannot do this that Harré will not afford a factual status to force. Newton's second law – mass × acceleration = force – is not to be seen then as an empirical generalisation about observables in the world. It is a definitional device which enables us to connect up facts about the motions of bodies. The proposition 'there are forces' is not, on this account, to be understood as stating a fact of dynamics.

One has to distinguish direct and indirect derivation of a concept from observation. A scientific concept is said to be directly derived from observation if its immediate referent is capable of being perceived. Thus, for example, colour concepts would be directly derived from observation, as the referents of colour words are capable of being perceived. In contrast to this, indirect derivation is said to occur when the immediate referent is not capable of being perceived, but is the result or product of an intellectual operation. The concept of force would be derived in this latter way. The concept which is indirectly derived is regarded as a function of concepts which are directly derived from observation. The term 'force' is used to *mean* the product of mass and acceleration. By performing this intellectual operation, the scientist is in a better position to connect up the facts of motion within a unified theory. This is the role that force is said to play; it does not take on the role of a term which has a direct referent.

According to Harré, when the concept of force has been constructed, a new theoretical concept is thereby formed. It is not a mere refinement on already established observational concepts and neither is it reducible to mass × acceleration. This latter claim is more difficult for him to sustain, as given that force is *defined* in terms of the product of mass and acceleration, it is difficult to see why it cannot be reduced to mass × acceleration.

An objection that may be brought against Harré's account of force as a purely theoretical concept is that we can directly measure it. Is it not the case that in the spring-balance we measure force in the same way that we measure length or velocity? And if this is the case, is there not a strong ground for saying that the concept of force is directly derived from observation? Harré's answer to this is that the argument rests on a misunderstanding of the nature of the spring-balance. It is essentially the same type of instrument as the kilo-watt-hour meter. It is essentially a computer and depends on Hooke's law for its success in measuring force. The units of force, pound weight, are not determined by instruments like the KWM, but are derived from concepts used for calculating forces. We cannot directly measure force in the way we can measure length. Any method of doing so will involve the kind of definitions typical of the second law of motion.

A reticular theory can be defined as a set of relationships between refined observational concepts mediated by one or more theoretical concepts which are to be understood wholly in terms of the complex observational concepts of the theory. Dynamics and geometrical optics could be regarded as examples. The essential point to clarify is that such theories are held not to *explain* phenomena. Their role is not explanatory; they are useful devices for making calculations or predictions. If this is the case, the next question to ask concerns the concept of causality which reticular theories presuppose. Here we need to distinguish two senses of causation: the maximal and the minimal sense.

The maximal sense incorporates the following characteristics:

(1) The idea of agency or productivity, that is, the cause actually *produces* the effect. The cause makes the effect occur.

(2) Each specification of a cause that we make in explaining the occurrence of some effect is open in the sense that it can be expanded by giving more details of the actual mechanism by which the cause produces the effect.

(3) When we specify a cause, we are specifying a set of necessary conditions for the occurrence of the effect. Each specification can be treated in this way as each specification refers to an element which, if absent, would prevent the effect from occurring. The set of necessary conditions is open. This means that if we are identifying a cause of a phenomenon, say an ultra-violet lamp in a greenhouse causing plants to flower, there are other background conditions which must also hold (in this case, the temperature, humidity, regular watering and so on). All these conditions would themselves have causes, and so on, *ad infinitum*. When we pick out the cause of

a phenomenon we assume stability in these background conditions. This means that we can never describe a set of conditions such that the description of the effect *follows* from them. What we can do is select a set of necessary conditions which will suffice for the practical production of the effect assuming a background of relative stability.

The second sense of causation is the minimal sense and it has the following Humean characteristics:

(1) The cause is observable and so is the effect, but the relation between them is not observable. The reader should refer to the section on necessary connection (p. 300). The minimal sense involves Hume's principle that all we can observe in a serial chain are the events that severally compose it.
(2) The connection between cause and effect is a conceptual one. It is a connection made in our minds and manifested in our language. It is not what the scientific realist would call a 'real' connection. Hume expressed the matter by referring to it as a habit of mind brought about through the repetition of conjunctions.

It is the model of minimal causation that reticular theories fit in with. A non-realist philosopher of science will want to say that the laws of motion are reticular. The concept of force which relates phenomena in the laws of motion is entirely theoretical. The relation is conceptual not observable. Harré puts much emphasis on the idea of observability. Let us now consider how a scientific realist might argue against Harré's non-realist account of the laws of motion and especially the concept of force.

The account that the realist will want to give will involve the maximal sense of causation. He will want to say that the laws of motion are explanatory in the sense that the theory of the virus is explanatory. It actually explains the occurrence of certain symptoms by giving a straightforward factual account of the virus. It is an account which refers to actual items in the world. Similarly, with the kinetic theory of gases, you have an account of the actual constitution of gases and this tells you *why* Boyle's Law holds. Is it not open to the realist to claim that force *produces* acceleration (first characteristic of maximal causation), just as a virus produces symptoms of a disease or as molecules of a gas produce pressure on the walls of a container? In other words, the realist can claim that the concept of force is so effective[10] in producing accurate predictions that we must accept that there actually are forces which are responsible, in the full-blooded sense of agency, for causing the motions. The realist is claiming that the effectiveness of the concept of force justifies treating the term 'force' as a term which denotes a real item which is involved in the physics of motion. Given that the realist's claim is that even though force is unobservable, it is such a powerful concept that it must be admitted as a denoting term, it is not a sufficient answer to merely reiterate the point concerning the unobservability of forces. Harré is aware of this limitation of the unobservability thesis and offers an alternative argument. He suggests that the desire to treat the concept of force in a realist manner is anthropomorphic in origin. His claim is that the concept of force can be eliminated from dynamics without any loss of empirical content. The elimination of the concept does not result in our missing out on a fact of dynamics. Harré holds that every mechanical phenomenon is an interaction and every mechanical problem is reducible to the task of finding the velocity, acceleration and position of masses after interaction given their values before interaction, or to the complementary problem of working back to an initial state from one's present knowledge. In Newtonian mechanics, the action-reaction principle holds and on Harré's non-realist account, the matter is expressed by saying that since action and reaction are equal and opposite, force never appears in the answer to a mechanical problem. It only occurs as a part of the working out of the answer rather than the answer itself. For this reason it is not to be given a realist interpretation. The realist might object that all Harré has done is to *stipulate* what a mechanical problem is rather than providing a method for what constitutes a mechanical problem. If he had done this, he might have found that 'force' was an indispensable concept for the setting out of the method.

A realist might also claim that a comparison can be made between the use of the concept of force in mechanics and its use in instructing someone to ride a bicycle. He could claim that the concept is not eliminable from this latter usage. Harré does not afford much importance to this. He thinks it is wholly anthropomorphic to say that you can use the concept in situations where there are organisms who feel sensations of force; we cannot argue from this to its use in inorganic situations. The realist would argue that there was a close relation between the two uses of the concept. Harré holds that when we talk about force in relation to sentient creatures, we have to be talking about sensations. The realist will hold that what we feel is felt by sensations but is not itself a sensation; it is this force with which physics is concerned. Thus the realist is claiming that such a usage is not anthropomorphic in the way Harré suggests and he might seek to justify this by pointing out genuine cases of anthropomorphising, such as the use of the concept 'magnetism' in relation to attraction felt by people to one another and saying that this kind of case needs to be distinguished from the one of 'force' in relation to sentient creatures.

A word ought to be said here concerning the use of Ernst Mach's method for the elimination of concepts from science (*The Science of Mechanics*) to which Harré acknowledges a debt. Mach attempted to show that concepts like 'force' and 'mass' were eliminable from physics. Ultimately he arrives at a phenomenalistic account of science. The irreducible objects of scientific enquiry are groups of sensations. On this account the force experienced via sensation in the realist's rejoinder to Harré will simply *be* the sensations. No distinction will be drawn between sensations and force. The term force which the realist says denotes a real term we feel will just be a convenient term used to denote a certain kind of sensation.

Although Mach's phenomenalistic thesis is sophisticated. It faces the problem which all such theses face, namely, that of reconciling their account of what science is with what scientists understand themselves to be actually doing. Surely, science is not just the recording and predicting of one's sensations. Scientific accounts concerning human pre-history are not usually regarded as hypothetical records of sensations that would have occurred had a sentient being been present or recordings that might have been reported on a machine.

Finally, in connection with Mach, I want to indicate a crucial distinction between his philosophy of science and that of the realist. For Mach, concepts such as force are summative: they connect up the facts. A good scientific theory is one in which the facts are connected up in the simplest way. Summative economy is the criterion for a good theory. This should be contrasted with the realist case which holds that a good theory is the one which fits the facts better than its competitors. It may, of course, be the case that the theory which best fits the facts is not as simple as its competitors, but, for the realist, it is still the best. Simplicity is desirable but it is not the criterion of truth in science.

Returning to our discussion of Harré, the realist will want to attack the initial distinction between reticular and explanatory theories. According to Harré, when we have a theory that actually explains (as opposed to reticulates), every relation among observables is mirrored by a corresponding relation among theoretical concepts. In a genuine explanation, we do not use theory to *form* relations, but to actually account for relations that are already known. Thus, in the example of mechanics which we have been discussing, 'force' forms a relation; we are said not to discover a new relation, rather we form or make a relation. This is the essence of a reticular theory. But when we explain a phenomenon, we do not form new relations, rather we explain the ones we already have. This method of setting up the distinction can be attacked. It can be argued that any kind of theory involves the forming of relationships between theoretical entities, and, if you are a realist, you will want to say that the *discovery* of relationships is the business of scientific theorising. On this line of argument, no line is to be drawn to separate reticular from explanatory theories. The realist position is that even in what Harré refers to as reticular theories, theoretical entities are not there solely for the purpose of forming relationships. They have a descriptive function regarding real items operative in a system.

There is another way of distinguishing reticular from explanatory theories to which Harré refers. This involves the claim that, as far as explanatory theories are concerned, we can have competing theories. But the distinction breaks down as you can also have competing theories concerning the alleged reticular concept of force. Faraday's theory of electro-magnetic force involved the claim that lines of electro-magnetic force were lines of strain in the ether; whereas the action at a distance theory did not require any medium. It can certainly be claimed that such theories compete and yet they are held by Harré to be reticular and, as we have seen, competition is a supposed characteristic of explanatory theories.

Harré tells us (*Philosophies of Science*, p. 89) that a non-realist theory seems to be appropriate for the concepts of force and light rays. I now want to examine briefly the case for giving a non-realist account of geometrical optics. Here we turn to the work of another philosopher, Steven Toulmin.

Toulmin wants to offer a non-realist account of geometrical optics. Suppose we ask what exactly is discovered when a scientist discovers that light travels in straight lines. We want to know what kind of discovery this is. Toulmin's argument is that it is a new way of looking at old phenomena. The rectilinear propagation principle grew out of the following:

(1) Our experience of phenomena such as light and shade
(2) Various practical skills and techniques developed as a result of our experience of the phenomena.
(3) Out of those regularities in optical phenomena that are not stated but are assumed and enshrined in ordinary language.

To take some examples concerning our experience of light and shade, shadows moving with the sun and lengthening as it sets are part of our experience. Concerning the second, the making of sundials is an example of a skill resulting from such experience. Concerning the third, examples of such regularities would be that water does not flow up hill (this is connected with our knowledge of up and down), if you put your hand in a fire, then it will burn (this is connected with our expectations in the world) and the shortest way to get across a field is to follow your nose (this is supposed to involve the concept of straightness).

Toulmin wants to say that these are the principles from which the rectilinear propagation principle of light emanates. The next issue raised concerns the nature of the inference from these principles to the rectilinear propagation principle of light. Toulmin tells us that it is not a logical passage and in this he is at one with Popper. In attempting to elucidate the nature of this inference, Toulmin claims to be exposing what he refers to as the 'Man Friday Fallacy'. By this he means that the discovery of the rectilinear propagation principle of light and other such theoretical discoveries are not to be compared with Crusoe's discovery of a man on the island or to our earlier example of a zoologist's discovery of the whereabouts of giant turtles. So what is the difference in these cases? The rectilinear propagation principle of light differs from the case of Crusoe in that you cannot come face to face with light, whereas Crusoe could come face to face with the man. Crusoe's conclusion can be established once and for all. Crusoe reached his conclusion by applying a familiar kind of inference to new data. The inference takes the form: (1) footprint, (2) footprint means man, therefore, (3) man. In this case the kind of inference is old; it is the data that are new. In the case of geometrical optics the position is reversed. It is not the data which are new but rather, the inference. It is by this inference that we are led to look at familiar phenomena in a new way. According to Toulmin, these differences mean that when we say that we have discovered that light travels in straight lines, this should not be taken to mean that whereas once we thought nothing was travelling, we now find that there is something. To think this would, according to Toulmin, commit the Man Friday Fallacy. It is not like the case of Crusoe in which he thought there was no one else on the island, but found that there was. For Toulmin, this is not the model we use for understanding the nature of a theoretical discovery such as the rectilinear propagation principle of light. Toulmin goes on to tell us that in addition to avoiding the Man Friday Fallacy above, we must also avoid thinking that the discovery of the rectilinear propagation principle of light involves the discovery that something is travelling in one direction rather than another. What the optical discovery amounts to is that one can talk profitably about something travelling in these circumstances. In other words, this way of looking at an optical phenomenon is a profitable one. These differences indicate a major divergence from the Crusoe case. In the case of Crusoe, the language in which the inferred conclusion is expressed is the language of everyday life. However, in the case of geometrical optics, terms such as 'light' and 'travelling' are given new uses and new senses in the statement of the theory. After the discovery of the rectilinear propagation principle of light, we use 'shade' and so on as effects of light in a new sense. A crucial feature of the rectilinear propagation principle of light is the coming to think of light in a new way and coming to ask new questions which are now possible and intelligible.

There are a number of criticisms that the realist would want to make of Toulmin's theories. The realist will accept that there are differences between the case of Crusoe and the scientist but he will not afford them the same significance as Toulmin does. He will not want to say that a realist interpretation involves committing of the Man Friday Fallacy. On a realist interpretation, the rectilinear propagation principle of light does involve the claim that something has been discovered to be travelling, whereas before it was thought that nothing was travelling. Toulmin regards this as a misunderstanding. As we have seen, he says that we can see the man but we cannot see the light. His reason for making this claim seems to be because there is no such thing as coming face to face with light. However, there are cases where we do not see anything travelling but would still want to say that something was travelling. In the case of the transmission and reception of television signals we find that something is capable of travelling which we did not know previously. We do not actually see the signals though we do use their effects. When we fire a bullet from a gun we do not see the bullet in flight, but we would certainly say that something was travelling. How do such examples compare with the case of light? We cannot see light in the straightforward sense that one can come to see a bullet, and perhaps a supporter of Toulmin might want to say that rather than seeing light, it is light which enables us to see anything. The realist will admit that seeing light is different from seeing physical objects, but again he will want to discount the importance of this difference. It could be argued that there is a sense in which you can see light. Thus, for example, you can see a beam of light from a headlamp in the dark, you can trap light on a screen, it can be scattered through a prism and the effects of this scattering can be seen. We would, of course, need to import theoretical backing for the claim that light was being seen, but we would also need at least some theory in the case of seeing a bullet. The realist will claim that this fact that you need more theory in the case of light makes no alteration to the reality of what is seen. The plausibility of the realist's position here rests on the assumption that when we see anything, there is a level of description at which we can be said to be adopting *some* theory about low-level theory. To try and make this clearer, imagine a case where it would be unproblematic to say that something was travelling when we thought it was not. If we came across what we thought was a disused railway track and then we saw an engine shunting along it, we would have discovered something travelling where we thought nothing was and we would have come face to face with the engine. Now on the realist's account above, this coming face to face with the engine will involve us in holding some theory, namely, low-level theory. A supporter of Toulmin could question this. He could say that this is not a *scientific* theory in the sense that the rectilinear propagation principle of light is a scientific theory. He can protest that the realist's distinction between high and low-level theory is masking differences.

The use of these terms implies that the scientist and the ordinary man are doing the same thing, namely, theorising albeit on different levels. The seeing and recognising of an *engine* as distinct from an object, certainly involves an interpretation, but are interpreting and theorising the same activity? The realist would probably not want to regard them as the same, but would want to say that in order to interpret we involve ourselves in at least low-level theorising. If one finds such a view attractive, then one must face the difficulty of saying that if animals interpret their environment, then it will follow that animals theorise. In other words, creatures which are incapable of using language will be said to hold theories. Perhaps the problem with the realist's argument lies in making the claim that in order to interpret we must theorise instead of saying that in order to theorise, we must interpret. These two claims need to be distinguished.

In regard to Toulmin's other point concerning the different ways of talking, the realist reply would be to agree that we come to regard 'light' in a new way, but, unlike Toulmin, he would go on to say that the profitability of this new way of talking is due to the fact that it is an accurate representation of the nature of light. In other words, it fits the facts well. The realist is saying that this explains the profitability of the new way of talking, whereas Toulmin cannot say *why* it is more profitable. The non-realist may regard scientific theories as models which permit certain references and generate new questions. The value of the model would be seen in terms of its utility in these areas. The realist will want to say that there comes a time when the utility is so marked that a model is not just a model but an accurate representation of the nature of the phenomenon under investigation. I shall leave the reader to ponder the following remark of the physicist Niels Bohr in connection with this topic: 'When it comes to atoms, language can be used only as in poetry. The poet, too, is not nearly as concerned with describing facts as with creating images.'

▶ A note on objectivity

The above remark by Niels Bohr belies a quite common view, namely, that science is concerned with describing facts, whereas other human activities such as art or poetry are not. They are more concerned with emotion and images and therein lies their subjectivity. The objectivity of science lies in its dealing with matters of fact. Such a view as this is a matter of great philosophical debate and is by no means universally accepted. Non-realist philosophies of science would argue that the notion of a theory-neutral fact is an incoherent concept. This is not to deny that science deals with facts, but should be understood as meaning that the facts dealt with by science are internal to the practice of science. It might also be claimed that there are other facts, such as artistic or moral facts, that are dealt with equally objectively by other disciplines. Such a view as this will involve the claim that the criteria of objectivity and subjectivity are internal to the many different areas of human activity and it is logically illegitimate to attempt to impose across the board, standards for all subjects. Thus, according to this thesis, you cannot say that art or poetry are subjective, whereas science is objective. They are not to be characterised as attempts to answer the same questions and, therefore, cannot be judged by the same standards. Indeed, this can be pushed a stage further and one could say that in order to judge, one must do so from a particular vantage point. There is no absolute vantage point from which to survey all areas of human activity. There are just the vantage points themselves and you cannot judge one by using the standards of another.

Perhaps this issue is best clarified by the use of examples. Charles Babbage, generally regarded as the inventor of the analogue computer, wrote a letter to Tennyson regarding Tennyson's poem 'The Vision of Sin'. In this letter, Babbage wrote that, 'in your otherwise excellent poem, there is a line which reads: Every moment dies a man, every moment one is born. If this were true, then the population would be at a standstill.' Babbage went on to give a more accurate figure, to two decimal places, declaring that even that was not completely accurate, but was sufficiently accurate for poetry. This well illustrates the absurdity that can arise when standards of truth and meaning become confused. All one can say of Babbage's comments in regard to *poetry* is that they are irrelevant.

A similar example concerns a lady in Matisse's art studio. After looking at one of the paintings, she exclaimed that surely this woman's arm is too long. The artist replied, 'Madame you are mistaken, that is not a woman, that is a picture.'

Harré in *The Philosophies of Science* (pp. 23–4) attempts to locate the objectivity of science in the nature of the imagination used by the scientist. It is a rationally controlled and disciplined imagination and this is presumably to be contrasted with other forms of imagination which are characteristic of other areas of human activity. But how plausible is this dichotomy? Surely, it is quite in order to describe a work of austere sculpture as the exercise of a disciplined imagination controlled by rational principles regarding form and perspective.[11] Can we not also draw a distinction within literature between those works of fiction in which an author exercises a disciplined imagination from other works in which an author allows imagination to run away with him? [12] The difficulty lies in understanding what it would mean to say that *all* uses of imagination within literature are irrational or ill-disciplined in contrast to its use in science. The problem here is that if we are to characterise one course of action or way of thinking as irrational in comparison to others, we must first of all be able to say that they aim at the same goal. In the case of literature and science, this would be a difficult claim to understand. You might try to specify the goal by appealing to notions such as 'truth' or 'capturing or representing reality', but notions such as reality also have their place in literature and other areas. Some philosophers would want to say that they are all internal to the respective activities. In other words, it is not the sole prerogative of science to capture reality and this is why we can understand and accept the remarks of human practices if given within the practice. The reality is exhausted by the conceptual system which constitutes the practice.

Harré sees science as the construction of a picture of the world. In addition, to the disciplined imagination, he also appeals to the severe discipline of the experimental method in distinguishing science from the creation of artistic works. This idea can be criticised on the ground that the artist, sculptor and poet experiment. The nature of the experimentation can differ but it does not follow that the nature of the difference is to be located in the fact that one is disciplined and the others are not. It would be false to say that the arts are characterised by a general attitude of carelessness or by a slap-dash approach. Besides, when they do show such an approach it can be reorganised or criticised, and this would be difficult to account for if it were a permanent defining feature.

However, it is open to the scientific objectivist to complain that the experimenting of the artist or the poet simply does not add up to a method. He can allow that they do experiment but he can say that the principles of experimentation cannot be specified in the methodical manner in which they can be for science. He might claim that this is due to the importance of the individual artist or writer. There is an irreducibly individualistic element which is absent from science. One way of arguing for this position is to say that if Leonardo had not painted the Mona Lisa, then no-one else would have, whereas, if Kepler had not claimed that the orbit of Mars was elliptical, then someone else would have. The philosophical controversy centres on how this is to be interpreted. The fact that an activity involves an irreducibly individualistic or personal element does not entail that it is legitimate to characterise that activity as subjective. Although it involves a personal element, it cannot involve just *any* personal element and must, therefore, be distinguished from idiosyncrasy.

Another way of attempting to locate the objectivity of science lies in the direction of claiming that science is the attempt to construct a picture of the world as it would be if there were no human beings. If one takes this view, then it will become paramount to give an account of theoretical entities in such a way that they have a directly referring role; hence the importance of our previous discussion. When one says that the totality of scientific proposition constitutes a complete account of the world as it would be without sentient creatures, we would need to say that the theoretical entities referred to in such propositions refer to real existents rather than that they are convenient fictions which are useful given the concerns of sentient creatures when making predictions and ordering their lives.

Questions

1 Perception and Knowledge

1. (a) What are the main differences between Rationalism and Empiriism?
   (b) To what extent may Descartes be described as a Rationalist?
2. Discuss the claim that physical objects are not really coloured.
3. (a) What conclusions does Descartes draw from the example of the melted wax?
   (b) How justified are those conclusions?
4. (a) State any form of the argument from illusion.
   (b) Discuss the validity of the argument you have stated.
5. (a) What does Russell take the immediate objects of perception to be?
   (b) Evaluate his arguments for saying this.
6. (a) What does Hume take the contents of the mind to be?
   (b) Discuss critically his classification of those contents.
7. (a) What are Russell's criticisms of Berkeley?
   (b) Do the criticisms go far enough?
8. Are there any good arguments to show that we are not directly aware of physical objects?
9. Discuss the role of inference in perception.
10. (a) What is Russell's solution to the problem of *a priori* knowledge?
    (b) Does his solution have any unacceptable implications?
11. (a) How does Russell distinguish knowledge by acquaintance and knowledge by description?
    (b) Why does Russell think that knowledge by description is so important?
12. (a) What is Linguistic Phenomenalism?
    (b) Discuss two arguments which might be used to show that it is an inadequate solution to the problem of perception.
13. (a) How does Hume explain our acquisition of knowledge?
    (b) Are his own examples always consistent with his account?
14. (a) What does Ayer hope that the verification principle will achieve?
    (b) Does it?
15. Discuss Ayer's claim that all *a priori* propositions are analytic.
16. (a) What does Russell mean by 'universals'?
    (b) What is his theory of universals meant to explain?
17. (a) What is the purpose of Descartes' method of doubt?
    (b) Is the method a reasonable method?
18. How does Hume distinguish knowledge, belief and fiction?
19. Discuss Russell's account of the limits of philosophy.

The following are more difficult:

20. (a) What is Russell's theory of descriptions?

    (b) Why is it important?

21. 'Ayer's phenomenalism is just Berkeley's idealism without God.' Discuss.

22. (a) What is the problem of universals?

    (b) Discuss two solutions to it.

2 Problems in the Philosophy of Mind

1. Can you justify a claim to know that another person is angry?

2. What does Descartes take the essence of the self to be? How well do his arguments support his conclusion?

3. Is it true to say that a computer can think?

4. 'Thinking is the firing of neurons.' Discuss.

5. Is the concept of an unconscious mind an intelligible one?

6. 'If he ran away, then he must have been afraid.' Discuss.

7. 'Causal explanation is appropriate for natural science, but when it comes to social science we must explain actions in terms of reasons.' Discuss.

8. (a) Does Descartes establish that the mind and body are separate?

   (b) Are all the arguments in *Meditation* VI consistent with this claim?

9. 'The concept of a person cannot be analysed into something more fundamental.' Can it?

10. 'I don't see why there are any problems concerning the relationship of the mind and the brain. To talk about one is the same as talking about the other.' Discuss.

11. Discuss critically A. J. Ayer's treatment of the problem of other minds in chapter 7 of *Language, Truth and Logic*.

12. (a) How does Hume in the *Enquiry* attempt to solve the free will problem?

    (b) Give two criticisms of his attempt.

13. (a) Give two reasons why a philosopher might opt for the thesis of physicalism.

    (b) Discuss critically *one* version of physicalism.

14. 'If determinism is true, then no one can be praised or blamed.' Does this have to be true?

15. (a) Distinguish Cartesian doubt from sceptical doubt.

    (b) Discuss the logical viability of Cartesian doubt.

16. Do after-images exist?

17. What does it mean to say that a mental state is the *same thing* as a brain state?

18. 'If I cannot doubt that I am in pain, then my knowledge is absolutely certain.' Is it?

19. Does Descartes' approach to philosophy have any unacceptable presuppositions?

20. Has behaviourism resolved problems in the philosophy of mind?

21. 'I know what I feel because I know what to say.' Discuss.

22. Does the problem of other minds have any practical relevance?

23. Discuss whether a physicalist can give an adequate account of the qualitative aspects of our experience.

24. Assess the claim that mental states are caused by and realised in the structure of the brain.

25. Discuss the claim that the mind-body problem is insoluble.
26. Can purely psychological criteria account for personal identity?
27. Assess the importance of memory in determining personal identity.

3 The Philosophy of Religion

1. (a) What do you understand by 'God'?
   (b) Discuss the logical viability of the concept.
2. 'The order we see around us could have come about only as the result of intelligent planning.' Discuss.
3. (a) Give a clear and concise statement of one version of the ontological argument.
   (b) What criticisms can be made of the argument you have stated?
4. Must the universe have had a first cause?
5. Has Hume shown that a belief in miracles is always irrational?
6. (a) What is the problem of evil?
   (b) How successful is the free-will defence in disposing of the problem?
7. Is there an inconsistency in maintaining that God is omniscient *and* that we can act freely?
8. 'Science and religion are at war.' Discuss.
9. (a) What do you understand by 'religious faith'?
   (b) Can such faith have a rational foundation?
10. Discuss critically any version of the cosmological argument.
11. Does religious experience provide a valid ground for 'belief in God?
12. (a) Describe Descartes' reasoning in *Meditation* V which leads him to say that God exists.
    (b) What status does Descartes afford to the proposition 'God exists'?
    (c) Evaluate his reasoning.
13. (a) State Hume's objections in the *Enquiry* to the design argument.
    (b) How damaging are those objections?

The following are more difficult:

14. Can the concept of a miracle be elucidated solely in terms of a breach of a law of nature?
15. 'Religious language cannot be used to express any fact about the world.' Discuss.
16. Is the proposition 'God exists' logically necessary?
17. Has Kant disposed of the ontological argument?
18. Are there any similarities between having faith in God and having faith in another person?
19. (a) Is Swinburne's argument from design an improvement on Paley's?
    (b) In what ways, if any, is Swinburne's argument defective?
20. Must there be evil?

4 An Introduction to Ethics

1. Does Plato's ethical theory provide us with absolute values upon which no one could disagree?
2. Discuss critically Plato's thesis that knowledge is virtue.

3. (a) What is Plato's theory of Forms?
    (b) What are the ethical implications of the theory?
4. How important is the concept of 'function' in Aristotle's ethics?
5. In what ways, and to what extent, may Aristotle's ethical theory be described as relativist?
6. (a) Discuss Aristotle's distinction between voluntary and involunary action.
    (b) What are the ethical implications of the distinction?
7. Aristotle held that pleasure was a good but not the chief good. Evaluate his reasons for saying this.
8. (a) What is Aristotle's doctrine of the mean?
    (b) Assess the ethical importance of the doctrine.
9. 'The only measure of right and wrong is the greatest happiness of the greatest number.' Discuss.
10. (a) What are the differences between rule- and act-utilitarianism?
    (b) Do either of them have any morally unacceptable implications?
11. (a) Why does Ayer say that value judgements are nonsensical?
    (b) Evaluate his reasons for saying this.
12. (a) What is meant by saying that value judgements cannot be derived from factual ones?
    (b) Is a distinction between facts and values always easy to draw?
13. Discuss any two attempts to bridge the fact-value gap.
14. Discuss the view that moral judgements entail commands on oneself and others.
15. How important is universalisability in morality?
16. *Can* you perform an act which you sincerely believe to be wrong?
17. (a) How might a utilitarian approach the problem of animal experimentation?
    (b) Does this approach have any unacceptable implications?
18. 'In assessing the moral worth of an action it is the motive not the consequences that we must consider.' Discuss.
19. (a) What does Sartre mean by 'bad faith'?
    (b) Discuss the importance of the concept in his ethics.
20. Discuss Sartre's account of the role of decision-making in morality.
21. (a) Why does Sartre say that man's responsibility is awesome?
    (b) Are we as responsible as Sartre claims?

The following are more difficult:

22. Discuss the view that an action can have moral worth if and only if it emanates from what Kant called a 'goodwill'.
23. (a) Why is the Form of the Good so important in Plato's ethics?
    (b) Discuss Aristotle's criticisms of the Form of the Good.
24. Are there any restrictions on what can count as a moral principle?
25. Discuss the claim that goodness cannot be defined.

5 Social and Political Philosophy

1. 'The only real base for authority of the state is force.' Can such a claim adequately account for what we understand by political obligation?
2. (a) What does it mean to say that laws are the expression of the general will?
    (b) How intelligible is the notion of a general will?

3. 'In a state of nature there are no rights or obligations.' Discuss.
4. Discuss the claim that in a democracy each person is the author of the law.
5. How reasonable is it to explain the origin of the state by appealing to an initial pact between the people and the sovereign?
6. (a) What are the main differences between open and closed societies?
   (b) Which of the conceptions applies to modern Britain?
7. Are there any circumstances where it is justifiable to break a law of a democratic society?
8. (a) State Mill's libertarian principle.
   (b) How might this principle be applied to the case of freedom of publication?
9. 'The only rights are legal rights.' Discuss.
10. Is it legitimate to describe Mill's libertarian principle as an ideological one which serves a particular class interest?
11. (a) Why does Mill think that freedom of opinion is so important?
    (b) How good are his arguments to show its importance?
12. Discuss the claim that Marxism is the only genuine way of gaining a scientific understanding of society.
13. (a) What are the main features of Marx's materialist conception of history?
    (b) Discuss two criticisms that could be made of such a conception.
14. (a) Show how Marx applies the concept of dialectic to history.
    (b) How convincing do you find this application?
15. Discuss critically Marx's concepts of alienation and false-consciousess.
16. Could it ever be legitimate to overthrow an elected government?
17. (a) Discuss how Mill's individualism has played a role in our legislation.
    (b) Are there any cases where it should not have a role to play?

6 The Philosophy of Science

1. 'If the theory can be falsified, then it is scientific.' Discuss.
2. Assess the adequacy of Mill's principles of inductive inference.
3. (a) What is the problem of induction?
   (b) Can the problem be solved?
4. Assess the role of observation in the formulation of scientific theories.
5. 'Science can be distinguished from other human enterprises in terms of its objectivity.' Discuss.
6. Is there a logic of scientific discovery?
7. To what extent, if any, are paradigms useful in understanding the development of science?
8. 'The only necessity is logical necessity.' Discuss.
9. Using any scientific theory you have studied, assess whether it can support a non-realist view of science.
10. How important is methodology in understanding the nature of science?
11. Discuss the adequacy of Hume's theory of causation.
12. (a) Illustrate what is meant by the imaginative leap of the scientist.
    (b) Assess the importance of imagination in science.

Notes

1 Perception and Knowledge

1. The reader should consult Chapter 4 for an account of Plato's theory of knowledge.
2. Descartes invented co-ordinate geometry.
3. Hume admits that there might, however, be practical differences as it is far more difficult to conduct experiments with people than with physical objects. Knowing that you are part of an experiment can affect the outcome of the experiment.
4. Although Newton made many hypotheses, he said that much of his own work (that is, making hypotheses) contravened his methodological principle. Compare with Hume's remark, 'Newton trod with caution and therefore more secure steps, the only road that leads to true philosophy'.
5. For Hume, to say that A is the cause of B means that A and B are constantly conjoined in our experience.
6. In discussing G. E. Moore on sense-data, Ayer has claimed that the term 'seems' should not be understood in its everyday sense but merely as a logical device which prevents entailment. Thus it should not be understood as implying the real possibility of mistake. But Ayer also says: 'Let us say, *more cautiously*, [my italics] that it seemed to Moore that he saw his hands.' Now Ayer cannot have it both ways for the use in the ordinary sense of 'seems' is precisely to introduce caution. The real issue here is whether such caution can be justified and whether there is some specifiable point where it cannot be. See A. J. Ayer, *Russell and Moor:, The Analytical Heritage* (Macmillan, 1973), p. 172.
7. A. J. Ayer, *The Foundations of Empirical Knowledge* (Macmillan, 1940), Chapter 1.
8. Reid's reply to Hume, *Essays on the Intellectual Powers of Man*, II (Macmillan, 1944), p. 14.
9. A. J. Ayer, *The Problem of Knowledge* (Pelican, 1974), pp. 94–5.
10. See Susan Stebbing's *Philosophy and the Physicists* (London, 1937), pp. 51ff and C. W. K. Mundle's *Perception: Facts and Theories* (Oxford, 1971), p. 94. For a full and comprehensive discussion of colour, the reader is advised to read Mundle's book. Stebbing pays little attention to the issue of colour.
11. See B. Russell, *Principia Mathematica* (Cambridge University Press, 2nd edn, 1916), p. 66.
12. Ayer, *Russell and Moore: The Analytical Heritage*, p. 38.
13. See G. Frege, 'The Thought: A Logical Inquiry' in *Philosophical Logic*, ed. Strawson (Oxford University Press, 1973), pp. 17–39.
14. L. Wittgenstein, *Philosophical Investigations*, I (Oxford University Press, 1953), pp. 65–7.
15. See Chapter 4 of the present volume, 'An Introduction to Ethics'.
16. Reprinted in the Pelican 1974 edition.

2 Problems in the Philosophy of Mind

1. Rene Descartes, *Meditations*, II (Penguin Classics edition, 1973), p. 103.
2. *Ibid.*
3. *Ibid.*, p. 105.
4. Descartes uses 'imagine' to cover all forming of pictures in the mind's eye.
5. Strictly, one should not talk of 'conscious' experiences unless one is also prepared to talk of unconscious ones.
6. D. Hume, *Enquiry Concerning Human Understanding* (Bobbs-Merrill, 1951), pp. 76–7.
7. He does not have to claim that such a state of affairs is *physically* possible. It is sufficient for such a state of affairs to be describable. The supposition does not involve him in a contradiction.
8. J. J. C. Smart, *Philosophy and Scientific Realism* (International Library of Scientific Method, 1963), pp. 92–105.
9. Saul Kripke, 'Naming and Necessity' in *Semantics of Natural Language*, ed. Harman and Davidson (Dordrecht: Reidel, 1972).
10. Patricia Smith Churchland, *Neurophilosophy* (MIT Press, 1986).
11. U. T. Place, *The Philosophy of Mind*, ed. V. C. Chappell (New Jersey, 1962).
12. The reader might like to consider the linguistic consequences those theories have for the case in which a mirror system enables you to observe your own brain states. He should also compare the use of the personal pronoun in talk about mental states on the one hand and brain states on the other.
13. J.-P. Changeux, *Neuronal Man: the biology of the mind* (Pantheon, 1985).
14. We are, of course, assuming for purposes of this argument that the question, 'How does the mind work?', is an intelligible question which will yield (ultimately) an answer in terms of some general principles. The reader should think carefully about this assumption.
15. Daniel Dennett, *Essays on Freedom of Action*, ed. Ted Honderich (Routledge & Kegan Paul, 1978).
16. *Ibid.*, pp. 159–60.
17. Reported in the *Sunday Times* magazine, 7 September 1978.
18. Strawson, *Individuals* (Oxford, 1959). See also 'Persons' in *Essays in Philosophical Psychology*, ed. Gustafson (New York, 1964).
19. That is, where the possibility of doubt is logically precluded.
20. A. J. Ayer, *Language, Truth and Logic* (Pelican, 1974), ch. 7.
21. Wittgenstein, *Philosophical Investigations* (Oxford, 1953; Blackwell paperback, 1975).
22. This should not be confused with questions about the origins of language. We are concerned with a *private* language. Besides, it would be odd to suppose that language began through a simultaneous decision by a group of individuals to go in for the practice of naming. Perhaps it is when a group used signs in a particular way that they begin to formulate the concept of a name. This would at least avoid questions such as, 'when was this particular sign used as a name?'. I can tell you when the expression 'QE II' was first used as a name, but not the expression 'food'.
23. Remember that there is no *possibility* of a check by external observers. This

distinguishes the case from that of any rule of behaviour one might decide to follow.

24. See F. Waismann, *The Principles of Linguistic Philosophy* (Macmillan Papermac, 1971), pp. 22–7.

25. I am not going to discuss the claim that '*I know* that I am in pain by direct acquaintance' as it is unclear what question this would answer. It is not clear to the author that the question 'How do I know that I am in pain?' is a well-formed question. It is hard to see how an answer could consist in the provision of a *method.* Methods need to be followed.

26. E. Bedford, 'Emotions' in *Essays in Philosophical Psychology*, ed. Gustafson (New York: Anchor, 1964; Macmillan paperback, 1973).

27. See R. S. Peters, *The Concept of Motivation* (Routledge & Kegan Paul, 1974).

28. Nowadays many psychologists would not make such a claim even for habitual actions.

29. See: J. B. Watson, *Behaviourism* (New York, People's Publishing Co., 1924), pp. 155–65; Wittgenstein, *Philosophical Investigations* I, p. 476; Kenny, *Action, Emotion and Will* (Routledge & Kegan Paul, 1976), pp. 22 ff.; James, *Principles of Psychology* (New York, 1950), p. 450 (for a causal account in reverse).

30. William James, *Varieties of Religious Experience* (Fontana Library, 1960).

31. See Freud's *Complete Psychological Works*, vol. III (Hogarth Press, 1966; New York: Macmillan).

32. It is, of course, true that relationships which did not appear to be sexual in character can turn out to be sexually motivated, and Freud has made us more aware of this possibility. It does not follow from this, however, that all such relationships are like this or could be like this.

33. Glover, *Basic Mental Concepts* (Oxford University Press, 1972), p. 1.

34. MacIntyre, *The Unconscious: a conceptual analysis* (Routledge & Kegan Paul, 1976), ch. 3.

35. See the criticism of Flew in Chapter 3 of this volume, in the discussion of the Problem of Evil.

36. Honderich (ed.), *Essays on Freedom of Action* (Routledge & Kegan Paul, 1978), p. 207.

37. B. F. Skinner, in *Psychology: The Study of a Science*, ed. S. Koch, vol. II (New York: McGraw-Hill, 1959), p. 375.

38. See R. S. Peters, *The Concept of Motivation* (Routledge & Kegan Paul, 1974) for a most readable statement of this position.

39. Their use of language involves the use of some rules.

40. Peter Winch, *The Idea of a Social Science (ISS)* (Routledge & Kegan Paul, 1977).

41. Alan Ryan, *The Philosophy of the Social Sciences (PSS)* (Macmillan, 1976).

42. *Sunday Times*, Weekly Review, January 1981 and J. H. Crook, *The Evolution of Human Consciousness.*

43. K. Popper, *The Poverty of Historicism* (Routledge & Kegan Paul, 1976), pp. 105 ff.

44. 'Laws', that is, in a scientific not a legal sense.

45. The most complete statement, together with a number of replies, occurs in the *American Journal of Behavioural and Brain Sciences* (1980). Simpler statements can be found in the *BBC Reith Lectures* (1984) reprinted in *The Listener*, especially recommended are the editions of 8 and 15 November 1984.

3 The Philosophy of Religion

1. Note the identification of spirit with mind.
2. Hume's *Dialogues* (Hafner Publishing Co., 1966), p. 157.
3. William Paley, *Natural Theology* (Bobbs-Merrill, 1963).
4. See Hume's *Enquiry* (Bobbs-Merrill, 1951), pp. 145–6.
5. Hume, *Dialogues*, V, p. 207.
6. See Hume's *Enquiry*, S VI.
7. *Dialogues*, II, p. 185.
8. In order to be clear about which series Aquinas is working with.
9. *Psalms* 14:1.
10. See J. Barnes, *The Ontological Argument* (Macmillan, 1972).
11. J. H. Hick, *Arguments For The Existence of God* (Macmillan, 1976), pp. 76–8.
12. I. Kant, *Critique of Pure Reason* (Macmillan Study edition, 1973), pp. 500–7.
13. Norman Malcolm, *The Philosophical Review* (1961).
14. See MacIntyre, 'Visions' in *New Essays in Philosophical Theology*, ed. Flew and MacIntyre (SCM study edition, 1972).
15. *Enquiry*, pp. 129–30.
16. Ninian Smart, *Philosophers and Religious Truth (PRT)* (SCM Press, 1964).
17. See Barth, *Church Dogmatics*, 111/3 (Edinburgh: T. & T. Clark, 1953), p. 311.
18. There is, of course, the exception of *a priori* knowledge, but that is not the issue here.
19. St Augustine, *Confessions*, VII (Westminster Press, 1955), 5.
20. Hick, *Evil and the God of Love* (Fontana, 1974), pp. 366 ff.
21. *Ibid.*, p. 370.
22. *Ibid.*, p. 376.
23. *Ibid.*, pp. 182–3.
24. Forsythe, *The Justification of God* (Latimer House, 1948), p. 69.
25. Flew, in *New Essays in Philosophical Theology*, ed. Flew and MacIntyre, pp. 144–70.
26. Mackie, 'Evil and Omnipotence' in *God and Evil*, ed. N. Pike (Prentice Hall, 1964).
27. Hick, *Evil and the God of Love*, p. 291.
28. F. R. Tennant, *Philosophical Theology* (Cambridge University Press, 1930).
29. Wittgenstein, 'God does not reveal Himself *in* the world', *Tractatus Logico-Philosophicus* (Routledge & Kegan Paul, pbk, 1974).
30. J. R. Lucas, *The Freedom of the Will* (Oxford, 1970), Ch. 14.
31. N. Pike, *God and Timelessness* (London, 1970), ch. 4.
32. Mr. J. I. Daniel in an unpublished paper.
33. *Ibid.*
34. Spencer, *Evolutionary Ethics* (Longman, Rees, 1873).
35. This does not mean logical necessity.
36. Hick, *Faith and Knowledge* (Macmillan, 1988).
37. A non-religious example may be taken from Tolstoy. The choice of whether to propose marriage would be such an example. If the man could have proposed but did not, then that memory may remain with the woman.
38. There is also the problem that strength of belief might be measured in terms of

the occurrence of religious experiences and whether such experiences occur could be said to depend on how strongly you believe.

39. See for example, A. J. Ayer, *Language, Truth and Logic*, ch. 6.
40. Winch, *The Idea of a Social Science* (Routledge & Kegan Paul, 1977).
41. An account of rising from the dead in terms of emerging from a cataleptic state would not be an account *within* religious language.

4 An Introduction to Ethics

1. There is no clear distinction in Plato between 'necessarily true' and 'always true'.
2. 'Opinion' here includes what we would call knowledge via the senses.
3. B. Russell, *The Problems of Philosophy* (Oxford University Press, 1974), p. 53. Russell uses the term 'universal' in order to avoid any incorrect mentalist connotations which might be associated with Plato's term 'Idea'.
4. Compare with Stevenson, *Seven Theories of Human Nature* (Oxford University Press, 1973), p. 25.
5. F. M. Cornford, *The Republic of Plato* (Oxford University Press, 1942), p. 207.
6. A. E. Taylor, *Plato* (Methuen, U.P. 1971); R. L. Nettleship, *Lectures on the Republic of Plato* (Macmillan, 1929).
7. The reader should consult A. E. Taylor's *Plato* pp. 506–7 for a discussion of this issue.
8. The exercising of thought means that use of reason in theoretical studies. The obedience to a rational principle means the propriety of our passions to their right objects, the discipline of the emotions, in accordance with a rule, principle or end formulated by reason.
9. J. Bentham, *An Introduction to the Principles of Morals and Legislation*, ch. I.i in *Utilitarianism*, ed. M. Warnock (Fontana, 1973).
10. G. E. Moore, *Principia Ethica* (Cambridge University Press, 1976), p. 67.
11. Philippa Foot, in *Theories of Ethics*, ed. p. Foot (Oxford University Press, 1974).
12. Richard Hare, 'The Promising Game' in *Theories of Ethics*, ed. p. Foot, pp. 115–27.

5 Social and Political Philosophy

1. J. W. Allen, *History of Political Thought in the Sixteenth Century* (Oxford University Press, 1966), p. 436.
2. Jean Jacques Rousseau, *Political Writings* (C. E. Vaughan, 1915), pp. 305–6.
3. See Rousseau, *Social Contract* (Everyman, 1930) I, V.
4. *Ibid.*
5. Mill in M. Warnock, *Utilitarianism*, introduction, p. 16.
6. J. S. Mill, Essay on Bentham in *Utilitarianism*, p. 112.
7. *Ibid.*, p. 113.
8. *Ibid.*, pp. 113–14.
9. See J. R. Lucas, *Democracy and Participation* (Penguin, 1976).

10. All page references are to the Fontana paperback edition of *Utilitarianism*.
11. One is here reminded of Voltaire's remark that although I disagree with what you say, I will defend to the death your right to say it.
12. Benjamin Gibbs, *Freedom and Liberation* (Sussex University Press, 1976), p. 100.
13. *Ibid.*, p. 101.
14. *Karl Marx: Selected Writings in Sociology and Social Philosophy*, ed. T. Bottomore (Penguin, 1963), p. 67.
15. K. R. Popper, *The Open Society and its Enemies*, vol. II (Routledge & Kegan Paul, 1962).
16. Here 'cannot' is to be understood in a causal sense.
17. *Karl Marx, Selected Writings*, p. 250, see also p. 176.

6 The Philosophy of Science

1. It might explain if there was something in the room which caused baldness, but that's not the point now.
2. I say to some extent because there were shortcomings evident to many at that time with Aristotle's physics.
3. It is possible to interpret this method as constituting a separate employment of the first two methods. If you wish to pursue this, see Copi, *Introduction to Logic* (Prentice Hall, 1993).
4. If the reader wants to see a good example of how this works in practice, then consult Copi's example of Pasteur and the discovery of anthrax vaccine.
5. *The Logic of Scientific Discovery* (Hutchinson, 1975), p. 59.
6. Bring out the obvious case against the creativists.
7. Ayer's assertion that 'no finite series of observations is ever sufficient to establish the truth of a hypothesis beyond all possibility of doubt' demonstrates the problem of induction.
8. Thus the singular proposition, 'This is not a unicorn', does not falsify, 'There are unicorns'. The falsification can only be done by a universal proposition, 'There are no unicorns', but in order to know the truth of this, we should have to be able to scan the entire past, present and future states of the universe. This we cannot do.
9. If you achieve the same results by performing different operations, we would account for this by saying that the same thing was being measured in either case. But if length is *defined* in operational terms, then it follows that you have two different concepts. How plausible is it to say that you have two concepts of length? Surely, what we should say is that there are two ways of measuring a thing, length).
10. This procedure assumes that we have already established the principle that explanatory power implies a reality claim.
11. Assuming that we need refer to imagination at all.
12. We must also take account of the fact that 'unimaginative' is a critical term.

Bibliography

Allen, J. W., *History of Political Thought in the Sixteenth Century* (Oxford University Press, 1966)

Anselm's *'Proslogion'*, tr. M. J. Charlesworth (this includes Gaunilo's reply) (Clarendon Press, 1965)

Aquinas, *Summa Theologica* (Eyre & Spottiswoode, 1966)

Aristotle, *Nicomachean Ethics*, tr. Sir David Ross (Oxford University Press, 1966) (*The Works of Aristotle* series)

Augustine, *Confessions* (Westminster Press, 1955)

Austin, J. L., *Sense and Sensibilia* (Oxford, 1962)

Ayer, A. J., *The Foundations of Empirical Knowledge* (Macmillan, 1940)

Ayer, A. J. *Language, Truth and Logic* (Pelican, 1974)

Ayer, A. J., *The Problem of Knowledge* (Pelican, 1974)

Ayer, A. J., *Russell and Moore: The Analytical Heritage* (Macmillan, 1973)

Barnes, J., *The Ontological Argument* (Macmillan, 1972)

Barth, K., *Church Dogmatics* (T. & T. Clarke, 1953)

Bentham, J., 'An Introduction to the Principles of Morals and Legislation', in *Utilitarianism*, ed. M. Warnock (Fontana, 1973)

Berkeley, G., *Principles of Human Knowledge* (Dent, 1919, Everyman edition)

Bradley, F. H., *Ethical Studies* (Oxford University Press, 1927)

Bridgman, P. W., *The Logic of Modern Physics* (New York: Macmillan, 1954)

Broad, C., *Five Types of Ethical Theory* (Routledge & Kegan Paul, 1962)

Buehler, J. (ed.), *The Philosophy of Peirce* (Kegan Paul, Trench Trubner & Co., 1940)

Burke, E., *Reflections on the French Revolution* (Dent-Dutton, 1964, Everyman edition)

Butler, J., *Of Personal Identity* (Heinemann, 1931)

Changeux, J.-P., *Neuronal Man* (Pantheon, 1985)

Chappell, V. C. (ed.), *The Philosophy of Mind* (New Jersey, 1962)

Churchland, P. S., *Neurophilosophy* (MIT Press, 1986)

Copi, I. M. *Introduction to Logic* (Prentice Hall, 1993)

Cornford, F. M., *The Republic of Plato* (Oxford University Press, 1942)

Crook, J. H., *The Evolution of Human Consciousness* (Oxford: Clarendon Press, 1980))

de Mariana, J. and Bodin, J., quoted in W. Durant, *The Story of Civilisation, Vol I The Age of Reason*, chs 1 and 2 (Heron Books, 1974)

Descartes, R., *Discourse on Method* and *Meditations* (Penguin Classics, 1973)

Durant, W., *The Story of Civilization* (Simon & Schuster, New York 1935; Heron Books, 1973)

Flew, A. G. N. and Macintyre, A. (eds), *New Essays in Philosophical Theology* (SCM study edition, 1972)

Foot, P. (ed.), *Theories of Ethics* (Oxford University Press, 1974)

Forsythe, J. *The Justification of God* (Latimer House, 1948)

Foster, J., *The Immaterial Self* (Routledge, 1996)

Freud, S., *Complete Psychological Works* (Hogarth Press, 1966)

Gaunilo, *Proslogion*, trans. M. J. Charlesworth (Clarendon Press, 1965)

Gettier, J., in A. Phillips-Griffiths (ed.), *Knowledge and Belief* (Oxford University Press, 1976)

Gibbs, B., *Freedom and Liberation* (Sussex University Press, 1976)

Glover, J., *Basic Mental Concepts* (Oxford University Press, 1972)

Gustafson, D. (ed.), *Essays in Philosophical Psychology* (New York: Anchor, 1964; Macmillan Paperback, 1973)

Hare, R. M., *The Language of Morals* (Oxford University Press, 1975)

Harman and Davidson (eds), *Semantics of Natural Language* (Dordrecht: Reidel, 1972)

Harré, R., *Matter and Method* (Opus, 1975)

Harré, R., *Philosophies of Science* (Oxford, 1978)

Hart, H. L. A., *The Concept of Law* (Oxford University Press, 1961)

Hegel, G. W. F., *Logic* (Oxford University Press, 1975)

Hempel, C. *Philosophy of Natural Science* (Englewood Cliffs, Prentice Hall, 1970)

Hick, J., *Faith and Knowledge* (Macmillan, 1966)

Hick, J., *Arguments for the Existence of God* (Macmillan, 1976)

Hick, J., *Evil and the God of Love* (Fontana, 1974)

Hick, J. and McGill, A. (eds), *The Many Faced Argument* (Macmillan, 1968)

Hobbes, T., *Leviathan* (abridged) (Fontana, 1971)

Honderich, E. R. (ed.), *Essays on Freedom of Action* (Routledge & Kegan Paul, 1978)

Hudson, W. (ed.), *The Is-Ought Question* (Macmillan, 1969)

Hume, D., *An Enquiry Concerning Human Understanding* (Bobbs-Merrill, 1951)

Hume, D., *Dialogues Concerning Natural Religion* (Hafner Publishing Co., 1966)

Hume, D., *Treatise of Human Nature*, ed. L. A. Selby-Bigge (Oxford, 1888)

Jackson, F., 'What Mary didn't know', *Journal of Philosophy*, lxxxiii(5), 1986

James, W., *Principles of Psychology* (New York, 1950)

James, W., *Varieties of Religious Experience* (Fontana Library, 1960)

James, W., *The Will to Believe and Other Essays in Popular Philosophy* (New York: Dover Publications, 1956)

Kant, I., *Critique of Pure Reason* (Macmillan Study Edition, 1973)

Kant, I., *The Groundwork* (Liberal Arts Press, 1949)

Kenny, A. *The Five Ways* (Arcadia, 1972)

Kenny, A., *Action, Emotion and Will* (Routledge & Kegan Paul, 1976)

Kline, M., *Mathematics in Western Culture* (Penguin, 1988)

Koch, S. (ed.), *Psychology: The Study of a Science* (New York, McGraw-Hill, 1959)

Kuhn, T., *The Structure of Scientific Revolutions*, enlarged edn (Chicago Press, 1990)

Locke, J., *Essay Concerning Human Understanding* (Dent, 1972)

Lucas, J. R., *Democracy and Participation* (Penguin, 1976)

Lucas, J. R., *The Freedom of the Will* (Oxford, 1970)

Mach, E., *The Science of Mechanics*, trans. T. J. McCormack (Open Court, 1960)

Macintyre, A., *The Unconscious: a conceptual analysis* (Routledge & Kegan Paul, 1976)

Malcolm, N., *The Philosophical Review* (1961)

Marx, K. and Engels, F., *Collected Works* (Lawrence & Wishart, 1975)

McGinn, C., *The Problem of Consciousness* (Scribner, 1991)

McGinn, C., *The Making of a Philosopher* (Scribner, 2002)

Melden, A., *Rights and Right Conduct* (Basil Blackwell, 1970)

Mill, J. S., *Utilitarianism* (including *On Liberty*), ed. M. Warnock. (Fontana, 1973)

Moore, G. E., *Principia Ethica* (Cambridge University Press, 1976)

Mundle, C. W. K., *Perception: Facts and Theories* (Oxford, 1971)

Nagel, T., *The View from Nowhere* (Oxford University Press, 1986)

Nettleship, R. L., *Lectures on. the Republic of Plato* (Macmillan, 1929)

Nidditch, P. (ed.), *The Philosophy of Science* (Oxford University Press, 1982)

Ogden, C. K. and Richards, I. A., *The Meaning of Meaning* (Routledge, 1924)

Paley, W., *Natural Theology* (Bobbs-Merrill, 1963)

Papineau, D., 'Brains and Feelings', *Richmond Journal*, 2003

Pascal, B., *Pensées* (Penguin Classics, 1995)

Passmore, J., *A Hundred Years of Philosophy* (Penguin, 1975)

Peters, R. S., *The Concept of Motivation* (Routledge & Kegan Paul, 1974)

Pike, N. (ed.), *God and Evil* (Prentice Hall, 1964)

Pike, N., *God and Timelessness* (Routledge & Kegan Paul, 1970)

Plamenatz, J., *The English Utilitarians* (Oxford, 1949)

Plato, *Republic*, commentary by F. M. Cornford (tr.) (Oxford University Press, 1942); *Phaedo, Gorgias, Timaeus, Symposium* are available in many editions, including LOEB and Penguin

Popper, K. R. *The Open Society and its Enemies* (Routledge & Kegan Paul, 1962)

Popper, K. R. *Conjectures and Refutations* (Routledge & Kegan Paul, 1963)

Popper, K. R., *Logic of Scientific Discovery* (Hutchinson, 1975)

Popper, K. R., *The Poverty of Historicism* (Routledge & Kegan Paul, 1976)

Reid, T., *Essays on the Intellectual Powers of Man* (ed. Woozley) (Macmillan, 1944)

Robson, J. M. (ed.), *Collected Works of J. S. Mill* (Routledge & Kegan Paul, University of Toronto, 1979)

Rousseau, J. J., *Political Writings* (C.E. Vaughan, 1915)

Rousseau, J. J., *Social Contract* (Dent-Dutton, 1930; Everyman edition)

Russell, B., *Human Knowledge: Its Scope and Limits* (London and New York, Unwin, 1948)

Russell, B., *Principia Mathematica* (Cambridge University Press, 1912)

Russell, B., *The Problems of Philosophy* (Oxford University Press, 1974)

Ryan, A., *The Philosophy of the Social Sciences* (Macmillan Students Edition, 1976)

Ryle, G., *The Concept of Mind* (Hutchinson's University Library, 1949)

Sartre, J.-P., *Being and Nothingness,* tr. Hazel Barnes (Methuen, 1957)

Sartre, J.-P., *Existentialism and Humanism* (Eyre Methuen, 1974)

Searle, J. R., *The Reith Lectures 1984* (BBC Publications, 1984); see also *American Journal of Behavioural and Brain Sciences* (1980)

Searle, J. R., *Intentionality* (Cambridge University Press, 1985)

Searle, J., *The Rediscovery of the Mind* (MIT Press, 1992)

Searle, J., *The Mystery of Consciousness* (Granta Books, 1997)

Searle, J. and Anscombe, G. E., in P. Foot (ed.), *Theories of Ethics* (Oxford University Press, 1977)

Shoemaker, S., *Identity, Cause and Mind* (Cambridge University Press, 1984)

Shoemaker, S. and Swinburne, R., *Personal Identity* (Blackwell, 1984)

Smart, J. J. C., *Philosophy and Scientific Realism (PRT)* (International Library of Scientific Method, 1963)

Smart, N., *Philosophers and Religious Truth* (SCM Press, 1964)

Sosa, E. (ed.), *Causation and Conditionals* (Oxford University Press, 1977)

Spencer, H., *Evolutionary Ethics* (Longman, Rees, 1873)

Stebbing, L. S., *Philosophy and the Physicists* (London, 1937)

Stevenson, C. L., *Ethics and Language* (Yale University Press, 1944)

Strawson, P., *Individuals* (Oxford, 1959)

Strawson (ed.), *Philosophical Logic* (Oxford University Press, 1973)

Strawson, G., *Mental Reality* (MIT Press, 1994)

Swinburne, R. W. (ed.), *The Justification of Induction* (Oxford University Press, 1976)

Swinburne, R. W., *The Existence of God* (Clarendon Press, Oxford, 1979)

Taylor, A. E., *Plato* (Methuen, 1971)

Tennant, F. R., *Philosophical Theology* (Cambridge University Press, 1930)

Toulmin, S., *The Philosophy of Science* (Hutchinson, 1967)

Urmson, J. O., *Berkeley,* Modern Masters Series (Fontana, 1972)

Vaughan, C. E., *Studies in the History of Political Philosophy* (Manchester University Press, 1939)

Waismann, F., *The Principles of Linguistic Philosophy* (Macmillan Papermac, 1971)

Warner, R. and Szubka, T. (eds), *The Mind–Body Problem* (Blackwell, 1994)

Warnock, M., *The Philosophy of Sartre* (Hutchinson, 1966)

Watson, J. B., *Behaviourism* (New York, People's Publishing Co., 1924)

Winch, P., *The Idea of a Social Science* (Routledge & Kegan Paul, 1977)

Wittgenstein, L., *Philosophical Investigations* (Oxford University Press, 1953; Blackwell, 1988)

Wittgenstein, L., *Tractatus-Logico-Philosophicus* (Routledge & Kegan Paul, 1974)

Name Index

Subject and Concept Index